# Wedding Days

## When and How Great Marriages Began

## SUSAN J. GORDON

*For my husband, Ken, and in memory of my grandmother,*
*Etta Lambert Billow. His love never lets up; hers never let me down.*

For Cecilia + Leo —
Best Wishes in
celebration of your
wedding day —
January 27th.

Oct. 22, 2021

# ACKNOWLEDGMENTS

**M**OST MARRIAGES BEGIN WITH GIANT leaps of faith. I was blessed to wed an incredibly loving and devoted man. Ken participated in every facet of this book, fully sharing (and seeming to enjoy) all the research and work. His extraordinary energy, enthusiasm, and encouragement never wavered – in spite of countless pressures from his own work, and the major "distractions" of our two sons' weddings within a six months' span. Night after night, Ken met me at the library after work and spent hours helping me discover rich and valuable material. He is a gifted and indefatigable researcher and lover of history; I might have written this book without him, but I never could have accomplished it so well or so joyously.

Thanks and my unconditional love go also to my sons and daughters-in-law—Edward and Patrice, Peter and Melissa – helpmates and devoted partners whose relationships and love have led their (unbiased) mother to predict that great things will surely be achieved in their own marriages.

Special thanks also go to my very dear friend Gail Gitman, who often dropped everything to search meticulously for much needed and sometimes obscure information, to create complicated charts, and to lend a sympathetic ear to my occasional frustrations. At the Authors Guild, enthusiasm, good humor, wise advice and patience were generously offered by Johnny Chinnici of Digital Services during the time spent putting the new, updated edition of Wedding Days in perfect order.

The lifelong love and marriages of my aunts and uncles, Muriel and Maynard Petkun and Selma and Leo Berkowitz, have always been inspirations to me. Other close friends and relatives, including Carol and Mike Dyer, Rose-Marie and Jeff Foster, the Gethin-Jones family, Paul Gitman, Barbara and Jeff Gullotta, Maury and Gerry Kaplan, Elaine and Bob Klein, Barbara and Ken Leish, Georgia and Bill Pollak, Barbara and George Quint, and Pat Tomassi also contributed useful information and endless support.

# SEEING LOVE
## AN INTRODUCTION

THIS BOOK IS A CELEBRATION of marriage and a toast to 366 couples throughout 1,500 years of recorded history – husbands and wives who have achieved greatness and made a difference in our lives. It focuses on the courtships and marriages of artists, composers, writers, statesmen, explorers, athletes, scientists, inventors, performers, musicians, monarchs, and philanthropists, and cites their major accomplishments. Wealthy or poor, royal or obscure, they all began their marriages with timeless dreams of hope for the future and heartfelt prayers for a joyful, productive, and satisfying life together.

My earliest memories of weddings and new marriages were not stories my parents told me about how they fell in love and were married, but glimpses into other people's lives. When I was about 5 years old, I saw a young couple driving in a blue convertible trailing tin cans and old shoes. I was riding in my father's car, a rare event since my parents had already been separated for 3 years and were on the verge of a divorce.

The blue convertible sped by with its "Just Married" sign stretched across the trunk. As the young man turned the steering wheel deftly with one hand, he caressed the neck of his yellow-ponytailed bride with the other. In an era before seat belts, she snuggled right beside him and closed her eyes. This must be what love looks like, I remember thinking. I must be seeing love.

A few years later, my aunt and I were driving on a country road outside of Boston. It was a gloriously bright springtime afternoon, and as we passed a steeple-topped church on a hillside, the doors flew open and a bride and groom rushed out in a whirl of white. The wedding guests followed, throwing rice at the happy couple. The bride tossed her bouquet to cheering girlfriends, waved to everybody, and then hopped into a car with her new husband and drove off.

I, who had no personal experience seeing love between a man and a woman in my own home, remembered the newlyweds in the car, saw the couple dashing out of the church, and could only conclude that surely, this was love. Because if it isn't love right then, on the very day you are married … when is it?

Fortunately, I grew up to celebrate my own marriage to a man I continue to fall in love with after more than 50 years. I first saw Ken when I was the new girl in high school. Eight years passed before we married, after going steady, breaking up, and getting back together again. But all along I knew that Ken was the smartest, funniest, and most passionate young man I ever dated – the one I knew I'd never get tired of seeing every single morning and the one I most definitely wanted to be the father of my kids.

Neither Ken nor I came from whole families; neither of us saw our parents grow old together. Doing research on great marriages has been meaningful to both of us; it's also been heartwarming, eye-opening, and full of surprises.

Marriage was on my mind a while ago, when my two sons became engaged to wonderful young women. I thought about famous people throughout history; what kinds of marriages had they had?

Thinking about George and Martha Washington, Paul and Linda McCartney, and Ozzie and Harriet was easy, but what about other well-known people? I knew about Daniel Boone; was there a Mrs. Boone? What role did she play in her husband's trailblazing expeditions? Was there a Mrs. Dostoyevsky? Mrs. Rembrandt? Did comedian Henny Youngman really mean it when he said, "Take my wife"? And what kind of wife inspired a 17th century shah to commemorate her death by building the Taj Mahal?

I also thought about great women. Who did Annie Oakley marry? Who married Grandma Moses and Betsy Ross? What kinds of marriages did writers Agatha Christie and Laura Ingalls Wilder have?

I began reading lots of biographies and I uncovered great information: Charles Darwin married his first cousin; Marc Chagall's future in-laws told their daughter she would starve if she married that worthless painter; future president Andrew Johnson's wife taught him to read and write; the original Siamese twins married two sisters ... and fathered 21 children!

I also learned about significant couples who were well known in their own time but are mostly forgotten now. Few people know about the 19th century English circus performer Andrew Ducrow and his bareback-riding wife, Margaret, or African-American investigative journalist Ida B. Wells and her equally committed husband, Ferdinand Barnett, or Berthy Kinsky von Suttner, who founded European pacifist organizations with her husband, Artur, and in 1903 became the first woman to win the Nobel Peace Prize. I'm happy to bring their stories to life again.

From Pocahontas to Priscilla Presley, no woman ever forgets her courtship and wedding day. Even 53 years after Julia Dent married Ulysses S. Grant in 1848, the former first lady still smiled and said, "Never shall I forget ... that hot August night...."

Not much has changed throughout the centuries. Brides and grooms have always had last-minute jitters; parents have always felt no one is good enough for their "perfect" child; living together is nothing new; step-parenting has always been tricky; intermarriages have always taken place; and some people don't find their ideal mate until their second or third trip down the aisle.

For the most part, first meetings were unremarkable. Future sweethearts met in grammar school, college, railway cars, and art classes, at lectures, dances, and church choir rehearsals, or after a messy divorce. Introductions were made by siblings, classmates, business associates, and rivals. Some couples fished each other out of lakes, nursed each other through illnesses, or spotted each other at garden parties or across proverbial crowded rooms.

I have been pleased to discover a good number of long-lasting Broadway and Hollywood marriages, belying the myth that actors are too self-absorbed to settle down and be happy with one other person. I also enjoyed learning that many well-known figures, such as Rembrandt, Bach, and Darwin, literally thrived in the married state.

Some marriages were relatively short; others lasted more than 50 years. While it's true in many cases that only one spouse – frequently the husband – achieved greatness, it probably wouldn't have happened if his partner hadn't taken care of the house, the kids, and him, creating a satisfying, secure environment conducive to the flowering of genius.

What actually went on between husbands and wives can only be conjectured as we study their autobiographies, letters, and journals, as well as historical analyses and "facts" provided by others. Difficulties in determining the accuracy of information about someone else's life are greatly compounded when studying a marriage. Now it's not just one life we are trying to understand, but two – in a deeply complicated, extremely private relationship. All we know is what we are told or can see for ourselves; what we understand best is the work they have done – what these people have achieved and left for us and future generations.

The information in this book was collected from more than 2,000 books and other sources. Wedding dates have been determined through efforts of serious scholarship and are as exact and reliable as possible. When no firm date exists, I've selected one based on the best evidence available, and this has been noted in the entry. Sometimes different source materials present conflicting information; they might refer to the date a marriage license was issued instead of the date of the actual wedding ceremony. Other times, researchers simply make mistakes. I welcome readers' help with new information for subsequent editions.

Most stories describe how these amazing couples' marriages began, but sometimes the spotlight shines on their accomplishments. In many cases, these people were young and ambitious when they married, but they had not yet found fame in their chosen careers. Their listed names are the ones they had at the time they were wed. Since this book is about husbands and wives, children are mentioned only to make a point about the parents.

This is not a complete list of great marriages throughout history, because there wasn't enough room to include all of them! Nor is this book the last word on marital happiness. Times weren't always good, and many of these couples had their share of sadnesses. Some had extramarital affairs and some, eventually, were divorced. But for a variety of reasons, in most cases they stayed together, and that unique combination of marital passion, support, happiness, and peace helped him, her, or them achieve something truly wonderful.

Everyone's here – reluctant bridegrooms, frazzled brides, interfering fathers, meddling mothers, helpful aunts, and rich, controlling relatives threatening to change their wills. And century after century, in the center of all these melodramatic maelstroms are young couples bent on matrimony, proving again and again that true love "conquers all." My unending fascination with "seeing love" has caused me to search for the couples' own words and to use them whenever possible. Virtually every quotation (including those beneath their names) comes from their letters, journals, recorded conversations or published work; their words can help us all see love.

I hope these stories will inspire you to read more about these celebrated two-somes' lives. Let their favorite phrases become your good-luck expressions. Name your kids after them, use the same colors for your wedding celebrations, eat the same foods, and honeymoon in the same places.

After everything is said and done, no one is luckier than those who are lovers. "Take any streetful of people buying clothes and groceries, cheering a hero or throwing confetti and blowing tin-horns," wrote the poet Carl Sandburg 10 years after marrying his beloved Paula. "Tell me if the lovers are losers ... tell me if any get more than the lovers...."

More than 350 years ago, Sir Richard Fanshawe told his wife, Anne: "My life and fortune shall be thine, and every thought of my heart."

You, too, should be so lucky.

# JANUARY

# JANUARY 1

## WILLIAM HENRY GATES III & MELINDA FRENCH

*"She made me feel like getting married.*
*Now that is unusual!"*

BY THE TIME BILL ASKED MELINDA to marry him, the Harvard College dropout was almost 38 years old. He had risen quickly to the top of the burgeoning software industry, and by 1987 he was the billionaire co-founder and chief operating officer of Microsoft.

Dallas-born Melinda was 29, and first met Bill at a Microsoft press event in New York City. She had just joined the company in Seattle, soon after completing her MBA at Duke University.

Previously, Bill had dated other women at work, where some employees jokingly wore "Marry Me, Bill!" t-shirts. But his growing relationship with Melinda was kept top-secret outside the company until they became engaged in 1993. Bill's billionaire friend, Warren Buffet, greeted them on a Sunday night after their chartered jet landed in Omaha. Forthwith, Buffet took them to a jewelry store he owned, where they selected a magnificent engagement ring.

New Year's Day 1994, Bill and Melinda were married on the Hawaiian island of Lanai. Her wedding gown was white silk organza enhanced with pearls, and he wore a white dinner jacket over black pants. The ceremony took place at the 12th hole of "The Challenge at Manele," a golf course overlooking the Pacific Ocean, and was officiated by the Chancellor of Seattle University. Country music singer Willie Nelson entertained the newlyweds and 130 invited guests at a celebratory luau that ended with spectacular fireworks. But few outsiders caught even a glimpse of the nuptials because Bill had booked all the helicopters that flew over the 140.5 square miles island, and reserved all the hotel rooms, too.

Following in the philanthropic footsteps of Andrew Carnegie and John D. Rockefeller, Bill and Melinda established Bill & Melinda Gates Foundation to fund and support worldwide worthy causes through grants in education, health, and financial aid for the poor. They plan to give away 95% of their great wealth before they die. Even so, they'll be very rich!

# JANUARY 2
## ANSEL ADAMS & VIRGINIA ROSE BEST
### *"Be yourself – I truly mean YOURself"*

IT'S DIFFICULT TO KNOW WHAT ANSEL fell in love with first at Yosemite National Park in California – the valley or Virginia Best. Her father was a landscape painter who kept an old Chickering piano in his art studio inside the park. Ansel was an accomplished pianist who gave concerts as well as lessons. He visited the Bests often, to practice his music and to photograph the scenery and the young woman who had captured his heart. By the time he was 26, however, he and Virginia began to realize that photography, not music, would be his life's work.

"Know that I love you," he wrote to her shortly before their wedding in 1928. Ansel also described the "acoustically correct" studio he wanted, with plenty of wall space for pictures and workrooms for him and Virginia, too. He wanted lots of friends around him, as well as "green things – and the air of the hills."

They married at Best's Studio, 6 years after they had met. Virginia wore her best dress, which was black. Ansel wore knickers and his "trusty basketball shoes," along with a coat and tie. The best man almost lost the wedding ring, dropping it into the snow while putting snow chains on the honeymoon car.

Both sets of parents approved wholeheartedly of the match and were delighted to attend the marriage ceremony. The family had grown, wrote Ansel's father subsequently, having "taken into … our hearts one of the finest girls in the whole world."

It didn't take long for Ansel to become one of the best-known and most beloved photographers of the American West. Even today, many of his sharply focused pictures of majestic landscapes remain unparalleled and magnificent. From sunrises in the towering Sierra Nevada Mountains to moonrises over tiny western towns, his pictures are breathtaking and evocative. In 1940 Ansel helped establish the photography department at New York's Museum of Modern Art.

## JANUARY 3
## JOHN MARSHALL & MARY WILLIS AMBLER
*A lock of hair brought him back*

JOHN'S FATHER LIKED BOASTING ABOUT HIS son, an intrepid colonel fighting in the Revolutionary War. His Yorktown, Virginia neighbors – especially the Ambler sisters – were impressed until John came home on a furlough and they saw he was an unsophisticated frontiersman in buckskin, friendly and pleasant but definitely unpolished.

Fouteen-year old "Polly" Ambler was dazzled, however, and vowed to seek him out at a society ball. She knew that her mother, Rebecca Burwell Ambler, had once been courted by the young law student, Thomas Jefferson, but had rejected him to marry Polly's father, an older and more established suitor, instead. Polly sensed that John also had a potential for greatness, and she hoped he'd wait for her until she grew up.

John was 27 when he came home a few years later. As a war hero, lawyer, and member of the Virginia House of Delegates, he could have won one of the many wealthy and eligible young widows. Instead, he chose Polly.

He proposed to her shortly before her 17th birthday. She teased him and declined, thinking he would ask again. But John was too deeply hurt to speak, and Polly burst into tears as she watched him ride away on his horse. Fortunately, a cousin who had witnessed the incident surreptitiously managed to snip off a small lock of Polly's light brown hair, race after John, and give it to him. He took it as a sign that Polly had changed her mind – which, of course, she had.

They married soon afterward, in 1783, in an Ambler cousin's home in Hanover County. Polly wore an off-the-shoulder white brocaded dress with shirred sleeves. Around her neck was a fine gold locket containing that precious lock of hair.

Eighteen years later, John became Chief Justice of the United States.

# JANUARY 4
## IRVING BERLIN & ELLIN MACKAY
### *"Always...."*

*"Irving Berlin Weds Ellin Mackay – Elopers Speed Away,*
*Rich Father Ignored For Composer by Society Bud ....*
*Broadway's King of Jazz ... crossed labyrinths of social*
*And religious difference and carried off the youngest*
*daughter of Clarence H. Mackay, multimillionaire ...."*
*Headlines blared in 1926.*

THE 37-YEAR-OLD RUSSIAN JEWISH IMMIGRANT proposed to 21 year-old Ellin on New Year's Eve. Four days later, on a foggy, fairly mild Monday morning, she put on a gray suit and an orange hat, slipped out of her father's apartment, and took her first subway ride downtown to the marriage chapel at City Hall, where she married Irving. They spent a few days in Atlantic City after the wedding, and then sailed to Europe for a two-month honeymoon.

"Don't think our marriage was sudden," Ellin told reporters. She'd been interested in Irving ever since she first heard his music. But love meant everything to her, she declared. "I'm happy because I've done exactly what my heart told me to do."

Ellin's father made no public statements, although he was hounded by the press. But he drew up a new will, cutting his daughter out of her share of his $10-million estate. After the stock market crash of 1929, the fortune was worthless.

Irving gave Ellin much more – the copyright to his new song, "*Always,*" which he had dedicated to her for a wedding gift. Eventually, it was worth hundreds of thousands of dollars, as were many other songs she inspired him to write, such as "*Blue Skies,*" "*Cheek to Cheek,*" and "*Remember.*"

Clarence Mackay didn't speak to his son-in-law for years. Although he mellowed after he lost his wealth, he was never comfortable with his daughter's marriage to a Tin Pan Alley Jewish songwriter. Years later, Ellin liked to say, "Certainly, I married out of my social order. I married up."

# JANUARY 5
## ETHELBERT NEVIN & ANNE PAUL
### *"My melodies are you"*

"THE HAPPIEST EVENT OF HIS LIFE was his marriage, on the fifth of January, 1888, to Miss Anne Paul .... Their lives flow along.... Happily because of the love and devotion they bear to one another," wrote "Bert's" mother several years after the wedding at St. Peter's Episcopal Church in Pittsburgh. Guests were ushered into "a veritable Christmas forest" filled with holiday trees and overhanging boughs as a choir of children and adults marched in pairs down the center aisle, singing the bridal chorus from *Lohengrin*. Bert's wedding gift to Anne was his new song, "Oh! That We Two Were Maying!"

He had quit college eight years earlier and headed for Boston, the center of American music at that time. Although his father had objected, his mother, also a musician, never doubted her son's choice of a career. One day, he would become a concert pianist and composer. Bert's first collection of melodies was published within a year of his marriage, by Gustav Schirmer's Boston Music Company. Many of his best-loved pieces, including the poignant scores for Eugene Field's famous poems, "Wynken, Blynken, and Nod," and "Little Boy Blue" were inspired by his love for Anne and their two children.

In a contemporary newspaper article, novelist Willa Cather described visiting the Nevins and listening to Bert play. Anne, she believed, was a good deal like her husband's music, with the same "idealism and delicate sympathy and sweetness." Bert agreed with Cather. "My life is yours and yours alone," he wrote Anne afterwards. "My melodies are you; my harmony is you!" He was working on a piece called "Love Song," which began:

> Thy presence brings to me sweet rest,
> Thy hands bring soothing to my brow,
> Thy words such sympathy avow,
> Thy going leaves me all unblest.
>> Abide with me.

# JANUARY 6
## GEORGE WASHINGTON & MARTHA DANDRIDGE CUSTIS
### His "agreeable consort"

AMERICA'S MOST FAMOUS GEORGE AND MARTHA probably met at a dinner party in Williamsburg, Virginia, where the wealthy young widow lived with her son and daughter. George was 26; Martha was a year older. Remarriage was not in her best interests, because it meant relinquishing control over her late husband's estate. But Martha wished for a loving and energetic partner and a good stepfather for her children.

When not away at war, George had been living alone at Mount Vernon. He was 6'2" tall and tended to be shy. Martha was quite short, and she enjoyed social gatherings. She also was intelligent, affable, and a good listener. George's size might intimidate others, but Martha thought nothing of pulling him down by his coat lapels when she had something important to say.

They were married in 1759 at St. Peter's Church, near Martha's home. She wore a white quilted silk and satin dress and was driven to the church in a coach drawn by six horses. George wore his regimental regalia and rode beside Martha on his horse.

Shortly before the wedding George resigned his military commission and planned to settle down at Mount Vernon as a gentleman farmer. He wrote, "I am now ... fixed at this seat with an agreeable consort... and hope to find more happiness in retirement than I ever experienc'd amidst a wide and bustling World." In time, he would reenter that "world" however, as commander-in-chief of the Continental army and then as president of the world's first constitutional democracy when he was 57-years old.

George had been a lucky man in battle; during the French and Indian War, two horses had been shot out from under him and at least four bullets had struck his coat, although he remained unharmed. Martha had been lucky, too. She had married "well" the first time. Now she had "done well" again, although she didn't know it. Yet.

# JANUARY 7
## GEORGE BURNS & GRACIE ALLEN
### *"Say goodnight, Gracie"*

BEFORE GEORGE AND GRACIE BECAME A comedy team, they'd both been working in vaudeville – she as a dancer and he as a song-and-dance man. George had also been part of a roller-skating act. But in the 1920's, their humorous routine became their ticket to fame, with Gracie as the scatterbrained wife and George as the patient, reflective, and always somewhat amused straight man and husband. Earning 5 dollars a day on the well-known Orpheum circuit, they delighted audiences across the United States and eventually performed on radio and television, and in motion pictures.

George proposed to Gracie in San Francisco on Christmas Eve, 1925. They were married two weeks later in Cleveland. For 20 dollars, he bought his bride a ring which surprised him by changing colors the longer it stayed in his pocket! Gracie became sentimentally attached to that ring and always wore it, even when she and George could afford more expensive jewelry.

Privately, he called her "Googie" and she called him "Nat" or "Nattie" because his real name was Nathan Birnbaum. Over the years, George wrote many books about his life with Gracie. In *Gracie: A Love Story*, he told readers that in most marriages, the really important questions were simple: 'How do you feel?' 'Is the soup hot?' Those kinds of things kept a marriage together.

Gracie adored George and projected her characteristically zany, cockeyed confusion when she described him to Blanche, their friend and neighbor on *The George Burns and Gracie Allen Show* on television: "George has more sex appeal in his whole body than most men have in their little finger."

Every show ended the same way: He'd tell her "Say good night, Gracie," and she'd reply, "Good night, Gracie."

# JANUARY 8

## HENRI MATISSE & AMELIE PARAYRE

*He always loved the way she looked*

AMELIE WAS A DRESSMAKER AND MILLINER in Paris when she met Henri, and she continued working after they married in 1898 so he could keep on painting. Right after the wedding they went to London to visit the art museums; then they traveled to Toulouse and Corsica to visit her family. They spent a year in the south of France, where Henri fell in love with the Mediterranean light and bright colors that he painted over and over again throughout his long career.

Returning to Paris, Amelie continued working at her shop. Henri painted in their small apartment and in nearby parks, and studied sculpture at night. Periodically, he found work painting theatrical scenery. One year he painted miles of laurel leaves along the cornices of the Grand Palais of Paris exhibition hall.

Amelie was "very lovely ... erect, with a good carriage and the possessor of beautiful dark hair that grew charmingly, especially at the nape of her neck," Henri wrote years after they married. He also admired her "pretty throat and very handsome shoulders." She was his model for the bright pink-faced woman with red hair in "The Green Line," "The Woman with the Hat," "The Guitarist," and many other works.

Henri worked feverishly and slept restlessly; when he woke up in the middle of the night, Amelie would talk softly or read to him until he fell asleep again. "Despite the fact that she was timid and reserved, she was a person of great kindness, force and gentleness," he said.

Amelie never forgot one of Henri's gifts, which he gave her when they had very little money. He bought her a mounted butterfly with iridescent blue wings, saying it was because the beautiful color reminded him of the intense and magnificent light of the Mediterranean and their first year of marriage, when they lived beside the sea.

# JANUARY 9

## LOUISE DILWORTH BEATTY & SIDNEY HOMER

*"Two musical waifs threw their fortunes together"*

TWENTY-TWO-YEAR OLD MISS BEATTY WAS DETERMINED to learn "all about music" when she came to Sidney's studio for singing lessons in 1893. She thought he was extremely bright and handsome, and he was enchanted by her demeanor and voice. "It was not like the contralto voices I had heard .... It was low but it had the sparkle and brilliance of a great dramatic soprano," he wrote years later in their autobiography. Eventually she became an internationally famous American contralto singer.

Sidney began taking meals at the boardinghouse where Louise lived, on Boylston Street in a Boston suburb. They talked incessantly about music and attended concerts and operas together. She inspired him to write music, and he encouraged her to sing.

Their wedding in January 1895 was followed by a reception at her sister's house in Arlington, Massachusetts. Driving to catch a train to "the snowy wilds" of the Baldpate Inn, they wondered why strangers on the streets waved and smiled at them, until they noticed a little shoe – announcing they were "just married" – that had been tied to their coach's roof by one of the wedding guests.

After their daughter was born in 1896, the Homers sailed for France, where they spent borrowed money and a small inheritance on advanced vocal training for the new mother. Louise deftly turned her wedding dress into an evening gown for concert performances in Paris. In 1898, she made her European operatic debut in *La Favorite*, while Sidney and their daughter listened and applauded.

Although Sidney continued to compose, he was primarily devoted to his wife's singing career. Louise rarely missed a performance – despite having 6 children! She sang Emilia in *Otello* at New York's Metropolitan Opera House in 1902, only 5 weeks after giving birth to a son. By 1909 she had made more than 50 recordings.

# JANUARY 10

## JULES VERNE & HONORINE DE VIANE MOREL

*Flying to the moon was less daunting than getting married*

"THE MERE THOUGHT OF INVITING FRIENDS to the marriage service makes my hair stand on end in horror!" wrote the future author of books about fearless exploits under the sea and incredible trips to the moon. In 1857, Jules' farfetched fantasies seemed less frightening to him than being married before a crowd of people.

Honorine was a 25-year-old widow with 2 small children when she and 29-year-old Jules met at her sister's wedding. They fell in love quickly, but Jules had not yet realized his creative genius as a writer. Although he'd sold some short stories and written a few plays, he worked primarily as a stockbroker.

They married at the Church of St. Eugene in Paris. The groom was somewhat dazed and later wrote, "I didn't know where I was, and I handed out money to everyone …. Someone shouted for the bridegroom! They meant me!"

A few days later, he and Honorine stood before the statue of Venus de Milo in the Louvre, and he introduced his bride to "the only woman of whom you need ever be jealous."

Long before polar explorations, spaceships, airplanes, helicopters, escalators, automobiles and motion pictures were realities, Jules was imagining them. Honorine didn't complain when he came home at night from the stock exchange and sat down to write. She enjoyed reading his manuscripts and sometimes rescued "failures" he had hurled into the fireplace.

After 5 years Jules sold *Five Weeks in a Balloon* to a publisher. He quit his job (which he hated) and continued writing more than 65 books, including *Journey to the Center of the Earth*, *20,000 Leagues Under the Sea*, and *Around the World in 80 Days*, as well as essays, short stories, geographical works, plays and librettos.

# JANUARY 11

## DR. BENJAMIN RUSH & JULIA STOCKTON

### *"my Sweet Julia"*

BENJAMIN AND JULIA FIRST MET IN 1763, when he was an 18-year-old student at Princeton and she was 4 years old, apparently lost in the commencement crowd. He recognized the little Stockton girl immediately and carried her to her father's house, "listening with great pleasure to her prattling all the way." Benjamin and Julia didn't meet again for 12 years; by then, he had become a surgeon and physician and a delegate to the Continental Congress in Philadelphia.

Julia's father, also a congressional delegate, invited Dr. Rush home to dinner and reintroduced him to his daughter. That evening, Julia charmed Benjamin by singing Scottish tunes. She was 16, he later reminisced, with "a complexion composed of white and red, a countenance at the same time soft and animated, a voice mild and musical." He visited the Stocktons' estate, Morven, every week and gently prodded his Philadelphia patients to please pay his bills; after all, he was planning to be married!

After a wedding at Morven in 1776, the Rushes settled down on Walnut Street in Philadelphia. A few months later, Julia visited her family. Benjamin missed her terribly. "My loveliest girl," he wrote. "I think, write, talk, work, love – all, all – only for you."

That summer, Benjamin and other Continental Congress delegates signed the Declaration of Independence. The subsequent years were hard; there was a long, painful war and many illnesses, including a yellow fever epidemic that paralyzed Philadelphia in 1793. Julia and Benjamin corresponded constantly whenever they were apart. She was his most sincere and trusted friend, as well as "the dear right side of my heart."

Shortly before their wedding, Benjamin had asked the artist Charles Willson Peale, to paint Julia's portrait. In it she is elegantly seated, plucking lute strings. Probably, she is singing a simple Scottish tune to delight her beloved husband.

# JANUARY 12

## CHARLES WILLSON PEALE & RACHEL BREWER

*Her face was the kind "that painters love to imitate"*

WHEN CHARLES WAS THIRTEEN, HE QUIT school and became a saddler's apprentice in Annapolis, Maryland. He had already shown artistic talent, drawing complicated designs for his widowed mother's fine needlework and making pictures on glass with colored inks. The saddler taught him how to carve leather and wood, enabling Charles to set up his own shop soon after he and Rachel were married in 1762. Neither of them suspected that one day he would paint the portraits of virtually every famous citizen in the newly established United States of America.

Rachel was the 14-year-old sister of Charles' friend John Brewer, who lived by the South River. On the night Charles first met Rachel, he showed up unexpectedly after dark. "Go around the back, you impudent baggage!" Rachel called when Charles knocked on the front door. She thought he was an itinerant tradesman until her brother rushed out to greet him, but Charles quickly accepted her apologies when he looked into her dark brown eyes.

They struggled financially during the first years of their marriage, because Charles owed money to creditors who had helped him set up his business. Besides saddlery, he learned how to upholster furniture and paint signs. Then Charles bought his first art book and supplies, after being inspired by the portrait painters he met in Philadelphia. Whenever he sold someone a saddle, he offered to paint the customer's portrait, too. Eventually, a group of Maryland gentlemen were so impressed with Charles's self-taught skills that they sent him to school in London to study art. When he returned to Maryland, the years of struggle were over.

Charles never tired of painting pictures of his beautiful Rachel. They named their sons Raphael, Rembrandt, Titian and Rubens – inspiring them to become painters, too.

# JANUARY 13*
## SIR KENELM DIGBY & VENETIA STANLEY
*"Two hearts with mutual desire"*

TWO YEARS AFTER KENELM AND VENETIA were secretly married in 1625, the future English naval commander, natural scientist, and diplomat began writing his *Private Memoirs*. He called himself "Theagenes" and his beloved Venetia "Stelliana." Their story, in the form of an allegorical romance, was first published 200 years later.

Childhood friends, they had played together near the Digbys' Buckinghamshire estate, but Kenelm's mother disliked Venetia and encouraged her son to go abroad when he was 17. Before his departure, he and Venetia stole away from a hunting party and spent a passionate afternoon in a secluded wood. Her eyes were hazel, her cheeks rose pink, and her face framed by "heartbreaker" curls. There could be no other woman in Kenelm's life, he swore. Exclamations of love, rapturous kisses, locks of hair, and a diamond ring were exchanged.

At a masked ball in Angers, France, Marie de Medicis, the middle-aged queen mother of Louis XIII, took a liking to Kenelm and aggressively tried to seduce him. Escaping her clutches, he fled to Italy and circulated rumors of his death. He also wrote to Venetia, telling her the truth. Unfortunately, Kenelm's letter miscarried; others were either lost or intercepted by his mother.

For 2 years, Venetia thought Kenelm was dead. Eventually, she moved to London and became engaged to someone else. Kenelm howled when he found out and threw a bracelet made of Venetia's hair into the fire. Why didn't she wait? Had she doubted his love? He returned to England, vowing never to see her, but when their paths crossed accidentally, he was hooked again. "The sun seemed to grow pale at her appearance, as being dazzled by a greater light than its own."

Venetia was furious, believing he had tricked her. They fought and separated. A few weeks later, Kenelm slipped into her bed and awakened her with love. Soon afterward, they were married.

---

*Date approximate.

# JANUARY 14
## JACK BENNY & SADIE MARKS
### *A great team*

THE FORMER BENJAMIN KUBELSKY MARRIED HIS beloved Sadie at a friend's apartment in the Clayton Hotel in Waukegan, Illinois in 1927. Sadie fainted right after the rabbi pronounced them husband and wife, and it took an hour and a half to revive her. Then they called Sadie's folks in California, who wished the new couple luck but doubted the marriage would last.

After a quick celebration, the newlyweds raced to Chicago, where Jack had a part in *The Great Temptations*. Sadie spent the first part of their wedding night sitting in the audience watching Jack on stage. "But I was so tired from all the hectic running around during the week …. I fell asleep long before the first curtain," she wrote in *Jack Benny: A Biography*.

The couple first met in Vancouver, British Columbia, where Jack was performing. His friend Zeppo Marx (one of the famous Marx Brothers) invited him to a Passover seder at the Markses', Zeppo's distant relatives. Fourteen-year-old Sadie flipped for 27-year-old Jack right away, but he forgot about her until they went out on a blind date 5 years later. By then she was selling hosiery in a department store and was "exquisitely lovely," he recalled. Too shy to talk about romance, the lovesick entertainer bought silk stockings by the gross instead.

Eventually, Jack achieved stardom on radio and television shows, with Sadie playing his devoted wife, "Mary Livingstone." Although Jack portrayed a violin-playing, self-deprecating skinflint, he actually was quite generous, kind, and sentimental. Sadie was just like him.

Before their wedding, Jack's father had his late wife's wide gold wedding ring cut into 2 narrow bands – one for Jack's wife, and the other for his sister, who was also getting married. Sadie wore that precious ring forever. "Until the day Jack died, he was … holding my hand," she wrote. "Jack thought I was everything, and I thought he was everything."

# JANUARY 15

## DANNY THOMAS & ROSE MARIE CASSANITI
### *Making Room for Danny*

ROSE'S ITALIAN FAMILY DID'NT LIKE THE "Turk" their 17-year-old daughter had met in Detroit, where they both were entertainers on *The Happy Hour Club* radio show. Marry him, her father warned, and you'll find yourself living in a tent!

Danny (whose Lebanese name was Amos Jahoob) thought the petite dark-haired singer was a knockout, so he walked a mile out of his way each day just to hop on board her streetcar and ride with her. Rose knew he had very little money and burst into tears when he spent his last nickel buying her a candy bar.

In 1936 they were married by an Italian priest in a Belgian church on Mack Avenue in Detroit. But joy was mitigated by sadness when Danny lost his job. Ready to quit show business, he got a chance to perform in Chicago after praying to Saint Jude, patron saint of lost causes. Danny became a night-club emcee, USO performer, and movie actor, but being a comedian suited him best and brought him fame and financial success.

Danny often claimed that his 3 kids – including Margaret Julia, who grew up to be Marlo Thomas – created the title for his television show, "Make Room for Daddy," which ran from 1953 to 1964. Just like the fictional character he portrayed, their own father was an entertainer on the road a lot. Whenever Danny was away, the kids slept with their mother in their parents' bedroom. When he came home, it was "make room for Daddy!"

Twenty-five years after Rose and Danny married, he stood outside his mansion with his family, watching celebrities and friends at the silver anniversary party he and Rose were hosting. Pointing to the very large, luxurious tent suspended over the swimming pool, Danny couldn't resist reminding his father-in-law of his dour prediction, made so long ago.

# JANUARY 16*
## LAFCADIO HEARN & SETSU KOIZUMI
### *Coming home, in a foreign land*

TWENTY-FIVE-YEAR-OLD SETSU, THE DAUGHTER OF A samurai, became Lafcadio's inspiration and constant source of love. When Lafcadio first arrived in Japan in 1890, he was a restless, shy, and insecure journalist, essayist, and novelist, born in Greece and educated in England and France. He had gone to the United States when he was a young man but never felt at home anywhere until he came to the Orient. Entranced by the beauty, solitude, and ancient customs of Japan, he was 40 when he began teaching Western literature there.

As soon as Setsu met Lafcadio, she was deeply impressed by his sensitivity, kindness and honesty. He "was an extremely honest man," she wrote. "He did not have the least evil in his mind.... During his childhood he had always been teased by malicious people until he cried. The keening of his sensibility was astonishing."

They married some time in January, 1891, in a traditional Japanese ceremony that included an exchange of rice wine before witnesses. As a proper Japanese son-in-law, Lafcadio accepted the responsibility of caring for his wife's parents as well as for his own wife and the children they would have. They lived in a traditional Japanese "birdcage house" on a lake in Matsue. "There is no such thing in Japan as privacy," he wrote. "There are no secrets. Every earthly thing a man does is known to everybody, and life is extravagantly, astoundingly frank." He began dressing and acting more and more like a native. Eventually, he became a Japanese citizen, adopting the name, Koizumi Yakumo.

Most literary biographers believe Lafcadio produced his best works in Japan because of his sympathetic observations of Asian life. He revived interest in Japanese folktales and was instrumental in bringing Japanese philosophy and art to Western audiences.

---

*Date approximate.

# JANUARY 17
## ALEXANDER CALDER & LOUISA JAMES
*Passionate about art, and Louisa*

THE NIGHT BEFORE THEIR 1931 WEDDING in Concord, Massachusetts, "Sandy" showed Louisa's relatives some of the wire sculptures he had made of circus animals that could oscillate, roll, hop, or twitch. Some people were shocked; others were amused and wondered just who was this young man Louisa was marrying? When the reverend arrived the next day, he apologized for missing the show. "But you are here for the circus today," Sandy said wryly.

Although he was the son and grandson of artists, Sandy didn't intend to become one, too. After graduating from Stevens Tech in New Jersey, he tried a few "regular" jobs for a while, but when his parents offered to pay for drawing classes at New York's Art Students League, Sandy found his passion.

Inspired by Mondrian's shapes, Miro's forms, and other abstract art, Sandy began making stationary structures called "stabiles," and sculptures that moved, called "mobiles."

He met Louisa on a transatlantic voyage. Her father was aloof and unimpressed with the young man who called himself a "wire sculptor," but back home, Louisa invited him to their Cape Cod summerhouse. Later, she visited his Greenwich Village studio and was fascinated by his sculptures and drawings. One day she would create magnificent hooked rugs based on Sandy's designs.

They fell in love quickly but waited 2 years until Sandy – who traveled back and forth from Paris to see Louisa – was selling enough art to feel financially secure. Shortly before the wedding, he gave her a gold ring he had designed for her.

They sailed for Paris and lived in Sandy's small apartment at 7, Villa Brune. Louisa quickly got used to the contraptions Sandy hung around their home. All the door latches had been rigged with strings and wires; from the bathtub he could open the front door, just by moving his hand!

# JANUARY 18

## WASHINGTON ROEBLING & EMILY WARREN
### *"A strong tower to lean upon"*

WASHINGTON AND EMILY MET AT A Union army officer's ball during the Civil War, 10 years before he and his father designed and began building New York City's Brooklyn Bridge.

"Miss Emily Warren… has captured your brother Washy's heart," he wrote his sister back home in Troy, New York. To Emily he said, "I think we will be a pair of lovers all our lifetime."

They were both 26 when they married in Cold Spring, New York, soon after Washington's honorable discharge in 1865. For a while, they lived in Ohio, where the Roeblings built the Cincinnati and Covington suspension bridge. Afterwards they studied steel mills and bridges in Europe, and Emily learned engineering. Then the Roeblings won the contract to build what would be called "The Eighth Wonder of the World."

During the 14 years that it took to construct the Brooklyn Bridge over the East River, the elder Roebling died and Washington became chief engineer. Tragically, he encountered "the bends" in 1879, after staying underwater too long in one of the caisson chambers. Bedridden and weak, he could no longer supervise completion of this mammoth project.

"At first, I thought I would succumb," he later wrote. "But I had a strong tower to lean upon, my wife, a woman of infinite tact and wisest counsel."

Emily became her husband's spokesperson, inspector, and messenger, consulting with workmen and bringing them instructions. In an eloquent and impassioned plea, she convinced the board of trustees not to replace Washington with another chief engineer.

Washington supervised the construction process from the bay window of their home at 110 Columbia Heights in Brooklyn. On May 24, 1883, the bridge was completed. Crowds cheered, bands marched, and fireworks soared over the water. Dignitaries including President Chester A. Arthur and New York Governor Grover Cleveland congratulated the Roeblings personally. Their parlor was filled with refreshments and flowers; some people said the celebration resembled a wedding.

# JANUARY 19
## FRANCIS SCOTT KEY & MARY TAYLOE LLOYD
*The sweetest smile*

THE FUTURE AUTHOR OF "THE STAR-SPANGLED BANNER" was a 22-year old Virginia lawyer in 1802 when he married Mary at Chase House, her father's mansion in Annapolis, Maryland. Always a poet at heart, Francis fell in love with Mary soon after his uncle Philip introduced them. Mary's golden hair, merry dark eyes, and sweet disposition inspired her beau to pen some sonnets. In "To Mary," Francis wished,

*Perhaps she'll value more my love,*
*Perhaps give more of hers to me,*
*Perhaps may greet me with a smile,*
*More sweet, if smile more sweet can be.*

After their wedding, they moved to Washington, D.C., where Francis joined Uncle Philip's law firm. They went home for Francis's sister's wedding to Roger B. Taney, who eventually became a U.S. Supreme Court justice.

The Keys remained with their children in their Georgetown home on Bridge Street throughout most of the War of 1812, even during an oppressively hot summer when the British attacked and burned the city. When a prominent doctor friend was imprisoned on a British ship anchored near Fort McHenry in Baltimore harbor, Francis and another volunteer went to negotiate Dr. Beane's release. Afterwards, the British prevented the 3 Americans from departing until after the fort was bombarded.

The American flag waved all day over the fort, until darkness fell and it could be seen no longer. At "dawn's early light" in the smoke of battle, Francis stood on the deck of a ship and began jotting down the words of what would become America's most patriotic song. He continue writing at home, shaping his words to fit the melody of "Anacreon in Heaven." A few weeks later, his poem appeared in a Baltimore newspaper. The editors accurately predicted that his song was "destined long to outlast the occasion" that had produced it.

# JANUARY 20
## RICHARD E. BYRD & MARIE AMES
*He named a new land after her*

WHEN RICHARD AND MARIE WERE GROWING up in Virginia, the future aviator and polar explorer often told her about famous adventurers who had "conquered" mountains, oceans, and faraway lands. Someday, Richard vowed, he would explore the North Pole. In 1900, when he was 13, he visited a family friend in the Philippines, becoming the youngest person to travel around the world alone.

He went to Virginia Military Institute and then to Annapolis, where his athletic career was ruined by serious leg injuries, but Marie's "TLC" helped heal his disappointments. Why not become a flyer? She suggested, when they learned that Admiral Peary had reached the North Pole on foot. She told Richard that he could explore far-off lands from the air, mapping out huge areas still unexplored.

Marie and Richard married in 1915, when he was a naval attaché stationed in Washington, D.C. during World War I. His brothers, Tom and Harry, were best men at the wedding. (Eventually, they also married their childhood sweethearts and were best men at each other's weddings, too.)

Richard's greatest achievements began in the 1920's, when he became the first man to fly over the regions of both the North and South Poles. He also piloted the first airmail flight across the Atlantic and organized the first full-scale exploration of Antarctica. Leading a group of scientists, reporters, and photographers across vast wastelands of ice and snow, the explorers established "Little America" as their base of future operations. Richard's expedition went on to discover and claim new regions in Antarctica under the flag of the United States.

When Richard established "Marie Byrd Land" in 1929, he named it for the woman "who has backed and helped me every foot of the way, who has shouldered much of the burdens… and whose understanding has made my many expeditions possible."

# JANUARY 21

## CASPAR DAVID FRIEDRICH & CAROLINE BOMMER

*With Caroline, "more time is spent eating, drinking, sleeping, joking, laughing"*

CASPAR WAS A RESPECTED 44-YEAR OLD German Romantic painter when he married Caroline, who was 25. He'd always been a serious man whose early experiences with death and loneliness inspired much of his art. Caroline brought great joy into his life, but his works remained introspective and filled with allegory and symbolism.

They married in 1818 in Dresden, where Caspar was a member of the Academy of Art, and Caroline became his primary model. He painted her standing on faraway fields and waving goodbye from a ship heading toward a distant port. Her figure dominates "Woman Before the Setting Sun" in which we see her from the back, facing the sun which has dropped behind a mountain. Caroline's arms are spread out; both she and sun are the givers of light and of life. Probably, Caroline was already pregnant. In 1819, their first child, Emma, would be born.

"On the day Caspar is painting air, he may not be spoken to," said Caroline, who became her husband's dearest friend and lover. She understood his great need for solitude and the long walks he often took in the moonlight. Caspar believed that God was everywhere and that Nature should be revered. At Christmastime they decorated their home with evergreen branches, rather than cut down a tree unnecessarily.

In the 1830's he painted "Evening Star." In the golden tones of late afternoon, Caroline crosses an open field with one of their daughters, and their son Gustav Adolf stretches his arms toward the sky.

"Close your physical eye," Caspar suggested, "so that you first see your pictures with your spiritual eye. Then bring to light what you have seen in the dark so that it is passed on to others from the outside to the inside."

# JANUARY 22

## SIR RICHARD BURTON & ISABEL ARUNDELL
### *"One soul in two bodies"*

A
T THIRTY, RICHARD WAS TALL AND broad, with thick dark hair and arched eyebrows. His head was leonine and his black eyes were piercing and magnetic. He was half-Irish, half-English, but he looked quite exotic.

He first met Isabel by chance, on the ramparts of the French city of Boulogne, when she was 18 and traveling with her mother and sisters. The dashing and mysterious English officer's glance was mesmerizing. Hadn't a fortune-teller told her, "You will cross the sea and be in the same town with your Destiny and not know it?"

Neither one spoke, but Richard stared at Isabel with his dark, penetrating eyes. He did not know about the Gypsy's predictions, or that Isabel would always save the gloves and sash she wore a few nights later when they danced at a society ball.

Soon afterwards, Richard left for Mecca disguised as an Arab merchant. No white man had visited Mecca before, and he wrote about his travels in books that brought him fame. Future works would include translations of *The Arabian Nights* and *Kama Sutra*, in which he restored much of the passion and eroticism missing from other versions.

Isabel's conventional Victorian mother opposed her daughter's infatuation, but Isabel would not give up. "If Richard and I never marry," she wrote, "God will cause us to meet in the next world; we cannot be parted; we belong to each other." Years passed. Isabel rejected other suitors and promised Richard she would wait for him. On he went – from Mecca to Medina, to India and the American West – until at last he returned to her.

They married in 1861, 11 years after their first encounter. "My darling," Isabel said, "I have read every word you ever wrote, and I would rather have a crust and a tent with *you* than be queen of all the world!"

# JANUARY 23

## EDWARD THE CONFESSOR & EDITH GODWINE
### *Aka Eadward and Eadgyth*

EDITH WOULD HAVE BEEN THE FIRST TO say it wasn't easy being married to someone who was "holier than thou." Still, clerics had given the chubby albino king of England his saintly nickname, and he tried his best to live up to it.

Everyone was glad when Edward ascended to the throne, replacing that wretched Dane, Harthacanute, who had treated England shabbily. Once England was back in the hands of a native-born king, Edward decided to seek a good wife.

Edith's father, Godwine, the pushy and powerful earl of Wessex, introduced Edward to his eldest daughter. Edward thought that the 24-year old maiden was bright as well as beautiful, as well as suitably God-fearing. She thought he was affable and gentle, although somewhat pale.

They married on a Wednesday in 1045, and straightaway Edith was crowned. As part of her "morning gift," which brides customarily received after the wedding night, Edward gave her Winchester and Essex.

Most of the time, their kingdom was at peace. Edward and Edith devoted themselves primarily to religion and supervised early construction of Westminster Abbey. Edith gave grammar lessons to local scholars and was also an accomplished spinner and embroiderer. She stitched elaborate robes for Edward. The king admired her work profusely but usually hung the garments in the back of his closet. A creature of habit, he preferred putting on his plain old robes over and over again, confessing softly that Edith's were a bit too showy.

When the monarchs didn't produce an heir, rumors and speculation arose. Some said that Edward and Edith were too pious to find time for sex, others said they didn't like sex, and some silly fools said they never had sex at all! But Edward and Edith, like every wise couple, kept their private life private.

# JANUARY 24

## KING EDWARD III & PHILIPPA OF HAINAULT

*"Hay, hay, the White Swan, by God's soul I am thy man!"*

AFTER PHILIPPA'S UNCLE AND HIS DUTCH mercenaries fought with Edward's troops against the Scots in Northumberland, he invited the 14-year old future king and his mother to drop by, sometime, for a visit.

Perfect timing, thought Queen Isabella, a forceful and bossy woman. She'd been considering possible brides for her son; why not the flaxen-haired, 13-year old daughter of the wealthy and powerful Count William of Hainault, Holland, and New Zealand? There were 3 other sisters, equally apple-cheeked and pretty, but Edward preferred Philippa. Like other Plantagenets, he was fair-haired, blue-eyed and tall. Philippa thought he looked like an angel.

Back in England, Isabella coerced her husband, Edward II, to abdicate. Young Edward was crowned in January 1327, and that fall, he and Philippa were married by proxy in her Flemish home. In December, the bride sailed to England for a rousing reception in London and a ride across snow-covered country roads to York, where the archbishop formalized her marriage to Edward in 1328. Edward didn't remain under his mother's wicked thumb much longer. By the time he was 18, he had executed her paramour and forced her into retirement.

*"Honi soit qui mal y pense"* (Evil to him who evil thinks), said Edward, making it the motto of the Order of the Garter. He had so much confidence in Philippa, he made her regent whenever he went overseas. In 1346 she assembled her own army and drove back Scots who invaded again. She could be bellicose, and also just; after Edward laid siege to Calais in France, Philippa persuaded him to rescind the executions of 6 town leaders.

Edward would be the first English king to make women an integral part of court life. He and Philippa encouraged the arts, especially poetry, and like all happy parents, they encouraged their children to marry for love.

# JANUARY 25

## JOSIAH WEDGWOOD & SARAH WEDGWOOD
*"two married Lovers, happy as this world can make them"*

"I YESTERDAY PREVAILED UPON MY DEAR Girl to name the day, the blissful day! when she will reward all my faithful services, & take me to her arms! to her Nuptial bed!" Josiah wrote to his good friend and partner, Thomas Bentley, in 1764. Josiah and "Sally" were 3rd cousins who had known each other since childhood, yet they did not marry until he was 34 and she was 30 years old.

Josiah had learned about pottery-making while apprenticed to his older brother, Thomas, and became a master potter by 1759. That year, he opened his own small factory, Ivy House, in Burslem, England, and produced cream-colored "Useful" ware, decorated with simple designs. Many potteries existed in England then, but Josiah soon earned a reputation for perfection. His spouts poured evenly, his lids fit properly, and all his handles were easy to grip.

A year after Josiah and Sally married, he received his first royal order – a tea service for Queen Charlotte and King George III. Sally gave birth to their first child, Susannah, who would one day become Charles Darwin's mother. More children would be born to the Wedgwoods, but Sally also maintained an active role in her husband's business. Evenings, he showed her new designs and products, and she visited his factory and shops often. They were a liberal-minded couple, involved in community life and supportive of the American and French Revolutions.

Josiah's partnership with Bentley represented an ideal combination: Josiah was a perfectionist craftsman, and Bentley had extensive knowledge of classical and Renaissance art. Their early black basalt vases painted with red classical figures led to the development of what would become the most famous Wedgwood pottery – neoclassical white clay patterns and cameos superimposed on the flat surfaces of vases, mugs, bowls, platters and teapots.

# JANUARY 26
## MADELEINE L'ENGLE & HUGH FRANKLIN
*Always "more than music"*

WHEN THE FUTURE NEWBERRY AWARD-WINNING AUTHOR of *A Wrinkle in Time* and other exceptional children's books first met the man who would one day become famous as Dr. Charles Tyler of TV's soap opera, *All My Children*, he was a struggling actor and she had just gotten a bit part in the same play.

After graduating from Smith College, Madeleine moved to Greenwich Village in New York City and supported herself by selling stories and poems, and appearing in theatrical productions. In 1944, she was thrilled to win even a small role in a touring company production of Chekhov's *The Cherry Orchard*. Hugh was cast as the student Trofimov; she was the maid and thought the handsome dark-haired actor would never notice her. But at the end of the first day, Hugh asked her out for dinner. They talked until almost 2:00 am. When Madeleine got home, she was sure she had met the man she wanted to marry.

The road company traveled across the United States, led by the acting stars, Eva Le Gallienne and Joseph Schildkraut. Madeleine kept writing in her spare time and eventually completed her first novel. When the show's run was over, she and Hugh kept in touch and saw each other whenever he was in New York.

In her memoir, *Two-Part Invention*, written many years later, Madeleine described an evening when Hugh played music from *Swan Lake* on her phonograph and recited lines from a poem by Conrad Aiken:

*Music I learned with you was more than music,*
*And bread I broke with you was more than bread.*

And then he proposed. They were married in an Episcopal church in Chicago in 1946 during the run of *The Joyous Season*, in which they both were performing. After the ceremony, Hugh and Madeleine raced back to the theater in time for the next show.

# JANUARY 27

## GEORGES ROUAULT & MARTHE LE SIDANER
### *"Faithful Marthe"*

WHEN GEORGES AND MARTHE MARRIED IN 1908, he was 36 and working on his series of paintings of judges and tribunals. He and Marthe had met at the home of mutual friends in Paris. She was a witty and well-born pianist from Saint-Malo who had been raised to appreciate art. Her mother was a musician, her father was a sea-faring captain who also painted and sculpted, and her brother was a Pointillist painter.

Georges was born in Paris during the brutal Franco-Prussian War of 1871, and the bombings may have foreshadowed his dark, serious paintings. Most likely, his greatest influence was a devoted grandfather who taught him to appreciate the art of Rembrandt, Daumier, Monet, and other masters, and who gave him the courage to find his own style. George's teenage apprenticeship to a stained-glass maker also made an impact on his future work, especially those pictures in which bright colors are separated by thick black lines.

Marthe got along well with the Rouault family, which was fortunate, because during the first years of their marriage, the young couple lived with Georges's parents in Versailles. His beloved grandfather died soon after the wedding, but his grandmother gladly watched over her great-grandchildren so Marthe could give piano lessons and supplement the family income.

Although Georges reproached himself for not earning enough money, Marthe didn't complain about having to work. She often played music at gatherings of friends and especially admired the works of Ravel and Debussy. Georges painted park scenes in Versailles as well as landscapes, religious subjects, clowns and other performers. He also wrote poetry about his "Faithful Marthe" and their four children – Genevieve, his "chiming bell," Isabelle, his "little dove," Agnes, a "little pigeon," and his son Michel, "frail pillar of the house." Some of Georges's work was published in Apollinaire's new magazine, *Soirees de Paris.*

# JANUARY 28

## KURT WEILL & LOTTE LENYA

*With Lotte, life and music were never dull*

A LTHOUGH THE MARRIAGE OF KURT WEILL, AN introverted and brilliant German-Jewish composer and musician, and Lotte Lenya (born Karoline Bismauer), a street-smart, extroverted and highly talented Viennese singer and dancer with freethinking attitudes towards sex, was rarely peaceful, their union – especially their early years together – inspired Kurt to produce 7 works for the stage and more than a dozen concert pieces and scores within 3 years. In many cases, he wrote his music for Lotte's gravely voice, which he loved "like a very force of nature."

Kurt was 24 and writing *Der Protagonist*, a tragic opera, in Berlin in 1924 when he first met 26-year old Lotte, who'd been asked to meet his train and accompany him to a well-known dramatist's home. Kurt had broken away from his conservative family, and here was Lotte – homely yet magnetic, a bohemian artist with an anti-bourgeois attitude. Soon after their 1929 marriage in a civil ceremony at Berlin's city hall, he wrote his parents, saying that living with Lotte made his music "more confident much freer, lighter – and simpler." A year later he began collaborating with Bertoldt Brecht, who wrote the libretto for *The Threepenny Opera* while Kurt composed the music, including the song, "Mack the Knife."

In the 1930's Kurt and Lotte lived apart at times, but emotionally and psychologically, they were always attached. They left Berlin in 1933, divorced in Italy, and then sailed to America together. In 1936 they bought a pair of wedding rings in Woolworth's and remarried in New York. He wrote scores for Hollywood films and Lotte performed in plays and in radio productions. In her later years, Lotte appeared in films such as *From Russia With Love*. After Kurt's death in 1950, she dedicated herself to protecting and preserving his work, and eventually donated everything to Yale University.

## JANUARY 29

## CHARLES DARWIN & EMMA WEDGWOOD

### *"My wonder Charley"*

THE FUTURE AUTHOR OF CLASSIC THEORIES on evolution and natural selection saw no problems in marrying his first cousin. A few weeks before their wedding in 1839, other things worried him terribly. "I wish the awful day was over," Charles wrote Emma. "I am not very tranquil when I think of the procession; it is very awesome."

The ceremony was conducted by another cousin, John Allen Wedgwood, at St. Peter's Church in Shrewsbury, Charles's birthplace. Having a friendly relation guide him in repeating those hallowed vows of matrimony helped Charles get through the service and begin life with the woman he would call his "greatest blessing."

Charles had doubts about marriage in general and had composed a list of pros and cons. Not marrying meant "freedom to go where one liked," and "not forced to visit relatives, or bend to every trifle," but marriage could bring a "constant companion" and "object to be beloved and played with – better than a dog anyhow." "Only picture to yourself a nice soft wife on a sofa with good fire, & books & music perhaps," he concluded. "Marry – Marry – Marry Q.E.D!"

Charles and Emma were both 29 when they married. She wore a gray-green silk dress and a white bonnet trimmed with feathers. Afterwards, they dashed off for a train to London, eating sandwiches and toasting their future with bottled water.

Their first home was Macaw Cottage at 12 Upper Gower Street in Bloomsbury, not far from Regent's Park. They often took long walks and looked at the animals (especially the apes!) in the Zoological Gardens nearby. Charles's father encouraged his son's research by giving the young couple financial help during their early years.

Although Charles never shared Emma's deep religious faith and she couldn't accept his views on evolution, it didn't stop her from helping out whenever possible and proofreading his *The Origin of Species* before publication.

# JANUARY 30

## SALVADOR DALI & "GALA"

*"Muse of the Surrealists"*

ALA AND DALI MET ON THE beaches of Cadaques, Spain, in July 1929. She and her husband, French surrealist poet Paul Eluard, had been part of the circle of artists drawn to Paris in the rich, creative years after World War I. Now their marriage was virtually over, and Gala sought a new artist to cling to and inspire.

Dali was 25, flamboyant, outrageous, eccentric, and extravagant. He pomaded his hair, painted in the nude, and often wore pearl necklaces and ribbons around his wrists. Gala was in her mid-thirties, with long black hair, piercing dark eyes, and a highly liberal attitude toward sex. She slithered when she walked and resembled a mysterious and exotic panther. No one knew her exact age, or details from her past. "The secret of all my secrets," she said, "is that I do not tell them."

If Dali was bizarre, so was Gala. In Paris she had stirred the passions of many young artists, inspiring them to create radically new work. She believed Dali was a genius, but on the verge of madness. She would help him keep a grip on reality while he unleashed his wild visions on his canvases. Soon he began work on "The Accommodations of Desires," a haunting glimpse into the world of dreams.

Dali's fascination with Gala never ceased. "I fixed in my memory the value of every grain of her skin…. Her back ravished me with the delicacy of the joints…. Her hair, her intimate hair, her odors, intoxicated me," he later wrote in *The Secret Life of Salvador Dali*.

In 1934, Dali's "The Persistence of Memory" attracted worldwide attention, and he was offered his first one-man show in New York. But since Americans were too conventional to accept his exotic mistress, Dali and Gala were married in a civil ceremony in Paris shortly before they sailed. Witnesses included their landlord, landlady, and … Paul Eluard.

# JANUARY 31

## WILLIAM TEMPLE & DOROTHY OSBORNE

*"Dear, shall we ever be happy, think you?"*

WILLIAM AND DOROTHY HAD A BRIEF shipboard romance while crossing the English Channel on the way to Saint-Malo France in 1648. She was 21, beautiful and spirited, and traveling with her adolescent brother, Robin. William was 20, good-looking, cultured and charming, and on his way to the continent to continue his education. They had met shortly before embarkation, on the Isle of Wight. Civil war raged in England, and King Charles I was imprisoned by Cromwell's forces nearby. One night, Robin scratched an anti-Cromwell message on a window-pane, and the next morning the 3 travelers were arrested.

When Dorothy took the blame for her younger brother, William was deeply impressed and touched. She was set free after a scolding, and the 3 were soon on their way again. Voyaging together, Dorothy and William became inseparable, talking about literature, music, art… and love. He lingered with Dorothy and her family in Saint-Malo for several months until his father learned about the romance and wrote – Leave for Paris now, as planned!

The young lovers corresponded; would they ever meet again? A few years later, the Osbornes returned to Chicksands, their ancestral home in England. Other men courted Dorothy, including Cromwell's son Henry, but no one could match her beloved William. She teased him about marriage, writing that the perfect husband should not be "a traveled monsieur whose head is all feather inside and out…. He must not be a fool, nor peevish, ill natured, nor proud nor covetous, and to all this must be added, 'he must love me.'"

In 1651 they became secretly engaged in London. He sent her a gold ring, inscribed, "The love I owe/I cannot showe."

At last William's father softened, Dorothy's father died, and they married in 1655. William became a great statesman and author, and Dorothy – Lady Temple – was his loving hostess and helpmate.

# FEBRUARY

# FEBRUARY 1

## JULIA MARGARET PATTLE & CHARLES HAY CAMERON

*"his constant tenderness has sweetened every hour"*

J ULIA MARRIED CHARLES IN 1838 IN Calcutta India, where her father served in the Bengal civil service. She was 22, witty and bright; Charles was 42 and a member of the Indian Law Commission and Council for Education. Julia knew that their marriage would be passionate at a time when few Victorians wrote or even spoke about sexuality. Charles had published his "Essay on the Sublime and Beautiful" about the power of sexual attraction. Rejecting most of the conventions of expatriate English society, they helped establish universities in India and admit Indians into the civil service.

The Camerons and their 11 natural and adopted children lived in India, Ceylon, London and the Isle of Wight. Julia wrote poetry and translated famous German works into English, but when her children gave her a wooden camera and darkroom equipment, photography became her life's work. "From the first moment," she wrote, "I handled my lens with a tender ardour, and it has become to me as a living thing."

Soon, Julia's photography took priority over household affairs. She invited – and sometimes summoned – servants, family members, houseguests, even strangers to sit before the camera, often for as long as 5 or 7 minutes. The Camerons' chicken house became Julia's "glass house" or studio, and the coalhouse nearby served as a darkroom. She called her photographs "theophanies" – representations of God in human beings. She won medals for her work and photographed such notable Victorians as Browning, Darwin, and Tennyson.

Julia favored close-ups of the face, deliberately blurring the rest of the body, and often created symbolic scenes with religious or literary themes. Her friends dressed up and posed as people from the Bible, history, or great works of literature. Charles, with his long white beard, was a perfect Merlin in her series of illustrations for Tennyson's *Idylls of the King*.

# FEBRUARY 2

## SAMUEL CLEMENS & OLIVIA LANGDON

### *"Darling Livy"*

S AM AND "LIVY" PROBABLY WOULDN'T HAVE met if he hadn't sailed with her brother Charles to Europe and the Holy Land in 1867. In Charles's stateroom was a picture of Livy; Sam saw it and claimed he fell in love on the spot. Six months later, he greeted the entire Langdon family at New York City's St. Nicholas Hotel, while he was working on *The Innocents Abroad*. He showed them the sights, including Steinway Hall where Charles Dickens read from his book, *David Copperfield*. At 22, Livy was 10 years younger than Sam. Her devoted father, a wealthy coal magnate, knew "Mark Twain" was a celebrated journalist and author, but was the "Wild Humorist" right for his daughter? Livy also had doubts; the first time Sam proposed, she turned him down.

The Langdons returned home to Elmira, New York, and Sam went on the lecture circuit, writing to Livy and devouring every word she wrote back. Livy represented perfection to Sam. Like Tom Sawyer and other male characters he created, Sam believed such cultured and refined women were made to "sivilize" rough-edged men like himself. He also enjoyed her affectionate family; his had always been cold and reserved.

For the next 2 years, he visited Livy whenever possible, until at last she confessed that she loved him, too. They married in 1870 in the Langdons' front parlor. The next day, family and friends rode with them on a train to Buffalo, where they expected to settle in rented rooms. Instead, their sleigh pulled up in front of a private house, bought and furnished by the Langdon family.

Married life was blissful, and Sam wondered why on earth he had waited so long to marry. If he had the chance to do it over, he wrote, "I would marry in early infancy instead of wasting time cutting teeth and breaking crockery."

## FEBRUARY 3

## SAMUEL RICHARDSON & ELIZABETH LEAKE

*Riding "double" is better than "single"*

SAMUEL BEGAN WRITING HIS CLASSIC NOVELS *Pamela* and *Clarissa* a few years after he married "Bett" in 1733. They had met 10 years earlier, when he worked for her printer father in London before Samuel's first wife died. No children survived that marriage, but Samuel would have many daughters with Bett. Although he occasionally "complained" about being the only man in an all-female household, in truth he loved it.

Women always liked Samuel. They confided in him, and shared some of their private thoughts. "I was not more than 13," he later wrote, "when some … young women … having a high opinion of my taciturnity, revealed to me their love-secrets, in order to induce me to give them copies to write after, or correct, for answers to their lovers' letters." Their requests inspired his most significant literary achievement – *Pamela*, the first English-language novel – a story told in a series of letters written by Pamela Andrews, a young woman who successfully defends her virtue and honor.

Samuel and Bett lived at Blue Ball Court near Salisbury Square. She was a devoted and capable housekeeper, although he fretted that she "had a Love of bed on mornings." He rose early, and often wrote during the quiet hours. He loved to eat but hated to exercise. After he gained a lot of weight, his doctor convinced him to buy a "chamber horse" which was a large chair set on a wooden board, flexible in the middle, with braces for the arms and a footstool for the feet.

Samuel "worked out" on his "horse," reading, dictating, and writing parts of his novels there. Sometimes, Bett sat with him. The chamber horse "rides double better than single," he joyfully recounted to a friend.

Educated at an early age in the delights of love and passion, Samuel appreciated all the good things in life and encouraged others to feel the same way.

# FEBRUARY 4

## SAMUEL CUNARD & SUSAN DUFFUS

*Sail away with me ...*

M RS. DUFFUS ENCOURAGED THE ROMANCE BETWEEN her daughter and Sam Cunard, who courted Susan for a year before they were married in 1815. He'd grown up in their Halifax, Nova Scotia, neighborhood and had always been bright, energetic, and resourceful. One day, he would make a fine catch for her Susan. No one realized that he would also revolutionize ocean transportation.

Sleigh bells announced the arrival of wedding guests at the Duffuses' mansion on a cold, snowy day. The wedding in the grand drawing room was followed by a festive banquet. Sam and Susan set up housekeeping in a 4-story house on Brunswick Street and filled it with furniture he had bought in London.

Mr. Duffus was a prosperous tailor of custom-made military and naval uniforms for officers attached to the English forces based in Halifax. Sam's father owned a fleet of cargo ships that carried goods between England, New England, Bermuda, and Nova Scotia. Delivering mail to the military was a high-priority for years, but after Wellington defeated Napoleon in the summer of 1815, service was cut drastically.

Sam was as enterprising as Susan's mother had predicted; within months he had set up S. Cunard & Company, a packet service of fast boats for the British Postal Service, delivering mail to Boston as well as Bermuda. Five years later, passengers began traveling on Cunard ships. Under the blue flag with a white star in the center, Cunard's square-rigged cargo ships also carried New World lumber, food, sheep, and horses to Britain.

The shipping industry was booming, but other Halifax businesses suffered after Wellington's victory. Sam and Susan helped her parents financially after many English officers – who had been her father's valued customers – were sent back to England. Susan also assisted the governor's wife in collecting food and clothing for needy families and persuading the local government to finance soup kitchens.

# FEBRUARY 5
## JENNY LIND & OTTO GOLDSCHMIDT
### *"all my heart ever wanted"*

THE "SWEDISH NIGHTINGALE" WAS 25 WHEN she met Otto, a 16-year old music student at Leipzig Conservatory in Germany. She had been singing professionally for 7 years, and her powerful, vibrant soprano – with a range of 2 ¾ octaves extending to the G above high C – thrilled audiences everywhere.

The two musicians tried to suppress their passion for each other, as Otto accompanied Jenny at local concerts. "Isn't it cruel?" she wrote to a friend about Otto. "He is the first person that I could confidently … swear before God that I could make happy in every way and that I am really made for. But he is so young!"

Jenny left Germany and became engaged to a member of Sweden's Royal Opera Company. A few months later, P. T. Barnum invited her to tour with his show in America. Everything she sang, from operatic solos to "Home Sweet Home" and "My Old Kentucky Home" had audiences cheering and begging for more.

After her 93rd performance, Jenny was exhausted. She hated the circus atmosphere of Barnum's extravaganzas and persuaded him to terminate her contract. Then she began singing at small recitals and wrote to Otto, begging him to come to America and accompany her. Soon after he arrived, Jenny broke her engagement.

In 1852, Jenny married Otto in the Beacon Hill, Boston home of close friends. She wore a traditional Swedish wedding gown of white muslin, with a white veil secured by orange blossoms and myrtle. The silverware she had selected was engraved with the letter J encircled by an O, symbolizing her belief that with Otto, she would be surrounded by happiness.

After a month-long honeymoon in the mountains of western Massachusetts, Jenny gave 40 more concerts in America with Otto before they returned to Europe. Eventually, they made their home in England.

# FEBRUARY 6
## MARGOT FONTEYN & ROBERTO ARIAS
### *100 Red Roses*

THE 1955 MARRIAGE OF ONE OF Britain's prima ballerinas and a Panamanian diplomat may have surprised some of Margot's fans, but it brought her more happiness than all her years on the stage. Margot and "Tito" had met 8 years earlier at a party in Cambridge, England. They saw each other a few times. When they parted, he gave her a 1936 Panamanian coin honoring his father's second term as President of Panama, and she gave him an autographed picture of herself.

Six years later, Margot was in New York City performing in *The Sleeping Beauty* when Tito, now Panamanian delegate to the United Nations, reentered her life. He had married in Panama but was getting a divorce. "Will you marry me?" he asked her. She wondered … was he serious?

Tito wrote Margot long passionate love letters saying he'd never been able to forget her and had often consoled himself by believing that Margot's name was literally engraved on his heart. He sent her 100 red roses. A diamond bracelet. His chauffeur's services. Anything, if only she would marry him.

After dancing in *Daphnis and Chloe*, Margot flew to Paris with Tito, where they were married at the Panamanian consulate. The tiny room was meant for 10 guests, but more than 50 showed up! She forced her way through the crowd, searching for her parents. Swarms of newspaper photographers surrounded her, noisily clamoring for attention as their flashbulbs exploded and camera shutters banged. She could barely hear the consul general performing the ceremony. What should have been the loveliest and most meaningful day of Margot's life was "worse than a prize fight," she recalled in her autobiography.

After a honeymoon in the Bahamas, they lived in London. Margot continued to dance, and Tito was ambassador to the Court of St. James's.

# FEBRUARY 7

## AMELIA EARHART & GEORGE PALMER PUTNAM
*For the fun of it*

ON THE DAY IN 1931 THAT Amelia married George at the Putnams' Noank, Connecticut estate, the famous 33-year old aviatrix handed him a note stating, "I shall not hold you to any medieval code of faithfulness to me, nor shall I consider myself bound to you similarly." The woman who had soared above the clouds, free as a bird, said she could never endure "the confinements of even an attractive cage."

The 45-year old heir to a publishing empire respected his bride's hard-won independence and freedom. He also accepted her decision to keep her maiden name. They had met in 1928, soon after Charles Lindbergh flew non-stop to Paris. The publisher G. P. Putnam's Sons was looking for a female flyer to accompany male pilots bound for Europe on a Fokker plane as part of a publicity campaign. Amelia grabbed the opportunity. After they took off in June, one of the pilots drank so excessively on a layover in Newfoundland that Amelia – dubbed "Lady Lindy" by the press – stepped in to fly part of the way.

Afterward, George invited Amelia to stay at his lavish home in Rye, New York, and write about her accomplishments. She also lectured about flying, tested new equipment, and became a magazine columnist. He divorced his first wife in 1929 and helped guide Amelia's career. The more time the spent together, the more they fell in love. Still, it took 6 proposals of marriage from George to win Amelia, although she insisted on terminating the union after one year if either partner was unhappy.

That never happened. Instead, Amelia, one of the best-known feminists of her time, continued flying in air races and in award-winning nonstop and cross-country flights. Eventually, she set records flying solo from Newfoundland to Ireland, Hawaii to the U.S. mainland, and Mexico City to Newark.

# FEBRUARY 8
## RAPHAEL SOYER & REBECCA LETZ
### *"How autobiographical my 'art' is"*

REBECCA'S FRIEND AND FELLOW TEACHER, FANNY Soyer often spoke of her 3 talented brothers – Isaac, and the twins, Raphael and Moses – but it was Raphael who captured the young teacher's heart. At 32, he still lived at home with his family, and would be the last brother to marry, in 1931. For inspiration, Raphael roamed the streets of New York City. Frequently, he painted scenes of people without hope – vagrants, men standing outside missions, people sleeping in parks or under bridges.

Rebecca was tall and slender, with red hair wrapped in braids around her head. She modeled for Raphael, as did dancers, actresses, other artists, and Lower East Side bohemians. Many of his paintings revealed a keen appreciation of female sensuousness. He liked painting women in intimate settings – sleeping, sitting, or conversing in small groups. He also made money illustrating books and painting portraits.

In 1929, Raphael brought "Dancing Lesson," a painting depicting his sister, brothers, mother and grandmother to a gallery in Manhattan. The director was impressed and told him, Bring back a dozen like this and I'll give you a show.

Raphael's paintings sold quickly, enabling him to rent studio space with other artists. Rebecca helped out by sewing curtains for the art windows. After his 3rd one-man show, Raphael was invited to teach at the Art Students League. At last, he and Rebecca could afford to marry.

In the early years, Raphael and Rebecca had little money, but they managed to travel to Europe before their children were born. They Soyers always talked about political events and believed that art should never be censored. They supported the anti-fascists during the Spanish Civil War and spoke out against war and Naziism as members of the American Artists Congress.

If Raphael isn't painting, he's sick," said Rebecca many times. Aside from his family, his art was his life.

# FEBRUARY 9
## ETHAN ALLEN & FRANCES MONTRESOR BUCHANAN
*"partner of my joys, my dearest self"*

T HE FAMOUS AMERICAN REVOLUTIONARY WAR GENERAL and leader of the Green Mountain Boys was 46 when he proposed to "Fanny," a 24-year old war widow. She was bright, beautiful and witty, and although she had a temper, she also had a passion for life. Ethan's first wife had died, but his second marriage would be as joyous as his first one had been disappointing and sad.

He met Fanny in Westminster, Vermont in January 1784. Ten years earlier, her late stepfather had sided with the British in New York and posted a reward for the capture of Ethan and other "Green Mountain outlaws, dead or alive." If Fanny remembered the incident, she dismissed it now.

A month later, she was standing on a chair in her mother's home, putting dishes into a china closet, when Ethan entered. "Fanny," he declared, "if we are to be married, now is the time, for I am on my way to Sunderland."

"Very well," Fanny answered, stepping down from the chair. Their engagement lasted only as long as it took them to walk into the dining room, where Vermont's Chief Justice Moses Robinson was having breakfast with some lawyers. They were lighting their pipes when Ethan asked Robinson to marry them then and there.

Are you sure? asked Robinson. Of course! Ethan said. He'd taken Fort Ticonderoga with less thought. After the ceremony Ethan and Fanny rode in a sleigh across the Green Mountains to the home he shared in Sunderland with his brother, Ira. Later, Ethan and Fanny moved with their children to Burlington, where he concentrated on writing for the rest of his life. Besides philosophical treatises, he penned sweet romantic verses:

*Dear Fanny wise, the beautiful and young,*
*The partner of my joy, my dearest self,*
*My love, pride of my life....*

# FEBRUARY 10

## QUEEN VICTORIA OF GREAT BRITAIN & PRINCE ALBERT OF SAXE-COBURG

*"My dearest dearest dear"*

"MONDAY, FEBRUARY 10 – THE LAST TIME I slept alone," wrote Victoria on the morning of her wedding in 1840. Three days before, she had sent carriages to fetch Prince Albert from Gotha, Germany. The Channel crossing was rough, and when he arrived, onlookers said his face was the color of a wax candle.

He was tall; she was small and thought him "beautiful." He was motherless; she was fatherless. They both were 18 and about to begin one of the most romantic marriages in royal history.

The Archbishop of Canterbury and York and the Bishop of London officiated at the wedding on a cold, rainy day at the Chapel Royal of St. James's Palace. When someone asked why only 3 Tories were on the extensive guest list, Victoria replied, "This is *my* marriage and I will only have those who sympathize with me!"

The evening before the wedding, she and Albert dined together, read the marriage service, and practiced putting on her ring. She thought a full rehearsal was unnecessary but regretted it later. Her bridal train wasn't long enough for her 12 bridesmaids to carry, and they "all huddled together and scrambled rather than walked along, kicking each other's heels and treading on each other's gowns." As for Albert, he never knew when he was supposed to stand, sit, or kneel.

But Victoria looked appropriately regal in a white satin dress trimmed with orange blossoms and lace, a diamond necklace, and a sapphire brooch from Albert. Like other royal brides, she did not conceal her face behind a veil. One hundred wedding cakes made by various London confectioners were served at the reception. The grandest cake was 9 feet around its circumference, and 16 inches high.

Honeymooning at Windsor Castle, Victoria wrote about the "happiest day of my life…. I *never never* spent such an evening!… He clasped me in his arms and we kissed each other again and again! His beauty, his sweetness and gentleness – really how can I ever be thankful enough to have such a *husband*!"

# FEBRUARY 11
## RICHARD TUCKER & SARA PERELMUTH
### *"by my side all the way"*

SARA ALWAYS WAITED IN THE WINGS whenever "Ruby" left the stage of New York's Metropolitan Opera House, even if only for a quick wardrobe change. The internationally acclaimed Jewish tenor sang many roles, including Canio in *Pagliacci*, Rodolfo in *La Boheme*, and Don Alvaro in *La Forza del Destino*. After the rousing finale, Sara usually heard the audience's "bravos" and boisterous pleas for "encore!" before her dark-haired, smiling husband appeared backstage. Holding hands, they walked to Ruby's dressing room and welcomed adoring fans. Ruby autographed playbills as Sara jotted down the names and addresses of those who brought gifts or requested photographs.

Years later, Ruby's lifelong enthusiasm for opera continued through the Richard Tucker Foundation, established by Ruby's family to assist young opera singers.

"The American Caruso" began dating Sara in 1943, when her uncle gave him her phone number. The younger sister of tenor Jan Peerce, Sara was impressed by Ruby's magnificent voice, especially after he serenaded her in a Romanian restaurant on the Lower East Side. His clothes were shabby and his income low, but Ruby convinced Sara and her parents that he would become a *hazzan* or cantor and a great opera singer, and make everyone proud of him.

He married his "dearest Kitten" on a Tuesday in 1936 at the Grand Mansion, a Ludlow Street banquet hall partially owned by the Perelmuths. After a storm-tossed honeymoon cruise to Bermuda, the newlyweds returned to Manhattan. Ruby worked in the fur district, sang at bar mitzvahs and weddings, and became a part-time cantor. Sara worked too, enabling them to buy voice lessons for Ruby and occasional opera tickets. At last, the man who would become of the 20th century's greatest tenors could take his wife to the Metropolitan Opera. They sat in the audience, but both knew that one day, Ruby would be singing center stage.

# FEBRUARY 12
## FRANS HALS & LYSBETH REYNIERS
### *Her "Jolly Hans"*

I N THE HALS FAMILY REGISTRY, BABY Sara's birth was recorded 9 days after Frans married Lysbeth in 1617. Maybe their wedding was held in a hurry, but they remained happily together for the next 52 years, and had 8 more children, including 3 who became painters.

Frans had been married before, but his wife had died after 5 years, and he didn't seem to regret it. Now in his mid-30's, he hoped to find a sweet, affectionate wife and raise a family. In Haarlem, the Netherlands, Frans became a member of the painters' guild, established an art school, and married Lysbeth in Spaarndam, a small city nearby.

The most lucrative field for an artist was portrait-painting. Wealthy Dutch burghers wanted pictures of themselves and their growing families, and they also bought paintings to decorate their homes. Frans was able to capture the fleeting expressions of his sitters – even the stolid merchants whom he painted so often. Some men belonged to shooting clubs, which were groups of volunteers who gathered together socially during peacetime and assembled posthaste for the national defense. Frans' "Banquet of the St. Joris Shooting Company," done in 1616, has long been considered a masterpiece, magnificently depicting 13 men in high, stiff ruffled collars who are sitting at a table.

Frans rarely spent much time sketching, but got right to work with his paintbrush and colors. In most of his pictures, everything happens in the foreground. His figures look you straight in the eye. Frans painted for the viewer, as if he were saying, Here it all is, right up front.

Although Frans always enjoyed his schnapps, a close look at the details of his paintings shows that he never shortchanged his art. Lysbeth was spirited and strong-minded herself, and happy to see Rubens, Van Dyck, and other painters who visited their home.

# FEBRUARY 13*

## PRINCESS ELIZABETH OF ENGLAND & PRINCE FREDERICK OF BOHEMIA

*Father of the Bride (almost) breaks the bank*

ON THE "CAN YOU TOP THIS?" list of elaborate wedding celebrations, the nuptials of Elizabeth and Frederick surely rank among the highest.

They met in 1612, when Frederick visited England. The teenaged princess's beauty and charm had been celebrated by court poets, and the Elector Palatine of Bohemia wasn't disappointed. Although their marriage was "arranged," the young couple had truly fallen in love. Later on, Elizabeth was called "The Queen of Hearts" by her subjects.

Sadly, wedding preparations were interrupted by the sudden death of Elizabeth's brother Henry, the Prince of Wales, but the celebrations that followed softened the nation's grief. A mock naval battle involving 36 ships, 500 sailors and 1000 musketeers took place on the Thames River. Fireworks exploded above 4 floating castles, and giant puppets of St. George, a beautiful maiden, and a fire-eating dragon hurled torches at each other until, one by one, they burst into flames. Masked balls, theatrical productions, and other spectacles took place before the 1613 wedding.

Frederick's entrance at Whitehall Chapel was heralded by trumpets. Elizabeth followed, wearing a richly embroidered silver gown and a gold crown embellished with diamond and pearl pendants swinging gently against her waist-long hair. Her bridesmaids numbered 16, to match her age in years, and they walked behind her in white satin dresses. Someone likened the sight to a constellation of stars trailing behind a glorious moon.

Royal pockets were turned inside-out to pay for all the merry-making but King James still remained more than 50,000 pounds in the red. The royal exchequer was completely bankrupt, and his royal highness was forced to levy taxes to help make ends meet. Elizabeth was mortified when the new groom's household was temporarily dismissed, and her father left town for a while to avoid further embarrassment.

---

*Date approximate; the wedding pageant lasted more than a week.

# FEBRUARY 14

## CHARLES BOYER & PATRICIA PATERSON

*Lifelong love after a whirlwind courtship*

COUNTLESS LOVERS HAVE CHOSEN VALENTINE'S DAY as the perfect wedding day – and that includes couples who have known each other only 22 days.

Charles Boyer, the 34-year old suave French actor with impeccable charm, thought he was past the age of falling in love when he met Pat at a Fox Studio lunch party on January 23, 1934. Already, he'd become a success on the French stage and in silent movies in America. When the "talkies" began, Charles learned English, and with his velvet voice and captivating dark eyes he was soon playing leading film roles.

That winter, Charles was in Hollywood to film *Caravan*. He wasn't looking for romance, but he found it in 24-year old Pat, a vivacious blond English musical comedy actress. Her breakthrough role in the movie *Bitter Sweet* had brought her to California and the brink of stardom the previous year.

If Cupid ever shot his arrow into anyone, it was Charles. As soon as he saw Pat, he couldn't think of anyone else. Other beautiful actresses were at the party, but he looked only at her. Pat was intrigued by his continental charm and French accent, and they began seeing each other right away. Charles had always avoided "affairs of the heart," but not seeing Pat, even for a day, was unbearable.

They talked about getting married and all the reasons it was better not to do it – until they jumped into Charles's Plymouth roadster, drove to Yuma, Arizona, and were married by a justice of the peace. After a one-night honeymoon in a nearby motel, they went back to Hollywood. Charles's friend, singer Maurice Chevalier, threw a party for them and their stunned but delighted friends.

Who says whirlwind courtships never work out? These 2 sweethearts were married for more than 40 years, and their love for each other never wavered.

# FEBRUARY 15
## FYODOR DOSTOYEVSKY & ANNA SNITKINA
### *"Fedya" and his "Golobchik"*

ANNA BEGAN WORKING FOR FYODOR IN 1866 when the 45-year old Russian author needed a stenographer to help him meet the deadline for his new novel, *The Gambler*. Almost 2 years had passed since his first wife's death, and he was still visibly depressed. Anna arrived at his St. Petersburg home every weekday morning wearing her best – and only – dress, which was black. The color suited Fyodor's serious mood. He paced his study as he spoke, and pulled on his long hair when stymied for a word or phrase.

After several hours of intense work, they'd take short breaks. Anna made *pastila*, Fyodor's favorite dessert of dried apricots, pears, and peaches, which they ate while drinking tea. He spoke about his hard life and 5 years of imprisonment as a political criminal. Creditors hounded him; he had been forced to pawn family valuables. But Anna had a soothing effect on Fyodor, and gradually he grew to care for her. He called her *"Golobchik,"* an affectionate term meaning "little bird."

Her job ended when *The Gambler* was completed on time. A week later, Fyodor asked Anna to come back so he could dictate *Crime and Punishment*. He also confessed that he missed her deeply. Many years later, Anna wrote in her *Reminiscences*, "I won't try to convey the words full of tenderness and love that he said to me then; they are sacred to me. I was stunned, almost crushed by the immensity of my happiness and for a long time, I couldn't believe it."

They married in 1867 in Ismailovsky's Cathedral in St. Petersburg. Fyodor's stepson, Paul, was the only person to protest, saying the "old man" should have asked him first!

With Anna, Fyodor finished *Crime and Punishment* and wrote *The Idiot*, *The Brothers Karamazov*, and other great works. She gave birth to 3 children but also continued to be Fyodor's secretary, stenographer, copyist, and financial manager.

# FEBRUARY 16

## JAMES MONROE & ELIZABETH KORTRIGHT
### *"dear Eliza"*

THOMAS JEFFERSON WAS THE FIRST ONE to notice that James was in love, because his letters had become brighter and more optimistic. After 3 years in the Congress of the Confederation, James had come home to Virginia to hang up his lawyer's shingle in Fredericksburg. But he kept going back to New York City, where he had met Elizabeth at a party. Within a year, they were engaged.

At 19, Elizabeth was the beautiful and aristocratic daughter of a well-regarded New York merchant who had been a British captain during the Revolutionary War. Her friends had always predicted that Elizabeth would marry well, and were somewhat disappointed when she accepted James's proposal in 1786. (They changed their minds later, when he became the 5th president of the United States!)

Perhaps it was his energy and devotion to their new nation that attracted Elizabeth to James. He dressed poorly; once he came calling in a worn-out coat and shapeless breeches, and she said teasingly that he looked like a "woodman." He also refused to wear a powdered wig.

Jefferson was glad that the new couple would be settling not very far from his home at Monticello. Fredericksburg's solid population of merchants and businessmen needed good lawyers. Although practicing law never interested James very much, he knew it would bring financial security. He and Elizabeth found a home only a short walk from the office, which enabled him to come home quickly after work. Within a year, a daughter was born, "who tho' noisy, contributes greatly to our amusement," he wrote.

To strangers and people she barely knew, Elizabeth appeared reserved and at times too formal, but with James and her immediate family she was affectionate and loving. Their marriage became extremely close, and both hated parting from the other, even for a day.

## FEBRUARY 17

## ALICE LEE ROOSEVELT & NICHOLAS LONGWORTH
### *"Princess Alice" and "Nick"*

"PRINCESS ALICE" WAS OUTSPOKEN, ARGUMENTATIVE, PEEVISH, beautiful, demanding – and the favorite daughter of President Teddy Roosevelt. Fashion-conscious women wore "Alice blue," her favorite color, and everyone danced to the popular song, "Alice Blue Gown." In 1904, when she turned 18, her name was linked with eligible monarchs, military officers, Harvard and Yale football players, and former Rough Riders.

Alice met "Nick" at a Washington dinner party. The Ohio congressman was a clever and self-confident man-about-town who would one day become speaker of the House. Fifteen years older than Alice, he most certainly attracted her attention. They saw each other often but kept their relationship light and fun-filled.

In 1905 Alice was invited to join the secretary of war and a large contingent of political figures – including Nick – on a 4-month-long boat trip to visit heads of state in the Far East. When it ended, they were engaged, and she wrote in her dairy, "I love you with everything that is in me, Nick, Nick, my Nick." Then she told her parents that she wanted to be married in February 1906 – only 2 months away – which didn't give her stepmother, Edith much time to make the arrangements.

The weather was unseasonably warm that Saturday as 1000 invited guests arrived at the White House. Alice's wedding dress was white satin trimmed with lace that had enhanced her late mother's wedding dress, and with a long train of white and silver brocade. Not wanting to be upstaged by anyone, Alice refused to have any bridesmaids in her wedding party.

At noon, the Marine Band began playing, and TR escorted his daughter down the aisle. When the bishop asked, "Who gives the bride away?" the usually loquacious president was speechless.

## FEBRUARY 18
## ALEXANDER PUSHKIN & NATALYA GONCHAROV
### *Torment and bliss*

THE WEDDING OF THE FUTURE NATIONAL poet of Russia was postponed many times before his bride's grasping, meddlesome mother finally relented and let him marry her precious daughter. Long ago, the Goncharovs had been wealthy, but their riches had been squandered by reckless descendants. Now widowed, Mrs. Goncharov was determined that her daughter marry well. Who was this worthless poet? Just a scribbler with no steady income!

Natalya was 16, beautiful, and deeply attracted to Alexander's genius. He was 29 and knew she wasn't brilliant, but he wanted a wife and a home.

*My desires have been fulfilled.*
*The creator has sent you to me, you my Madonna,*
*The purest example of purest loveliness.*

But Mrs. Goncharov listed her demands. Natalya needed a large trousseau; could Alexander provide it? He struggled to get enough money together, but Mrs. G. postponed the wedding anyway, and made more demands. Alexander sold poems and short stories. He mortgaged his property. But time and again, the wedding was delayed. When he and Natalya did marry in Moscow in 1831, the bridegroom was so shaky and exhausted as they exchanged rings, one slipped out of their hands. He bent down to pick it up, bumping into the lectern and knocking a crucifix and Bible to the floor. Then Alexander's candle went out. "All the bad omens," he muttered nervously.

Married life did not prove blissful until they packed their bags that May, leaving town – and Mrs. Goncharov – for a rented house in Tsarskoe Selo. Finally, Alexander could enjoy Natalya and finish *Eugene Onegin*, his greatest work. He also wrote other poems, including one in which he tells his wife,

*How sweeter far are you, my meek, my quiet one –*
*By what tormenting bliss is my whole soul undone….*

# FEBRUARY 19

## THOMAS HART BENTON & RITA PIACENZA
### *They "fooled them!"*

"MY HUSBAND IS A GENIUS," RITA often said, even when they had very little money and lived on the top floor of a walk-up apartment near Union Square in New York City. Tom eventually achieved greatness as a painter and muralist, focusing on themes from American history. But what kept them going in the early years was the money Rita earned designing hats and writing a sewing column for *Ladies' Home Journal* magazine. She also recognized the value of Tom's paintings more quickly than he did, and sometimes sold works that he had discarded.

Rita was 17, dark-eyed, attractive, and wearing a red hat when she signed up for Tom's adult education class in drawing at a Manhattan public school in 1917. He was 29 and loved looking at her. After class he often sketched her face from memory. Once they became friends, Rita took Tom home to meet her family, and he began dropping by for Sunday dinners.

Neither set of parents was thrilled. The Piacenzas didn't think it was right that Tom didn't have a "real" job and would be relying financially on Rita. The Bentons said ... well, she was *only* the daughter of Italian immigrants. After all, Tom's father had served in the Confederate army, and his great-uncle and namesake was *the* famous Thomas Hart Benton, United States senator and writer.

Fortunately, by the time Tom and Rita married at St. Francis Xavier Church in New York in 1922, everyone agreed that "family" was "family." Mr. Piacenza insisted on cooking the celebration dinner. That June, the newlyweds went to the island of Martha's Vineyard in Massachusetts, and summered with other artists, writers, and musicians.

In Tom's autobiography, he recalled that some of his friends were surprised to learn that he had married, thinking he'd never be content with one woman permanently. "I fooled them," he wrote. "Or it might be better to say, my wife fooled them."

# FEBRUARY 20
## ARTHUR ASHE & JEANNE MOUTOUSSAMY
*Remembering love*

ARTHUR WAS IMMEDIATELY ATTRACTED TO THE beautiful photographer who asked to take his picture at a United Negro College Fund benefit in October, 1976. Jeanne worked for NBC, and although she liked the tennis star, she didn't expect anything serious to develop with someone known as a "carefree bachelor."

His father couldn't believe how much Jeanne looked like Arthur's mother, who had died when he was 6 years old. Arthur hadn't realized it, and yet he felt, somehow, that memories of his mother played a part in his falling in love with Jeanne. He gave her a red rose (his mother's favorite flower) on their first date, and married her 4 months later.

Arthur had hoped to marry someday, but he knew it would have to wait until he had fulfilled his dream as a professional tennis player. Jeanne was bright, thoughtful, and independent, and she seemed to accept the fact that much of their dating would be on the telephone. Arthur called her often from Europe, Australia, and everywhere else he traveled on tours. She enjoyed his quiet sense of humor. Instead of proposing formally when he came home that winter, he slipped an engagement ring into an envelope and stuck it inside her medicine cabinet. Three days passed before she noticed it!

Arthur had surgery to remove bone chips from his heel shortly before he married Jeanne in 1977. Their friend, Reverend Andrew Young, who was the United States Ambassador to the United Nations, performed the ceremony at the U.N. Chapel in New York City. Jeanne hoped that her work would still be judged simply on its own merits, not praised because now she was Mrs. Arthur Ashe. She continued to succeed, eventually producing works such as *Daddy and Me*, the touching and poignant book she wrote with their young daughter about losing a parent at a young age.

# FEBRUARY 21

## MARTIN VAN BUREN & HANNAH HOES

*Everything was "OK" between them*

A LTHOUGH MATTY STARTED OUT AS A LAWYER, he was active in politics even before he married his Dutch sweetheart, "Jannetje," in 1807. In 1800, when he was 18, he campaigned for Thomas Jefferson and began associating with political groups in New York City.

Upstate in Kinderhook, New York, bridegrooms traditionally invited the entire town to their weddings, and hosted elaborate celebrations. But Matty was frugal and somewhat shy, so he and Jannetje were married at her sister's home in Catskill across the Hudson River, with only their immediate families present.

Within a year, they bought a house on Warren Street in the nearby town of Hudson. In March 1808 Matty was appointed surrogate judge of Columbia County. He attended court sessions in Albany and New York City, sometimes sleeping in poorly heated, dilapidated inns. He rode the circuits rain or shine but was always grateful to come home to his Jannetje, the 4 sons they eventually had, and their clean and comfortable house.

Matty and Jannetje never forgot that first summer after their marriage, when Robert Fulton's steamboat, the *Clermont*, completed its maiden round-trip voyage between Albany and New York City. Until then, few people sailed on rivers, but a new age of transportation and commerce had begun in America. In 5 years, Matty was elected to the New York State Senate. In 1837 he became the 8th president of the United States and the first one born in the new nation.

No one's sure when the American expression, "OK," was first used, although many historians think it referred to "Old Kinderhook," Matty's nickname in political campaigns. But perhaps its original use was more personal – when Jannetje asked Matty to do something, his response was like that of countless husbands. He'd look at his dear wife and say, "OK!"

# FEBRUARY 22

## AARON MONTGOMERY WARD & ELIZABETH COBB
### *A real family business*

"MONTY" MET ELIZABETH IN CHICAGO IN the 1860's, when his childhood friend George married Elizabeth's sister. Although Monty was tempted to follow his future brother-in-law into retailing, he had ideas for something better. Growing up in Michigan, he had worked in a general store where customers always complained about limited selections and high prices. Yet they had no choice but to shop there; it was the only store in town.

After he moved to Chicago, Monty wondered, Why not establish a mail-order business and sell goods to small-town people directly, with payment on delivery? He'd need a catalog and a store located near a railroad station. He talked it over with his friend Elizabeth, and they decided he would carry shoes, farm equipment, carpets, nails … everything. Elizabeth said she'd help out in any way she could.

Monty opened his first mail-order store in 1871, right before the Great Chicago Fire. Confronted by so much devastation, many businessmen gave up, but not Monty. He started raising capital again, despite George's dire prediction that he'd go broke within a year.

Five days after Monty's 28th birthday in 1872, he and Elizabeth were married. They rented a small shipping room on North Clark Street, assembled a one-page price list, and sent it to almost half a million Midwestern farmers. Monty visited many towns, introducing himself and encouraging people to order from his catalog. Elizabeth's family pitched in, too. Her brother worked in the packing rooms, her father was the night watchman, and her mother put together samples to send to customers, and also helped with the bookkeeping. Pretty soon, George swallowed his pride, gave Monty his life's savings, and was made a partner in the growing business.

By the end of the 19th century, the Montgomery Ward catalog was one of the most widely read publications in American history.

# FEBRUARY 23

## HUGO BLACK & JOSEPHINE FOSTER
*A "sweet" and "spiritual" nobility*

JOSEPHINE AND THE FUTURE U.S. SUPREME COURT justice had both grown up in Birmingham, Alabama, but they didn't meet until Hugo came home after serving in World War I. That summer, Josephine postponed her plans to study journalism in New York and joined the Yeomanettes, a women's branch of the navy. Hugo, a labor lawyer, was living in a bachelor apartment on a very steep hill. One day, he recalled in his autobiography, he saw a brown-haired, beautiful young lady walking up the hill in a close-fitting, eye-appealing dress.

Later, he saw her at a dance and at the home of mutual friends. Her escort lost track of Josephine after Hugo got her attention, and they spent most of the evening "hiding" behind a potted palm. There was something about the way she walked, smiled, and listened, he remembered. She seemed to have "a sweet" and "spiritual nobility about her."

The Fosters were somewhat disappointed when Josephine announced that she wanted to marry Hugo. She was only 21 but he was almost 35 and his family was not well connected, socially. Other beaux pursued her, but Josephine remained steadfastly committed to Hugo. She'd never known a man who exuded so much confidence. "Everyone in that false society we lived in felt he was common," she said. But Hugo was so brilliant, she knew he would surpass them all.

She wore a blue suit and a gray hat when they married at her parents' Birmingham home in 1921. Three years later, Hugo was elected senator from Alabama. In 1937, he was appointed to the U.S. Supreme Court and was Justice Black for the next 34 years. He believed that freedom of speech and religious liberty were absolute rights, and that the 14th Amendment made the entire Bill of Rights applicable to everyone.

# FEBRUARY 24

## THOMAS ALVA EDISON & MINA MILLER
### *A Morse code proposal*

TOM MET MINA NOT LONG AFTER his first wife died. The famous inventor was lonely; his daughter was at boarding school, and his 2 young sons were living temporarily with their aunt. At 38, he was a millionaire, having invented the phonograph, the incandescent electric lamp, and the quadraplex telegraph which sent 4 messages at one time. Most people were awed in his presence, but Mina wasn't intimidated. She was only 18 but looked him straight in the eye. The "Wizard of Menlo Park" was impressed!

"Got to thinking about Mina and came near being run over by a streetcar," he wrote in his journal after Mina returned home to Ohio and he headed for Florida. "If Mina interferes much more, will have to take out an accident policy." He wrote to her often and visited her the following summer. Her protective parents wouldn't let him spend time alone with their daughter, so he taught her Morse code which enabled them to communicate privately by tapping on each other's palms, even in a room full of people.

One day he tapped his marriage proposal on Mina's hand and she tapped back … yes!

The Millers rolled out a red carpet on their front lawn in Akron and decorated the parlor with huge bouquets of calla lilies and palm leaves for the 1886 wedding. In the library, dozens of pink carnations spelled out "E—M." Tom got the jitters and told Mina, "I'm getting pretty scared – I wonder if I will pull through. I know you will, women have more nerve than men."

She walked down the aisle wearing a white silk dress edged in lace, with a diamond pendant suspended from a pearl necklace. After the reception they boarded a train for their honeymoon and new home in Fort Myers, Florida. More revolutionary inventions would follow, but for now Tom devoted all his attentions to the bride he affectionately called "Billy."

## FEBRUARY 25*

## HEINRICH STEINWEG (STEINWAY) & JULIANNE THIEMER

### *Perfect harmony*

"HENRY" AND JULIANNE MET IN SEESEN, Germany, at the foot of the Hartz Mountains where the blond-haired girl lived with her family. Julianne loved music and soon fell in love with the young stranger who played the organ in the village church on Sundays. It's said that she pumped the bellows and Henry played the organ at their own wedding in 1825, right before the ceremony began.

Henry had been born in Wolfshagen Germany, but by the time he was 15, he was orphaned and alone in the world. He joined the army and fought against Napoleon at the Battle of Waterloo. Years later, veterans remembered a soldier who sat around the campfire strumming soothing melodies on his homemade zither. Although no one knew his name, most probably it was Henry.

He had learned the trades of cabinetmaker and organ builder and had a natural fondness for music. He built a small 2-stringed piano and gave it to Julianne as a wedding gift. After a fire destroyed many parts of Seesen, the craft guilds relaxed their restrictions against outsiders. Henry went into business building furniture and repairing organs, and he began making bigger and better musical instruments.

He and Julianne had 7 children who played in their father's workshop as he hummed sweet tunes and crafted his pianos. In time, he developed a piano with purer and more vibrant tones than the tinkling sounds made by harpsichords. In 1839 one of Henry's pianos was played at the State Fair of Brunswick and awarded a first-prize medal. Eventually, the "Steinway tone" would become a standard to which all other piano manufacturers aspired.

Henry and Julianne's son Charles was the first to go to America. The rest of the family followed in 1851, and "Steinway and Sons" began producing their remarkable instruments in Astoria, New York.

---

*Date approximate.

# FEBRUARY 26*

## MARIA MONTOYA & JULIAN MARTINEZ

*Working together, with the clay*

MARIA AND JULIAN GREW UP IN the 1890's in the pueblo of San Ildefonso, near Santa Fe, New Mexico. By the time they married in 1904, Maria's perfectly round, hand-built clay pots were already considered exceptional. Julian had various jobs but had not yet discovered his true calling as a painter. Many years later, Maria remembered that her uncle couldn't understand why she wanted to marry Julian. He wasn't a farmer and he had no trade. But that didn't matter to Maria. To put it simply, she just loved him.

They married twice – in an all-day Pueblo ceremony during which Maria ground corn into a fine meal and brought it to her future mother-in-law, and then in a religious ceremony at the Catholic church. Two months later, Maria and Julian boarded a train for the St. Louis World's Fair, where they spent the next 4 months demonstrating pottery-making and traditional dances with other Pueblo Indians. The trip exposed them to new art forms and the ways of the outside world.

Back at San Ildefonso, Julian worked as a maintenance man at a Santa Fe museum and helped out at a nearby archeological dig. Some days he brought home unusual pieces of black pottery he had found. With the curator's encouragement, Maria began reproducing the pots and Julian painted designs on them. They experimented with firing techniques and discovered how to carbonize the pottery, giving it a lustrous, metallic black finish that, when juxtaposed with Julian's matte painting, produced unique black-on-black ware.

Eventually, Julian became governor of the pueblo, and Maria became a world-famous potter. "He helped me with everything," Maria said. "Oh, we had a nice life…. We were working together."

---

*Date approximate.

## FEBRUARY 27

## MARY MONTGOMERIE LAMB & HENRY SYDENHAM SINGLETON

*"My soul seems to rise and rejoice to the chime of a marriage bell"*

WHEN HENRY MARRIED MARY IN 1864, he sensed from the beginning that his beautiful, bright and charming young bride would become more than a typical English wife and mother. Mary had written poems and stories ever since she was a child, even though her parents had discouraged her. Henry gave her the best gift any husband can offer – the freedom to develop her talents. No wonder she described him as

*Love of my Life! Dearest of my desires! –*
*The one who kindled in my breast those fires*
*Which neither time nor tide can dull or dim.*

They married 3 days after Mary's 19th birthday and settled at Hazely Heath, Hampshire. Mary began working on a series of poems focusing on love and nature. She also birth to 2 sons and 2 daughters, and within 8 years her first poetry collection, *From Dawn to Noon*, was published under her nom de plume, "Violet Fane," which she took from a character in one of Disraeli's novels.

Mary and Henry made frequent trips to London and became well known in society. Besides poetry, she also wrote essays and novels. A good friend, W.H. Mallock, called her a "London Sappho." But Henry was her soulmate, as she wrote in "Song":

*There is a luster in thine eye*
*Which only sheds its beams for me,*
*There is a language in thy smile*
*Which others may not see…*
*Thou hast a beauty of thine own*
*Which others do not care to see –*
*There is a secret in thy heart,*
*'Tis only told to me.*

# FEBRUARY 28

## FIORELLO LA GUARDIA & MARIE FISHER
*"I lost a good secretary and got a bum cook!"*

I N A WELL-KNOWN SCENE IN the 1959 hit musical, *Fiorello*, the main character sits at his office desk on a cold December night and barks orders at his faithful secretary, Marie. Suddenly he pauses; no one has ever been as loyal and trustworthy as she, and yet he has never really noticed she's a woman … until now. When Marie puts on her coat and leaves, Fiorello runs after her. You're fired, he tells her, since how could he propose marriage to someone who works for him?

The script may not be entirely accurate, but it closely resembles Fiorello and Marie's brief courtship when he was a United States congressman for New York's 20th District, and working in Washington D.C. They were married 2 months later, at his Q Street apartment and he went right back to work on Capitol Hill after the wedding breakfast. When the Speaker of the House declared that congratulations were in order to Mr. LaGuardia, he was very touched.

The marriage in 1929 was no surprise to most of Fiorello's friends. Marie was 33 and had been his private secretary for the past 15 years. Ever since his first wife died in 1921, Marie had been the most important person in his life aside from his children.

He was 46, high-strung, talkative, and bursting with energy; she was soft-spoken, reliable, and reticent. Marie quit work right after the wedding, but she remained an active assistant in Fiorello's future campaigns and activities. Together they made an unbeatable team in their private lives and in politics.

Although Fiorello was, technically, a Republican, party allegiance meant little to him. He represented the "forgotten" people – immigrants, the aged, and others without political clout. "Who's Afraid of the Big Bad Wolf?" became his theme song, and 5 years after he married Marie, he became the most beloved and hardworking mayor of the City of New York.

# FEBRUARY 29*

## ADAM & EVE

*Really made for each other*

I T DIDN'T TAKE LONG FOR ADAM to realize that he had found the girl of his dreams. Eve was young, friendly, and eager to start a relationship, although she hadn't gone out with men before. Adam also had no dating experience, but like most guys, he didn't want Eve to know it. He slicked back his hair and tried to act suave and sophisticated. The garden was very nice, he said, with interesting walks, secluded spots to sit and chat, and any number of places for a quick bite of something to eat....

Eve knew she had finally met Mr. Right and that Adam came from a good family. So what if it was an "arranged marriage?" There was nobody like Adam.

Their wedding was a simple affair. The bride kept her own name and didn't wear anything except a few white blossoms in her hair. She carried a magnificent bouquet of flowers, but there was no one to toss it to. The menu was strictly vegetarian and the very short guest list eliminated all troublesome seating arrangements. Every day was sunny, so weather was not a problem. Since nobody worked, the ceremony did not have to be held on a weekend.

They wrote their own vows, after discussing and debating words like "obey" and whether or not a "woman's place" was only in the home. Walking down the aisle to their favorite tune, "If You Were the Only Girl in the World, and I Were the Only Boy," Adam and Eve concluded that only one promise had to be made: they would love each other, no matter what.

Eventually, the honeymoon period was over. It's hard to say just how long it took, since the passage of time hadn't been figured out yet. But Adam and Eve would look back on the early years of their marriage, when life was peaceful, beautiful and simple … just like paradise on earth.

---

*Date Approximate.

# MARCH

# MARCH 1
## GEORGE BANCROFT & SARAH DWIGHT
### *"dearest Sally"*

GEORGE AND SARAH KNEW EACH OTHER only a few months before he confessed his love in the spring of 1826. She was the daughter of a wealthy Springfield, Massachusetts family, and he was a brilliant scholar teaching school at Round Hill Academy in nearby Northampton. When Sarah's father, Jonathan Dwight, learned about George's proposal, he drove straightaway to the academy for a serious talk.

Eight years would pass before George published Volume One of his life's work – his monumental *History of the United States*. Writing it would take more than 30 years, while he held various jobs and government posts, including secretary of the navy under President James Polk. But now, at the age of 26, George was unsure about his future plans but he knew he could not live without his books, his research … and Sarah.

George told his future father-in-law about his experiences in Europe where, after graduating from Harvard at the age of 17, he had studied with leading romantic poets and writers including Goethe and Lord Byron. He had also been impressed by German historians who taught him how to maintain objectivity and search for true historical sources. By the time he returned to America, George yearned for a satisfying academic life, solitude, and a loving wife.

Mr. Dwight was so impressed with George's intelligence and ambitions that he offered him the greatest gift: part-time employment in one of the family's businesses, giving George time to work on his own.

The engagement would last almost 10 months, a period filled with frustration and the fear that perhaps Sarah would change her mind. "Of all the human beings, on you my affections unite," he told her. At last they married at the Dwights' gracious home in Springfield in 1827. The wedding was followed by a reception and ball at George's house in Northampton.

# MARCH 2

## ROBERT MORRIS & MARY WHITE

*"partner of my happy moments and sharer of
my sorrowful hours"*

A LTHOUGH ROBERT WAS A PROSPEROUS PHILADELPHIA businessman when he married "Molly" in 1769, neither could have predicted that within 7 years he would be financing the American Revolution!

When they met, Robert was 35 and almost twice Molly's age. His partner, Thomas Willing, had invited many socially prominent families, including the Whites, to a ball at the Assembly Hall. Other young men besides Robert asked the brown-eyed, willowy Molly to place their names on her dance card, but he soon swept her off her feet. She was charming, gracious, and unaffected; Robert was confident, warm, and sincere. Their personalities never changed throughout the long years of their happy marriage. Their home on Front Street and their country estate, The Hills (which contained the first privately owned icehouse in America), were popular centers of gaiety, open for parties as well as political meetings.

Five years earlier, Robert, who imported British products and exported American goods, had joined other frustrated colonists in resisting England's Stamp Act. When war broke out, he became a member of the Continental Congress. He also began financing munitions and naval armaments.

Robert's honesty was well known and respected, and by 1780 he was superintendent of finance for the new confederation, lending and borrowing money for the public cause. He also raised money by selling war bonds, even if it meant going from house to house to do it. Sometimes, the only security Robert could offer was his own good name and reputation.

Hundreds of candles glittered in the crystal chandeliers of Philadelphia's Christ Church on the day Robert and Molly married. Church bells chimed as the bride and groom exited the chapel. They rang again for liberty in 1781, when the British finally surrendered at Yorktown.

# MARCH 3

## ELIAS HOWE & ELIZABETH AMES

*Her "necessity" was the "mother" of his invention*

FOUR YEARS AFTER ELIAS MARRIED ELIZABETH in 1841, he completed the first operating model of a sewing machine. They had met in Boston, where he was working in a machine shop. Three years earlier, at the age of 16, Elias had left his parents' farm for the textile mills of Lowell, Massachusetts. Elias had been born lame, which made farm work difficult, but he always liked tinkering with complicated machinery. Soon, he advanced from bobbin boy to making and repairing the cotton looms.

The Panic of 1837 forced many mills and factories to close down, so Elias and a few friends headed for Boston, where he fell in love with his dear Elizabeth and eventually made his fortune.

At that time, all garments were sewn by hand, and workers were paid for each completed piece. Tailors and seamstresses spent hours hunched over worktables, but by the end of the day they had produced very little. Elizabeth always believed that Elias's own physical disability made him sensitive to the sadness in other people's lives. He couldn't bear watching his wife take care of their home and family all day long and spend her evenings sewing garments to sell to neighbors when he *knew* he could make a machine to do it faster, and better.

The problem was money. Elias needed his job at the machine shop and worked on his invention only late at night, when he was exhausted. Fortunately, his friends recognized his genius and provided financial support for the Howe family so Elias could concentrate on his sewing machine.

Like many inventors, Elias didn't become wealthy overnight. Crafty imitators began infringing on his patent, but after years of litigation, he won thousands of dollars in past royalties and guarantees for future royalties as they were accrued.

## MARCH 4
## RONALD REAGAN & NANCY DAVIS
*"My life really began when I met Nancy"*

WHEN NANCY CAME TO HOLLYWOOD IN 1949, her greatest ambition was not to be a famous film star. Instead, the future first lady hoped to have a successful, happy marriage. She met Ronnie a few months later. Already, he was a president – of the Screen Actors Guild – and strongly opposed to Communist sympathizers. Nancy was very interested in political issues, and admired every word Ronnie said. He was also attracted to her, but his 8-year marriage to actress Jane Wyman had just ended and he wanted to be single for a while. He did, however, give the name "Nancy D" to a new foal born at his ranch.

He was 41 and Nancy was 30 when they married in 1952 in a small ceremony at the Little Brown Church in the San Fernando Valley. Actor William Holden was best man, and his wife Ardis was matron of honor. Nancy wore a grey wool suit with a white collar and a small flowered hat with a veil. They spent their wedding night at the Mission Inn in Riverside and honeymooned in Phoenix, Arizona. On their way back to California, they drove through a sandstorm which tore apart the canvas top of their convertible. Even then, Nancy and Ronnie were a team: he drove the car as she held the top down!

For a while, they lived in Nancy's Brentwood apartment and then settled into a comfortable but conventional home at 1258 Amalfi Drive in Pacific Palisades. Within 14 years, Ronnie would forgo Hollywood and the television career he had developed, switch from being a Democrat to a Republican, and run for the governorship of California. He'd never been elected to public office before, but with Nancy at his side, he was unbeatable.

Eventually, he dedicated his autobiography to her and wrote, "To Nancy: she will always be my First Lady. I cannot imagine life without her."

# MARCH 5

## JACOB RIIS & ELIZABETH NEILSEN

*"Two, we would beat the world!"*

SIXTEEN-YEAR-OLD ELIZABETH KEPT JACOB'S LOVE NOTES even when her parents insisted that she reject his marriage proposal. Wounded and impetuous, her 21-year-old suitor sailed from Denmark to America, carrying the immigrant's classic dream that someday he would make his fortune and marry the girl back home. He struggled for several years, finding work as a coal miner, carpenter, brick-layer, and traveling salesman. Often, he slept in 5-cents-a-night flophouses and ate only when he earned enough money for a meal. But Jacob kept writing to Elizabeth. After he landed a job as a cub reporter for a New York news association, he knew that he had found his vocation.

Scraping together some money, Jacob proposed marriage to Elizabeth again. She didn't answer for months, but at last she agreed, having come to believe "that we are meant for one another." He sailed home immediately.

They were married in the Domkirke, the oldest church in Ribe, in 1876. Elizabeth wore flowers her friends had "loved up" and nurtured in their own tiny winter gardens. As she and Jacob rode in a carriage toward the dock and the boat to New York, "her head was leaning trustfully on my shoulder and her hand was in mine; all was well," he later recounted.

They settled in Brooklyn, and Jacob got a job with the New York *Tribune*. Covering street life and local issues, he was so horrified by the bleak lives of hard-working poor families living in overcrowded, rat-infested tenements that he devoted himself to improving their situations. With articles, photographs, and books such as *How the Other Half Lives*, he stirred the social conscience of many New Yorkers, which led to vast improvements in child labor and sweatshop laws, as well as housing and school conditions.

# MARCH 6

## EDWARD JENNER & CATHERINE KINGSCOTE
*She rescued him … so he could save millions*

DR. JENNER WAS 38 WHEN HE MARRIED the young woman who had saved his life. His older brother Stephen conducted the wedding ceremony in 1788 in a small country church in Berkeley, England, not far from the place where Catherine had found Edward 2 years earlier.

He had been riding to the village of Kingscote in a snowstorm to attend to a pregnant woman in labor. As Edward pushed on through the blizzard, he knew that he would probably die if he lost his way or fell off his horse. Reaching the house, Edward knocked on the heavy front door and collapsed.

When he awakened, he was in a warm room, and wrapped in a blanket. A sweet-faced 23-year-old woman with large gray eyes was watching him. It was Catherine. Not only had she rescued Edward, but she had also helped his patient deliver a healthy child. Edward and Catherine talked about medicine, music, and poetry for hours until he fell asleep on the floor, by the fire. When he recovered, she invited him to come back with his violin so he could accompany her while she played her spinet piano. With more time to talk, Edward told her he'd never wanted to be anything but a doctor. Even now, he would not have thought about marriage if Catherine hadn't entered his life.

He'd become obsessed with smallpox, the scourge of the 18th century. Even people who survived the disease suffered deeply and were disfigured by scars. Primitive inoculations required patients to be isolated for weeks, and the treatments produced great pain and suffering, and sometimes death.

After years of research and testing, including experimental inoculations on his own children, Edward confirmed that injecting people with cowpox vaccine immunized them from smallpox. By 1801 smallpox was virtually gone from Western civilization.

# MARCH 7

## ADOLPHUS BUSCH & LILLY ANHEUSER
### *"Darby and Joan"*

IN 1911 LILLY AND ADOLPHUS CELEBRATED their golden wedding anniversary by decorating their Pasadena, California home with hundreds of golden flowers. Thirty-eight relatives sat on golden chairs and ate from golden plates. Adolphus placed a diamond, pearl, and gold tiara on Lilly's head and said his successful career would never have happened without her help and understanding. Then the man who created the "King of Beers" told her she would always be his queen. Other celebrations were held that night in 35 cities including St. Louis, where 13,000 employees and business associates of the Anheuser-Busch company danced to a 50-piece band, ate countless ham sandwiches, and drank more than 40,000 bottles of Budweiser at the Coliseum downtown.

Even before the joyful couple grew old, people called them "Darby and Joan" after the deeply happy elderly pair in an old English song. Adolphus met Lilly soon after he and his older brother, Ulrich, came to St. Louis from Germany and set up a brewer's supply store. One of their best customers was Eberhard Anheuser, whose daughters, Lilly and Anna, soon fell in love with the brothers. After a double wedding ceremony in 1861 at St. Louis's church of the Holy Ghost Evangelical Lutheran, Eberhard hosted a lavish reception for the 4 newlyweds. That morning, Adolphus had closed a major deal and made enough money to take Lilly to Europe for their honeymoon.

Soon Ulrich and Anna moved to Chicago, where he continued in the brewing supply business. Adolphus enlisted in the Union army but was discharged after 3 months. He and Lilly studied brewing techniques in Germany and Bavaria and learned about Louis Pasteur's achievements. Back in America, Adolphus was the first brewer to pasteurize beer.

In 1864, Eberhard invited him to help manage his brewery, and 15 years later, the Anheuser-Busch Brewing Association was established.

# MARCH 8
## CHARLES BEARD & MARY RITTER
### *"pure happenstance"*

WHEN CHARLES MET MARY, SHE WAS SOAKING wet. Years passed before the two scholars teamed up in "life-long partnership" and became internationally known historians, but that day marked the beginning. Mary and a few DePauw University friends had been paddling a small boat on an Indiana lake when suddenly they capsized. Within seconds, Charles was pulling Mary out of the water, helping her wring her skirt dry, and gently brushing twigs out of her hair. In later years, he looked back on that time as "pure happenstance, and knew he had been blessed with good fortune.

They married in 1900 and took a bicycling trip through Europe that spring. The next 2 years were spent at Oxford University in England, where Charles had helped establish a "free university" for working-class students. Among their friends was suffragist Emmeline Pankhurst, who lived nearby, as well as other socialists and labor sympathizers. Change was in the air as the new century began, and Mary hoped to see more women involved in work and politics.

Back in America, she and Charles enrolled in graduate programs at Columbia University, marched in suffrage parades, and expounded their views in progressive political journals. The Beards believed that a solid understanding of *past* history could positively affect the course of *future* history, a philosophy reflected in one of their major works, *The Rise of American Civilization*, written in the 1920's.

After many years, Mary confessed to still being deeply in love with Charles and delighting in their "orgies of co-authorship." "I loved sitting at home with my darling every night and being at his side all the days," she wrote. No one could fully understand their "mutual happiness in working, jabbering and getting such exercise as we took in our simple ways. THIS IS AN ABSOLUTE TRUTH."

# MARCH 9

## NAPOLEON BONAPARTE & JOSEPHINE TASCHER DE BEAUHARNAIS

### *"To Destiny!"*

JOSEPHINE WASN'T IMPRESSED WHEN SHE MET Napoleon. The French army officer was somewhat shy and inexperienced, 6 years younger, and several inches shorter than she. Her late husband has been guillotined the year before, during the Reign of Terror. Josephine had been imprisoned, too, but was released days before her own scheduled execution. Virtually penniless, with 2 children to care for, she borrowed money from relatives, fixed herself up, and looked for a new and suitable protector.

When Napoleon was promoted to brigadier general, she focused all her attentions on him. At 32, her body was still voluptuous. She flattered and teased him, beguiled and seduced him, making him half-mad with passion: "To live with Josephine is to live in Elysium," he wrote. "A kiss on your mouth, your eyes, your shoulder, your breasts, everywhere! everywhere!"

They married in Paris in 1796. Signing the wedding contract in the mayor's office, Napoleon added 18 months to his age and Josephine subtracted 4 years, making them both – for the moment – 28 years old. Afterward, they walked back to her apartment; her children were with relatives, but her pet dog Fortune was at home.

The tiny black-faced pug had a nasty disposition and snapped at everyone except his mistress. He snarled when Napoleon entered the house, and barked ferociously when he climbed into Josephine's bed. Next, he nipped at Napoleon's heels, sinking his teeth into his legs. Napoleon tried tossing the little monster out the door, but Josephine blocked the way, insisting that her sweet pet always slept beside her and getting married wasn't going to change that.

Two days later, Napoleon and his troops departed for Italy and conquered it in record time. Eight years later, he and Josephine were emperor and empress of France. She never parted with the wedding ring he gave her; inscribed inside were the words, "To Destiny!"

# MARCH 10*

## GUSTAV MAHLER & ALMA MARIA SCHINDLER
### *"Wonne uber Wonne"*

GUSTAV COULDN'T TAKE HIS EYES OFF Alma at a dinner party in Vienna in 1901. He was 41 and an internationally known composer and conductor. She was 22, intelligent and incredibly beautiful. They began sharing stories, discussing music, and arguing about famous works. The next day, Gustav wrote the first of many love poems for her. The great man was so befuddled, he left his shoelaces untied and forgot his own phone number. All he could think about was Alma.

He wrote passionate letters to her, filled with longing for "the dearest and most sublime object of my life… my peace, my heaven in which I can constantly immerse myself."

"There was a magic circle round us which quickly encloses those who have found each other," Alma wrote almost 50 years later. A landscape painter's daughter, she understood the insecurities that plagued artists, and the unpredictability of life in the public eye. No matter how famous Gustav became, much of his work was misunderstood because it was a departure from typical romantic 19th century music. But Alma stayed with him, nurturing him through bouts of depression and inspiring him to compose magnificent symphonies.

"I want to become the sort of person you wish and need!" she wrote, reluctantly agreeing to give up her own musical ambitions for him. By Christmas, 1902 they were engaged. The news leaked out, and audiences stared at Alma, not the stage, when Gustav conducted operas.

"We're consumed with desire," she wrote in her diary. "It's sapping all our strength." A few days later – *"Wonne uber wonne!"* (Joy beyond all joy!). She was pregnant with their 1st child when they married at Vienna's Karlskirche and honeymooned in St. Petersburg, where Gustav conducted 3 concerts.

Gustav's life was transformed. Soon he was composing his Fifth Symphony, generally considered his sunniest work. Alma's influence was magical.

---

*March 9 has also been cited.

# MARCH 11

## RUSSELL BAKER & MIRIAM NASH

### *It wasn't "in the cards" but ...*

RUSSELL WAS A 24-YEAR OLD REPORTER for the *Baltimore Sun* when he married "Mimi" in 1950. Years later, in *Growing Up* and *The Good Times*, he described their relationship and all the times he had told her marriage wasn't "in the cards."

They first met one night in the parlor of a rooming house as he was dropping off his blind date. "This is Mimi," his date said. Those words changed Russell's life forever. But his mother wasn't happy when he brought Mimi home; after all, she lived alone, wore makeup, probably bleached her hair, *and* she was only 19. In those days, most women were either "good" or "bad," and Russell's mother implied that Mimi was the latter.

Russell didn't think he would marry Mimi, but he couldn't give her up. Exasperated by his stubbornness, after 3 years she moved to Washington to start a new job and hopefully a new life. A year later, after breakups, mix-ups, and passionate reunions – which Russell subsequently described as "the routine stuff of Hollywood's romantic comedies" – he realized that he wanted to marry Mimi after all.

"What a lovely spectacle she was when I first saw her at the altar," he recalled. She wore a beige suit with a dark blue hat, and he felt rather spiffy in a blue suit with padded shoulders and wide lapels. They were married in a church near his mother's home on Marydell Road in Baltimore, and took the train to New York for a short honeymoon at the Hotel Commodore. Within 5 years, Russell was writing for *The New York Times*. His columns were poignant, personal, universal, introspective, irreverent, and humorous – often all at the same time. In 1979 he became the first humorist to win the Pulitzer Prize for Commentary.

# MARCH 12
## PAUL MCCARTNEY & LINDA EASTMAN
### *He saw her standing there*

L INDA, A ROCK BAND PHOTOGRAPHER, MET Paul backstage at Shea Stadium in New York, where the Beatles were performing to sellout crowds in 1965. They crossed paths again at London clubs and at Brian Epstein's press party for the Sergeant Pepper album. Hordes of photographers vied for the attention of the famous musicians, but blond-haired, attractive, mini-skirted Linda was often the only one able to get close to them.

She'd always been comfortable around celebrities, especially because her entertainment lawyer father had been bringing them home when she was growing up. Linda was 18 when her mother died, and her feelings of devastation and loss were similar to those Paul had felt at 14, when his own mother died.

Within 2 years, he had fallen in love with Linda and her young daughter, Heather. They began living together in Paul's house at 7 Cavendish Avenue in St. John's Wood, London, and filled it with dogs and cats, as well as ducks, geese, and chickens in the yard.

In 1969, the band was on the verge of splitting up, and no other Beatles attended Paul and Linda's brief wedding ceremony at the Marylebone registry office in London. But throngs of reporters and fans stood outside. That summer, soon after Linda's next baby, Mary, was born, the family moved to Scotland and withdrew from public life. This inspired rumors that Paul had died.

How Paul and Linda met and married isn't, in the long run, half as interesting as the fact that they managed to stay together through experiences that could easily cause less stellar couples to separate. More than 20 years later, Paul was quoted as saying, "I twisted Linda's arm and she agreed to marry me...." She was afraid that it wouldn't work out, but he kept saying, "Aw, come on, it will be fine. Don't worry." And he never stopped telling her that.

# MARCH 13

## JAMES DALTON TRUMBO & CLEO BETH FINCHER
### *"under cloudier skies or sunnier"*

ALTON'S FIRST WORDS TO CLEO WERE an order: coffee and a
hamburger. She worked at a popular drive-in restaurant near Hollywood, and he was a 32-year-old, up-and-coming novelist and screenwriter. Dalton was so transfixed by the adorable carhop that he proposed
marriage when he paid the bill.

Barely 20, Cleo had enough self-confidence and good humor to think,
This guy can't be serious. But Dalton persisted, dropping by the drive-in night
after night. When Cleo suddenly ran off with a boyfriend and got married,
Dalton did some investigating and found out that her "husband" was already
married! Cleo was crushed, but she also was eternally grateful to Dalton. It
took a year for her to officially disentangle herself from the cad she had "married," and marry Dalton in his mother's apartment in 1938.

Cleo had always been impressed by his energy, enthusiasm, and determination to win her. Those qualities helped them weather terrible times
9 years later, when Dalton, now one of the highest-paid writers in filmdom,
was jailed for 11 months along with other members of the "Hollywood Ten"
after refusing to disclose his political views and testify before the House Un-
American Activities Committee investigating Communists.

On their 13th wedding anniversary, Dalton wrote to Cleo from a prison
cell, where he predicted, "We shall have many good years together, under
cloudier skies or sunnier..." because their love would "make its own climate—
the climate of springtime... as I think of you."

Blacklisted from Hollywood for years, he eked out a living by writing stories anonymously. As "Robert Rich," he wrote the screenplay for *The Brave
Bulls*, which won an Academy Award in 1957. Subsequently, Dalton wrote
the screenplays for *Spartacus*, *Exodus*, and other hit movies under his own
name again.

# MARCH 14

## DON RICKLES & BARBARA SKLAR

*"I married a Valium"*

THE WORLD-FAMOUS MASTER OF INSULT jokes didn't marry until he was 38-years old. Barbara always knew that Don was a likable guy, in spite of his talent for hurling offensive remarks at everyone from the fat man sitting at a front row table in a Las Vegas nightclub, to Frank Sinatra himself, in Hollywood.

"What do you eat for dinner? Furniture?" Don asked the overweight man. And even though Don had never met "Ol' Blue Eyes," he certainly grabbed Sinatra's attention by politely suggesting that the crooner make himself at home by slugging someone.

No one escaped his barbs... except Barb. So what if he had said that marriage was no better than "laying in a dam watching a beaver eat your jacket..." Even his mother – "the Jewish Patton" – was a target, although Don loved her deeply, too. In fact, after he and Barbara married in 1965, they remained in his old apartment, right next door to Etta Rickles. Barbara let her mother-in-law still be the boss about a lot of things, which convinced Don that his new wife was a "saint."

Barbara had been his film agent's secretary, and she saw Don whenever he dropped by. He'd been looking for someone for a long time, and when he finally found her, he married her. A few months later, he debuted on Johnny Carson's famous *Tonight Show* and had the chutzpah to greet his host with "Hello, dummy!" The audience, and Johnny, loved "Mr. Warmth," whose career picked up dramatically. Meanwhile, Barbara took care of their home and two kids; later on, she traveled with Don often. Just as private as he was offstage, she kept him company, helped out in his dressing room, and was always his number-one fan.

# MARCH 15

## ELIZABETH TAYLOR & RICHARD BURTON
### *"Le scandale"*

NEITHER RICHARD NOR ELIZABETH EVER FORGOT the first time they met, at a party in Los Angeles in 1953. She was 20 and he was 28. "She was unquestioningly gorgeous," he wrote years later. "She was, in short, too bloody much, and not only that, she was totally ignoring me." Elizabeth's first impression was that "he was rather full of himself."

The film and stage stars met again 10 years later on the set of *Cleopatra*, a motion picture remembered, primarily, for running millions of dollars over budget and for the real-life romance of "Antony" and "Cleopatra" – aka Dick and Liz. Although she teasingly called him "Gramps" and he addressed her as "Pudgy," their love scenes were passionately hot. She was not quite 30 and wed to her 4th husband, singer Eddie Fisher. That marriage, as well as Dick's to Sybil Burton, went on the rocks by the time the film was released. Dick and Liz became an item in gossip columns everywhere.

One of Richard's first gifts to Elizabeth was a necklace of ancient Egyptian scarabs, probably made during Cleopatra's time. When they married in 1964, Elizabeth wore a low-cut yellow chiffon gown enhanced by another gift – a huge emerald brooch.

The ceremony was held in their hotel suite in Montreal's Ritz Carlton. The following day, they flew to Toronto, where Richard was starring in a production of *Hamlet*. When the curtain came down that night, he invited Elizabeth to join him on the stage, where he introduced her to the audience. Then he quoted Hamlet's words to Ophelia in the nunnery scene – "I say we will have no more marriages!" The audience went wild. Within 5 years, Elizabeth and Richard were probably the best–known and best-paid acting team in the world.

# MARCH 16

## ROBERT MITCHUM & DOROTHY SPENCE

*There never was anyone else…*

THE SEXY HOLLYWOOD STAR WITH SLEEPY eyelids found his perfect wife when he was in his teens, and was married to her for more than 50 years.

Bob quit high school in New York when he was 14, in the early 1930's. He worked at odd jobs, and hitchhiked around the country. His family moved, too, to Rising Sun, Delaware, where he met Dorothy on one of his visits. By then, he was 16 and she was 14, already tall and slender, with a serene disposition. Just being around her made Bob feel less lonely. At first, she was put off by his wise-guy demeanor, but gradually she discovered his gentleness underneath.

Dorothy's parents didn't like the brash and smart-alecky young man, and forbade her to see him. He didn't admit that his limp was from gangrene he'd gotten while working on a chain gang, but they sensed that his background had been unconventional. Bob hung around Dorothy for as long as possible, and then headed to California, where he practically stumbled into acting at a local playhouse. He wrote to Dorothy often, warning her not to get serious with other men because someday, he would come back to marry her.

They were 22 and 20-years old when Bob came east in 1940. On a Friday night, they drove to Dover, Delaware and knocked on the door of a Methodist minister who married them amid the odors of cabbage his wife was cooking on the stove.

Bob and Dorothy's honeymoon trip was a bus ride to Los Angeles. Years of financial struggle and the births of 2 children followed. His first acting break was playing bad guys in Hopalong Cassidy westerns. In 1945, Bob's Academy Award nomination for best supporting actor in *The Story of G.I. Joe* put him on the road to stardom.

# MARCH 17

## FRANKLIN DELANO ROOSEVELT & ELEANOR ROOSEVELT

*"Well, Franklin, there's nothing like keeping the name in the family."*

—THEODORE ROOSEVELT

UNCLE TEDDY SAID HE'D BE DELIGHTED to give away the bride when Eleanor married his distant cousin, Franklin, in 1905. As president of the United States, Teddy also said they could have their wedding at the White House, but Eleanor preferred an aunt's Manhattan town house at Fifth Avenue and 76th Street. Okay, said Teddy, as long as they got married on St. Patrick's Day, when he'd be in New York marching in the parade. Onlookers swarmed around the president and blocked nearby streets when he arrived at 3:30PM, preventing some guests from getting to the ceremony on time.

"Try and forget the crowd and only think of Franklin," Eleanor's aunt advised the nervous bride. "If you are wise, you will drink a cup of strong tea half an hour before you go downstairs. It will give you color and make you feel well. *No* sugar or cream in it!"

White lilacs, lilies, and roses decorated the townhouse. An orchestra played the wedding march as 6 bridesmaids wearing cream-colored taffeta dresses descended the circular staircase. Eleanor followed in a stiff white satin dress, and carried a bouquet of lilies of the valley. Her Brussels lace veil was secured to her hair by a diamond crescent comb. Around her neck was a "dog collar" of pearls with diamond bars, a gift from Franklin's mother. Under a bower of pink roses and palms, the couple recited their marriage vows loudly, so their voices could be heard over the din of bagpipes outside the windows.

The honeymooners spent a quiet week alone at the Roosevelt family's home in Hyde Park, postponing an extended trip to Europe until the summer, when Franklin would be on vacation from his studies at Columbia Law School. (He, too, had been under a lot of stress, and failed 2 courses that semester!)

## MARCH 18
## JOHN LOCKWOOD KIPLING & ALICE MACDONALD
### *"Ruddy's" parents met by a lake*

A LICE HAD DARK RED HAIR AND blue eyes, and was witty and insightful. She often spoke in a rush, her sharp mind moving more quickly than her words. By contrast, John was serene and smiling, somewhat forgetful but incredibly kind and gentle. Before he met Alice, he'd been working as a sculptor during construction of London's Victoria and Albert Museum in the 1860's, and would be immortalized in a large group portrait there.

He then came to Staffordshire and was designing pottery in nearby Burslem when Alice's minister brother, Frederick, invited him to a gathering of local artists and scholars. The picnic was held by Lake Rudyard, and that's where John met Alice. Later, they commemorated that romantic spot by naming their first child after it.

They were determined not to marry until they could stand on their own feet financially. Both were 27 when they boldly decided that John should accept the position of architectural sculptor at the Jeejeeboy School of Art in Bombay. They would leave for India as soon as they were wed.

Alice's younger sister, Georgiana, who had already married the painter Edward Burne-Jones, handled all the arrangements for the wedding, held at St. Mary Abbot's church in London on a blustery day in 1865. Because Alice's father's health was poor, Frederick gave away the bride. Renowned writers and artists, including Charles Algernon Swinburne, the two Rosettis, and Ford Maddox Ford attended the reception, though Alice and John had already slipped away and boarded a waiting ship.

For the next 30 years, Alice wrote poems and articles for magazines and local newspapers in India, and supported all her husband's artistic endeavors. Later, she would also influence their dear son "Ruddy," who would be permanently inspired by that exotic land.

# MARCH 19
## JOHN CASSAVETES & GENA ROWLANDS
### *His leading lady*

GENA MET JOHN IN NEW YORK City in 1953, soon after she left the University of Wisconsin in her junior year and enrolled in the Academy of Dramatic Arts. He had graduated 3 years before but saw her performing in a studio production. She was radiantly beautiful and determined to become an actress. He was bright, intense, and passionately in love with the theater, with acting … and with Gena. They were married in 1954 at the Little Church Around the Corner in Manhattan. She was 19 and he was 24.

At first, they performed separately as well as together in television drama series such as *Kraft Television Theater* and *Lux Playhouse*, and acted in plays on and off Broadway. But by his late 20's, John was eager to become an independent filmmaker and put a unique spin on his own productions.

The couple moved to Hollywood in 1958 and worked together on some of John's projects. He'd already produced *Shadows*, a grainy, poignant black-and-white film that grew out of a series of drama workshops he conducted. Many of John's other films featured Gena or close friends such as Peter Falk and Ben Gazzara. Sometimes, the scripts were only loosely written drafts open to interpretation and improvisation by the cast, but he wrote *A Woman Under the Influence* in detail, tailoring it specifically for Gena. They promoted the film themselves until it was booked into theaters coast to coast. It won awards and citations, and an Academy Award nomination for Gena.

Some critics called their marriage tempestuous, providing John with rich material for his films, but he and Gena remained devoted to each other. Next to John, "other people look squinched up," she said. Referring to his Greek ancestry, she added, "he's my Mediterranean madman, and I wouldn't have it any other way."

# MARCH 20
## JOHN LENNON & YOKO ONO
### *Life as Art, Art as Life*

A FEW DAYS AFTER BEATLE PAUL McCartney married Linda Eastman in 1969, John and Yoko decided to do the same thing. As they drove around London in John's white Rolls-Royce, they considered various sites for their momentous event. Why not the Channel ferry between England and France? Or perhaps a very grand ceremony performed by the Archbishop of Canterbury, no less. But that would take a lot of time to arrange and besides, it was unlikely that the archbishop would agree.

Instead, John and Yoko flew to the island of Gibraltar and were married in a 3-minute private ceremony. Both were dressed in white: John wore a sweater, jacket and pants; Yoko wore a mini-dress, kneesocks, and a wide-brimmed hat. They held lit cigarettes and sported white tennis shoes. She was 36 and already had a daughter; he was 28 and had a son.

Within the hour, the newlyweds were on a plane to Paris, where the press surrounded them at Le Bourget airport. They stayed a few days, had lunch with painter Salvador Dali, and then were off to the Netherlands, where they staged a week-long "bed-in" for peace at the Amsterdam Hilton's Suite 902, pleading for the world to "Give peace a chance" and end the war in Vietnam. They produced a short documentary film called *Honeymoon*, as well as *Wedding Album*, a collection of recordings, photographs, and mementoes about their momentous day.

They had first met 3 years before, in a London art gallery where Yoko's avant-garde work was being exhibited. John was impressed by her bizarre conceptions and creations, and eventually he financed some of her shows. The other Beatles were never comfortable with Yoko. But she and John became a powerful team, expressing themselves through musical and visual works of art.

# MARCH 21

## BENNY GOODMAN & ALICE HAMMOND DUCKWORTH

### *Let's dance!*

T HE "KING OF SWING" WAS AN internationally known clarinetist and bandleader when he and Alice married on the first day of spring in 1942. Benny was a 32-year old bachelor, and Alice was 35 and had recently ended her marriage to a member of the British Parliament. She had 3 daughters, and would have 2 more with Benny.

They'd met in England in 1934, when Alice's brother, music writer and producer John Hammond brought Benny and other leading jazz musicians together to cut records. A year later, after a routine evening playing dance music at the Palomar Ballroom in Los Angeles, Benny and his new band broke loose with wild improvisational sounds of pulse-pounding music... and the new era of "swing music" was born! In the late 1930's Benny was one of the first white bandleaders with an integrated band, featuring outstanding African-American musicians such as Lionel Hampton and Jess Stacy.

For a long time Benny had been focused on his career, and people often joked that he was "married" to his music. By the early 1940's it had made him rich and famous. As the great-great granddaughter of Cornelius Vanderbilt, Alice was wealthy, too, but her upper-crust background didn't stifle her interest in show business and in the personable and ambitious clarinet player. She helped Benny smooth out some of his rough edges, and although their families wondered sometimes what brought the society girl and jazz musician together, their relationship proved to be loving and long-lasting.

They married in Nevada and headed for California. Benny later said, "Hardly anyone thought the marriage would work. Alice had been married before to a rather staid Englishman and was used to a home life. We spent our first 3 months under 73 different roofs on the road."

# MARCH 22

## J.R.R. TOLKIEN & EDITH MARY BRATT
### *His "Luthien"*

"RONALD" MARRIED EDITH IN WARWICK, ENGLAND in 1916, shortly after he left for military service in World War I. They had met 8 years earlier in a boardinghouse in Cheltenham, when he was 16 and she was 19. Bright, impressionable, but also lonely and orphaned teenagers, they became very close in the years they lived together.

Edith was a talented pianist whose family was distantly related to Sir George Grove, editor of the well-known dictionary of music. Ronald's guardian, Father Francis, discouraged his relationship with Edith because she wasn't Catholic, but by the time Ronald left to study at Oxford, he believed that Edith would wait for him and that they would marry one day.

Few people knew how he felt about Edith, but Ronald never stopped dreaming about her. In the meantime, however, she became engaged to another man because she lost hope that Ronald would ever return. Soon after his 21st birthday, Ronald hurried back to Cheltenham and convinced Edith that she never should have doubted his love.

Three years later, there was time only for a short honeymoon in Somerset before Ronald left for France. While it's difficult to know where writers find their inspirations, it's likely that the darker parts of *The Lord of the Rings* were inspired by Ronald's experiences in trench warfare. Perhaps he created Middle Earth to escape the frightening realities of 20th century life.

After the war, he and Edith lived on Northmore Road in Oxford, and eventually he became the Merton Professor of Linguistics and Literature at Oxford. He wrote *The Hobbit* and the *Rings* trilogy there and was known as a kind and generous teacher and man. As Edith's life brightened, she became a proper don's wife, keeping house and raising their 4 children. Ronald compared her to his character Luthien – "the fairest maiden that has ever been."

# MARCH 23

## LOUIS BRANDEIS & ALICE GOLDMARK
### *"we have found each other"*

L OUIS AND ALICE FELL IN LOVE in the summer of 1890 at a family gathering in New York's Adirondack Mountains. The future U.S. Supreme Court justice was a brilliant and introspective 33-year old lawyer who had settled in Boston after graduating from Harvard Law School. His distant cousin Alice was 23, brown-eyed and slender. Since Louis often worked 7 days a week, his brief holiday in the mountains was a blissful time.

They took long walks, read together, and became inseparable. As moths fluttered against Alice's window screen late at night, she opened her diary and wrote about Louis: "His eyes are always upon me. We go down to the river and he tells me his story – we have found each other."

By the time they parted, they were planning their engagement. Alice returned to New York City, and Louis began searching for a home for them in Boston. They corresponded constantly, and he admitted that ever since he had left for college 17 years before, he had "stood alone – rarely asking – and less frequently caring, for the advice of others." Now everything had changed. Without Alice, Louis felt incomplete. "I feel myself... growing more into your soul," he confessed. "And I am very happy."

"If the 23rd were not fixed immutably, I should... break away and carry you off," he said, one week before the wedding.

Alice's brother-in-law, Dr. Felix Adler, founder of the New York Society of Ethical Culture, conducted the ceremony at the Goldmarks' apartment in 1891. After honeymooning in the Berkshires, Alice and Louis moved to 114 Mt. Vernon Street, near Boston Common and Louis's office on Devonshire Street.

Louis often represented needy clients without charging them fees. Alice also was involved in social causes and set up night-school classes for working people.

# MARCH 24*

## ANNE DUDLEY & SIMON BRADSTREET

*"My head, my heart, mine eyes, my life, nay more"*

*If ever two were one, then surely we,*
*If ever man were lov'd by wife, then thee;*
*If ever wife was happy in a man,*
*Compare with me ye women if you can.*

SO BEGINS ANNE'S WELL-KNOWN POEM, "To my dear and Loving Husband," written in Massachusetts Bay Colony about 1650. She would have been a writer, no matter where she lived – "I am obnoxious to each carping tongue / Who sayes my hand a needle better fits" – but her poems are the first known works of exceptional literary value to have been written in colonial New England.

Childhood sweethearts, Anne and Simon married in England 2 years before they sailed with her parents to America in March 1630, on John Winthrop's flagship, the *Arabella*. March is also the month of Anne's birth, as well as the beginning of springtime, so it is chosen, here, as the month of her wedding. She was 16 and he was 24-years old. They were married for 44 years, during which time they lived in various parts of the Massachusetts Bay area and raised 8 children in an atmosphere of love and respect for education and literature. Future descendants would include 19th century author and lawyer Richard Henry Dana, and U.S. Supreme Court Justice Oliver Wendell Holmes, Jr.

The Puritans believed that marriages could end only with death. But Anne also hoped to be remembered on this earth. She wrote to her adored husband:

*Thy love is such I can no way repay,*
*The heavens reward thee manifold, I pray.*
*Then while we live, in love lets so persever,*
*That when we live no more, we may live ever.*

---

*Date approximate

# MARCH 25

## THOMAS MOORE & ELIZABETH DYKE

### *"those endearing young charms"*

TOM'S UPPER-CRUST FRIENDS WERE SURPRISED WHEN he married "Bessy" in 1811. The 31-year old composer-poet was cultured and handsome enough to have married any number of wealthy women in London. He'd met Bessy, a poor but beautiful young actress, in Kilkenny, Ireland, 3 years before. Tom usually wrote the music for theatrical productions, but that season he and Bessy performed together in a play. Although she was not well-educated, Bessy was talented, spirited, kindhearted and adoring.

Tom had always been passionate about music, and had also written rhymes since childhood. He'd left Ireland for London when he was 20 and found patrons, including the Prince of Wales. Soon the young Irishman was playing music, singing at social gatherings, and writing poetry.

After he married Bessy, Tom decided to give up depending on the precarious nature of patronage. For a while, he and Bessy lived with friends. Then they moved to a small house he called "a nutshell of a thing" in the country, where he devoted himself to "the quiet pursuit of literature." A publisher advanced him money to write "*Lalla Rookh*," a long, lyrical poem about an oriental romance. It would become one of his most famous works and rank him alongside Lord Byron and Sir Walter Scott. But Tom's *Irish Melodies* – over 100 pieces of lyrical beauty – became the crowning achievement of his life.

He was thinking of Bessy when he wrote:

*Believe me, if all those endearing young charms*
*Which I gaze on so fondly to-day*
*Were to change by to-morrow, and fleet in my arms,*
*Like fairy-gifts fading away,*
*Thou wouldst still be ador'd, as this moment thou art,*
*Let thy loveliness fade as it will,*
*And around the dear ruin each wish of my heart*
*Would entwine itself verdantly still.*

# MARCH 26

## LESLIE STEPHEN & JULIA PRINSEP DUCKWORTH
### *"such a wife as no language can describe"*

'LORD, WHAT A CRANKY BRUTE I am!" Leslie wrote a friend in 1877. His wife had died 2 years before, leaving him dejected and with a young child in their home near London's Kensington Gardens. A few months later, Leslie's news was brighter: "Mrs. Duckworth is our neighbor almost, and I have been seeing her…. Her children have been playmates of my poor little girl, who needed playmates very much…. We are to be married before very long… and if I am not happy… it will be my own fault."

Julia, too, had been widowed. "I was only 24 when life all seemed a shipwreck," she wrote Leslie after they became friends. She did not intend to marry again. It took a long time to accept his proposal, but one evening, she suddenly looked up at Leslie and announced that she wanted to be his wife and would do her best to be a good one. Their marriage would be happy, and she would give birth to 4 more children, including future writers Virginia Woolf and Vanessa Bell.

On Sunday afternoons, Leslie and Julia hosted salons for aspiring and well-established poets, artists, musicians, and novelists. Julia was particularly delighted to listen to her young guests talk about their romances and friendships.

As a respected Victorian man of letters, mountaineer, biographer, historian, and first editor of Britain's *Dictionary of National Biography*, Leslie encouraged young writers such as Robert Louis Stevenson, Thomas Hardy, and Henry James. Julia wrote, too, including *Notes For Sick Rooms*, a sympathetic and helpful book about how to care for ill people.

Many years after March 26, 1878, Leslie could still say, "Not a fibre in me but thrills at the thought of all the goodness lavished upon me since that day."

# MARCH 27

## PRINCE KHURRAM & ARJUMAND BANU BEGAM
### *"Chosen One of the Palace"*

I N 17TH CENTURY INDIA, ROYAL WEDDING dates were determined by the emperor's astrologers. Khurram and Arjumand had to wait 5 years for an auspicious day to marry. During that time, they were not permitted to meet or even see each other.

In 1607, the 16-year old prince was walking through the Royal Meena Bazaar in Agra, near the palace harem. Vendors hawked jeweled silks, perfumes, and amulets, and young men flirted with innocent young women until strict fathers chased them away. Outside one of the striped tents was the prime minister's lovely 15-year old daughter. Arjumand's voice was soft as rain trickling down a gentle hillside. Her long eyelashes fluttered when she laughed, and Khurram was enchanted by her.

They married in 1612 in a glorious ceremony at the bride's home. Dancers swayed and dervishes whirled; dignitaries arrived in palanquins and on the backs of elephants. Everyone feasted until long after midnight, and the emperor proclaimed that his daughter-in-law would be called Mumtaz Mahal – "Chosen One of the Palace."

Khurram, too, took a new name when he inherited his father's throne. As Shah Jahan, "King of the World," he ruled over a vast empire with Mumtaz, his closest companion and most trusted political advisor. She was wise and compassionate, and encouraged him to sponsor new developments in music, architecture, and painting. Tragically, she died in 1631, after giving birth to their 14th child.

After a long period of mourning, Shah Jahan decreed that a mausoleum as perfectly formed and beautiful as his beloved wife be built beside the Yamuna river. It took 20,000 workers 22 years to create the exquisite Taj Mahal, which the poet Rabindranath Tagore called "a teardrop on the cheek of eternity." It still stands today, a tribute to undying love.

## MARCH 28
## FELIX MENDELSSOHN & CECILE JEANRENAUD
*He composed his "Wedding March" after his wedding!*

"I HAVE JUST BECOME ENGAGED TO Cecile Jeanrenaud," Felix wrote his mother 6 months before his wedding in 1837. "I feel quite dizzy... Oh, how wonderful and happy I feel!"

They had met in Frankfurt, Germany, when Cecile was 19 and he was 27. Felix was already a famous composer, and she had imagined he would be a humorless and boring old man playing fugues on the piano. Instead, she found Felix elegant and good-looking, with dark curly hair and dark eyes.

Until then, he had been living alone in Leipzig. Felix had been romantically involved before, but had never thought seriously about marriage. One night, his sister Fanny sat him down and said, Felix, it's time you got married. Of course, he told her, I will. Someday. When he directed a series of choral concerts that year, little did he know that the blue-eyed, blond soprano would become his wife!

He proposed to Cecile at the end of summer in a grove of beech trees outside of town. They were wed the following March at the Reformed French Church of Frankfurt, where her father was the pastor. Honeymooning in the Rhineland, Felix and Cecile filled a diary with stories and drawings of their first weeks together. The diary, which is now in Oxford's Bodleian Library, still contains a withered nosegay of violets that she had placed in his buttonhole, inspiring him to compose "a delightful allegretto."

"The weather this evening is magnificent and the whole landscape lies before us without a trace of fog," wrote Cecile. "We lie under the young trees which are planted around a church, we sing, dance on the thin grass, count the many islands in the Rhine... and love each other very much."

# MARCH 29

## CLARK GABLE & CAROLE LOMBARD
### *"Maw" and "Paw"*

IN 1939 CLARK WAS MGM'S "KING of Hollywood," and Carole was one of the most glamorous and talented film stars and comediennes. Clark had been married twice before, and after Carole's untimely death he married twice again, but most film buffs agree that she was the love of his life.

They met on the set of *No Man of Her Own* in 1932. It was Clark's comedy role, but his blond co-star soon put him at ease. They called each other "Maw" and "Paw" and played practical jokes on each other. The day film work ended, Carole handed him a large ham.

She was almost 30 and he was 38 when they got married in Kingman, Arizona, on Clark's first day off while filming *Gone With the Wind*. MGM had been squeamish about "Rhett Butler's affair," and assisted Clark in getting his wife, Rita, to agree to a divorce.

Hollywood's latest lovebirds moved into a secluded white brick "farmhouse" on 20 acres in the San Fernando Valley. They planted citrus trees, rode, hunted, and fished. Carole wasn't thrilled about cooking over campfires or spending the night in a sleeping bag (once, she was bitten by a rattlesnake) but she did it for Clark. No woman pleased him as much as she did, and throughout their marriage they adored each other.

During World War II, Carole toured the United States selling war bonds. One night, when her plane was due back in Los Angeles, Clark tucked a blond department store mannequin into Carole's side of their bed as a gag. But Carole never made it back... and the "King" never got over it. He said he wanted to be buried beside her; 18 years later, he was.

## MARCH 30

## LAURENCE STERNE & ELIZABETH LUMLEY
### *"My dear Lawrey"*

"OUR COUSIN BETTY LUMLEY IS MARRIED to a Parson who once delighted in debauchery," wrote Matthew Robinson to his sister in 1741. Laurence may have been a high-spirited, rowdy student at Jesus College, Cambridge, but few pupils took their studies seriously. He became a clergyman after graduation, not because he was particularly devout, but because he needed a career. Writing had always been Laurence's favorite occupation, and one day he would write the great novels, *Tristam Shandy*, and *A Sentimental Journey*.

Matthew's sister's reply was more favorable: "Mr. Sterne has a hundred a year living, with a good prospect of better preferment. He was a great rake, but... has varnished his character.... I wish they may live well together."

Laurence and Elizabeth had met in York, not far from Sutton-on-the-Forest where Elizabeth, who had inherited a tidy income from her late father, lived in a cottage on Little Alice Lane. She invited Laurence, the lively new vicar, for dinner often, and they spent evenings talking about music and song. He courted her for 2 years. When Elizabeth left town to visit relatives, she encouraged him to stay at her cottage.

"The hour you left," he wrote her, "I took to my bed.... One solitary plate, on knife, one fork, one glass!—I gave a thousand pensive, penetrating looks at the chair thou hadst so often graced... then... took out my handkerchief, and clapped it across my face, and wept like a child."

When Elizabeth returned, she became seriously ill. She told Laurence that if she died, all she owned would go to him, but he nursed her back to health. They married on Easter Monday, and Elizabeth saved "Lawrey's" love letters for the rest of her life.

# MARCH 31

## WILLIAM MICHAEL ROSSETTI & LUCY BROWN
### *"my dearly loved wife"*

THE ROSSETTI AND BROWN FAMILIES HAD been close for many years in Victorian London, and were uncharacteristically surprised when William and Lucy announced their engagement. Her father, Ford Madox Brown was a well-known painter and the Anglo-Italian Rossettis were known for their Pre-Raphaelite philosophy of art. As an art critic, biographer, and man of letters, William provided financial and emotional support to his family, which included the poets Dante Gabriel and Christina.

"For several years preceding 1873 I had a warmly affectionate feeling for Lucy Brown," wrote 44-year old William in his typically restrained fashion. An artist like her father, Lucy painted watercolors such as "Romeo and Juliet in the Vault," and took care of the family home in London. It was there "that I first met my future wife," William wrote, "a quiet candid-looking little girl, aged less than 7, modestly self-possessed." Now she was 30 and happy to accept William's proposal shortly after she returned from a trip to Italy.

"I decided that I would not again part with Lucy, if I could help it," he recorded in his diary. He was relieved when she agreed to live with the Rossettis in their house on Euston Square, but this event may have prompted William's sister Maria to escape the embarrassment of spinsterhood by joining a convent. Christina was delighted, however, saying he had brought a "fresh spring of happiness... into our family." Dante's gift would be a portrait of his new sister-in-law, painted the following summer.

Lucy and William were married as agnostics on a Tuesday in 1874, and they honeymooned in Italy and France. Lucy gave birth to 7 children within 7 years, but she continued to exhibit her art and became involved with feminist causes. She later wrote a life of Mary Shelley, and he wrote a life of Keats.

# APRIL

# APRIL 1

## GENE AUTRY & IDA MAE SPIVEY

### *No fooling!*

N OT UNTIL AFTER THEIR SPUR-OF-THE-MOMENT WED-
DING did Ina realize she had married the future singing cowboy on
April Fools' Day. Gene was 23 and she was 18 in 1932, and as they
sat together in the corner booth of a St. Louis restaurant, he convinced his
blue-eyed bride that he was as serious about marriage as she. She *had* wondered, since he proposed on their 4th date!

They'd been introduced by Ina's uncle Jimmy, who had worked with Gene
before he began singing and playing his guitar on the *National Barn Dance*
radio show. Like Gene, Ina had grown up in Oklahoma, but she lived with
Jimmy and his family while studying music at a college in Springfield, Missouri. Gene said she had "skin like rose petals," and fell for her right away.

The well-known humorist Will Rogers had listened to Gene perform when
he was an amateur, and suggested that he try singing professionally. By the
time Gene married Ina, he was making $35 a week which was a good salary
during the Depression. Soon they were on their way to Hollywood, where he
began appearing in motion pictures.

The 1935 movie, *Tumbling Tumbleweeds* secured Gene's career. Two years
later, he was voted the top western-movie star, an accolade he held for the
next 6 years. Wearing his spotless white 10 gallon hat, Gene appeared in
more than 100 western films and television shows. Later, he founded the California Angels baseball team.

In 1938, Gene sang about the cowboy's declaration that no woman could
ever hurt him "As Long as I've Got My Horse," although he always loved Ina
more than Champion, his famous steed. If not for Ina, Gene might not have
recorded "Rudolph, the Red-nosed Reindeer," which reminded her of the
story of the ugly duckling. More than 2.5 million records were sold the first
year, and it's still a popular Christmas song.

# APRIL 2

## JACQUELINE SUSANN & IRVING MANSFIELD

*Lovely them*

BEFORE JACKIE BECAME A WELL-KNOWN AUTHOR, she was a Broadway actress appearing in plays such as Clare Booth Luce's *The Women*. Jackie met Irving in 1937 at a party for theater people in New York City. She'd left home in Philadelphia after winning her parents' reluctant blessing for her to skip college and study acting instead. Two years later, at the age of 18, she married Irving in her parents' apartment. He was a press agent and theatrical producer, but he wrote "writer" as his profession on the marriage license, possibly to soothe his somewhat worried in-laws.

After the ceremony, the rabbi said he hoped Jackie and Irving would establish a traditional home, but for the most part, their "homes" would be hotel suites. "If I wanted a cook, I would have married one," said Irving, pointing out that it took 4 years to notice that their hotel apartment even had a kitchen!

The radio personalities Goodman and Jane Ace gave the newlyweds a portable typewriter as a wedding present, and 7 years later, Jackie sat down to write. First, she wrote the play, *Lovely Me*, with a friend; later came *Not Tonight, Josephine*, about being "owned" by a French poodle. Not until she was almost 50 did Jackie write the best-selling novel, *Valley of the Dolls*. The characters were modeled after recognizable Hollywood stars, and show business lifestyles involving drug abuse, alcoholism, extramarital sex, and homosexuality quickly captured the public's attention.

Irving organized an elaborate publicity tour, and Jackie promoted her book, selling millions of copies. Another best-seller, *The Love Machine*, followed. Writing 2 number-one novels back to back quickly made her rich and famous, despite reviewers' negative criticisms. "I'd like to have the critics like me," Jackie said. "I'd like to have everybody like what I write. But when my book sells, I know people like the book. That's the most important thing."

# APRIL 3

## F. SCOTT FITZGERALD & ZELDA SAYRE
### *his "darling heart"*

T HEY MET AT A DANCE FOR soldiers in Montgomery, Alabama on a warm summer night in 1917. "Scotty's" army uniform was Brooks Brothers' finest. If he looked a bit forlorn, it was because he had just learned that a former girlfriend had married someone else.

The incredibly beautiful daughter of a local judge was being whirled around the floor by one of Scotty's friends. Zelda smoked and drank liquor, shocking her parents and most people in the small southern town. But these young men at the dance were from faraway places, and Scotty was a writer, something Zelda deeply wanted to become. He pursued her intensely, and proposed marriage as soon as he was discharged.

Zelda stalled him, wanting to be sure that Scotty could support her. He headed for New York City, got a job and sold his first novel, *This Side of Paradise* at the age of 23. "I AM IN THE LAND OF AMBITION AND SUCCESS AND MY ONLY HOPE AND FAITH IS THAT MY DARLING HEART WILL BE WITH ME SOON," he wrote in a telegram.

Still, it took another year of mad dashes back to Montgomery, arguments, reconciliations, phone calls, and frantic letters before Zelda told him, yes.

The ceremony was held in 1920, in the rectory of Manhattan's St. Patrick's Cathedral the day before Easter Sunday. Zelda wore a dark blue suit and hat and carried a bouquet of orchids and white flowers. Their honeymoon began at the Biltmore Hotel, but they whooped it up so much that the management finally asked them to leave.

They were young, good-looking, rich and successful, but with their nonstop parties, trips to Europe, and outrageous behavior, they became a tragic couple. Even so, Zelda and Scotty embodied the Jazz Age of the Roaring '20's, and he wrote all about it.

## APRIL 4

## WILLIAM PENN & GULIELMA MARIA SPRINGETT
### *"a match of Providence's making"*

WILLIAM AND "GULI" WERE MARRIED IN 1627 in a Quaker ceremony at a 14<sup>th</sup> century hunting lodge in Chorley Wood, England. Under the oak beams of a large white-plastered room, they sat beside each other, facing the Friends at meeting. As the silence deepened, the bride and groom stood, took each other's hands and, in the presence of God and the congregation, promised to love and be faithful to each other for as long as they lived.

Their words were simple and included no vows of obedience. No rings were exchanged, and no wedding attendants participated. Sunlight streamed through the casement windows, and when William and Guli sat down, the other Friends approached them, giving blessings and encouragement. Forty-six witnesses signed the wedding contract, along with the bride and groom.

Two years earlier, when William and Guli first met, he was 25 and she was a few months older – a "spinster" who was beautiful as well as intelligent. From her mother she had learned a great deal about medicine and surgery, and she used her skills to help the sick. Their courtship had been interrupted by William's arrests and imprisonments for preaching Quakerism and writing religious treatises, but now there was time to spend 5 months alone at a honeymoon cottage called Basing House.

Ten years later, King Charles II gave William a huge tract of land which would become Pennsylvania. In his "Holy Experiment," William brought Quakerism and the concept of free public education to the American colonies.

William often sent loving notes to Guli, especially on his voyages to the new world. Fearing he might never see her again, he wrote, "My love – that neither sea nor land nor death itself can extinguish or lessen toward you – most endearingly visits you with eternal embraces, and will abide with you forever."

# APRIL 5

## POCAHONTAS & JOHN ROLFE

*Native American Princess Marries Future Tobacco King*

IN 1614 THE YOUNG INDIAN PRINCESS whose story still fascinates people stepped into a small Jamestown, Virginia church decorated with wildflowers, and became the wife of an English settler. She wore a muslin dress and tunic, a white veil, and a string of freshwater pearls given to her by her father, Powhatan.

Pocahontas was probably 17 and John was in his late twenties when they married. He'd been married before, but his first wife died soon after they arrived at the Virginia colony. By the time of the wedding, Pocahontas had been living with the English settlers for almost a year, after she was captured during feuds with her father. But she was treated respectfully, more like a guest than a prisoner, and was considered resourceful and intelligent. Interested in learning English ways, Pocahontas accepted Christian instruction and was baptized as Rebecca.

Make peace with the English, she encouraged her father. When she was 10 years old, she had convinced him to spare the life of John Smith. Now, John Rolfe, who had been experimenting with tobacco seeds brought from the West Indies, became friendly with Pocahontas and they began to care for each other. He wrote to Governor Sir Thomas Gates for permission to marry her.

With Pocahontas, John said, "My hartie and best thoughts are, and have a long time bin so intangled and inthralled in so intricate a laborinth, that I was even awearied to unwinde myselfe thereout." Wisely, the Governor agreed to the union, believing that it would bring the Indians and English together and end the bloodshed. It took a while for Powhatan to acquiesce, but he finally recognized that the settlers were here to stay and for the time being, anyway, there would be peace.

# APRIL 6

## JOHN GLENN & ANNA MARGARET CASTOR
*Childhood sweethearts from 'way back*

"A NNIE" AND "BUD" GLENN GREW UP and went to high school together in New Concord, Ohio in the 1930's. She was dark-haired and beautiful, and he had red hair and freckles. Although Annie was outgoing, she had a serious stutter that wasn't corrected until many years later. Bud adored her, and throughout much of their life together, he was her "voice" in public.

When Bud was 16, his father gave him a 1929 roadster. Bud painted "The Cruiser" red and drove Annie everywhere. Their friends knew how much Bud liked going at top speeds, so they weren't surprised in 1962 when he circled the earth 3 times in less than 5 hours on *Friendship 7*, the first manned American orbital space flight.

World War II had begun while Bud and Annie were students at Muskingum College, and he enlisted in the Navy Air Corps. Patriotism ran high in their hometown, which John later described as "a real-life version of *The Music Man*." After his basic training ended in 1943, he married Annie in a small ceremony attended by their families and friends. Following a short honeymoon, they lived on an air base in Cherry Point, North Carolina.

John flew 59 missions in the Pacific. Later, when he became a Marine test pilot, he and Annie lived in El Centro, California. When John was elected to the United States Senate in 1974, he won by the largest margin in Ohio's history.

John always called Annie "the real rock of the family," and never left her without feeling the pain of separation. Whenever he was about to leave on a dangerous mission, they'd make light of it. He'd say, "Well, I'm going to the corner drugstore to buy some chewing gum," and Annie would smile and answer, "Don't take too long."

# APRIL 7

## CHARLES DE GAULLE & YVONNE VENDROUX
### *He changed her mind about soldiers*

CAPTAIN DE GAULLE WAS INTRODUCED TO the Vendroux family and their 20-year old daughter, Yvonne, at an art exhibition in Paris in 1920. She was dark-eyed and petite, with masses of black hair swept up and away from her oval face. Yvonne had already rejected another military man because she didn't want to spend her life traipsing from one garrison town to another. But 30-year old Charles was intelligent, well-mannered, impeccably dressed, and very tall. She took his arm, which he had gallantly extended, and they walked off to look at the paintings.

He and Yvonne talked about art and poetry. He also described his service during World War I and how he'd been wounded several times and taken as a prisoner of war by the Germans. Yvonne's family was from Calais, where her father owned a biscuit factory. Charles was originally from Lille but had grown up in Paris where his father was a professor of philosophy and literature.

Two weeks later, they met again at a ball at the Palace of Versailles. After Charles cut in for a waltz, he and Yvonne danced continuously in the glittering ballroom. By the end of the 6th waltz, they were engaged.

Standing between statues of Saint Louis and Charlemagne, they were married at the church of Notre-Dame de Calais the following spring, shortly after Charles's military service ended. Arm in arm, they exited the church under the drawn sabers of fellow officers. The reception included an 11-course dinner, music, and more waltzes.

After honeymooning at Lake Maggiore in northern Italy, the de Gaulles settled in an apartment on the Left Bank in Paris. Charles taught and wrote on military history and tactics. After the fall of France in 1940, he became commander of the Free French Army; by 1959, he was president of the Fifth Republic.

# APRIL 8*

## FLAVIUS PETRUS SABBATIUS JUSTINIANUS & THEODORA

### *His "gift" from God*

NO ONE KNOWS THE EXACT DAY in 525 (or, possibly, 524) that Justinian, heir to the throne of Byzantium, married Theodora, a comic actress and exotic dancer, but it seems fitting to imagine that this famous couple of early Christianity was married close to Easter time.

He was Emperor Justin's 40-year-old nephew, and she was the 25-year-old daughter of the bear keeper at the Hippodrome. Theodora had long dark lashes, a voluptuous figure, a lusty sense of humor, and great intelligence. Justinian loved her to distraction and gave her plenty of money, property, power, and independence – things few women of her time ever had. That's because he wanted Theodora as his colleague as well as his consort.

For a few years, she had been his mistress because he couldn't legally marry someone so far beneath his rank. But in 524 he managed to have the law changed, and married Theodora within a year. The Emperor had no complaints; he, himself, had loved and wed a former courtesan. Theodora even managed to charm the bishops, who were impressed by her theological knowledge and convictions.

She could be resolute and ruthless, compassionate and charitable. She established hospitals for the poor, set up refuges for homeless girls, and opened an unused palace on the Bosporus for poor and abused women. If not for Theodora, Justinian probably would have lost his throne 7 years later, during the Nike riots between hostile factions of government.

As emperor, Justinian was the political and spiritual leader of Byzantium. With his "revered wife's" help he brought 200-year-old Constantinople to its economic and cultural heights and strove to restore the empire of ancient Rome. Today, in the church of San Vitale in Ravenna, Italy, Justinian and Theodora remain in all their glory, peering down through time from golden mosaics crafted and installed almost 1500 years ago.

---

*Date approximate.

# APRIL 9

## SOPHIA LOREN & CARLO PONTI
### *I do, I do … I do, I do!*

SHE WAS TALL, GODDESSLIKE, AND NEAPOLITAN; he was pint-sized, balding, Milanese and married… but their relationship became a lifelong love affair and romance.

Sophia Scicolone first met Carlo at a beauty contest in Italy when she was 15 and the Italian film producer was 38. She won second prize, but he offered something better – the chance for a career in movies. She and her mother had worked as extras in *Quo Vadis* that year. Photos of Sophia were also appearing in the *fumetti*, which were soap-opera-like strips in daily newspapers. Still, she and her family were very poor. But Carlo, in his partnership with Dino de Laurentiis, had discovered other stars, and now he was offering Sophia a real contract.

At first, the cameramen disliked her imperfect looks: her mouth was too wide; her nose too long; and her hips too broad. Sophia changed her last name to Loren, but she refused to change her features, and Carlo began to realize they would become part of her fame.

They married twice – first in September 1957, after Carlo's Mexican divorce. But five years later, that marriage was annulled when the Italian government refused to recognize it and charged Sophia and Carlo with bigamy. In 1960, with the help of Carlo's ex-wife, they remarried in Sevres, a Paris suburb.

Sophia had been filming *The Countess From Hong Kong* in London when she slipped into Paris and managed to evade the press long enough to marry Carlo in a small, simple ceremony. She wore a yellow dress and carried lilies of the valley. Later, she remarked, "To be finally married after 8 years… certainly had importance, but… I couldn't help but feel that Carlo and I had really been married for a long time."

# APRIL 10
## LUCRETIA COFFIN & JAMES MOTT
### *Equal and abiding respect*

THE GIRL WHO BECAME AN OUTSPOKEN Quaker abolitionist and advocate for women's rights met her future husband in French class in 1809. Usually, boys and girls were separated, but those in training to be teachers took some special classes together at the Nine Partners Boarding School in Dutchess County, New York. Lucretia was from Nantucket, Massachusetts, and James came from Mamaroneck, New York.

Often called a "spitfire," Lucretia was tiny, outspoken, and somewhat impulsive; James was tall, serious, and contemplative. They were a deeply loving couple throughout their long marriage, always sharing a double bed and bemoaning the nights when one was away traveling and they had to sleep apart.

They married in a Quaker ceremony at Philadelphia's Pine Street meeting home in 1811, where 175 witnesses signed the marriage certificate. Lucretia's family had moved to the city a year earlier, and now her father invited James to work with him in his retail business, changing its name to "Coffin and Mott – Merchants."

Lucretia became a Quaker preacher after the tragic death of their 3-year old son. While raising 5 other children, she formed a women's anti-slavery society in Philadelphia with James' encouragement and support. He stopped selling cotton goods because they were made with slave labor, and their home became a stop on the Underground Railroad. Although angry protestors occasionally threw rotten eggs and rocks at the Motts' house, they persisted in advancing their principles. In 1840 they were delegates at the World's American Anti-Slavery Convention in London. After they returned, they met with President John Tyler and futilely tried to convince him to support emancipation.

After many years of happy marriage to James, Lucretia wrote down her philosophy of matrimony, and often gave it to newly engaged couples: "In the true marriage… the independence of the husband and wife is equal, their dependence mutual and their obligations reciprocal."

# APRIL 11

## GILBERT DE LAFAYETTE & ADRIENNE DE NOAILLES
### *"My dear heart"*

GILBERT WAS ORPHANED BY THE TIME he was 13, but he inherited a great fortune, making him a very eligible bachelor. Marriages between aristocratic French families were often arranged in the 18th century, and the Duc d'Ayen de Noailles had 5 daughters. He and Gilbert's great-grandfather signed their agreement before they told Gilbert or Adrienne about it. The young couple was lucky, for they also fell in love.

In 1774, 400 guests attended the ceremony of the 16-year old marquis and his 14-year old bride in the candlelit chapel of the Hotel de Noailles, her family's home near rue St. Honore in Paris today. After a lavish reception, friends and relatives escorted the newlyweds to a bedroom. Everyone lingered for a while around the 4-poster bed until the duke mercifully closed the curtains and ushered the teasing guests outside.

Gilbert and Adrienne were old enough to marry, but too young to live independently, so they stayed with her family for several years. Gilbert became a captain at a garrison in Metz. Three years later, he sailed to America and, at the age of 20, became a volunteer major general in Washington's Continental Army, fighting bravely in the Revolution. He played an important part in the American colonists' victory at Yorktown, and subsequently hung a copy of the United States Constitution on a wall in his study.

Although Gilbert was a wealthy aristocrat, when he returned to France he became a lifelong supporter of freedom. Even so, when the Reign of Terror began, Gilbert fled Paris but was captured by right-wing émigrés. He spent the next 5 years in an Austrian prison, out of touch with his family, who were in danger, too.

Adrienne was imprisoned for a year in Paris; then she and 2 daughters managed to get to Austria, where they joined Gilbert voluntarily for his last 2 years in prison. Someday, they fervently believed, their good name would be restored. And it was.

# APRIL 12

## ANTOINE DE SAINT-EXUPERY & CONSUELO SUNCIN DE SANDOVAL

### *"Saint-Ex" and "Poussin"*

IN THE 1930'S "SAINT-EX" WAS PART of a bunch of foolhardy flyers who often flew without instruments through windstorms and bad weather. Although he is best remembered for his 1943 classic, *The Little Prince*, his writings also include *Night Flight* and *Wind, Sand and Stars*.

He met Consuelo in Buenos Aires, one of his mail delivery stops, when he was 30. She was a very attractive 28-year old widow from San Salvador, with large, expressive dark eyes and a rich imagination. Stories of their courtship varied, but Consuelo often said they became involved after Saint-Ex took her and a small group of people up in the air for a ride. He asked her for a kiss. When she refused, he threatened to crash the plane if she didn't… so she did.

She was petite, extravagant, passionate, and unpredictable, and she liked to say her family was descended from Spanish royalty. Saint-Ex was tall and bearlike and attracted to Consuelo's wildness and lack of inhibitions. He brought her to Paris within a year, causing his mother to say, Marry Consuelo; this living-together business is very embarrassing! His writer friend Andre Gide noted that Saint-Ex had written a new book and brought home a fiancée: "Read one, seen the other. Congratulated him heartily, but more for the book; I hope the fiancée is as satisfactory."

They married in 1931 in a small chapel in southern France. Consuelo wore a black lace dress and mantilla and red roses in her black hair. Her Pekingese dog was one of the attendants. After honeymooning on the Riviera, Saint-Ex resumed flying and Consuelo, whom he called "mon poussin"—my chick—awaited him either in Paris or their Casablanca apartment.

# APRIL 13

## CHANG AND ENG BUNKER & ADELAIDE AND SALLIE YATES

*The ultimate double wedding*

WHEN CHANG AND ENG WERE BORN in Siam in 1811, their parents never expected that their sons, who were attached at the waist, would become world-famous celebrities, loving husbands, and the fathers of 21 children.

For a while, curiosity seekers flocked to the village of Meklong, where the "Siamese twins" lived, but generally the boys' childhoods were uneventful and calm. At first, they walked like tipsy drunks, but later on they ran, swam and even mastered complicated dances. What was difficult was deciding where to go, but Chang was more assertive and usually got his way because Eng was easygoing and placid.

When the twins were 18, they joined a traveling exhibit and sailed for Europe and America. They toured for years, making enough money to support their family and purchase a farm in Wilkesboro, North Carolina. They were 31 when they adopted the last name, Bunker (after the famous hill) upon becoming naturalized American citizens. Around that time, they also met the Yates family and their daughters, Adelaide, 18, and Sallie, 19.

Adelaide and Chang were quickly attracted to each other, but it took months for Sallie to fall for Eng. Certainly, the prospect of being married to two men and never being alone with either one would have given most women pause. But once the sisters agreed to the twins' marriage proposals in 1843, they never wavered. After their parents overcame the initial shock, they hired the local parson and made all the arrangements. A lively dinner-dance celebration followed the wedding ceremony. Then the 4 Bunkers retired to a very large bed in their new home, where the phrase, "alone together," was given new meaning. Years later, they moved into 2 farmhouses within walking distance of each other in Mount Airy. Chang and Eng alternated houses, spending 3 days in each place with each wife and family.

# APRIL 14

## PIERRE-AUGUST RENOIR & ALINE CHARIGOT
### *Madame Renoir ... at last*

IN PIERRE'S 1883 PAINTING, "BESIDE THE SEA," Aline wears a lace-trimmed blue dress and bonnet, and sits in a yellow wicker chair by the Guernsey cliffs. She holds a pair of knitting needles, and a soft pile of yarn rests on her lap. Aline stares directly at the artist, and his painting confirms that he adores her.

Four years before, she was a 19-year old dressmaker working with her mother on the rue St. George in Paris, not far from Pierre's studio. When Aline began modeling for him, she didn't understand anything about art, but she loved to watch him paint. Pierre was 38, with strong feelings about the physical proportions of a face. "Never marry a woman with a large chin. She'd rather be torn to pieces than admit she was in the wrong," he advised his son Jean, who became a film director. But Pierre liked Aline's looks, especially her almond-shaped eyes and well-balanced head. She also had a light step, and he said she "could walk on grass without hurting it."

Aline lived with Pierre for years as his common-law wife, partly because his wealthy patrons – on whom he depended – would not have approved of his marriage to a "peasant." The couple was always hard-pressed for money. When their first child was born in 1885, Pierre paid the doctor with a painting instead of cash.

By 1890 Pierre was more optimistic about his financial future, and before family and friends he married Aline in the town hall of the 9th Arrondissement. They stayed in Paris until July and then went to the country for the summer. Relaxed and at peace, Pierre immortalized his new bride and their child in "The Apple Seller" series of paintings.

# APRIL 15

## LORD RANDOLPH CHURCHILL & JENNIE JEROME

*"the sky is bluer than I have ever seen it*
*since I first met you"*

THE NIGHT BEFORE JENNIE MARRIED RANDOLPH in 1874, her thoughts resembled those of countless brides: "This is the last time I shall wind this clock… this is the last time I shall look in this old mirror. Soon nothing will be the same for me anymore: Miss Jennie Jerome will be gone forever."

A maid brought her a breakfast tray in the morning, but Jennie barely touched it. Then her corset was pulled as tightly as possible – without causing her to faint during the ceremony. Her wedding dress was white satin, trimmed with yards of Alencon lace. A tulle veil covered her from head to foot. At 20, she was marrying 27-year old Lord Randolph Churchill, 3rd son of the 7th duke of Marlborough, at the British Embassy in Paris. He had proposed to her 3 days after they met.

His parents disapproved of the Brooklyn-born daughter of "flashy" self-made Americans and only consented to the union on the condition that Randolph run for Parliament and *win*. He'd never worked hard before, but his announcement that he would earn a living "in England or out of it," if that's what it took to marry Jennie, convinced them that he was serious.

"This was a love match if ever there was one," wrote their son Winston, born later that year. Fortunately, Jennie's father provided her with a generous dowry, although he balked at the British custom of giving husbands control of the money and insisted that Jennie receive part of it regularly.

The marriage was not ideal in every way, but it produced young Winston, whom his mother recognized as an exceptional child. She assisted in launching his career in literature and politics and, and helped him become one of the 20th century's most outstanding politician-statesmen.

# APRIL 16

## NEWELL CONYERS WYETH & CAROLYN BOCKIUS
### *"she's just the girl I want"*

"N.C." AND CAROLYN MET AT A sleighing party one wintry evening in 1904, in a scene as magical and evocative as his book illustrations. Twenty-two years old, he was studying art at the Wilmington, Delaware art school run by the famous illustrator, Howard Pyle. That fateful night, snow was falling heavily, causing the young couple to huddle close together. For N.C., it was bliss.

He first mentioned Carolyn to his parents in a letter he wrote a few days later. Like most young men embarrassed to share their romantic feelings, N.C. simply said that a "Miss Bockius" had invited him to church on Sunday. Soon he was visiting the Bockius house regularly. By spring, he and Carolyn were packing picnic baskets and taking long walks in the Brandywine countryside.

He kept talking about Carolyn in his letters, but couldn't admit his growing love. Back home in Needham, Massachusetts, Mrs. Wyeth sensed that her son had more on his mind than art and wrote back, asking if he was concentrating enough on his work. "Mama," he replied. *"please* have faith in me…. Do you think I would do anything rash?"

He didn't marry Carolyn until more than a year later – after she'd won his parents' approval. N.C. and Carolyn spent the weeks before their 1906 wedding painting, papering, and fixing up their future house at 1331 Shawcross Avenue in Wilmington. That spring, he worked on his "Solitude Series" of paintings, which were very well received. Commissions for his book illustrations began coming regularly. When *McClure's* magazine offered N.C. $4,000 a year for magazine covers and story illustrations, his financial future was secured.

In 1908, he and Carolyn moved to a farm in Chadds Ford, Pennsylvania, the future home of their 5 children, including the artists Henriette and Andrew. A few years later, N.C. began a series of illustrations for children's classics, starting with *Treasure Island*.

# APRIL 17

## NORMAN ROCKWELL & MARY BARSTOW

*She read to him while he painted*

SOON AFTER NORMAN'S FIRST MARRIAGE ENDED, he left New York for a California vacation and met Mary, a 22-year old school-teacher. Still depressed, he was in no mood to think about romance. Anyway, he wondered, who would want him? He was divorced and "thirty-six years toward the grave," he wrote in his autobiography. But Mary liked Norman right away. They decided to marry within weeks, but waited a few months to please her parents, who hosted the wedding in the garden of their Alhambra home in 1930.

A recent Stanford University graduate, Mary knew a lot about art. Norman was a high school dropout who already was a fairly successful illustrator, with his work on the covers of *Boy's Life* and other magazines. For many years, his pictures were on every front cover of *The Saturday Evening Post*.

Unlike Norman's first wife, Mary was sincerely interested in his work. They raised 3 children in their New Rochelle, New York home on Lord Kitchener Road, and she often kept Norman company while he painted. First, he made preliminary sketches, followed by a full-size charcoal drawing made from life, using friends and neighbors dressed in appropriate costumes as models. Next, another sketch was made in color. The final stages of a painting were reached in anywhere from 2 weeks to 2 months. During those long days, Mary often read to Norman; they enjoyed the works of Tolstoy, Dickens, Jane Austen, and Voltaire, as well as contemporary best-sellers.

Norman had the remarkable ability to create thoughtful, detailed pictures of American life, focusing on family relationships, romance, and age and youth. People were deeply touched by his heartwarming scenes during the Great Depression. Those who couldn't afford to buy art taped his magazine covers on the walls. Norman's most memorable series was "The Four Freedoms," painted during World War II and used to promote the sale of war bonds.

# APRIL 18

## GRACE KELLY & PRINCE RAINIER III OF MONACO
### *Hollywood Princess Weds Real-Life Prince*

S HE WAS EXTREMELY BEAUTIFUL, MORE REGAL in bearing than most blue-blooded women. Grace was filming *To Catch a Thief* on the French Riviera in 1955 when she met Prince Rainier, one of the world's most eligible bachelors. He gave her a private tour of Monaco's Palace Gardens, and came to see her in Philadelphia a few months later. Right after Christmas, he gave her the engagement ring she wore in her last film, *High Society*.

Gossip columnists called Grace a bricklayer's daughter, but by now her father, Jack Kelly, was extremely wealthy. What he didn't like was the old European tradition of paying a dowry for his daughter. At first Jack refused, saying Monaco must be in financial trouble and he didn't want Grace marrying some "broken-down prince." Finally, Jack came to accept the arrangement and probably paid about $2 million.

The civil wedding ceremony was held first, on April 18, 1956, in the throne room of Rainier's palace. Immediate families and close friends attended, and Europeans watched it on television. A religious ceremony followed the next morning at Monaco's Cathedral of St. Nicholas. Grace wore an ivory taffeta dress trimmed in Valenciennes lace. Tiny lace lovebirds were applied to the back of her veil, dotted with thousands of seed pearls. Since Rainier was royalty, his bride was expected to precede him to the altar. Jack Kelly escorted Grace down the aisle and was directed to a nearby pew. But the upstart American dad wouldn't leave his daughter alone at the altar and insisted, in a quiet, dignified way, on standing beside her until Rainier arrived.

The wedding was followed by parades and receptions for hundreds of guests, until the newlyweds sailed off for a 7-week Mediterranean cruise.

"We both understood what the marriage meant," Rainier said years later. "We fell in love…. A lot of people never thought it would last. I guess we fooled them."

# APRIL 19

## LAWRENCE WELK & FERN RENNER

### *Wunnerful! Wunnerful!*

THE BOYS IN LAWRENCE'S BAND SLEPT through his 1931 wedding to Fern. But it took place at 5:30AM, so it's no wonder that some well-wishers weren't awake for the ceremony!

Fern and the future leader of television's Champagne Musicmakers were married in Sioux City, Iowa's Sacred Heart Cathedral. Fern had just arrived from Dallas on the early morning train. By 10:00AM, they all would be heading for a gig in Wisconsin that night. The bride and groom weren't the only jumpy participants; it was the priest's first wedding, too, and he forgot to bless Fern's ring until after the ceremony was over.

Fern and Lawrence had met in Yankton, South Dakota a few years before, when she was a student nurse attending his radio concert. As he played the accordion and led his band through waltzes, polkas and other tunes, Lawrence couldn't take his eyes off the "prettiest girl I had ever seen… [with] great big brown eyes… fair skin and dark hair… and she looked very unimpressed by everything… around her," he wrote later.

He asked her out repeatedly until she accepted, providing she was home early enough to study. He promised to do almost anything, and actually arranged to have elective surgery in the hospital where Fern was training, because it meant spending a few days near her.

By the time they married, Lawrence's band had become well known in mid-western dance halls and on the radio, but as the Depression worsened, bookings became harder to get. Fern traveled with Lawrence as much as possible, and quickly learned to keep a mop and pail in their car so she could clean the dismal rooms they sometimes occupied. Later, he achieved fame as a big-name orchestra leader and TV host.

# APRIL 20
## EDMOND HALLEY & MARY TOOKE
### *"beloved wife"*

FANCIFUL BIOGRAPHERS HAVE SAID THAT EDMOND first saw "his" comet on his honeymoon in 1682, but probably it's not true. However, the blazing ball of light with a fiery tail, which eventually was called "Halley's comet," did appear over England that same year.

When Edmond met Mary 2 years before, he was 24 and she was the amiable and attractive daughter of a London bank official. Edmond and Mary often watched the night sky, and he jotted down notes about everything they saw. He probably also saw stars in Mary's beautiful eyes, because when he left for Italy, he wrote to her often. They were married at St. James's Church in London 3 months after his return, and moved to a house in the suburb of Islington, where Edmond set up his first observatory.

Edmond was cheerful, well-liked, and extremely happy at home. Mary adored him and even tolerated his pranks: when the young Czar Peter (who became Peter the Great of Russia) visited London, he and Edmond spent a lot of time talking and drinking together. Late one night, they got drunk. Peter jumped into a nearby wheelbarrow, and Edmond pushed him until he rolled down a hill and crushed a row of topiary hedges.

Edmond was very supportive of his friends. When Isaac Newton needed financial aid to publish his discourse on gravity and the laws of motion, Edmond solicited contributions to help Newton defray the costs.

As Edmond charted the frequencies and paths of comets, he noted that the comet he and Mary saw in 1682 had the same orbital characteristics as others that had been observed 76 years earlier… and 76 years before that. Eventually, he developed theories for predicting the motions and movements of comets and their counterclockwise orbits. True to his predictions, "Halley's comet" returns to our world every 76 years, and was last seen in 1986.

# APRIL 21

## OWEN WISTER & MARY CHANNING
### His "Molly"

FOUR YEARS AFTER "DAN" MARRIED "MOLLY" in 1898, he wrote *The Virginian*, a best-selling, highly acclaimed western novel whose central character is a handsome but nameless cowpunch who overcomes dangers and hardships and wins the heart of a pretty schoolteacher. It didn't take long before his words, "When you call me that, *smile!*" became part of American folklore, as did the image of the noble and lonely cowboy.

The first time Dan saw Molly, he was 10 and she was the newborn baby daughter of his mother's second cousin. Molly was a descendant of a signer of the Declaration of Independence and of the noted abolitionist and preacher, William Ellery Channing. Throughout her life, Molly was involved in social causes and reforms. She became a member of Philadelphia's Board of Education at the age of 26, a rare position for a young single woman to hold.

Dan's great-grandfather, Pierce Butler, had signed the U.S. Constitution for South Carolina, and his grandmother was the famous Shakespearean actress Fanny Kemble. A Harvard-educated lawyer, Dan had camped and hunted in Wyoming and Arizona for years. He gladly gave up his law practice soon after he sold his first western short story, "Hank's Woman," to *Harper's* magazine. The editors were willing to send him out west again to soak up the atmosphere and write more great tales. His friend, Teddy Roosevelt, said that Dan had "the power of the born story-teller" and read everything he wrote with great enthusiasm.

Dan and Molly were married in her parents' Germantown, Pennsylvania home on the day the Spanish-American War began. For the next 6 months, they traveled across the country, visiting relatives and historical sites, before settling down at 913 Pine Street in Philadelphia. They hung Fanny Kemble's portrait in the parlor and also displayed a few pictures by Frederic Remington, who illustrated some of Dan's western stories.

# APRIL 22
## ANDREW CARNEGIE & LOUISE WHITFIELD
### *"our cup runneth over"*

L OUISE WAS 30 WHEN SHE MARRIED the 51-year old millionaire in 1887. They had met 7 years earlier, but Andrew was too focused on work to think about marriage. Besides, he had promised his widowed mother that he wouldn't marry as long as she lived, and Mama Carnegie held her "Andra" to his word. However, he did enjoy taking Louise to concerts and the opera, and for carriage rides through New York City's Central Park. "Other young ladies were on my list," he wrote in his autobiography, but they "all faded into ordinary beings. Miss Whitfield remained alone as the perfect one beyond any I had met." Secretly engaged in 1886, he told no one – including Mama.

The powerful steel magnate had started out as a bobbin boy in a Pennsylvania cotton factory. After Andrew made his fortune, he began giving it away to worthy causes such as public libraries, colleges, art foundations, and the magnificent Carnegie Music Hall. Louise supported Andrew's plans to use his "surplus wealth" for the common good. Before they were married, she renounced most claims to his vast estate.

After their wedding New York City, they honeymooned in Britain's Isle of Wight and at a castle Andrew had rented in Scotland. "Happily married," wrote Louise, "two words fraught with the deepest meaning in the world." Andrew said, "She seems to have been made to turn the earth into a heaven for me." He often described her by quoting these lines from Shakespeare's *The Tempest*:

> *Full many a lady*
> *I've eyed with best regard: for several virtues*
> *Have I liked several women, never any*
> *With so full soul, but some defect in her*
> *Did quarrel with the noblest grace she owed,*
> *And put it into the foil; but you, O you.*
> *So perfect and so peerless are created*
> *Of every creature's best.*

# APRIL 23

## DIEGO RODRIGUEZ DE SILVA Y VELAZQUEZ & JUANA PACHECO

### Mi corazon (my heart)

J UANA WAS A LITTLE GIRL WHEN 10-year old Diego came to her father's house in Seville in 1610. The boy's parents had told Don Francisco Pacheco, a painter, that Diego was always sketching and that he seemed to have a strong understanding of light and shade – something that would later be called "chiaroscuro." The don studied Diego's paintings and invited him to be his apprentice; one day, Diego would become the preeminent Spanish painter of the 17th century.

For the next 6 years, Diego lived with the Pacheco family while he assisted the don in painting religious pictures for churches. Juana brought trays of food to the artists and lingered in the studio to watch them work. Diego did not intend to paint religious subjects all his life, he whispered to her. He wanted to portray living subjects – the people he saw in the streets, in shops, and inside taverns. His paintings were extraordinarily realistic; later, he would work exclusively from life.

In 1618, after Diego's apprenticeship concluded, he passed the examinations of the painters' guild in Seville and won the don's permission to marry Juana. Pleased and proud, the don gave the young couple several houses in the city, including one with sufficient room for Diego's own studio.

Diego was 18 and Juana was 16 when they married at the church of San Miguel de Sevilla. Poets and artists joined family and friends at a lavish wedding banquet hosted by the don, who subsequently arranged for his son-in-law to be presented to King Philip IV in Madrid. After the king appointed him court painter, Diego painted the royal family many times; in "The Maids of Honor," he included himself at work before an easel. In the king's service, he also traveled to Italy, where he bought paintings for the royal court and was inspired by the works of Michelangelo, Raphael, and Titian. But Diego never grew tired of painting his beloved Juana, who is immortalized exquisitely in his "Lady with Fan."

## APRIL 24

## EMPEROR FRANZ JOSEPH OF AUSTRIA & ELIZABETH OF BAVARIA
### *"Franzi" and "Sisi"*

THE 1834 MARRIAGE between the 23-year old emperor and 16-year-old princess was witnessed by hundreds of guests and more than 50 mitered bishops, and that's not all: the royal wedding night began in the presence of the newlyweds' mothers!

The bride was so nervous, she barely touched her food at the reception at Vienna's Hofberg Palace. When it ended after midnight, her mother, Ludovika, and mother-in-law, Sophia, escorted her down a candelabra-lit corridor to the bridal chamber. Sophia fetched Franz and brought him to his bride. By now, the new empress was cowering in the bed, and Sophia noted unpleasantly, "She hid her natural loveliness, for only a wealth of beautiful free-flowing hair buried in her bolster caught my eye, like a frightened bird lying low in its nest."

Like most sheltered young women of the 19th century, "Sisi" knew virtually nothing about sex. Mothers prided themselves on *concealing* the facts of life from their daughters, and new husbands expected them to shriek and carry on. Sisi and Franz barely endured the early days of their marriage but eventually became deeply attached.

Sophia had expected Franz to marry Sisi's sophisticated older sister. But at his most recent birthday party, he had kept dancing with Sisi, and waltzing her around the floor in her peach-colored gown. "She is as fresh as a newly peeled almond, and what a splendid crown of hair frames such a vision! How can anyone help loving such tender eyes and lips like strawberries!" he wrote afterwards. "I will marry Sisi!"

Whether or not their marriage fulfilled all of the young girl's fantasies, from the moment Franz took Sisi's hand as she stepped out of the flower-bedecked ship that brought her down the Danube to Vienna, he had found someone who would influence and love him for their entire married life.

# APRIL 25

## JEAN LOUIS AGASSIZ & ELIZABETH CABOT CARY
### *A brilliant and loving couple*

"LIZZIE'S" MOTHER SAW LOUIS FIRST. THE Swiss naturalist was attending church with the Lowells in Boston when he attracted Mrs. Cary's eye. Her matchmaking plans for her daughter dissolved when she found out that Louis had a wife and family in Europe. But within 3 years, his wife died... and Louis became terribly lonely.

He met Lizzie at a Cambridge dinner party in 1848, soon after he became a professor of natural history at Harvard. She was 26, well-educated, wealthy, and good-natured. Although Louis was 15 years older, his enthusiasm for life and his scientific work attracted her. He showed her his collection of fossils, crustaceans, mollusks, and coral, and talked incessantly about it. Natural history fascinated Lizzie. "You will see that I have eyes for its beauty, ears for its melody, and a heart to understand its teaching," she told him shortly after they became engaged.

She also had a heart for Louis's 13-year old son, Alexander, who soon arrived by ship. His two sisters also became very close to their new "mother."

"Lizzie looked lovely," wrote her sister after the wedding at King's Chapel in 1850. "She was dressed in green silk, with a white camel's hair shawl and a straw bonnet trimmed with white feathers on each side." After a gala reception at her parents' home, she and Louis walked to his house in Cambridge.

Eventually, Louis's collection would be kept at the Harvard museum he established, but now his materials were all over the house. Nothing perturbed Lizzie, not even live snakes in Louis's closet! Besides raising her 3 stepchildren and accompanying Louis on scientific expeditions, Lizzie was a pioneer of women's higher education and founded Radcliffe College at Harvard.

# APRIL 26

## ALBERT, DUKE OF YORK & LADY ELIZABETH BOWES-LYON

*The sun seemed always to be shining*

"YOU'LL BE A LUCKY FELLOW IF she accepts you," England's King George V told his son, "Bertie," after he proposed to Elizabeth in 1923. Years ago they had met at a children's birthday party; 5-year old Elizabeth had eyes like sapphires that brimmed with excitement. Bertie was 10, but his shyness and stammer made him dread royal get-togethers. He sat beside Elizabeth at teatime and was deeply touched by her calm acceptance of his handicap. She also gave him the cherries from her sugar cake.

Fifteen years later, they met again at his sister's wedding. Elizabeth was very fond of Bertie, but she knew that marrying into the royal family meant a life governed by rules and restrictions. When she finally accepted his proposal, she expected that they would simply be the duke and duchess of York.

No one anticipated that 13 years later Bertie's older brother, Edward, would give up his kingdom for the woman he loved, and that Bertie would become King George VI and Elizabeth his queen consort. Nor could anyone predict that Elizabeth, with her warmth, sincerity, and strong sense of duty, would help restore the monarchy to public favor after the shocking abdication.

The wedding was held at Westminster Abbey but was not broadcast on the radio because the archbishop of Canterbury feared that disrespectful Englishmen might listen in pubs and forget to remove their hats! Many British hearts were deeply touched, however, when the young bride placed her wedding bouquet on the Tomb of the Unknown Soldier, remembering those lost in the Great War.

Elizabeth would always be her father-in-law's favorite. April 26, he wrote, "was rather gray and inclined to rain, but as soon as the bride arrived at the Abbey the sun shone as it always does in her presence."

# APRIL 27

## RICHARD STARKEY & BARBARA BACH
### *"So blessed we're still together!"*

B Y THE TIME BARBARA MET RINGO Starr in 1980, the former Beatle was 40 years old, and had been divorced for almost five years. He was still a great drummer but less famous than he and his band mates had been in the 1960's. Barbara was a film actress, and also had been married before. After small parts in several films, she had starred as a Russian spy in the James Bond movie, *"The Spy Who Loved Me,"* in 1977, and a spy again, in *"Force 10 from Navarone"* the following year.

Back in 1965, 17 year-old Barbara had accompanied her younger sister to a huge rock concert at Shea Stadium in New York to see the Beatles. Barbara watched Ringo perform before thousands of cheering fans, but she never thought she'd ever meet *him*! (Coincidentally, Linda Eastman, Paul McCartney's future wife, was at the concert, too.)

Fifteen years later, Barbara and Ringo did meet, on the set of "Caveman," a silly comedy filmed almost entirely in Mexico. Ringo played "Atouk," a skinny, jittery caveman who yearns for "Lana," a beautiful maiden played by Barbara, who was the girlfriend of "Tonda," the tribe's leader.

Ringo and Barbara fell in love quickly, and became inseparable. In 1981, they were married in a civil ceremony held at the Marylebone Register Office in London, where Paul and Linda McCartney had tied the knot 12 years before. Ringo wore a black suit and bow tie, and Barbara wore a rose-trimmed ivory-colored wedding dress.

A reception was held at a club in Mayfair, where the groom played with Paul and George Harrison in an impromptu jam session—their first since the shocking, sudden loss of John Lennon, in late 1980.

On a rainy night that May, Ringo's car careened off a slippery English road, smashed into lampposts, and rolled over. "It was a miracle that we both got out alive," he recollected. Eventually, some pieces of the shattered glass were saved and put into lockets that Ringo and Barbara wore as remembrances of that terrible day in which—thankfully—they both survived. Years later, he says they are "so blessed we're still together!"

# APRIL 28

## ED SULLIVAN & SYLVIA WEINSTEIN
### *A really wonderful marriage*

I N 1926 SYLVIA WAS CELEBRATING HER high school graduation with friends at a New York City nightclub when she noticed a handsome young man with wavy hair and a wide smile. Ed was a sports reporter who frequented the clubs, looking for athletes to interview. He also was friendly with lots of entertainers whom he still knew years later when his Sunday-night variety show, *The Toast of the Town*, became one of television's most popular programs.

Ed asked the club's public relations man to introduce him to the attractive young woman. When Ed found out that Sylvia liked sports, he quickly invited her to upcoming tennis matches and a prize fight at Brooklyn's Ebbets Field. They dated for over 3 years, although Ed's Roman Catholic parents weren't happy that he was seeing a Jewish girl. Sylvia's family was more comfortable with the prospect of an interfaith marriage, especially because they realized how happy Sylvia and Ed were.

They married secretly at Manhattan's City Hall in 1930, intending to slip away to Atlantic City for 2 days before their "officially scheduled" wedding at a Catholic church. The news leaked out, however, so they told their parents before someone else beat them to it.

Two years later, Ed began writing "Little Old New York," a *Daily News* column that was soon syndicated nationally. He also hosted a radio variety show, introducing such stars as Irving Berlin and Jack Benny. *The Toast of the Town* (later, *The Ed Sullivan Show*) began in 1948 and debuted such performers as Jackie Gleason, Carol Burnett, the Supremes, and Elvis Presley.

Sylvia and Ed went nightclubbing almost every night and never tired of living in hotel suites. Years later he remarked that without Sylvia, he probably wouldn't have accomplished so much. "Hers has been the grim and the lonely job of waiting and watching," he told a biographer. "No matter what I've done, she's been there."

# APRIL 29

## PRINCE WILLIAM ARTHUR PHILIP LOUIS OF WALES & CATHERINE (KATE) MIDDLETON

### *"JUST WED"*

EVER SINCE WILL AND KATE ANNOUNCED their engagement in 2010, their joy was tempered by bittersweet memories of his mother, Diana. The Princess of Wales had died more than 13 years before, but her independent spirit, beauty, and tragic end still fascinated the world and the media. Wearing Diana's stunning white gold engagement ring with 14 diamonds encircling a 12-carat sapphire, Kate accompanied Will to Althorp in Northamptonshire where they placed flowers on his mother's grave a few days before the wedding.

Kate came from the village of Bucklebury, and Will spent his childhood in palaces. They had met at the University of St. Andrews in Scotland, where "William Wales" enrolled in 2001. Kate began that year, too, following a temporary upsurge in the number of female applications. Even though she was a commoner, she carried herself with elegance and decorum, and was not disconcerted by regal rules and traditions. Twenty-nine years old by the time she married Will, Kate had already captivated world attention *and* met the fussy standards of the royal family. Some people attributed her poise and self-confidence to the fact that she was almost 10 years older than Diana had been when she married Prince Charles in 1981.

The gorgeous bride arrived at Westminster Abbey in a white dress with a snug-fitting lace bodice and gently flowing satin skirt with a 9-foot train. Atop her head was a 1936 diamond tiara bought for his wife by the Duke of York (who became King George VI in 1938 after his brother renounced the throne). "You look beautiful," Will whispered to Kate. After the ceremony, the newlyweds headed to Buckingham Palace in a 1902 horse-drawn carriage. A few hours later, they took off in his dad's 1960 Aston Martin convertible, for a short drive over to Clarence House. The car was blue, but it was also "green" because it was powered by ethanol converted from surplus British wine! After the parties, the honeymoon, and Will's upcoming tour of duty in the RAF as Flight Lieutenant Wales, the couple would reside in North Wales as well as Kensington Palace, where Will recalled very happy times in his youth.

# APRIL 30*
## JOHANNES VERMEER & CATHERINA BOLNES
### *Sweet vrou Vermeer*

CATHERINA WAS FROM THE DUTCH TOWN of Gouda, about 15 miles east of Delft, a picturesque village of canals, tidy houses, and tree-lined streets where Johannes lived for his entire life. His paintings are small in scale, just like his hometown; household interiors are often the settings for his work. He focused on details such as a woman pouring milk, handling jewelry, sitting before a mirror, writing a letter.

Johannes was 20 and Catherina was one year older when they married at the town hall of Schipluy in 1653. Later that year, after he was admitted to the Guild of St. Luke as a master painter, Johannes could paint, teach art, and sell his work in Delft, just as his father, an art dealer and weaver, had done before him.

At first, he and Catherina lived with her mother, Maria Thins, who was legally separated from her husband but received an income from him. She had not been delighted when Catherina chose Johannes – probably because he was Protestant and she was Catholic – but Maria proved to be financially supportive and a loving mother for many years to come. Even so, the Vermeer family was fairly poor and occasionally was forced to sell Johannes's paintings to satisfy creditors.

Eventually, the couple established a home and studio for themselves and their 11 surviving children. Johannes's remarkable paintings covered the walls. He captured light in incredible ways. Vases, pitchers, casement windows, maps, and other objects of daily life are bathed in luminosity. A sense of stillness permeates his pictures. Ordinary events and objects are imbued with universal meanings.

Family belongings often appear in Johannes's pictures. No one is sure if Catherina modeled for her husband, but it's likely. Her yellow silk jacket is in "Woman with a Pearl Necklace," and "Lady with a Maidservant Holding a Letter." Most probably, Catherina posed for "Young Lady in Blue Reading a Letter."

---

*Date approximate.

# MAY

# MAY 1

## ELVIS PRESLEY & PRISCILLA ANN BEAULIEU
### *"Love Me Tender"*

LVIS'S ROMANCE WITH A TEENAGED GIRL grabbed everyone's attention in the 1960's. "The King of Rock 'n' Roll," who could have had countless women, was stuck on "Cilla," whom he first met in West Germany when she was 14 years old.

Cilla's stepfather was in the air force, and so was Elvis. But unlike other American GIs, Elvis lived in his own home at 14 Goethestrasse, near Bad Neuheim base. He met Cilla at a party. After his military discharge, she transferred to a school near Graceland, Elvis's mansion. Turning herself into his perfect dream, Cilla dyed her hair black, teased it to great heights, applied thick makeup, and did everything else that Elvis wanted.

Some people think Elvis's manager, Colonel Parker, had decided it was time for his boy to marry. After all, the colonel decided most things, and he certainly orchestrated the wedding as well. By 1967, Elvis was 32 and Cilla was 20 years old. The "king" was ready to take a "queen."

A Nevada Supreme Court justice performed the double-ring ceremony at the Aladdin Hotel in Las Vegas. Elvis wore a black brocaded jacket, vest, and dark trousers. Cilla wore a white organza wedding dress with a 6-foot train and a tulle veil. The bride and groom promised to love, honor, and "comfort" – not obey – each other. Their 6-tiered wedding cake was covered with pearl-studded red and pink hearts.

At their honeymoon getaway in Palm Springs, California, Elvis sang "The Hawaiian Wedding Song" as he carried his new bride across the threshold.

The colonel had disappointed many people – including the bride and groom, who couldn't invite everyone they wanted to be at their wedding. So a few weeks later, they put on their bridal clothes again and held a second celebration at Graceland for everyone who'd missed the main event.

# MAY 2

## BENJAMIN HENRY LATROBE & MARY ELIZABETH HAZLEHURST

### *"a woman of honor"*

THE FUTURE ARCHITECT OF THE UNITED States Capitol and Supreme Court buildings as well as numerous colleges, libraries, and churches came to America in the late 1790's after his first wife's death in England. The shock had left Ben despondent, but he found happiness in Philadelphia, in the architectural commissions he earned, and in Mary, who became his adoring wife.

They met when Ben was drawing up plans for a new Bank of Pennsylvania. Inspired by the Erechtheum of ancient Greece, he designed a splendid white marble edifice with porticos and columns, and began the American trend of Greek revivalism. Mary's father was a Philadelphia merchant much impressed with Ben's ideas and intelligence. Soon Ben was courting Mary, taking her on carriage rides to look at new sites and showing her already-completed buildings.

They married in her family's Philadelphia townhouse in 1800, when Mary was 29 and Ben was 36. His friend Thomas Jefferson sent congratulations, and subsequently enlisted Ben's advice about building the University of Virginia.

Mary insisted that Ben's young son and daughter, who had remained with relatives in England after their mother's death, now come and live with them. If anything, she would always be more forgiving and understanding of her 2 step-children than of the 5 she and Ben had together.

"The great feature," he wrote to his sister-in-law, "next to her benevolence, of my wife's character, is an undaunted firmness in the practice of what she deems right. She is in the highest sense of the word, *a woman of honor.*"

Ben was tall and muscular, but his health suffered when he overworked. Mary was the ideal artist's wife, respectful of his needs for solitude and inspiration, and wondrously proud of all that he created.

# MAY 3

## ALBAN BERG & HELENE NAHOWSKI

*"my faith is built on you"*

ALBAN FIRST SPOTTED HIS WIFE-TO-BE IN the standing-room sections of the Vienna Musikverein and Opera Houses in 1906. Like most students, they loved going to concerts but could rarely afford seats. Both were 21 years old. Helene was a gifted singer and pianist, although not as talented as Alban, whose operas and tonal compositions attracted worldwide acclaim before he was 35. But Helene's looks certainly were glorious: She was tall and slender, with long ash-blond hair. If she noticed him first, she didn't show it. But Alban kept popping up the musical performances she attended. At last, they started talking, and their lifelong passion began.

He begged her to stop seeing former beaux, but Helene needed time to sort out her feelings. Besides, her father, a practical civil servant, didn't like his daughter getting serious with an asthmatic musician and composer who lacked a financially secure profession. Helene and Alban met secretly at train stations, museums, and cafes, and sent each other lots of notes, which her sympathetic sister helped deliver.

"Well, I really *am* in love," he told Helene in 1907. He wrote heartfelt letters of entreaty to her father and after 4 years, Herr Nahowski finally consented to their union on the condition that they convert from Catholicism to Protestantism, so that a divorce – if necessary – would be easier to obtain!

Alban dedicated many works to his beloved Helene, including his operatic masterpiece, *Wozzeck*. "I owe it to you and *you alone*," he said. "*You composed* it and I only wrote it down."

Tirelessly, she championed his work, especially his unfinished opera, *Lulu*. "For 28 years I lived in the Paradise of his love," Helene said later. "Our souls were long ago joined together in … a union through all eternity."

# MAY 4

## HENNY YOUNGMAN & SADIE COHEN

*"Take my wife … please!"*

THE STAND-UP COMEDIAN WHO MADE THIS line famous was actually a very happily married man. He first met Sadie at Kresge's, a 5-and-10 cent store in Brooklyn where they both worked in the 1920's. Henny printed business cards and letterheads when he wasn't making music with his newly formed band, "The Swanee Syncopators." Directly across the store aisle was Sadie, selling sheet music and phonograph records.

It took months before Henny found the courage to talk to her or even learn her name. Sadie was red-haired, freckle-faced, adorable… and most likely, Irish – certainly not someone Henny could bring home to his Jewish mother. But one day when the band had been hired to play in Coney Island, he threw caution to the winds and invited Sadie to come and listen. That's when she told him she only dated Jewish boys!

They married in Brooklyn in 1928. Although Sadie's mother wasn't too impressed with her son-in-law's career, she gave the newlyweds space in her Chauncey Street apartment until they could afford their own. Henny's band kept performing but he was also having fun making wisecracks to the audience. One night, he filled in for an absent emcee and decided that comedy was better than music. Soon he became the "king of one-liners" which he delivered with rat-tat-tat speed, using his violin as a prop.

Henny's career really took off 8 years later when he began appearing regularly on singer Kate Smith's popular radio show. He first uttered his famous words about Sadie when she and some friends came to the studio shortly before showtime. They were gabbing so loudly, Henny couldn't concentrate on his script. Hoping someone could help the women find seats in the audience, he approached a stagehand and said, "Take my wife… please!"

# MAY 5

## MARY MARTIN & RICHARD HALLIDAY

*Her heart belonged to... Richard*

ALTHOUGH MARY WAS ONLY 25 WHEN she met Richard in 1939, already she was the divorced mother of a 7-year old son (future actor Larry Hagman) and a Broadway performer. Her big break had come in 1938, when she stole the show singing a blazing rendition of Cole Porter's "My Heart Belongs to Daddy" in the hit musical, *Leave it to Me*.

Richard had seen the play but he was feeling poorly and slept through most of Mary's performance. A story editor for Paramount Studios, he didn't notice her until a year later when she arrived on Paramount's Hollywood lot to appear in *The Great Victor Herbert*.

Richard was tall and thin with dark eyes and hair. Mary was petite and fair and thought he was "the most handsome, divine man I had ever seen." They dated on and off, drawn to each other but ambivalent about getting married. That didn't stop Richard from sending Mary cases of soap and cologne, and cryptic notes telling her to "keep it clean" whenever one of her former boyfriends came to town.

A few months before they married, he gave Mary a gold ring with a man's hand clasping a woman's; hidden in the man's palm was a ruby heart. "To MM from RH with...?" was inscribed inside. Soon after their spur-of-the-moment wedding in Las Vegas, he added, "Love! May 5, 1940."

As Mary's producer and manager, Richard arranged for her to ride a real horse galloping on a concealed treadmill in the play, *Annie Get Your Gun*, which toured for over a year. He also encouraged her to wash her hair on stage 8 times a week while singing "I'm Gonna Wash That Man Right Out of My Hair" in *South Pacific*. She dedicated her autobiography to him – "the one who taught me the meaning of the words, *heart* and *belong*."

## MAY 6

## LEW WALLACE & SUSAN ARNOLD ELSTON

*She was "a composite of genius, common-sense and all best womanly qualities"*

SUSAN AND LEW BOTH WERE AVID readers, although he confessed that he never liked school very much, preferring to draw pictures or read books of his own choosing. When they married in 1852, they settled in Crawfordsville, Indiana, where Lew became a prosecuting attorney who wrote in his spare time. His fame as a writer was ensured with the publication of *Ben-Hur*, his epic novel about the life of Jesus Christ. Susan wrote poems and magazine articles, as well as popular "tear-jerkers," such as *Ginerva: or the Old Oaken Chest*, and *Land of the Pueblos*, a collection of stories about life in New Mexico.

They'd moved out west from Indiana after the Civil War, when Lew became a major general and gallantly assumed command over thousands of Indian soldiers. He had begun writing *Ben-Hur* in Indiana, sitting beneath the trees beside their house. He continued to work on the book when he was the territorial governor of New Mexico. The remainder was written at night on an old pine desk in a back room of the governor's palace on the Plaza in Santa Fe. Lew completed the book in 1880, dedicating it to Susan, "the Wife of my Youth who Still Abides with Me."

The first draft of *Ben-Hur* had been written on slate, then copied onto paper, page by page. Never having visited the Holy Land, Lew learned about it from maps, journals, other books, and people he met who'd been there. Later, President Garfield appointed Lew as U.S. minister to Turkey, and he and Susan visited some of the sites he had described. They were astonished to see how accurate his depictions were.

When the Wallaces moved back to Indiana, Lew lectured about their experiences and continued to write. Avid fans of *Ben-Hur* often stopped by their house, hoping to meet the author of such a compelling novel.

# MAY 7*

## MALCOLM CANMORE, KING OF SCOTLAND & PRINCESS MARGARET

### *His saintly wife*

S EVERAL YEARS AFTER THE BATTLE OF Hastings, Malcolm stood on the beach of the Firth of Forth and watched a storm-tossed ship with tattered sails steer onto the shore near Dunfermline. Two Saxon princesses and their mother stepped onto the shore, assisted by Prince Edgar the Atheling.

Some say it was love at first sight for the king of Scotland, a widower in his late 30's with plenty of passion deep inside. On that fateful autumn day, when the wind was snapping tree branches and playing havoc with small boat moorings, Malcolm saw Margaret's winsome body shudder as she covered her shoulders with a shawl. It took all his strength to resist rushing to her instead of ordering his servants to bring the 4 voyagers to his stone fortress up on the hillside.

They had sailed for the Continent to escape William the Conqueror, but their ship had veered off course and gone north instead of west. They spent the winter in Malcolm's castle, eating dried meats and vegetables and drinking mead while listening to stories about how Malcolm had defeated the murderous usurper Macbeth and reclaimed the throne of his father, Duncan.

Although Malcolm's nickname was "Bighead," he could neither read nor write. But he was a brave and honest man, with a gentle heart in his warrior's breast. For months, he yearned for the 22-year old tall and stately Margaret, niece of the late (great) Edward the Confessor. Marry me, Malcolm implored her. The long winter gave her plenty of time to appreciate his sincere affections, valor, and fierce loyalties. By spring, Margaret gave him her answer.

In 1070 the bishop of St. Andrew's united the couple in glorious matrimony. Margaret, who would be declared a saint one day, helped to develop Christianity, culture, commerce, and art in her adopted land.

---

*Date approximate.

# MAY 8

## JOHN OPIE & AMELIA ALDERSON

*"my heart springs forward at the thought of
thy near approach"*

"A LMOST FROM MY FIRST ARRIVAL, MR. Opie became my avowed lover," Amelia wrote in her memoirs. The blue-eyed, auburn-haired neophyte writer was high-spirited and accomplished when she met the portrait painter at a London party in the autumn of 1797. He was 35 and recently divorced. Amelia was 28, somewhat old for an attractive single woman, but she had been raising younger siblings since her mother's death, and had just begun to attend social gatherings.

If other artists painted to live, John lived to paint. He'd been at it since his childhood in Truro, Cornwall, and by the age of 15 he had become a traveling portrait painter. One day the "Cornish wonder" would be a professor of art at London's Royal Academy. He lacked a formal education and was somewhat unpolished, but his feelings for Amelia were unabashed. He was in love! She adored him, too, although other men pursued her; none held a candle to John.

They were married at Marylebone Church in London in 1798 and settled at John's house at 8 Berners Street. Wedlock suited the Opies beautifully, as each inspired the other to excel in their arts. John's paintings of women seemed more graceful and sympathetic now, and although he was not as comfortable as Amelia with the soirees held in their home, his career benefited from the exposure.

"Fear makes you overrate others and underrate yourself," he told Amelia, encouraging her to become what she described as "a candidate for the pleasures, the pangs, the rewards, and the penalties of authorship." *Father and Daughter*, a "moral tale" was one of the many books she wrote. It was very well received in 1801 and continued to sell for the next 50 years.

John painted more than 500 significant portraits in his lifetime, including those of Dr. Johnson and Mary Wollstonecraft Godwin. He painted Amelia's portrait many times and illustrated some of her novels. Shortly before their wedding, he had written, "To love thee much better than I... is, I think, impossible."

# MAY 9

## SAM HOUSTON & MARGARET LEA
### *The eyes of Texas were upon her*

S AM WAS 46 WHEN HE MET 20-year old Margaret in Alabama in 1839. His first 2 marriages had been short-lived and over before 1836 when he defeated General Santa Anna at the Battle of San Jacinto and helped establish the Republic of Texas.

When Sam's term as first president of the republic ended, he returned to the practice of law. He was in Mobile Alabama promoting interest among speculators in new Texas town sites when he noticed a soft-spoken young woman with dark brown hair and magnificent violet eyes. Margaret was with her mother, a wealthy widow looking for profitable investments. But Mrs. Lea was wary of Sam, whose reputation included heavy drinking and a questionable financial situation.

Margaret, however, was thrilled to meet the famous Texan, who began courting her immediately. A few weeks later, he headed for Nashville and a short visit with his old friend, Andrew Jackson. Sam wrote to Margaret constantly, inviting her to come to Texas with her nay-saying mother. Mrs. Lea agreed, bringing one of her sons instead. Not only did Sam convince her that he loved her daughter, he also got her to buy tracts of land near Galveston! Back in Alabama, Margaret studied Spanish and stitched her trousseau. She carried a tiny picture of Sam with her all the time, inspiring her to write:

*Dear gentle shade of him I love,*
*I've gazed upon Thee till thine eye,*
*in liquid light doth seem to move,*
*and look on me in sympathy.*

In 1890, they married at her mother's gracious home. Many people thought the union wouldn't last any longer than Sam's previous marriages, but Margaret brought him joy, comfort, and 8 children. They were together for the rest of his life.

# MAY 10

## GILBERT STUART & CHARLOTTE COATES
### *Always together*

GILBERT HAD BEEN STUDYING ART IN London for 5 years when he became friendly with William Coates, a medical student who sat beside him in anatomy lectures. One weekend, William invited Gilbert to his parents' country home for Sunday dinner, and introduced him to Charlotte, his younger sister.

Shortly before the American Revolution, Gilbert had left his Rhode Island home and voyaged to London – the best place for a talented portrait painter to be in the late 18<sup>th</sup> century. He needed a regular income, as well as the guidance of a more experienced painter. An older, more established expatriate American artist named Benjamin West took Gilbert into his studio and helped him get established.

Charlotte fell madly in love with Gilbert, but her parents thought he was somewhat irresponsible. They tried to discourage their daughter from marrying him in 1786, not realizing that one day he would become the "Father of American Portraiture." Eventually, generations of schoolchildren would gaze at his fine portrait of George Washington whenever they saluted the American flag.

In 1794, Gilbert, Charlotte and their children sailed for America. The following year, the U.S. Supreme Court Chief Justice John Jay introduced him to the president in Philadelphia. George Washington was a restless man who disliked posing for portraits (and his new false teeth bothered him a lot). Even so, Gilbert was so congenial that Washington sat for 3 life portraits and Gilbert made many copies from them. His daughter Jane Stuart later recounted her mother's memories of Washington: "She saw him as he entered the hall door, when she was passing from the entry to the parlour, and she thought him the most superb looking person she had ever seen."

Gilbert liked his "Atheneum" portrait of Washington so much, he left it unfinished because he couldn't bear to part with it. (Mrs. Washington asked for it repeatedly, but he kept saying it wasn't ready yet!)

# MAY 11*
## ELIZABETH CADY & HENRY BREWSTER STANTON
### *Obey? No way!*

RECITING THEIR MARRIAGE VOWS IN 1840, Henry was somewhat startled when "Lizzie" promised to "love and honor," but refused to say, "obey." The wedding guests gasped. Back then, no one had ever heard of a bride omitting what every husband considered his rightful due.

There was a short silence. The minister looked at Henry, who gestured – Go on with the ceremony. Henry wasn't surprised. Ever since he'd fallen in love with Lizzie, he'd known that life with her would not be conventional.

The future reformer had received a fine education at Emma Willard's seminary in Troy, New York. Listening to women clients share sorrowful tales with her lawyer father, Lizzie also learned first-hand about injustices. Most girls were educated only to become useful wives and mothers; after marriage, their husbands controlled their property as well as their behavior.

Not Henry and Lizzie; they would manage just fine. That's what he told her parents, who had been steadfastly opposed to the union, saying Henry had no steady means of employment. (He already was an abolitionist and would later become a lawyer and journalist.) Lizzie was 25 and knew her own mind. She and Henry slipped away from her home in upstate New York and were married in New York City. Soon afterwards, they sailed for London to participate in an anti-slavery convention. Not much happened on the conference floor, where "strong-minded women" were shunned, but back at the boardinghouse Lizzie met Lucretia Mott and became firmly committed to the cause of women's rights.

Henry was the only man who protested the rejection of women delegates. When he and Lizzie returned to America, she campaigned effectively for passage of the married woman's property bill of New York State, and they devoted their lives to women's suffrage and other issues of discrimination – while raising 7 children.

---

*May 10 and 12 have also been cited.

# MAY 12

## SHOLOM (ALEICHEM) RABINOWITZ & HUDL LOYEFF
### *"he enchanted me"*

"OLGA'S" MARRIAGE CEREMONY TO THE WORLD'S most beloved Yiddish storyteller was performed in secret in 1883. She had been the 13-year old daughter of a wealthy Jewish landowner in Sofievka, Russia, when Sholom was hired as her tutor. He was 18, with wavy blond hair and blue-green eyes. In exchange for tutoring and handling secretarial affairs for Olga's father, Sholom received lodging, food, and time to write. He perfected his craft, creating short stories such as the "Tevye" tales, adapted in *Fiddler on the Roof* many years later.

Sholom tutored Olga for 3 years. They read the classics and popular literature, took long walks in the woods, and… fell in love. No day passed that they didn't see each other or yearn to do so. As he recalled in his autobiography, "The word 'romance' was too clichéd, the word 'love' too banal for what the young couple felt…. Not a cloud specked their blue sky."

But "Aunt Toibe," a spinster busybody, noticed that they had become inseparable. Toibe didn't mean to make trouble… but wasn't it her duty to ask Olga's father, Where was it written that a teacher and pupil must be so close all the time?

Olga's father fired Sholom. He had liked the young man, but if he was courting Olga, he should have asked for permission first! With her eyes full of tears, Olga watched Sholom depart down the road to Kiev. He sent Olga passionate love letters, which reached her father instead.

After 2 years, she begged a sympathetic cousin to locate Sholom and arrange a marriage. Afterward, her father accepted their decision and insisted that the newlyweds come home. Sholom adopted his pen name, which means "Peace among you," and began selling his stories to a new Yiddish magazine.

# MAY 13*

## ROBIN HOOD & MAID MARIAN

*"in solid content, together they liv'd"*

—FROM AN OLD ENGLISH BALLAD

T HE LEGENDARY ENGLISH OUTLAW MARRIED HIS "bonny fine mayde" in the late 12th century under a canopy of trees in Sherwood Forest, away from their peaceful homes in the north Midlands but safely out of the clutches of the treacherous sheriff of Nottingham.

Robin and Marian's romance began before the fateful day when he fled into hiding after killing one of the king's foresters in self-defense. Until then he'd been a nobleman named Robert Fitzooth, Earl of Huntington, and she the fair lady Matilda Fitzwater. Now he was an outlaw, condemned to death for treason. He changed his name, his appearance, and with the help of Friar Tuck, Little John, and other members of his band of "merry men," started robbing the rich and helping those in trouble.

Matilda pined for her sweetheart, knowing only that he lived somewhere in the dark forest. Her Robert was good-hearted, fair and honorable to all. Could he be the one they were calling "Prince of Thieves?"

Sometime in the joyous month of May, when lovers' hearts will surely break if they are not united, Matilda put on men's clothes and stole into the forest. If marrying Robert meant giving up her cozy life back home, so be it.

In a small clearing stood a handsome man dressed in green, with a peaked cap on his head and a quiver of arrows slung over one shoulder. Robin stuck an arrow into his bowstring, pulled and... heard the faint sound of footsteps behind him. Instantly he turned and grabbed the intruder. They tussled silently in the shadows, not even groaning lest they attract the sheriff's men. Finally, they quit and fell on the ground. "You're quite a fighter," Robin said. "Want to join me and my merry men?"

"Robert?" asked Matilda breathlessly. "Is that you?"

---

*Date approximate.

# MAY 14

## OSCAR HAMMERSTEIN II & DOROTHY BLANCHARD JACOBSON

*He missed the boat... but found true love*

OSCAR AND DOROTHY WERE MARRIED IN 1929 in the bridal suite of the Belvedere Hotel in Baltimore Maryland. They both had been married once before, but this marriage was for keeps. Wearing a gray dress with a fur-trimmed cape, Dorothy looked at "Ockie" and beamed. He looked at his auburn-haired, blue-eyed bride and knew he had found contentment at last.

Two years earlier, they had met on board the *S.S. Olympic* en route to London when she was 27 and he was a 31-years old lyricist. Oscar was limping after spraining both ankles in a touch football game with friends. His injuries had delayed his departure, causing him to cancel reservations on another ocean liner and take the same one as Dorothy. Aboard ship, their attraction was mutual, immediate, and intense. Soon after they reached England, Oscar wished he could ask Dorothy to marry him right then.

When he got back to New York, he and composer Jerome Kern adapted Edna Ferber's novel, *Show Boat*, for the stage. Their musical production dealt with serious topics such as racial prejudice, gambling addiction, and unhappy marriages, and it contained memorable songs including "Can't Help Lovin' That Man," "Make Believe," and "Ol' Man River." Oscar usually stood while writing his lyrics, saying it saved time when he needed to pace the floor. He had collaborated earlier with Sigmund Romberg in *Desert Song*, and would spend 27 years with Richard Rodgers following Kern's death.

It took Dorothy and Oscar 2 years to divorce their spouses and get married. After a wedding breakfast celebration, they sailed for a honeymoon in Europe on their favorite ship, *S.S. Olympic*, and promised they'd never part again. Oscar dedicated a new song, "Don't Ever Leave Me," to Dorothy.

She never did.

# MAY 15

## OSA LEIGHTY & MARTIN JOHNSON
### *"Home" would be schooners, rafts, and tents*

F EW COUPLES CAN CLAIM BEING CAPTURED by cannibals and escaping their clutches, but Osa wrote all about it in *I Married Adventure*, describing expeditions she and Martin took soon after their 1910 wedding. Osa had been 15 the year before, when she and her girlfriends attended Martin's film show and lecture near her home in Chanute, Kansas. He was a 24-year old photographer and adventurer who recounted tales of sailing the South Seas on board the *Snark* with writer Jack London. To a small-town girl from Kansas, Martin's stories were enthralling.

They married suddenly, on one of her visits to see him and his parents in Independence. That's when she heard him tell his business partner on the phone, "Big thing. I know that…. What?… Young? Well, maybe so, but she's got spirit and spunk!"

When Osa brought Martin home, her father declared, "You've got her, now take care of her!" But Martin's plans did not include settling down. "We're going around the world," he told Osa. She gulped and replied, "Well – all right, dear."

They sold their wedding gifts, presented film shows and lectures to raise money, and set off from San Francisco. They learned to sail, fly small planes, and photograph and film vanishing wildlife and native populations in Africa and the South Pacific. Whenever they'd gathered lots of material (and run out of money), they'd return to the United States and put on shows until they raised enough money to head off again.

Over the next 27 years, Martin and Osa made documentary films for the American Museum of Natural History in New York City, and published 18 books about their experiences. Osa also designed animal toys for the National Wildlife Federation.

# MAY 16

## EDGAR ALLAN POE & VIRGINIA CLEMM
### *'beautiful Annabel Lee"*

AFTER EDGAR'S MOTHER DIED, THE FUTURE poet and short story writer was raised by a merchant and his wife, who paid his tuition to the University of Virginia, but insisted that Edgar support himself otherwise. Gambling debts destroyed his finances, however, and he became destitute. One winter, he was forced to burn the furniture in his room for heat. At age 22, he left college and after a brief stint in the army, he moved in with his aunt, Maria Clemm, and her young daughter in Baltimore.

He was a sad-eyed, lonely young man, but Aunt Maria and cousin Virginia were caring and supportive. At last, "Eddy" felt as if he belonged to a real family. He sold some poems and stories, but his earnings were meager. For a while, he edited a literary magazine, but his book reviews were so scathing, he soon earned the nickname, "The Comanche of Literature."

As time passed, Eddy and Virginia grew closer. They played the piano, took walks in the garden, fixed dinner together, and became inseparable. When they married in 1836, he was 27 and she was 13, although the deputy clerk at the Richmond, Virginia marriage office kindly wrote "21 years old."

To Eddy, she would always be "my own sweetest Sissy, my darling little wifey." Biographers know relatively little about their private life, but they agree that these two were a loving and adoring couple.

"You know I love Virginia passionately, devotedly," he wrote to his aunt. "I cannot express the fervent devotion I feel towards my dear cousin – my own darling."

Eddy worked hard, editing various magazines and writing frightening tales such as "The Fall of the House of Usher" and "The Murders in the Rue Morgue," one of the first modern detective stories. In 1846 his poem "The Raven" was published in a New York newspaper, and his fame increased dramatically.

# MAY 17

## ANDREW JOHNSON & ELIZA MCCARDLE

*Always on his side*

A NDY COULDN'T SIGN HIS OWN NAME on the marriage certificate when he wed Eliza in 1827. Without her help, he might never have learned how to read and write. And he certainly wouldn't have become the 17th president of the United States.

Eliza was a 12-year old girl with soft hazel eyes and brown hair when Andy first saw her. He was 13 and had recently moved to Greeneville, Tennessee with his mother and brother. Andy worked as a tailor's assistant, and Eliza helped her mother sew quilts. She noticed Andy on Main Street and told her girlfriends, one day she would marry that good-looking fellow. Five years later, she did! It would be many years before the Johnsons ever heard of Abraham Lincoln, yet the name of their justice of the peace was Mordecai Lincoln – a cousin of Abe's father, Thomas.

The Johnsons' first home was the back room of the tailor shop, where Eliza read to Andy as he stitched. At night, she taught him reading, writing and arithmetic. When Andy's boss retired, he took over the shop, which became a meeting place for townspeople to discuss political matters. Soon, Andy discovered that he was a persuasive speaker. Within a year he was elected town alderman and then mayor. He also became a great reader, but he never learned to spell very well. "It is a man of small imagination who cannot spell his name more than one way," he explained to his secretaries.

Eliza was a calm, down-to-earth woman who never questioned her husband's integrity, even when Congress considered impeaching him as president. An old friend said, "Their union was fortunate and, by her aid, he was better prepared for the long encounter which fate held in reserve."

# MAY 18

## ANNE HARRISON & SIR RICHARD FANSHAWE

*"my life and fortune shall be thine, and
every thought of my heart"*

ICHARD WAS A 35-YEAR OLD STATESMAN and poet when he married Anne in 1644. She was 19 and a boisterous tomboy, or "hoyting girl," she wrote in her memoirs. "I thought myself a queen,' she said, "and my husband so glorious a crown that I more valued myself to be called by his name than born a princess."

They were married at Wolvercote Church, an ivy-covered stone edifice outside of Oxford, soon after Richard was appointed secretary of war by King Charles I. After Charles was beheaded in 1649, the Fanshawes sided with the Royalists and lived for many years in poverty and danger. They fled to Bristol with the king's court, but plague drove them to Truro and Penzance. Sailing to the Scilly Isles, they were robbed. Later, they were nearly shipwrecked en route to France, and Anne was almost taken into slavery by Turkish sailors.

In 1651 Richard was captured at the Battle of Worcester and imprisoned at Whitehall. For 3 months, until she was able to secure his release, Anne "visited" him every morning at 4 by standing under his prison window.

Following the Restoration, the Fanshawes regained much of their wealth. Richard became ambassador to Portugal and Spain, and he and Anne sailed to Madrid with their 5 children. He also had time to write poems and translate ancient texts including the writings of Horace.

The times were tumultuous, but Richard and Anne were happy. "Glory be to God," she wrote, "We never had but one mind throughout our lives. Our souls were wrapped up in each other's, our aims and designs one, our loves one, and our resentments one. We so studied one the other, that we knew each other's minds by our looks. Whatever was real happiness, God gave it me in him."

# MAY 19

## ROBERT LOUIS STEVENSON & FANNY VANDERGRIFT OSBOURNE

### *"Tusitala" and his 'Tiger Lily"*

R OBERT'S PARENTS REFUSED TO GIVE HIM money for a trip to California in 1879, and hoped that their 28-year old son would forget about Fanny Osbourne. She was 11 years older than he, married and the mother of 2 children.

They had become involved 2 years before at an artists' colony in France. Robert was writing stories, and Fanny had come to study art. But now she was deeply depressed; her youngest child had just died and her marriage was a failure. Back home in Britain, Robert's parents were distressed to look at him. His health problems were chronic, and now he was particularly thin and sickly.

Nothing could deter him from winning Fanny. He crossed the Atlantic and the United States soon after her divorce, and married her in San Francisco in 1880. Silver wedding bands were all he could afford, but he gave her some of his verses as a wedding gift. They spent 2 nights at the Palace Hotel, then headed north to Silverado and camped in a dilapidated cabin. They thought it all was an adventure.

In August, they returned to Scotland for a conciliatory meeting with his parents. Robert began writing something grand to please his new stepson, Lloyd. *Treasure Island* would be "about a map, a treasure, a mutiny, and a derelict ship…. No women in the story, Lloyd orders." Robert read chapters aloud to Fanny and Lloyd. The book became his first literary success.

He wrote more classics for children, including *A Child's Garden of Verses* and *Kidnapped*. It took him only 3 days to write the first draft of *The Strange Case of Dr. Jekyll and Mr. Hyde*. By 1888, wanderlust drove Robert and Fanny to take his widowed mother and Lloyd on a sailing adventure. They visited Australia and many islands, and settled down on 400 acres in Samoa.

# MAY 20

## JOHN GUTZON BORGLUM & MARY WILLIAMS MONTGOMERY

*Mount Rushmore, here we come!*

MARY WAS A PETITE WELLESLEY COLLEGE graduate who had just earned her Ph.D. at the University of Berlin when she met Gutzon onboard a ship to New York in 1901. He was 35, fairly short, and balding, and she was impressed by the American artist-sculptor's boundless energy and ambition.

When Gutzon was 22, he had married a 42-year old art teacher in California. Although Liza helped him start his career, eventually they drifted apart. She'd gone with him to Paris where he studied with Auguste Rodin, but when Gutzon sailed back to America, he was alone.

He set up a studio at 166 East 38th Street in Manhattan, and worked on sculptures for the 1904 St. Louis World's Fair. He also made angels and the Twelve Apostles for Manhattan's Cathedral of St. John the Divine, many statues of political and historical figures, and the colossal marble head of Abraham Lincoln for the rotunda of the capital in Washington, D.C.

Gutzon married Mary in 1909 and they moved to Borgland, an estate in Stamford Connecticut. Friends said that she stabilized his life and helped the excitable but brilliant man become less hotheaded. Still, he championed the causes of labor and always defended freedom of speech. In the late 1920's, Gutzon began his most ambitious work in the Black Hills of South Dakota.

Born in Idaho Territory, Gutzon always had a keen interest in western landscapes and American history. He jumped at the chance to sculpt massive busts of Washington, Jefferson, Lincoln, and Teddy Roosevelt into Mount Rushmore and he determined the ideal locations of the 60-foot high heads after years of drilling and blasting. A small village was erected for his work crew, alongside a home and studio for Mary and their children. The project took 14 years to complete and became one of the grandest man-made sculptures.

# MAY 21

## HUMPHREY BOGART & LAUREN BACALL

*She loved being "Mrs. Bogart"*

HORDES OF REPORTERS HAD DESCENDED ON the small town of Mansfield, Ohio by the time "Bogie" and "Betty" arrived on the Superchief train from California in 1945. A few days later, they were married at high noon at Malabar, the farm belonging to Bogie's novelist friend Louis Bromfield. Bogie cried throughout the entire 3-minute ceremony.

He and Betty had met on the set of *To Have and Have Not*. He was 44 and a major star whose gruff exterior masked a polished and gentle man. She was a stunning 19-year old model making her Hollywood debut.

"Have you got a match?" she asks him in the film. They are in a hotel corridor outside their respective rooms. Bogie searches through a table drawer while she leans against the door frame. "Here you are," he says, tossing her a box. It's a very short – but passionate – scene. Their real-life romance began just as quickly. By the time filming was completed, Bogie had left his 3rd wife. Eleven days after his divorce was final, he married Betty and began his happiest years.

She wore a pale pink suit with a brown chiffon scarf, brown shoes and belt, and she carried white orchids. Bogie wore a gray tweed suit, a wine-colored tie, and a white carnation in his lapel. He kidded that he was "something old;" "something new" was Betty's outfit; "something borrowed" was her mother's handkerchief; and "something blue" was Betty's slip.

"I felt as though I owned the world," she recalled in *By Myself*. "It seemed that everything that had ever happened to me had led to this day with him." Looking at Bogie, who was crying, she began crying, too.

## MAY 22

## AMOS BRONSON ALCOTT & ABIGAIL MAY

*"My husband, hallowed be the name, is all I expected,*
*[and] this is saying a good deal."*

BRONSON WAS A PROGRESSIVE NEW ENGLAND educator who observed his students carefully, much as he later kept detailed diaries about the 3 daughters he and Abby would have, including the famous author, Louisa May.

At 28, Bronson had started a private school on Salem Street in Boston, and hired 26-year old Abby as an assistant teacher. Like her boss, she thought children learned best by "doing," and she favored a relaxed, permissive atmosphere in the classroom.

It didn't take long before Bronson confided in his journal, "I do love this good woman, and I love her because she is good." He was tall and blond, with intense blue eyes. She had dark eyes and hair and was outspoken and spirited. Too shy to admit his feelings, he won her affection by showing her his writings.

Her parents were opposed to the marriage until Bronson's income was sufficient to support a family. Still, they became engaged. Abby described Bronson to her brother: "He is moderate. I am impetuous – He is prudent and humble – I am forward and arbitrary. He is poor – but we are both industrious – why may we not be happy?"

By 1830 Bronson could wait no more and wrote, "Providence bestows her bounties equally upon all, and it will be our folly alone if we do not obtain our share." He and Abby would manage. He was sure of it. Together, they won her parents' consent, and were married in Boston, at King's Chapel on Tremont Street. Afterwards, they walked to their first home, a boarding-house at 12 Franklin Street. Later, they received $2,000 from anonymous well-wishers. They never were told who sent it, but just knew it was from Abby's parents.

# MAY 23

## FRANCES MILTON & THOMAS ANTHONY TROLLOPE
### *"my future happiness on earth is at your disposal"*

"FANNY" MARRIED THOMAS ON HIS 35TH birthday in 1809, an era when all that was expected of an English lawyer's wife was that she manage the household affairs and bear his children. She gave birth to 5, including Anthony, one of the most prolific and well-regarded English writers of the 19th century.

Fanny and Thomas had been neighbors on Keppel Street in London, in homes a few doors away from each other. She and her sister had moved there from the country to keep house for their older brother. It was a bold move for women to take at that time; usually, they left home only to be married. Thomas had lived at Number 16, which became the model for some of his son's future books.

Fanny was 27, bright and lively, and thrilled by the cultural life of London. Thomas was a moderately successful barrister with good prospects, and she found him attractive, though somewhat reserved and quiet. In fact, he proposed to Fanny in a letter, saying he enjoyed her "society and conversation." Stiffly outlining the economics of his situation, he admitted that he didn't know how to express "the flippant nonsense... commonly used on occasions of this nature." Fanny wasn't worried about his unromantic tone, however. Deep feelings, she believed, were often difficult to express.

Life was good in the beginning, and all their children were born in the first 10 years. Fanny and Thomas genuinely loved each other deeply, but as time passed he mismanaged the family finances repeatedly by investing in foolish schemes and undesirable real estate. But Fanny was not the kind of wife to sit back and bemoan the family's misfortunes. She began writing books, beginning with *The Domestic Manners of the Americans*, to help support everyone, and for the next 20 years she produced a continual stream of well-received popular novels.

# MAY 24*

## ANDREW DUCROW & MARGARET GRIFFITH
### *Ladies and gentlemen, in the center ring...!*

N O ONE KNOWS FOR SURE WHAT first attracted Margaret to Andrew. Was it the way he juggled balls as he walked across the tightrope? Or his grand leaps over 7 horses?

Andrew's father had been the "Flemish Hercules," a circus "strongman" able to lift and hold between his teeth a table with his 5 children on it. By the age of 3, Andrew was tumbling and balancing himself on ropes, fencing, and riding horseback. At 15 he was chief equestrian and ropes dancer at Astley's Amphitheatre in London. Critics marveled at his discipline and courage. One said if Andrew were given the chance, he "would have danced on a rope stretched across the crater of Vesuvius during an eruption."

Margaret, too, came from a circus family. She met Andrew when he was appearing in a Liverpool circus with his "poses plastiques" – elaborate impersonations of antique statues in classical settings. Margaret watched all of Andrew's performances and soon was participating as an extra in many scenes. The famous writer, Charles Dickens, described her as "a lady rider of rare accomplishments and remarkable beauty."

She was saucy, delightful, and 20; Andrew was 25, blond-haired, good-looking and ambitious. They married in Holland in 1818 at the beginning of Andrew's 5-year tour of the Continent, which included a long stay with Franconi's circus in Paris.

When they came back to England, they had perfected amazing new "hippodramatic" acts such as "Cupid and Zephyr," "Cortez's Conquest of Mexico," and "Saint George and the Dragon." Margaret often rode in Andrew's spectacular processions as he performed incredible feats of daring such as standing up and riding 6 horses at one time, or leaping through hoops made of fire on his famous trick horse, Jack.

---

*Date approximate.

# MAY 25

## ANTON CHEKHOV & OLGA KNIPPER
### *"Dear, marvelous actress"*

"THE MOST IMPORTANT THING IN FAMILY life is love, sexual desire, one flesh; everything else is unimportant and boring," Anton told a friend 2 years before he met Olga.

Although the Russian writer's health was poor, his life was satisfying. His plays, *The Seagull* and *Uncle Vanya* were being presented and praised, and he was the author of numerous short stories. He was working on *The Three Sisters* when he became romantically involved with Olga, an auburn-haired Hungarian actress who often performed in his plays. At the age of 39, Anton had fallen in love.

He also was panic-stricken. A month before their 1901 wedding, he wrote to her from Yalta, promising to marry her as soon as he returned to Moscow if she swore to tell no one in advance. "I don't know why, but I am simply terrified of the wedding ceremony, and the congratulations and the glass of champagne you have to hold in your hand at the same time smiling vaguely."

Olga starred as Masha in the premiere of *The Three Sisters* at the Moscow Art Theater, and reviewers said it was superb! Members of the audience were weeping when the final curtain came down. But the playwright couldn't deal with a wedding!

Anton married Olga on a Friday at a small church in Moscow. At the exact same time, his friends were enjoying a special luncheon he had arranged elsewhere. By the time they figured out what had happened, the newlyweds had left the church, visited Olga's mother, and boarded a train to see the writer Gorky, under house-arrest in Nizhny-Novgorod. From there they continued to Axenovo for their honeymoon.

"We were so close to each other then," Olga reminded Anton in a letter a year later. And their 6-week honeymoon in the country had restored his fragile health, at least for a while.

## MAY 26

## ALFRED LUNT & LYNN FONTANNE

*Married to the theater, and to each other*

I N THEIR HASTE TO GET MARRIED in 1922, after delays caused by
runs of their respective plays, Alfred and Lynn raced downtown to the
marriage bureau in Manhattan with only 95 cents in their pockets. "Two
dollars, please," said the clerk, after conducting the ceremony.

The bride and groom were forced to borrow money from their witnesses,
who were 2 strangers they had corralled in the lobby. Then they kissed each
other, kissed the witnesses, and kissed the clerk! After celebrating with
chocolate sodas, they went home, got their wallets, packed some clothes, and
headed for a short honeymoon in Atlantic City, New Jersey.

Alfred had been eagerly awaiting his wedding day, but it unnerved him so
much, he forgot all his lines at his next performance. The stage manager had
to hide behind props and recite everything for him, while Alfred moved his
lips silently.

His love for Lynn had left him "unbalanced" before. When they first met
in 1919, he had stumbled down the steps while auditioning for parts in summer stock. The roles they won led to Alfred's breakthrough part as the title
character in Booth Tarkington's play, *Clarence*, and Lynn soon landed the
lead in the comedy, *Dulcy*, which established her career.

In 1924 they performed together in Molnar's romantic comedy, *The
Guardsman*. From then on, they were a great acting team. One critic wrote,
"Those who saw them on opening night, bowing hand in hand for the first
time, may well have been witnessing a moment in theatrical history."

Over the next 30 years Lunt and Fontanne appeared onstage together in
more than 18 plays in America and abroad. Their performance in the 1931
screen version of *The Guardsman* still gives theater lovers a glimpse of their
undeniable magic.

# MAY 27

## CHARLES LINDBERGH & ANNE MORROW

### *A secret wedding*

IN 1929, TWO YEARS AND ONE week after "Lucky Lindy" flew his *"Spirit of St. Louis"* solo from New York to Paris, he slipped into his future in-laws' Englewood, New Jersey home to marry Anne without attracting throngs of fans and reporters. The newlyweds escaped from their reception in a borrowed car, with the bride hiding on the floor. But the press caught up with them on their honeymoon yacht off the coast of Maine. Life with Charles, Anne realized, would always be in the spotlight.

They had met in 1927 in Mexico City, where Anne's father, the United States Ambassador, held a reception in Charles's honor. It had taken the 25-year old aviator 27 hours to fly there from Washington D.C., and meeting Anne was an unexpected delight. To show his appreciation, he took the Morrows for a plane ride over Aztec ruins.

The 20-year old Smith college student adored flying right away and subsequently realized that airplanes were one of the few places where she and "C" could be alone. Although goggles, helmets, and loud engine noises impeded conversations aloft, Anne wrote there was "a kind of bright golden 'bloom' over everything." Eventually, Charles taught her how to fly, operate the radio, and read charts and Morse code. She became an excellent navigator and radio operator, and helped Charles break his record for a transcontinental flight. Anne also became a well-respected poet, novelist, and essayist, writing about their adventures and her philosophical reflections.

Anne's well-connected and wealthy parents knew that Charles was considered a national hero, but all he'd ever been before was a barnstormer and stunt flyer walking on plane wings and doing other tricks in the air. Was this "glorified mechanic" right for their daughter? Maybe not, but because the Morrows loved her, they accepted Anne's decision and made her a small but beautiful wedding.

# MAY 28

## VERNON CASTLE & IRENE FOOTE
### *"Castles in the air"*

"I BELIEVE OUR LIVES ARE PLANNED in detail before we are born," Irene wrote, describing her fateful first meeting with Vernon. The future team of world-famous exhibition ballroom dancers met on a float in Long Island Sound in 1910. She was 18 and he was 24. They probably wouldn't have spoken to each other if a mutual friend hadn't swum over and introduced them.

Vernon was a British comedian performing on Broadway. He managed to get Irene a bit part in the play, but her scene was stolen by a then-unknown child actress named Helen Hayes who later admitted that she had a crush on Vernon, too. The following spring, Vernon and Irene married at her parents' New Rochelle, New York home on their anniversary day. After honeymooning in England, where they met Vernon's family, the Castles were back in New York in *The Hen-Pecks*, a slapstick comedy.

A year later they were in Paris, where "necessity made us dancers," said Irene, after promised roles in a play evaporated. Temporarily out of work, they danced so well at a supper club one night, the owner hired them to put on shows for the audience-diners. Soon, crowds of expatriates were coming to see and hear the latest American dances and melodies.

Ballroom dancing, especially to the tunes of Irving Berlin, was a popular pastime before World War I. Irene and Vernon created the "Castle Walk" by stepping up on the beat, rather than down, and also popularized the one-step, turkey trot, bunny hug, tango, and foxtrot. They toured cities across America and gave dancing lessons. When Irene cut her hair and put a band across her forehead, her devoted fans followed, calling their new look the "Castle bob" with a "Castle band."

# MAY 29

## LOUIS PASTEUR & MARIE LAURENT
### *All for science*

IN FEBRUARY 1849, LOUIS – THE FRENCH chemist whose name would become linked to his process of destroying dangerous microorganisms in food – wrote to the University of Strasbourg's rector, asking permission to marry his daughter, Marie. Explaining his modest background, Louis said he also supported his 3 sisters. "I have therefore absolutely no fortune," he added. "My only means are good health, some courage, and my position at the University."

He had arrived in Strasbourg 2 months before as acting professor of chemistry. Soon afterwards, he met Marie, and shortly after that, he proposed. Without her love, he confessed, "My work no longer means anything to me."

When they married 3 months later, at the Church of Saint Madeleine, he was 26 and she was 22, a cheerful blue-eyed girl who loved to sing and understood the fate of a scientist's wife: a limited income; acceptance that Louis's work always came first; knowing that even when Louis was home, he often was preoccupied.

Marie assisted Louis as much as possible, copying his notes and writing down his dictations, and he tried his best to explain things to her. But science was Marie's only rival. Louis had no other interests besides his work and family, even when they moved to the Sorbonne in Paris. On their wedding anniversary, many years later, she told their children, "Your father is absorbed in his thoughts, talks little, sleeps little, rises at dawn – in a word continues the life I began with him this day 35 years ago."

"The nights seem to me too long, yet I do not complain," Louis wrote to a friend. "I am often scolded by Madame Pasteur, whom I console by telling her that I shall lead her to posterity."

# MAY 30

## FREDRIC MARCH & FLORENCE ELDRIDGE
### *Favorite co-stars*

FREDRIC AND FLORENCE MARRIED IN MEXICO in 1927, and then toured 132 American cities with the Theater Guild Repertory Company. They'd been acting together since the previous year, when they met in the dining car of a train bound for summer stock productions in Denver, Colorado.

Unfortunately, Florence's springtime wedding tossed her out of the leading lady spotlight for a while, because the management said that a husband-and-wife team was unromantic and not good for business.

They never forgot that "brutal tour" across the United States, performing in "barns, gyms and saloons" and sleeping in seedy hotels, but Fredric also said, "It was fun for Florence and me, this working together constantly." It also improved their acting skills, enabling him to win a 5-year Hollywood contract. Although Florence was happier on Broadway, she gladly accepted film roles, especially when Fredric had a part, too. They were Bothwell and Queen Elizabeth in *Mary of Scotland*, Fantine and Valjean in *Les Miserables*, and Mr. and Mrs. Matthew Brady in *Inherit the Wind*.

She came from Brooklyn, was 25, and had always wanted to act. He was 29, from Racine, Wisconsin, and tried acting after giving up a humdrum job in banking. By 1937, Fredric was earning more than $450,000 a year and was one of Hollywood's highest paid actors. But he never gave up his love for the stage, and returned often to co-star with Florence. Even when a play flopped, the Marches were upbeat about it. In 1938 they apologized for *Yr. Obedient Husband*, by publishing a cartoon of 2 trapeze artists missing each other in midair and saying, "Oops, sorry!"

Always loyal to Florence, Fredric became so enraged at actress Tallulah Bankhead for deliberately upstaging Florence's performance in *The Skin of Our Teeth*, that he gargled loudly backstage during one of Tallulah's soliloquies.

# MAY 31*

## ALEXANDER SMITH & FLORA MACDONALD
### *"This happy bridegroom!"*

ALEX WROTE *A LIFE-DRAMA AND OTHER Poems* in 1853, when he was 23 years old. He had not yet met Flora, the Scottish lass from the Isle of Skye, but love and marriage were on his mind already when he wrote:

> *The lark is singing with the blinding sky.*
> *Hedges are white with May. The bridegroom sea*
> *Is toying with the shore, his wedded bride,*
> *And, in the fulness of his marriage joy,*
> *He decorates her tawny brow with shells,*
> *Retires a space, to see how fair she looks,*
> *Then proud, runs up to kiss her.*

Born in the Scottish Highlands, Alex became a lace designer like his father. But he also appreciated beauty that could be woven with words. Someday, Alex would visit the Hebrides, and when he did, he fell in love with Flora and brought her to Edinburgh. The rich images of Alex's poetry are as evocative and dreamlike as the intricate designs of fine lace. His *Life Poems* went through 4 editions in 3 years, providing him with a comfortable income and enabling him to quit the lace profession and concentrate on writing full-time.

He and Flora married in the spring of 1857 and settled at Wardie, near Granton. Alex wrote *City Poems* and *Dreamthorp* before beginning *A Summer in Skye,* a novel containing many poems about their life on the "misty isle":

> *… ring in the wind, my wedding chimes;*
> *Smile, villagers, at every door;*
> *Old churchyard, stuff'd with buried crimes,*
> *Be clad in sunshine o'er and o'er;*
> *And youthful maidens, white and sweet,*
> *Scatter your blossoms far and wide;*
> *And with a bridal chorus greet*
> *This happy bridegroom and his bride."*

---

*Date approximate.

# JUNE

# JUNE 1

## JUDITH LEYSTAR & JAN MIENSE MOLENAER
### *Two "lodestars" in art and matrimony*

EVEN BEFORE JUDITH AND JAN MARRIED in Holland in 1636, it was difficult to tell which paintings were hers and which had been made by him. The 2 artists probably met in Franz Hals's workshop and subsequently influenced and supported each other's work throughout their lives.

A few years before the wedding, Judith painted her self-portrait of a proud-looking, well-dressed young woman holding a violin and smiling. Her lips are parted and she might be saying, "I am Judith Leystar, a 23-year old painter, and I do not intend to marry until I have established my own workshop and studio, and have been accepted into the Haarlem Artists' Guild of St. Luke. (She became the first woman to do so.)

In Jan's "Self-Portrait in Studio," he holds a paintbrush and sits before an easel, and an old woman sits beside him. A gold coin rests in her lap; she is beseeching him. He looks us in the eye. Does the old woman represent the fleeting nature of life? Do her coins symbolize the emptiness of wealth?

Jan often painted pictures with double or hidden meanings, such as "Allegory of Marital Fidelity," which depicts good and bad qualities inherent in marriages. Judith's paintings focused on moral issues too, which was typical of Dutch painting at that time. She also painted flowers, still lifes, and portraits such as "Boy Playing a Flute," and "Jolly Topper." Usually, she signed her work with the symbol of a "leystar" or lodestar.

She and Jan were both 25 when they married in a church in Haarlem. They moved to Amsterdam and set up a studio together. Following the births of their 5 children, Judith painted less often, and concentrated instead on the family's business affairs. Her husband gave her power of attorney, enabling her to buy and sell properties for them.

# JUNE 2
## PRESIDENT GROVER CLEVELAND &
## FRANCES FOLSOM
### *"She'll do! She'll do!"*

MOST PEOPLE THOUGHT GROVER WAS KIDDING when the 40-something bachelor said he had waited for his future bride to grow up. "Frank" was the dark-eyed daughter of Grover's former law partner, who had died when she was 11. That's when "Uncle Cleve" became her legal guardian.

By 1886, Frank was 22, slender, intelligent, and imbued with "downright loveliness," a White House aide remarked years later. Grover was middle-aged and stodgy, but Frank adored him. Theirs would be the first White House wedding of a president in office. Soon after Frank graduated from Wells College, she became the youngest first lady and the most beloved since Dolley Madison.

The Blue Room was festooned with flowers as Grover escorted Frank down a wide staircase into the hall. Her white satin dress was enhanced by real orange blossoms bordering a white India silk overskirt. Around her neck was Grover's wedding gift – a magnificent diamond necklace.

After a 21-gun salute on the White House lawn and a buffet celebration, guests were given slices of wedding cake in white satin boxes autographed by the bride and groom. Reporters lurked in the shrubbery and spied on the newlyweds outside their honeymoon cottage in Deer Park, Maryland. Grover railed futilely against "key-hole journalism" and tried staying out of sight.

Nothing fazed Frank, who soon was hosting banquets, balls, and receptions for the general public, including special ones held on Saturdays to accommodate working women. The press admired Frank, as did the public, and it's been said that "Baby Ruth" candy bars were named after the Clevelands' eldest daughter.

When opponents vilified Grover during his reelection campaign, Frank defended him by saying she wished "the women of our country no better blessing than that their homes and their lives be as happy, and that their husbands be as kind and attentive, as considerate and affectionate as mine."

# JUNE 3

## EDWARD, DUKE OF WINDSOR &
## WALLIS WARFIELD SIMPSON
### *The woman he loved*

ONLY 16 GUESTS ATTENDED THE WEDDING of the ex-ruler of 500 million people in the British empire – the man who gave up the throne of England to marry "the woman I love" in 1937. Edward was 42 and Wallis was 41 when the small ceremony took place in the music room of the Chateau de Cande, a 16th century 50-room estate belonging to friends in the Loire Valley of France. Edward had desperately wanted a religious wedding, but no English bishop would perform it. At last, a vicar from Darlington England offered his services.

Wallis's 2-piece silk crepe wedding dress was created by Mainbocher in the color, "Wallis blue," and Schiaparelli designed her trousseau. Her wedding ring was made of Welsh gold, the same kind worn by British queens.

Originally the poor relation of an old Baltimore family, Wallis had been married twice before, which was why Edward couldn't marry her and still be king. Even so, she was a stickler for tradition. They needed an altar; a large chest was placed near the front of the room. "Something old" was a piece of antique lace stitched to the bride's lingerie. "Something new" was a gold coin recently minted for Edward's coronation, which Wallis placed in the heel of her shoe. "Something borrowed" was her aunt Bessie's handkerchief (Bessie was the only relative from either family to attend), and "something blue" was sapphire and diamond jewelry, and Wallis's dress, of course. Edward was his usual elegant self in a morning coat and striped trousers.

Following a wedding buffet celebration, they left in Edward's private railroad car on the *Orient Express* with 266 pieces of luggage. After a brief stopover in Venice, the honeymooners headed for a castle in Austria. Edward gave Wallis a diamond tiara as a wedding gift; at least she would always live like a queen.

# JUNE 4

## A. A. MILNE & DOROTHY DE SELINCOURT
### *"my Collaborator"*

ALAN MET "DAPHNE" AT HER 21st BIRTHDAY party in London, when he was 29. She laughed at all his jokes, and had "the most perfect sense of humour in the world," he wrote in his autobiography. After graduating from Cambridge, he sold freelance stories and poems to *Punch* until the famous humor magazine hired him as an assistant editor.

With a dependable, although modest, income, Alan and Daphne married in 1913 at St. Margaret's Church, Westminster, and took a 3-week honeymoon in Dartmoor. Soon after they settled in a flat in Embankment Gardens, Chelsea, Alan published his first book of essays and then served in France during World War I. When their only child – a son – was born, Alan chose his first name, "Christopher," and Daphne suggested "Robin" for the middle. On his first birthday they gave him a large teddy bear that was promptly named Winnie the Pooh.

Soon, the little boy had many stuffed animals, and his father was writing whimsical stories and poems about them – *When We Were Very Young* in 1924, and *Winnie-the-Pooh* 3 years later, introducing the now immortal characters Eeyore, Piglet, Kanga, and Roo. Although Alan also wrote plays and essays for adults, his biggest successes always were his books for children.

Many years later, Christopher Robin would remember his father kidding his mother by saying he married her only to avoid having to deal with plumbers and other petty household details. Daphne, however, could do little more than light a fire if someone else had built it!

That didn't stop Alan from dedicating his first book, *Once a Week*, to her: "To my Collaborator – Who buys the ink and paper, laughs and, in fact, does all the really difficult part of the business."

# JUNE 5*

## JOSEPH PENNELL & ELIZABETH ROBINS

### *On a bicycle built for two*

S HORTLY BEFORE ELIZABETH AND JOSEPH MARRIED in 1884, they resolved that they would "not allow anything to interfere with his drawing and my writing."

They had met 3 years earlier in a New York City magazine office. Joseph's assignment was to draw architectural etchings of historical buildings in Philadelphia, and Elizabeth was hired to write the text. Their first joint effort, "A Ramble in Philadelphia," appeared in the March, 1882 issue of *Century* magazine. Later, Joseph left for Europe to illustrate William Dean Howells's book, *Tuscan Cities*. He and Elizabeth corresponded often, and by the time he returned, they had decided to marry.

Elizabeth finished writing her *Life of Mary Wollstonecraft* shortly before the wedding. Joseph was 26 and she was 29 years old. They sailed for Europe in August and rode a tandem bicycle from London to Canterbury, stopping along the way so he could sketch and she could take notes. The following year, *A Canterbury Pilgrimage* was published, the first of many travel books they would produce together.

They settled in London, sending articles and drawings to American publishers and joining a circle of writers and artists including Henry James, George Bernard Shaw, and Whistler, who asked them to write his biography, *The Life of James McNeill Whistler*. Eventually, they visited most of Europe, and Elizabeth traveled by bicycle more than any other woman of her time.

The Pennells' work philosophy might have been summed up by Joseph in the introduction he wrote for a book about etchings: "Be yourselves, if you have anything in you, having studied... the great workmen of the past.... Do not copy them, but carry on their work... remembering they were known and hated, most of them in their day, because they did their work better than their fellows."

---

*Date approximate.

# JUNE 6
## OGDEN NASH & FRANCES LEONARD
*Love never let up*

OGDEN FIRST SAW FRANCES AT A dinner dance in Baltimore in November, 1928. He was so impressed by the attractive dark-haired young woman's delightful sense of humor during the cocktail hour that he surreptitiously rearranged the place cards at their table, so they would sit next to each other at dinner.

By the end of the evening, Frances's date was drunk and unfit to drive. Ogden suppressed his secret glee and gallantly offered to escort her home. He would become the famous author of humorous and satirical verses about marriage, children, family pets, politicians and other topics of everyday life. But nothing ever mattered as much to Ogden as winning Frances, who always encouraged and supported his work.

He lived in New York City, where he was a book editor and writer of poems and prose for *The New Yorker*. Soon began a 3-year courtship filled with hundreds of letters, phone calls, and mad dashes by train back to Baltimore to see Frances. Frequently, Ogden's dispatches contained wildly optimistic and humorous rhymes; by August, he declared he was a "silly lout, fumbling over phrases," and "The more I see you the more I love you, and the more I don't see you the more I love you."

They married in 1931 at Baltimore's Church of the Redeemer. Frances carried lilies and wore a long white satin gown with a veil that fitted snugly against her head and sailed down to the floor, encircling her. As Ogden predicted in one of the many poems she inspired, someday she might meet a better poet, but Frances would never know a "truer lover."

After a honeymoon in Canada, Frances and Ogden settled in New York City. Within a few years, he became a full-time freelance writer working at home, never far from Frances.

# JUNE 7

## EDWIN MUIR & WILHELMINA ANDERSON

*"This single song of love, this is A wonder."*

"MY MARRIAGE WAS THE MOST FORTUNATE event in my life," Edwin wrote in his autobiography 35 years after he married "Willa." Although Edwin's childhood on a Scottish farm had been idyllic, all was shattered after his family moved to Glasgow, where his parents and 2 brothers died before he was 20.

Thirty-two years old, he had resigned himself to a lonely life when he met Willa at a dance in Glasgow in the early spring of 1919. She was a 30-year old writer and a linguist, as well as vice-principal of a London teachers' college. Willa quickly became attracted to Edwin's brilliance and sincerity, and to the "blue flash in his eyes whenever he laughed." Edwin sensed with Willa, life could be joyous again:

*"Yes, yours, my love, is the right human face*
*I in my mind had waited for this long…."*

They were married at a registry office in London and honeymooned by the North Sea. Afterward, they took a flat near the British Museum. It was Edwin's first real home since his parents died. For the next few years, it was Willa, primarily, who saved Edwin from a nervous breakdown, helping him to recover by writing beautiful poetry. Through psychoanalysis, he became a great believer in dream analysis and discovered that tapping into childhood memories and dreams was an effective way to reach his deeper self.

Edwin and Willa often conversed in their own particular Scottish dialect or read the classics aloud to each other in the evenings. He worked as an editor and began writing essays, fiction, and criticism. Willa wrote novels, too, and eventually they translated many novels by European authors such as Franz Kafka's *The Trial* and *The Castle*, and the novels of Sholem Asch.

# JUNE 8

## DON MARQUIS & REINA MELCHER
### *His "favorite copy reader"*

ON WAS A MAGAZINE EDITOR IN Atlanta, Georgia when Reina, a freelance writer, literally walked into his life. He'd just published her latest story, and the slender blonde appealed to him right away. He took her out for an ice cream soda – an event his friends joked about afterwards, saying, Good grief, what won't men do for women?... Don's much more at home in a tavern, so what was he doing in such an "unwholesome" environment?

He was falling in love, he admitted later. Pretty soon, he and Reina were getting together regularly, talking about everything from "peach ice cream to speculation about the hereafter" and giving each other nicknames like "Tommy" and "Queenie."

Don had not yet created his famous twosome – archy, the philosophical cockroach, and mehitabel, the amoral cat. But the talented young man who would be compared to Mark Twain was warming up nicely, writing parodies, satires, witty poems and tall tales.

He and Reina married in 1909 and headed for New York the following winter. She wrote stories for magazines, and he got a job on a newspaper.

Then he was fired.

Reina persuaded Don to stick it out in New York, where they subsisted on "starvation diets" in a cold-water flat. Finally, one Saturday afternoon, another editor offered Don a job if he could write 4 humorous articles, 5000 words each, in 2 days. Don worked all day and night until Monday morning, when he passed out in front of his typewriter. Raina finished the job, tapping out the last 3000 words so well that "I can't tell to this day where my work stops... and hers begins," Don recalled years later. She delivered the manuscript to the newspaper office, and came home with a generous check.

# JUNE 9
## EDDIE CANTOR & IDA TOBIAS
*"Ida, sweet as apple cider"*

EDDIE STOOD OUTSIDE IDA'S HOME IN Manhattan the night her older sister got married in 1909. He was almost 17 and mad about Ida, but her parents had convinced her he'd never amount to anything.

Orphaned when he was a baby, Eddie had been raised in a Lower East Side tenement by his grandmother, Esther. But poverty didn't inspire the boy with bulging eyes and boundless energy to go into a good, solid business. Instead, he was going to be a vaudeville star – hardly an impressive occupation to a girl whose mother had warned her about all the ne'er-do-wells looking for romance instead of sensible jobs.

"Either forget about acting, or Ida will forget about you!" her father barked, but Eddie really wanted to perform. He sang, danced, and told jokes, and even worked as a singing waiter in Coney Island while another unknown named Jimmy Durante played the piano.

Somehow, Eddie had to make enough money to convince the Tobiases and Ida that he could be a worthy husband. He spent the next few years traveling with vaudeville troupes, doing comical skits and song-and-dance routines – and saving every penny he earned. Then he returned to Henry Street and married Ida, who had refused to marry anyone else.

Eddie would become a major radio, stage and film star who ended each show with his favorite song, "Ida." But right now, "it was June, the 9th of June, 1914.... June smiled and Ida smiled and I just grinned," he recalled in his autobiography. They spent $700 on a trip to Europe. Eddie said he didn't care that they traveled second class, "for I traveled with a first class wife."

# JUNE 10*

## REMBRANDT VAN RIJN & SASKIA DE UYLENBURGH
### *His goddess*

R EMBRANDT PROBABLY MET SASKIA IN AMSTERDAM while she was visiting her brother, Hendrick. Like Rembrandt, she had come from a small Dutch town and a family with many children, but her father was a wealthy lawyer and his was only a miller.

With the eyes of a true genius, Rembrandt began sketching Saskia. In the earliest picture she looks at us wistfully, her face partly shaded by a wide-brimmed straw hat adorned with flowers. Her head rests on one hand, and she holds a few flowers in the other. Rembrandt rarely painted flowers, except when he painted Saskia.

In another early painting, probably made shortly after their wedding in 1634, Saskia is costumed as Bellona, the Roman goddess of war. Although she is encumbered by heavy armor and her pose is somewhat stiff, modern x-rays reveal that Saskia was first painted in the nude... and "dressed" afterwards.

They married in a small church not far from Saskia's hometown of Leenwarden. Rembrandt was 33 and she was 21-years old. For a few months they lived with Hendrick, who occasionally represented his brother-in-law as an art dealer. Later, they rented rooms overlooking the Amstel River. Over the years, Rembrandt painted Saskia many times, often in costumes of goddesses such as Flora, the goddess of love, and prostitutes. Frequently, Saskia appears boisterous and flirtatious, as if she enjoys posing for her husband.

Not long after the wedding, Rembrandt painted them together in a tavern. She sits on his lap, and they look over their shoulders and smile suggestively at the viewer. Like the peacock feathers in his hat, their faces imply a sensually satisfying relationship. Although some think this picture is a typical Dutch allegory symbolizing the evils of too much drink and wantonness, others who believe in love say it represents Rembrandt and Saskia's rich private life.

---

*June 22 has also been cited.

# JUNE 11

## EDMUND SPENSER & ELIZABETH BOYLE
### *"all her body like a palace fair"*

EDMUND MARRIED ELIZABETH IN IRELAND ON St. Barnabas' Day, 1594, "so joyful a day, the joyfullest day that ever sun did see," he wrote. It was also the longest day of the year, according to the calendar then in use. Elizabeth was 25 and he was 42 years old. She was beautiful, well-educated, and blond, and would inspire her remarkable husband – known as "the Prince of Poets of His Tyme" – to write some of the finest Elizabethan love poems.

Two major works – "Amoretti" and "Epithalamion," are believed to represent stories of their courtship and wedding. Wooing Elizabeth was one reason why Edmund stopped writing his "Faerie Queene" for a while; he returned to it after their marriage, and mentions his wife in the 4th book. They met in County Cork, Ireland, where Elizabeth, an Englishwoman, had been living with distant relatives. Edmund wooed her for many months and would remark that the year it took to win her seemed much longer than all the 40 years he had lived before!

He describes her in "Epithalamion":

*Her goodly eyes like sapphires shining bright,*
*Her forehead ivory white,*
*Her cheeks like apples which the sun hath rudded,*
*Her lips like cherries charming men to bite.*

Their wedding and a sumptuous feast followed, until, at last ...

*Now bring the bride into the bridal bowers.*
*The night is come, now soon her disarray...*
*Lay her in lilies and in violets,*
*And silken curtains over her display,*
*And odoured sheets, and arras coverlets.*
*Behold how goodly my fair love does lie....*

# JUNE 12
## BERTHA KINSKY & ARTUR VON SUTTNER
### *"schatzchen (my treasure)"*

THE DAUGHTER OF A HIGHLY DECORATED Austrian field marshal, Bertha was Countess Kinsky, raised in an aristocratic world but helpless as her widowed mother squandered the family fortune at spas and casinos throughout Europe. In spite of her loss of income and social status, Bertha became an internationally respected writer, outspoken pacifist, and the first woman to win the Nobel Peace Prize, in 1905.

By the age of 30, she had resigned herself to spinsterhood after her fiancé died in an accident. Forced to seek employment, Bertha was hired as a governess to Baron and Baroness von Suttner's 4 daughters in Vienna. Within a year she was amorously involved with Artur, her pupils' handsome, 23-year-old brother, known as the "Sunshine boy." "When he entered a room, it immediately became twice as bright and warm as it was before," Bertha recalled in her memoirs.

Artur's parents were appalled and demanded that Bertha find work elsewhere. Reluctantly, she accepted a secretarial position in Paris with Alfred Nobel, the inventor of dynamite. The Swedish millionaire was quite taken with Bertha's beauty and intelligence, and might have proposed to her himself, if she had not been so in love with Artur.

In 1876 Bertha sold her last piece of good jewelry for a train ticket back to Vienna, where the lovers were tearfully reunited and ran off to be married secretly. They spent the next 9 years in the Caucasus, barely supporting themselves by giving language and music lessons, writing books, and covering the Russian-Turkish war for European newspapers.

Returning to Austria, Artur founded the League Against Anti-Semitism, and they both joined organizations advocating world peace. Bertha's 1885 antiwar novel, *Lay Down Your Arms*, became an international best-seller, praised by pacifists including Tolstoy, and established her as a major spokeswoman for peace.

# JUNE 13

## KATHE SCHMIDT & KARL KOLLWITZ

### *"life's comrade"*

"MY HUSBAND AND I DID EVERYTHING possible so that I would have time for my work," Kathe wrote in her memoirs. In late 19th century Berlin, such husbands were extremely rare. But Karl, a doctor, willingly helped care for their home and children, and encouraged Kathe to become an artist.

They met when she was 17, and he was a 20-year old medical student. Within a year, they were engaged. Marriage was delayed, however, until Karl established a practice, and Kathe pursued her graphic art studies in Munich and Berlin.

They married on Karl's 28th birthday in 1891 and moved into a 3rd floor apartment at 25 Weissenburgerstrasse in North Berlin. (They would live there for the next 50 years until the Nazis banned Kathe's work and their home was destroyed in World War II.) Kathe's art studio was on the ground floor next to Karl's medical office. Committed to the values of socialism, he worked for a workers' health insurance fund and took care of tailors and their families. He also treated elderly people and others with little money for medical care.

Kathe was particularly touched by the hunger and despair she saw in many of Karl's weary patients and their children. She began sketching them and making etchings, using the rolling pin from her kitchen to apply sufficient pressure. Her son Hans was born after she completed "Greetings," a joyful welcome to him, in 1892. The lines of the etching are unusually dark because the artist went into labor soon after she put the plate into its acid bath... and it stayed there for a long time!

She and Karl had been blessed to find each other; Kathe was not a typical "hausfrau," nor was Karl an ordinary husband.

# JUNE 14

## CAMILLE PISSARRO & JULIE VELLAY
### *A family of artists*

B Y THE TIME CAMILLE AND JULIE married in 1871, they'd been living together for 10 years. They had met near Paris, where she worked as a cook's helper for his parents, who strongly opposed their son's relationship with a servant. But the 30-year old Impressionist painter found Julie's energy and directness refreshing, compared to the "proper" behavior of other girls he knew, and very soon, he and Julie were romantically involved.

Throughout the 1860's they lived in flats in Paris and in the countryside, where life was more relaxed and studio space was less costly. Camille came to Paris to visit galleries and spend time with other artists such as Cezanne and Degas. Like Monet, Camille preferred painting directly from nature, bathing his scenes in glorious light and rich atmosphere. Julie worked for a florist and often posed for Camille, still a struggling artist. Although his parents weren't happy with the situation, they sent him money regularly.

Camille sold more and more paintings until the Franco-Prussian War began. He and Julie fled with their two children to a friend's farm in Louveciennes, Brittany, in 1870. Then they went to Norwood, England, where he painted many scenes, and the influential art dealer Durand-Ruel agreed to exhibit his work abroad.

By now, Camille was 41 years old, and his father had died. Julie was 32 and pregnant with their 3$^{rd}$ child. At last, his mother gave them her blessing, and they married at the city hall in Croydon. When they returned to Louveciennes, they saw it had been decimated by the war. Many of Camille's unframed paintings had been ripped and dirtied by soldiers butchering poultry. Village washerwomen wore his tattered canvases as "aprons." A claims lawyer hired by Camille's mother helped Julie and Camille collect money for the damages. Within a year, Camille was producing magnificent work again, such as "Orchard at Louveciennes." Eventually, 5 of their children would become artists, too.

## JUNE 15

## CARL SANDBURG & LILIAN STEICHEN

*"Your hands are sweeter than nut-brown bread*
*when you touch me"*

B Y THE TIME THE FUTURE PULITZER-Prize-winning poet and biographer of Abraham Lincoln was 29, he'd ridden freight trains, washed dishes, tilled fields, painted houses, fought in the Spanish-Civil War, and worked his way through college. In December, 1907, Carl met Lilian, whom he subsequently renamed "Paula," at the Social Democratic party headquarters in Milwaukee, Wisconsin. She was 6 years younger, and noticed that Carl rarely went anywhere without a book – often by Whitman, Shakespeare, or Emerson.

When he left on a business trip for the party, he wrote to her about socialism and sent her some of his poems. As the sister of photographer, Edward Steichen, Paula recognized Carl's incredible talents and wrote back to him—her "dear Poet-of-Our-World-Today"—to say that he was a far better poet than a socialist organizer.

Paula was Carl's "Ideal Woman" and "Dream-Girl," "tender as dew, impetuous as rain." Within 6 months they decided to marry. They didn't need much – just a small home with a coffeepot, a hat rack, a few chairs, and a flower vase. So what if Carl wasn't handy around the house? She'd take care of all the mundane chores; his only task was writing!

They married at a friend's home in Milwaukee and set up housekeeping in Appleton, Wisconsin. Paula considered wedding rings "barbaric" and reluctantly agreed to buy one (insisting on paying for it herself) to wear only when they traveled… although friends couldn't recall ever seeing it on her finger. She wouldn't promise to "obey," and they made a pact that if either partner ever wanted to end the marriage, that's all it would take to dissolve it. During a heated argument years later, Paula reminded Carl of their arrangement, but he said no, he'd stay in their marriage, and declared that he'd never go through all that wooing again!

# JUNE 16
## CHARLIE CHAPLIN & OONA O'NEILL
*She had a "luminous beauty"*

THE BRILLIANT FILM ACTOR, DIRECTOR, SCREENWRITER, and producer, the screen clown and "Little Tramp" who poked fun at fascism, moral hypocrisies, and human foibles married Oona when he was 54 years old. She was 18, and would be his 4th wife. In many ways, she also was the best thing that ever happened to him.

They met at a film agent's home soon after the 1940 release of Charlie's motion picture, *The Great Dictator*, in which he played the roles of a Jewish barber and a caricature of Hitler. Oona was the daughter of playwright Eugene O'Neill (who disapproved of the relationship), and a radiantly beautiful aspiring actress who understood and respected Charlie's intelligence and artistry.

Early in 1943, Charlie was embroiled in a nasty lawsuit and a paternity case. Oona provided him with a safe haven of love and sympathy. They married that year in the small village of Carpinteria, California, after successfully evading newspaper reporters. Incognito, the Chaplins honeymooned for 2 months in Santa Barbara, anxiously awaiting verdicts in Charlie's court cases. He was found not guilty of federal charges, and blood tests proved he was not the father of the plaintiff's child. But the adverse publicity saddened Charlie and Oona a great deal.

They lived quietly for the next few years. Oona decided not to pursue an acting career and gave birth to Geraldine, the first of their 6 children. Charlie concentrated on *Limelight*, the touching (and somewhat autobiographical) story of a down-and-out middle-aged comedian who falls in love with a beautiful young dancer. Later, the Chaplins settled in Switzerland, and Charlie continued to make films. At last, said Charlie's friend, the comedian Stan Laurel, he "got his fairy princess and they sure as hell lived happily ever after."

# JUNE 17
## JEAN-HONORE FRAGONARD &
## MARIE-ANNE GERARD
### *"The Pursuit of Love"*

S HORTLY BEFORE JEAN-HONORE MARRIED MARIE-ANNE IN 1768, he painted "The Swing," one of his most famous works. It was commissioned by a French baron who wanted a fanciful garden scene depicting his golden-haired mistress sailing on a swing pushed by a dutiful but foolish husband. On the grass beneath her, the happy baron reclines, and from his ideal vantage point he sees one tiny pink shoe kicked into the air, and his mistress's white-stockinged legs under her billowing skirts. Overlooking the charming dalliance is a statue of Cupid, with a finger against his lips.

Unlike the baron, Jean-Honore married his mistress, but it's pretty apparent that he seduced her first. Marie-Anne came to Paris in 1767, when she was 22. One of her relatives had arranged for her to consult with M. Fragonard, an established, 37-year old painter, about painting watercolors and miniatures.

She was charming, impressionable, and adorable, prompting him to offer very practical advice: Move in with me and I will teach you everything! In less than a year, they were married at the Church of St. Lambert at Vaugirard, Paris. Marie-Anne gave birth to a daughter 7 months later.

They lived in an apartment at the Louvre, home to King Louis XVI and Marie Antoinette, but managed to escape harm during the revolution. Jean-Honore's happy family life inspired him to paint scenes illustrating the joys of domesticity, such as "The Cradle," and "The Schoolmistress." Although some art critics have called his work frivolous, representing pre-revolutionary life in France, Jean-Honore was hardly a superficial man or painter. He cared for his elderly father, supported his family, and donated funds to the revolutionary cause. Marie-Anne and her sister Marguerite also helped the family financially by painting and selling miniatures.

# JUNE 18

## MARTIN LUTHER KING, JR. & CORETTA SCOTT
### *"M.L." and Miss Scott*

MARTIN WAS A MINISTER DOING GRADUATE work in philosophy at Boston University in 1952 when he met Coretta on a blind date. She was studying voice at the New England Conservatory of Music nearby. Since her fellowship covered only her tuition expenses, Coretta worked as a mail-order clerk and also cleaned houses for a family in exchange for room and board.

Martin was broad-shouldered and muscular, with almond-shaped eyes and a rich baritone voice. He looked steadily at Coretta as they ate lunch in a cafeteria near her school and talked about politics and philosophy. Each was impressed by the other's self-confidence and intelligence. "You're everything I'm looking for in a wife," he told her, and he proposed marriage right away. Coretta put off answering him, since it probably meant giving up her plans for a singing career. Finally, she realized that things might work out differently from the way she'd imagined, and she agreed to marry Martin.

Coretta's family was impressed by Martin's seriousness and determination, and while no one knew that within 10 years he would be the youngest person ever to win the Nobel Peace Prize, they all sensed that he wasn't going to be just an ordinary minister.

In 1953, Martin's father performed the wedding ceremony in the Scotts' garden. Coretta was 26 and Martin was 24 years old. A few months later, he became pastor of the Dexter Avenue Baptist Church in Montgomery, Alabama. In December, 1955, when Rosa Parks refused to give up her seat to a white passenger, Martin spearheaded a citywide boycott of buses by blacks that lasted for over a year and resulted in desegregated bus transportation. With Coretta beside him, Martin campaigned for voter registration and the end of racial discrimination in America.

## JUNE 19

## WILLIAM HOWARD TAFT & HELEN HERRON

*"the dearest sweetest boy that ever lived"*
*and his "guardian angel"*

"OH, NELLIE," WILL WROTE IN 1885. "I believe you can be happy with me." He was 28 and in love with the gray-eyed young woman who had brains as well as beauty. Although some men found Nellie a bit too outspoken, Will loved her energy and spirit. "Her capacity for work is wonderful," he told his father. But Nellie was cautious, believing "a woman is happier who marries exactly right – but how many do?"

Marrying each other *was* "exactly right." They remained best friends and confidants in the years ahead, when Will became governor of the Philippines, Teddy Roosevelt's secretary of war, and 27th president of the United States. Will would also be the only president to be Chief Justice of the U.S. Supreme Court after his term in office. Through it all, Nellie encouraged him and spurred him on.

They had met at a bobsledding party in Cincinnati, and Will began attending Nellie's salons for young intellectuals in town. He had graduated second in his class from Yale, and was studying law. Nellie was literary and musical, and had attended Miami University of Ohio. Her father, a close friend of President Rutherford B. Hayes, had taken her to Washington DC when she was 17, and she fantasized about becoming a first lady someday.

Like most well-bred women of that era, Nellie rejected Will's first two proposals, making him pine for her all the more. But at last she yielded to his fervent pleas, and they were married at her parents' home in 1886. Nellie wore a white satin gown with an embroidered bodice, and carried a bouquet of sweet peas and lilies. After a honeymoon tour of France, England, and Scotland, they settled down in Walnut Hills in Cincinnati.

# JUNE 20

## ALEC GUINNESS & MERULA SALAMAN
### *Lifetime roles as husband and wife*

ALEC WAS PERFORMING AS A WOLF and Merula was a tiger in a children's play called *Noah* when they met on the English stage in 1935. Three years later, the still-aspiring young players became engaged during a dress rehearsal for Shakespeare's *The Merchant of Venice*.

Although Alec's boarding school headmaster had declared that he wasn't the "acting type," by the time he married his auburn-haired fiancée he was 24 and on his way to achieving greatness as a stage and film actor for roles including Hamlet, Richard III, and Obi Ben-Kenobi in *Star Wars*. He would also win an Academy Award for his role in *The Bridge Over the River Kwai*, and be given a knighthood in 1959.

In 1938, en route to the marriage registry office in Reigate, south of London, Alec bloodied his hand on a rosebush while shaking hands with a well-known French actor. The wedding day was marred by first-aid treatments, but it also marked the start of a long and happy married life.

After a short honeymoon in Dublin, Alec and Merula took a walking tour of Donegal. They visited the director Tyrone (Tony) Guthrie and his wife, Judith, at their family's run-down but atmospheric Victorian country estate. On warm lazy mornings, Merula and Alec went rowing on a lake nearby, and she listened to him rehearse his lines for his upcoming role as Hamlet, which Tony would be directing soon for the Old Vic.

The actor John Gielgud also directed Alec that year – as Lorenzo in *The Merchant of Venice*. Critics said Alec performed splendidly, bringing new romance and passion to his role. It's not surprising: after all, he had just married Merula!

## JUNE 21

## RICHARD MILHOUS NIXON & THELMA RYAN
### *"dearest heart"*

I T'S UNLIKELY THAT "DICK" HAD HIS eyes on the White House back in 1940 when he married "Pat," but it's worth noting that their wedding was held in the presidential suite of a California hotel, where Presidents McKinley, Roosevelt, Taft, and Hoover had stayed. It also happened to be the same day that another president—Zachary Taylor—was married, 130 years before.

Dick and Pat had dated for 2 ½ years after they met as players in a Whittier community theater production, *The Dark Tower*. "It was a case of love at first sight," Dick said later. The young lawyer was entranced by the "beautiful and vivacious young woman with titian hair" who taught typing, and he told her someday he would marry her.

They went dancing and ice-skating – until he fell down too many times. He sent her poems and flowers. Some of their best evenings were spent grading papers together. He proposed to Pat at Dana Point, on a bluff overlooking the Pacific Ocean, not far from San Clemente. During their engagement, Dick wrote to her, saying she was "destined to be a great lady" and a great inspiration to him. "It is our job to go forth together and accomplish great ends and we shall do it too."

He was 27 and she was 28 when they married. Pat wore a rose-colored hat and an orchid from Dick pinned to her French blue lace suit. Afterward, they drove to Mexico in her car, stocked with cans of food from his parents' grocery store so they could save money on meals. Friends played a trick on them, however, by peeling off all the labels, so they never knew what they were going to eat!

On Dick's birthday the following January, Pat gave him a ceramic knight riding a dark horse, the symbol of a candidate who is unexpectedly nominated for political office.

# JUNE 22

## ANNIE OAKLEY & FRANK BUTLER

### *"Little Sure Shot" and Mr. Butler*

FRANK WAS MIGHTY SURPRISED TO MEET a 15-year old girl when he was introduced to a "crack shot from upcountry" challenging him to a shooting match on Shooter's Hill in Cincinnati. Phoebe Anne Oakley Mozee didn't doubt her abilities. Maybe the ruddy-faced Irish marksman was 10 years older and had won competitions. She'd been shooting quail in the woods for years and figured that hitting clay targets fired from a mechanical trap would be a breeze.

Onlookers placed bets on Frank and Annie; many doubted she would beat him… and were surely disappointed when she did. Frank was intrigued, however, and began courting Annie at her sister's house. A year later, in 1876, he married the pint-sized sharp shooter he would always call "little girl." They teamed up as "Butler and Oakley," performing in variety shows and circuses throughout the United States.

Annie had quit school by the age of 9, so Frank taught her to read as well as develop trick-shooting skills. By the time Buffalo Bill hired her for his Wild West Show, Frank had quit performing to become Annie's manager and coach. She could hit dimes, shatter glass balls tossed in the air, and slice the thin side of playing cards in half at 30 paces, often while doing cartwheels or riding horseback. She also perforated playing cards with 5 or 6 holes before they fell to the ground. Soon, theater stubs and other punch-marked tickets were nicknamed "Annie Oakleys."

Frank and Annie didn't have children, but they supported and educated 18 orphan girls. They also toured Europe many times. On one trip, Crown Prince Wilhelm of Germany insisted that Annie shoot a cigarette from his lips. She'd been performing that trick with Frank for years, and no one was prouder than he when she did it again… perfectly.

## JUNE 23
## RUTH BADER & MARTIN GINSBURG
### *"my life's partner"*

I T DIDN'T TAKE LONG FOR MARTY to realize that Ruth did many things well... but cooking wasn't one of them. Shortly after their 1954 wedding, he began studying recipes as well as law books, and assumed the role of family cook. More important, he became Ruth's "best friend and biggest booster," which is how she described him almost 40 years later, after her appointment as justice of the U.S. Supreme Court.

A Cornell University sophomore in 1950, Marty wasn't intimidated by the brilliant freshman who lived down the hall from his roommate's girlfriend. By Marty's senior year, he and Ruth decided to attend law school together. He began at Harvard the following fall, while she finished up at Cornell, as class valedictorian.

In 1954, they were married in Marty's parents' home in Rockville Centre, New York, and went to Europe at a time when you really could manage on $5 a day. Marty was drafted after they returned. He took a leave of absence from law school, and the future lawyers spent the next 2 years at Fort Sill, Oklahoma.

Ruth faced gender discrimination – an issue she fought, eventually, in lawsuits in the 1970's – while working in a Social Security office. After informing her supervisor that she was pregnant, Ruth was demoted to a lower-paying job.

She entered Harvard Law School in 1956 as one of 9 women among 500 students. The Ginsburgs hired a part-time baby-sitter for their young daughter and handled household chores along with their schoolwork. The next year, however, Marty became seriously ill. "Ruth was stuck with the care and feeding of one well-behaved small child and one not very well-behaved large child, obtaining and transcribing class notes for me, her own class schedule, and her work on the *Harvard Law Review*," he recalled later. "She persevered," however, "with grace and astounding stamina."

# JUNE 24
## THOMAS WOODROW WILSON & ELLEN AXSON
### *"My own darling"*

"THE FIRST TIME I SAW YOUR face… was in church one morning," Woodrow wrote Ellen after their 1883 engagement. He'd been visiting relatives in Rome, Georgia, and was attracted to the young woman sitting with 4 children. She was soft-spoken and beautiful, but her auburn hair was covered by a mourning veil. Woodrow thought she was a widow, but Ellen was actually the minister's daughter, caring for her siblings. She'd taken over all the housekeeping responsibilities after her mother died, and had resigned herself to a spinster's life. Meeting Woodrow would change all that, and give her a life beyond her dreams.

Woodrow was doing graduate work at Johns Hopkins University in Baltimore, and the idea of becoming governor of New Jersey *and* president of the United States was far from his mind when he courted Ellen. They went on picnics, searched for 4-leaf clovers, and talked about poetry and art. After he left, they corresponded but were too shy to mention love.

Serendipity united them a few months later, at the Eagle Hotel in Asheville, North Carolina. Both were waiting for train connections when Woodrow saw Ellen's face in the window of a restaurant, and rushed inside to find her. They lingered in Asheville for several days, enjoying the magic of being away from home and what Ellen would describe as "the joy of a sudden meeting and the pain of an imminent parting." By the time they said goodbye, they were engaged.

Two years later, the "shy little maid" who once "found it hard… even to whisper, 'I love you,'" married the reserved young man who was at last free from "all the dreariness of loneliness." The 1885 ceremony in Savannah was conducted by Ellen's grandfather and Woodrow's father. Afterwards, Ellen's 9-year old brother got into a fistfight with one of Woodrow's young cousins. The bride was horrified, but the groom thought it was highly amusing!

# JUNE 25

## JAMES THURBER & HELEN WISMER
### *No one was ever like Helen*

"JAMIE'S" LINE DRAWINGS AND STORIES OFTEN poked fun at overbearing, nagging wives, but Helen was not a "Thurber woman." Nor was Jamie a henpecked "Thurber man." He'd been unhappily married before, but in 1935 the "second time around" brought him great happiness.

Helen was a pulp magazine editor when she met Jamie at a party in Greenwich Village, New York. "Is sex really necessary, Mr. Thurber?" she asked the tall man with thick glasses, echoing words from his latest book. That caught his attention, and he laughed, but a year passed before they ran into each other again. Over the next 5 years, they became better acquainted, usually at gatherings with other writers and illustrators.

On the day after Jamie's divorce became final, he proposed to Helen at the Algonquin Hotel bar. Somewhat shocked, she got up, went to the ladies' room, came back and said yes. A month later, they were married by her father, a Congregational minister, and honeymooned in Menemsha on Martha's Vineyard, Massachusetts. Low on funds, Jamie wrote "The Departure of Emma Inch" in one day, and promptly sold it to *The New Yorker*.

Fans had worried that "wedded bliss" might dull Jamie's sharp-edged work, but it only got better. The human condition hadn't changed one bit, but Jamie's women had. *Let Your Mind Alone* contained fewer bad marriages, and wives often represented reason and common sense. When Helen objected to a particular scene in "The Secret Life of Walter Mitty," Jamie grudgingly accepted her opinion and rewrote it. Love and humor were vital in a happy marriage, he believed. "Remember laughter," he wrote in *The Thirteen Clocks* in 1950. "You'll need it even in the blessed isles of Ever After."

# JUNE 26
## CLAUDE MONET & CAMILLE DONCIEUX
### *Camille, always Camille*

CLAUDE PAINTED "WOMAN IN A GREEN Dress" in four days in 1866, when he was 26-years old. He hurried for two reasons – because he had to submit it in time for the next Paris Salon exhibition, and because he was enchanted with his new model, Camille.

The painting is not a conventional portrait. The young woman is seen from the back, and turns her head toward the artist. Her face is lovely, but the focus of the picture is the sweep of her long striped silk dress and short black velvet jacket. "Look at the dress," said Emile Zola, the writer. "It is both supple and solid, it trails softly, it lives…!"

Claude's bourgeois family was not impressed; so what if he was a "promising young painter?" He was practically destitute. For a while, they sent him small sums of money, but that stopped when Claude began living with Camille, whom they never liked. At times, Claude had to choose between having enough food and having enough painting materials. Camille bore his family's dislike stoically.

They moved to the country, where she posed for all four figures in his next painting, "Women in the Garden," and he began working outdoors all the time, concentrating on the effects of natural light. Camille sits on a riverbank in the painting, "The River." When it was exhibited in 1868, viewers said the light reflecting off the water was so intense, so *real*, it made their eyes tear.

Claude and Camille married in 1870, and two years later, they settled down in a cottage at Argenteuil with their young son, Jean. Camille continued to pose – holding a parasol, at the beach, in fields of poppies, anywhere Claude asked her to be. He painted her delicate features again and again, immortalizing his love and her beauty.

# JUNE 27

## IDA BELL WELLS & FERDINAND LEE BARNETT
### *"Call Me Thine Own"*

ALTHOUGH IDA AND FERDINAND'S 1895 WEDDING in Chicago was a typical affair, their marriage would not be conventional. Many years later, the poet Langston Hughes wrote, "Ida B. Wells married another crusader... and together they continued their campaign for equal rights for Negro Americans."

She was an African-American writer, and he was an African-American lawyer and widower with two sons. At 32, Ida was tall and elegant, with wide-set eyes and dark hair piled gracefully on her head. Ferdinand was also tall and good-looking, and a few years older than Ida. After a 3-day honeymoon they went right back to work.

They believed in racial equality but harbored no racial hatreds. Instead, they focused on specific issues of prejudice and discrimination, which Ida exposed as an investigative journalist. Before coming to the Windy city, she wrote bravely about lynchings in Memphis, Tennessee, and kept statistics on their frequency.

In 1893, the year she had met Ferdinand, he helped her and Frederick Douglass write and circulate an 81-page booklet lamenting the fact that black people were not represented at the Columbian Exposition being held in Chicago.

Months before their wedding, Ida went on anti-lynching crusades in British and American cities. Returning home in June, she found that faithful friends and Ferdinand had made all the preparations. "The large double parlors had been turned into a bower of beauty, filled with ferns and palms and roses," she wrote in her autobiography. They'd even gotten her a wedding dress!

As Ida Wells-Barnett, she became editor and publisher of the *Conservator*, the first newspaper for African-Americans in Chicago. Her campaigns for racial equality never stopped, even with the births of 4 children. Eventually, Ida met with Presidents McKinley and Wilson, and with members of Congress.

# JUNE 28
## HARRY S. TRUMAN & ELIZABETH WALLACE
### *"Dearest Bess"*

HARRY AND BESS'S 1919 WEDDING WAS held at Trinity Episcopal Church in Independence, Missouri, 6 weeks after his army discharge, 9 years after their courtship began, and 6 years after Bess said yes!

They'd grown up together in Independence. Bess was athletic, pretty, and popular, and had lots of beaux besides Harry. But he never wanted any other girl. "Please get ready to march down the aisle with me as soon as you decently can," he wrote from Europe. "I'm busted financially, but I love you as madly as a man can and I'll find other things." He also mentioned that he'd like to invite a few army friends to the wedding, if possible.

Bess wrote back and confessed that she, too, was eager to get married. Like Harry, she was 35-years old. "You may invite the entire 35th Division… if you want," she said. "I guess we might as well have the church full while we are at it."

The day was a scorcher. Flowers and wedding guests were wilting by the time bridesmaids wearing pastel-colored dresses proceeded to the altar at 4pm, followed by the groom in a 3-piece gray suit. In Harry's pocket was Bess's gold wedding ring, which he'd purchased at Tiffany's in New York City on his way home. She wore a white georgette crepe dress and picture hat, carried roses, and was escorted by her brother. After the ceremony, everyone celebrated with ice cream and punch. One of Harry's former army buddies wished him luck in a letter, saying he hoped that Harry's "new war" brought him as much success as the "old one."

The newlyweds drove off in Harry's roadster for a trip to Chicago, Detroit, and the beaches along Lake Huron. Their stay must have been pure bliss because "Port Huron" became Harry's special phrase to Bess from then on, referring to their happiness on their honeymoon.

# JUNE 29

## CHARLOTTE BRONTE & ARTHUR BELL NICHOLLS

*"As to my husband – my heart is knit to him"*

∽

"WOULD THAT CHARLOTTE'S LITERARY FRIENDS COULD have seen her," wrote her good friend Ellen after the wedding in 1854. "A halo of happiness seemed to surround her." Even before Charlotte and Arthur became engaged that March, her father, Reverend Bronte, had opposed their relationship. He didn't think that Arthur, a mere curate of Haworth Parish in Yorkshire, was worthy of Charlotte, already the well-known author of *Jane Eyre* and other works.

But Charlotte would not be swayed. Hadn't she dealt with sexual longings and the passion to be "absolutely bone of his bone, flesh of his flesh" in her novels? She was 38-years old and would marry for love. "Providence offers me this destiny," she said. Arthur adored her and would be a deeply devoted husband.

"Reader, I married him," she had written in *Jane Eyre*. Seven years after it was completed, she married Arthur before breakfast at the Haworth Church. When her father refused to give Charlotte away, her friend Miss Wooler stepped in and took his place. Only a few friends attended the ceremony, but news leaked out quickly and a crowd of villagers gathered outside the church to greet the newly-wedded couple. Charlotte wore a white embroidered muslin dress with a white lace veil and a bonnet trimmed with green leaves, and some people said she resembled a "snow drop."

Her life had changed remarkably. Now she would be wanted all the time, and that was a "marvelously good thing," she wrote afterwards. She had been writing since the age of 11, and stopped soon after her marriage. She and Arthur honeymooned in Ireland, touring the countryside and meeting his relatives, who said she had married one of the "best gentlemen in the country."

"No kinder, better husband than mine, it seems to me, can there be in the world," she concluded.

# JUNE 30

## ROBERT E. LEE & MARY ANNE RANDOLPH CUSTIS
### *His southern belle*

I T RAINED HEAVILY ON THE DAY Lieutenant Lee married Mary in 1831. The Reverend Keith arrived soaking wet, having traveled on horseback to the Custis mansion in Arlington, Virginia. The tall, thin minister stood in the grand foyer, puddles forming at his feet. Could anyone lend him dry clothing? The groomsmen, who were army friends of Robert's, had only their uniforms. The short, chubby father of the bride had spare civilian trousers and a coat, which he gave to the reverend. He put them on, but nothing fit well, causing some guests to titter.

At last, the drawing room doors were opened, and under a large beribboned floral bell suspended from the ceiling, the bridal party of 6 groomsmen and 6 bridesmaids filed in, followed by Mary and her father.

The future general of the Confederate army and his new wife shared a common heritage. Robert's father, "Light-Horse Harry," had fought with George Washington in the Revolutionary War, and Mary was the great-granddaughter of Martha Washington. Mary and Robert would name their first child George Washington Custis Lee.

Robert was 24 and had proposed to Mary by the dining room sideboard as she served him a piece of fruitcake. All afternoon, he'd been reading Sir Walter Scott's new novel to Mary and her mother. When he left the room for something to eat, mother encouraged daughter to follow him. It was Robert's only chance to be alone with her that day, and he surely made the most of it.

Mary was 23 and would always be one of the brightest lights in Robert's life. Years later, on their wedding anniversary, he wrote to her from a Civil War battlefield. "Do you remember what a happy day 33 years ago this was? How many hopes and pleasures it gave birth to!"

# JULY

# JULY 1
## DWIGHT DAVID EISENHOWER &
## MARY GENEVA DOUD
*She <u>really</u> liked Ike!*

LIKE MANY YOUNG COUPLES FACING WARTIME separations, "Ike" and "Mamie" moved up their wedding day in 1916. They'd known each other less than a year, and had met at a Texas army base where he was stationed. Ike was 26 and immediately taken with the "saucy" brown-haired girl with bright blue eyes. She was 19 and thought the junior officer was "just about the handsomest man" she had ever seen.

Ike telephoned Mamie the next day, and asked for a date. She said she was booked for weeks, but he persisted. When she added that she usually was home each day by 5 o'clock, he said he'd be there tomorrow. It didn't take long to convince her to cancel all future plans not involving him.

Both the bride and groom wore white when they married in her parents' home in Denver. Ike wouldn't sit down in his tropical dress uniform until after the ceremony, keeping the creases in his trousers razor-sharp. Mamie wore a dress of white Chantilly lace. As usual, her hair was in bangs over her forehead. They honeymooned at Eldorado Springs for 2 days and then went to Abilene, Kansas where she met Ike's family.

Mamie hung up a "Bless This House" plaque in their tiny apartment on the base, and displayed it in all their future homes. She rented a piano and encouraged Ike's buddies to drop by for beer and food, prompting them to nickname the place, "Club Eisenhower."

Ike and Mamie moved 35 times in the first 35 years of their marriage, and finally "settled down" for 8 years in the White House. She'd get upset when people said that as an army wife, she should be used to Ike's being away. "I never got used to his being gone," she explained. "He was my husband. He was my whole life."

# JULY 2

## KING CAMP GILLETTE & ATLANTA ELLA GAINES
### *Look sharp!*

KING WAS A CLEAN-SHAVEN TRAVELING HARDWARE sales-man when he married "Lantie" in Ohio in 1890. Her father, a wealthy oilman, listened to King's stories about life on the road, and was impressed by his determination to succeed.

King's mother, Fanny Camp Gillette, had written the *White House Cook Book*, and his father and brothers were always tinkering with one invention or another. So it's not surprising that when King started representing the Baltimore Seal Company, he accepted the advice of his boss, William Painter: "Think up something useful, like my 'Crown cork' bottle stopper." Painter had invented a non-reusable cork-lined tin cap that sealed in carbonation so well, it revolutionized the bottling industry.

One morning, in a hotel room in Boston, King realized that the blade of his straight razor was particularly dull. Stropping it on a strap wouldn't do enough; it needed professional sharpening by a barber or a cutler. On his way downtown, King impulsively purchased a small vise, pieces of brass, filing tools, and some very thin steel ribbon. Then he sent a telegram to Lantie, who was visiting relatives in Ohio, and said, "I HAVE GOT IT…. OUR FUTURE IS MADE!"

No significant improvements had been made to razor blades in a long time, but as America moved into the 20th century, efficiency experts were talking about ways to save time and money. King envisioned fashioning a 2-edged paper-thin razor blade so inexpensive to produce and purchase, it could be thrown away when it became dull. In 1903, he sold 51 razors and 168 blades. A year later – 90,000 razors and 12,400,000 blades. Lantie was thrilled, as was their son, baby "Kingie," who had hated Daddy's scratchy face and no longer yelped when Daddy kissed him!

# JULY 3
## LUCY APSLEY & JOHN HUTCHINSON
### *He could "beget love in anyone at the first"*

JOHN WAS ATTRACTED TO LUCY EVEN before they met in 1637. That spring, he had come from London to Richmond for the social "season." Impressed by all the scholarly books at the Apsleys' home, he was doubly awed to learn that they belonged to Lucy, who was out for the day. Afterwards, he called on the Apsleys several times, but Lucy never seemed to be at home. There's magic in that house, a friend warned him; men who got involved with the Apsley daughters usually ended up marrying them. But the more Lucy avoided John, the more he longed to see her.

She thought he would be conventional and superficial, like most young men she knew. She even told her footman to show him a pair of bridal shoelaces she'd worn to a wedding, implying that she herself was married. But John's intelligence and sincerity surprised Lucy when they met. He also had the "most amiable countenance, which carried in it something of magnanimity and majesty mixed with sweetness," she wrote later. They became inseparable, taking walks and discussing philosophy – and exasperating friends who envied the closed circle of love they soon built around themselves.

After they married at St. Andrew's Church in Holborn in 1638, John began studying for the ministry. Lucy gave birth to 2 sons and also translated 6 works of Lucretius into verse. Years later, she wrote *Memoirs of Colonel Hutchinson*, in which she described 17th century England during the civil war – a time when some Puritans sailed to the New World and others, such as John and Lucy, chose to stay and become caught up in those turbulent times.

Although Lucy was a Puritan, living an outward life of restraint and self-control, she wrote of John, "… never was there a passion more ardent and less idolatrous; he loved her better than his life, with inexpressible tenderness and kindnesses…."

# JULY 4

## JAMES JOYCE & NORA BARNACLE
*"yes, I said yes I will Yes."*

J AMES AND NORA WERE MARRIED IN London on his father's birthday in 1931, 27 years after they eloped and fled the religiously oppressive world of Ireland for the Continent.

They had met on June 10, 1904, on Nassau Street in Dublin. James was 22, writing and sometimes selling poems and stories. He was immediately taken with the red-haired 20-year old chambermaid from Finn's Hotel down the block. Six months before, Nora had run away from her family's home in Galway. Now, James asked her to meet him 4 days later. When she didn't show up, he sent a note, beseeching her for another "appointment… if you have not forgotten me! – James A. Joyce."

She hadn't forgotten. They went walking on June 16th, a day James would immortalize as *the* day on which the events of his famous novel, *Ulysses*, took place. By July, his letters to Nora were passionate: "Your glove lay beside me all night – unbuttoned – but otherwise conducted itself very properly – like Nora…. A twenty-five minute kiss upon thy neck. Jim."

October 8th, barely four months after they met, they left for Switzerland where he believed a job was waiting at a Berlitz language school. When they arrived, however, no job was available. James and Nora continued on to Pola, on the Adriatic Sea, and then to Trieste, where he gave language lessons and wrote most of his stories for *The Dubliners*. The following year, James worked at a bank in Rome and spent his spare time planning *The Dead*, and a story called *Ulysses*.

When Nora ran off with James, he hadn't even said that he loved her, although she had admitted that she loved him. But she knew she was the woman he had chosen to take with him, and that he was deeply happy she had agreed to go.

# JULY 5

## HORACE GREELEY & MARY CHENEY

*Love for "Hod" brought her back*

PRESBYTERIAN MINISTER SYLVESTER GRAHAM WAS TALK-
ING about his healthy crackers, and encouraging his audience to taste
them, when "Hod" glanced at the young woman sitting nearby. It was
1835, and he had been in New York City for 4 years. He had started out as
a printer but soon was writing articles and editorials for small newspapers.
Hod's new weekly magazine, *The New Yorker*, contained plenty of local news,
as well as poetry and stories. Now, he came to Graham's lecture as an interested journalist, but was distracted by Mary's astute questions and charm.
She was 22 years old, and had masses of dark hair he was sorely tempted to
touch....

"Have a Graham cracker?" she asked him.

The minister's prescription for good health seemed sensible: vegetarian
meals made with plenty of brown Graham flour; no coffee, tea or alcohol;
cold baths; loose clothing; and sleeping with the windows open. Mary lived
at Graham's boardinghouse; now Hod moved in, too. It enabled him to see a
lot of Mary.

She was a schoolteacher who'd grown up in Cornwall, Connecticut. Hod
was 24 and came from New Hampshire. He was enterprising, intelligent, and
on his way to becoming a well-known journalist, firebrand, and conscience of
the people, inspiring or infuriating many factions. During the Panic of 1837,
he'd be telling unemployed workers in crowded eastern cities to "Go west,
young man!"

Mary was bright, well read, and very knowledgeable about current events.
But after a few months she accepted a teaching position in North Carolina,
and left town. Hod missed her terribly, and wrote to her constantly. In spring,
1836, he described a house he'd rented at 124 Greenwich Street, large enough
for a literary salon on Friday nights. They could live there quite happily, he
wrote, if only she would marry him.

Mary wrote back right away, saying there was nothing she wanted more.

# JULY 6

## GEORGE, DUKE OF YORK, & PRINCESS MARY OF TECK

*"my sweet little 'May'"*

GROWING UP WITH AN OLDER BROTHER, "Georgie" never expected to become king of England. He also never thought he would marry his brother's fiancée, but that's exactly what happened. When Prince Eddy died suddenly in 1892, royal plans changed with remarkable speed, and Princess Mary received a second marriage proposal – from Eddy's brother, Prince George. His grandmother, Queen Victoria, pushed him to do it by giving him a dukedom, an income, and 2 houses. The next thing he needed was a wife. Write to "May," Victoria suggested gently.

Georgie and May were both painfully shy, but they spent time together on the French Riviera where their families had gone to assuage their grief. In 1893, the young couple were married in the Chapel Royal at St. James's Palace. Georgie's parents gave May a spectacular diamond necklace, which is what they had intended to give her in the first place.

The groom's mother, the Princess of Wales, faced a double sadness: her elder son had died, and now she had "lost" her beloved second son, too. She turned to her 3 daughters for comfort, and the 4 women banded together, excluding May from informal get-togethers and even barging in unannounced at the newlyweds' home.

May bore their treatment stoically, and Georgie was deeply grateful for this. Although he was still to shy to talk openly about love, he conveyed his growing feelings for May in a letter: "When I asked you to marry me, I was very fond of you, but not very much in love with you," he confessed. "but… I know now that … *I adore you sweet May*. I can't say more than that."

After King Edward VII died in 1910, Georgie became King George V, and May became his queen. They reigned for 28 years. (Watch the 2010 film, *The King's Speech*, and you'll understand even more!)

# JULY 7
## JIMMY CARTER & ROSALYNN SMITH
### *Best friends*

ENSIGN CARTER PICKED UP ROSALYNN AT her home on the day they married in 1946, and drove her to the Methodist church in Plains, Georgia. They arrived a few minutes late, Rosalynn remembered years later. The wedding march was being played as "Jimmy grabbed my hand and literally pulled me up the church steps."

The place was packed. No invitations had been sent, but it seemed as if everyone in town knew about the nuptials and wanted to be there. What no one knew was that these "small town kids" would eventually become president and first lady of the United States.

Rosalynn had fallen in love with Jimmy's picture before they met, because her best friend (and his kid sister) Ruth, had shown it to her. He was 20 when he came home from Annapolis one summer, and finally asked 17-year old Rosalynn to go out. As she recalled, in *First Lady from Plains*, "The moon was full in the sky, conversation came easy and I was in love with a real person now, not just a photograph." On the way home that night, she let Jimmy kiss her.

The following Christmas, he gave her a silver compact engraved with "ILYTG"—for "I Love You the Goodest," a phrase that became especially dear to them.

Their early married years were spent in the navy, moving from one base to another. Later, Jimmy described this time as "one of constant separation interspersed with ecstatic reunions." At first, Rosalynn deferred to Jimmy's needs and career, as most wives did in postwar America. But later, she asserted herself more and played an active role in family plans and decision-making. She and Jimmy became true partners – managing the family peanut business, serving in the governor's mansion, and in the White House, too.

# JULY 8

## GUSTAVE EIFFEL & MARIE GAUDELET

*His plans were extraordinaire!*

ALTHOUGH GUSTAV DIDN'T DESIGN HIS AMAZING tower until many years after he married Marie in 1862, he was known, already, as an up-and-coming French engineer. He hadn't intended to become one, but a few years earlier, his uncle, the owner of a successful vinegar factory in Dijon, had severed family ties after foolishly quarreling over politics. Realizing that he no longer was welcome in his uncle's business, Gustav joined a civil engineering company specializing in steam engines and other railway equipment.

Unlike some other families in town with more aristocratic lineage, the Eiffels were considered *nouveau riche*. Many parents didn't think Gustav was socially acceptable or good enough for their marriageable daughters. "I shall be satisfied with a girl with a medium-sized dowry and passable looks," as well as "a good disposition and simplicity of taste," he wrote to his mother. Marie, whose grandfather was a business associate of Gustav's father, was all of that and more.

He was 29 and she was 18 when they married in Dijon and moved to an apartment in Paris. A year later, their first child, Claire, was born, and she would be followed by 2 more daughters and 2 sons. Marie was sweet-tempered, loving and unpretentious, accepting her husband's long hours and frequent trips to oversee projects.

Within 5 years, he was designing iron arch girders for the Palace of Machines at the upcoming Paris Universal Exposition, held in 1867. By 1884, Gustav was known as France's master builder in metal, having planned and built many bridges and viaducts, as well as the steel interiors supporting Frederic Bartholdi's Statue of Liberty. Next would come Gustav's most incredible achievement, celebrating the centenary of the French Revolution. The Eiffel tower was intended to be a temporary structure, but it has remained the crowning glory of Paris.

## JULY 9

## NATHANIEL HAWTHORNE & SOPHIA AMELIA PEABODY

*"My beloved, you make a Heaven roundabout you."*

NATHANIEL AND SOPHIE FELL IN LOVE in 1838 but delayed their marriage for 4 years because of her fragile health and his reluctance to share his joy with his widowed, sorrowful mother.

Sophie and her sisters had read Nathaniel's *Twice-Told Tales* and invited him to visit them in Salem, Massachusetts. He lived nearby, and often took long walks through town, passing Gallows Hill and other sites of the 17th century witch trials. Nathaniel's family was descended from one of the "hanging judges," and thoughts about that dark time in history would always influence his work.

Nathaniel enjoyed spending time with the Peabodys, and was particularly drawn to Sophie's artistic talents, soft femininity, and gentleness. Within a year, they were secretly engaged and exchanging long, romantic letters, calling each other "dearest Wife" and "lovingest Husband."

"How happy were Adam and Eve," Nathaniel wrote. "All the infinity around them only served to press their hearts closer together," for they had no other people – such as his withdrawn, moody mother and Sophie's overbearing, protective family – to come between them.

Sophie was 33 when she married Nathaniel in the Peabodys' parlor on West Street, 5 days after his 38th birthday. After a brief celebration, they drove to Concord. "Every step the horses took, I felt better and not in the least tired," she wrote to her mother. "It seemed miraculous that I was so well."

Sophie's good health continued at The Manse, a home rented from Nathaniel's friend Ralph Waldo Emerson and decorated as a surprise by Louisa May Alcott's mother. Another unexpected wedding gift was a vegetable garden, dug and planted by Henry David Thoreau.

"Say what you will," wrote Sophie, "there never was such a husband to enrich the world since it sprang out of chaos. I feel precisely like an Eve in Paradise."

## JULY 10
## ISABELLA MAYSON & SAMUEL BEETON
### *"Bella figlia con amore"*

I N 1861, MOST ENGLISH WOMEN WHO read *Mrs. Beeton's Book of Household Management* probably imagined the author was a kindly, white-haired old lady – not a bright, spirited young woman. But Isabella was only 21 when she sat down to write her domestic encyclopedia, a year after she married Sam in 1856.

He had already made a name for himself in publishing, and Isabella's parents were pleased with the match. Four years before, Sam had arranged for a British edition of *Uncle Tom's Cabin* and invested his earnings in new publications such as *The Englishwoman's Domestic Magazine*, filled with articles about hobbies, crafts, and the latest fashions. Victorian women began buying it regularly.

Sam and Isabella corresponded daily from her home in Epsom to his London office. He was ardent, enthusiastic, and charming. She was romantic, energetic, and brimming with self-confidence. They courted for a year, and shortly before their wedding, she closed her last letter by saying, "Trusting you are perfectly serene and happy as your humble servant, and that I shall see you jolly on Thursday morning, believe me, my loved one, yours eternally, Bella."

After a 3-week honeymoon in France, Isabella set up their small house in Pinner, Middlesex, and joined Sam's staff. She wrote articles and collected information on household topics such as handling domestic help, keeping accounts, planning menus, solving legal problems, overseeing nursery care, hosting dinner parties, caring for invalids, polishing furniture, and getting out stains. When she and Sam realized that she had enough material for a book, she concentrated on it full-time. It was published in 1861, and more than 60,000 copies were sold in the first year.

"A place for everything, and everything in its place," Isabella wrote. Although few people know who first penned those oft-repeated words, all of us know that it's good advice.

# JULY 11

## ALEXANDER GRAHAM BELL & MABEL HUBBARD

*Read my lips – I love you*

"I HAVE DISCOVERED THAT MY INTEREST in my dear pupil has ripened into a far deeper feeling…. I have learned to love her," Alec wrote Mabel's mother in 1875. He'd been teaching her daughter visible speech, also called lip-reading, at her Cambridge, Massachusetts home. The 27-year old Scotsman had been too preoccupied by his scientific inventions to think about romance, but Mabel changed all that. Deafened by scarlet fever when she was 5 years old, she was now 17 and lovely to behold. On evening strolls, they'd pause under lampposts while Alec spoke and Mabel read his lips. Continuing their walk, she'd talk to him in the darkness until they reached the next lamppost, where Alec could reply.

His income was small and she was fairly young, so her parents asked Alec to wait at least a year before proposing marriage. "You can't support her on magnetism and electric wires," Mr. Hubbard said. "That, sir, is precisely how I intend to support her!" Alec declared. He hoped to figure out a way to enable deaf people to hear, and attempts to transmit sound from one place to another by means of electric current led him to invent the telephone.

Eager to marry Mabel, Alec tried selling some of his patents to the Western Union Telegraph Company, but they weren't interested. So Alec kept on working and taking financial aid from supporters – including Mr. Hubbard, who wasn't skeptical any more. Alec's telephone was still a novelty, and some even called him "Crazy Bell" when he married Mabel in 1877 in the Hubbards' parlor. The newlyweds honeymooned at Niagara Falls and visited Alec's family in Canada, where his cousins followed an old Scottish wedding custom of breaking oatcakes over Mabel's head.

She didn't know it, but financially, she was set for life. Alec's wedding gifts to Mabel were jewelry… and all but 10 of his 1,507 shares of Bell Telephone Company stock!

# JULY 12

## ISIDOR STRAUS & ROSALIE IDA BLUN

*"As we have lived, so will we die – together!"*

Ida and Isidor were young children when their families emigrated from Germany to the United States before the Civil War. Isidor's father opened a general store in Georgia, where his sons learned all about the retail business. Soon after war's end, Isidor and his brother Nathan, headed to New York City and rented space to sell crockery and glassware in a Manhattan department store owned by R.H. Macy. By 1896, they owned the entire store!

She was 22 and he was 26 years old when they married in New York in 1871. Isidor became a trusted friend and advisor to President Grover Cleveland, a U.S. Congressman from New York City in the mid-1890's, and a generous contributor to Jewish and secular causes. Ida was a traditional homemaker, caring for their large household, seven children, and Isidor. They wrote to each other daily, whenever they were apart.

In April, 1912, after touring Europe for several months, the Strauses set sail for home from Southampton England. Usually, they traveled on German ships, but this time, they booked passage on the maiden voyage of *RMS Titanic*. It collided with an iceberg on the fourth night, and sank the following morning. Roughly 2/3 of the 2,220 passengers and crew drowned in the Atlantic because of an insufficient number of lifeboats.

In the darkness of the ice-cold early morning hours of April 15th, when the time came for Ida to evacuate the ship and step into a lifeboat, she chose to remain aboard with Isidor. Crew members had urged him to leave, too, because of his poor health, advanced age, and first-class status, but Isidor refused to accept a life-saving seat ahead of women and children.

"We have been living together for many years, and where you go, I go," Ida told him, according to survivors who overheard her words. After 41 years of marriage, she would not be parted from her husband. Amid frenzied turmoil, cries of pain and grief, and prayers called out in a cacophony of languages, Ida confronted the existential reality that there was no more future, only *now*, and she made her decision. As the lifeboats pulled away from the doomed ship, witnesses recalled seeing Ida and Isidor on deck, clinging to each other in a warm embrace. Dying together was a very small part of their long-married life, but a final confirmation of their love. Today, a memorial fountain and sculpture in their memory stand in Straus Park on West 106th Street, not far from their home.

# JULY 13
## WALT DISNEY & LILLIAN BOUNDS
### *Mickey's parents*

WHEN WALT'S OLDER BROTHER AND BUSINESS partner Roy got married in April, 1925, Walt started thinking about matrimony, too. Until then, the 23-year old cartoonist had been too busy making animated films and setting up their new company in a small studio over a garage in Los Angeles.

Lillian had come from Idaho to visit her sister, found a job at the Disney studio, and decided to stay in California. She worked in the inking and painting department, copying cartoon drawings onto celluloid. Although Lillian's work was tedious, she liked the office, where everyone dressed informally and was on a first-name basis. Sometimes, on late rainy nights, Walt gave Lillian and another young woman rides home in his jalopy. Soon he was hanging around Lillian's work station all the time, and even bought a suit to impress her.

Three months after Roy's wedding, Walt and Lillian were married in her brother's home in Idaho. They spent their wedding night on a train bound for Seattle, where Walt made an emergency visit to a dentist for an infected tooth before he and Lillian embarked on a steamer to Long Beach, California. Walt relaxed aboard ship, enjoying the sea air and his new wife. He was wonderfully sweet, Lillian wrote her mother, and she was "divinely happy."

Walt assumed more responsibilities at work and changed the company's name to the Walt Disney Studio. He and Lillian settled into a $40-a-month one-room apartment with "kitchen privileges," within walking distance of his Hyperion Avenue offices.

Before they became the parents of two daughters, Walt and Lillian celebrated the "birth" of another "child" in 1928. Walt considered naming the little mouse Mortimer, but Lillian had a better idea – Mickey.

# JULY 14*
## WILLIAM OF NORMANDY & MATILDA OF FLANDERS
### *A new dynasty begins*

WILLIAM'S "CONQUEST" OF MATILDA HAPPENED LONG before he conquered England. He'd been a fearless fighter in Normandy, overthrowing power-hungry nobles in his own duchy several times before his 21st birthday. Then he met Matilda, the petite blond daughter of the count of Flanders, and niece of King Henry I of France. But she was not impressed with the "lowborn" young man who usually slept on stable floors, and she announced that she would rather be a "veiled nun" than marry him. Her opposition only inspired William to woo her more forcefully.

Some say that one day, in the town of Bruges, William dismounted from his horse, grabbed Matilda and pulled her down into the mud, where the two "lovers" rolled around for a few minutes. That done, William got up and rode off, and soon afterward Matilda agreed to marry him.

In another version, William stormed into her father's palace one night and tramped upstairs to Matilda's apartments. He seized her by the hair and dragged her about the floor. Then he leaped onto his trusty steed and rode off again. In either case, Matilda knew she was marrying a strong-willed man.

They probably married in 1053 in a church at Eu, by the Norman and Flemish border. Matilda was 21. She wore a fur-trimmed wool mantle and rode on a white mule. At 25, William was decked out in a red cape, purple boots, and a crown decorated with gold oak leaves.

Unlike many monarchs, William never took a mistress after marriage. He and Matilda were devoted to each other. He made her regent – a rare distinction at that time. They built monasteries in Normandy and hospitals for the blind and aged.

In 1066, after William's cousin King Edward the Confessor died, William won the Battle of Hastings and claimed England's throne. Matilda wasn't the least surprised!

---

*Date approximate.

# JULY 15

## THOMAS GAINSBOROUGH & MARGARET BURR
### *She loved posing for him*

IN 1745, MARGARET VISITED HER OLDER brother, who worked in the wool business in Sudbury, England. She'd already heard of his boss's artistic son, Tom, who'd been living in London for several years, struggling to establish himself as a portrait painter. But Tom's income was too unpredictable. Dejected and unable to support himself, recently he had moved back home.

Tom probably saw Margaret first in the woods of Suffolk County, where he took long walks and painted pastoral scenes of cows grazing in the fields or birds taking wing. He offered to paint Margaret's portrait and was delighted when she accepted. The sittings were frequent and protracted until, at last, a beautiful likeness was achieved. Margaret, it has been suggested, then smiled at Tom and hinted subtly that perhaps someday he might "own" the original! Her family history was somewhat mysterious; she never knew who her father was, but it's likely that he was an aristocrat because he had established a handsome lifelong annuity for her.

The following summer, when Tom was 19 and Margaret was 18, they traveled by coach to London and were married in Mayfair Chapel. No public art galleries existed at the time, so they were thrilled when Tom was commissioned to paint a scene of London on a Foundling Hospital wall, one of the few places for artists to display their work.

Soon he was longing for the countryside again, and they moved to the seaport town of Ipswich. Fortunately, Margaret's income enabled Tom to paint only those portraits or scenes that inspired him. His paintings were filled with the lyrical charm and wistfulness for which he became known. On the rare occasions when Tom and Margaret argued, he apologized by writing a note and signing it "Fox," his dog's name. Fox delivered the message to Margaret, and her dog Tristan brought back her reply.

# JULY 16

## MICHAEL J. FOX & TRACY POLLAN
### *"Alex" and "Ellen"*

By the time Michael met Tracy in 1985, the Canadian-born, 24-year old actor had already won 3 Emmy awards for his starring role as Alex Keaton in the TV sitcom, "Family Ties." Tracy was 25 when she joined the cast as Ellen Reed, an art student and Alex's onscreen girlfriend. His character fell in love, and the show's ratings soared!

"I suddenly had a partner," Michael recalled later, in a memoir. Although Tracy appeared in only 7 episodes, her impact on Michael would be life-long. She "had an earthiness, integrity, and talent that demanded I push my own work to a higher level."

Tracy was seriously involved with another actor, Kevin Bacon, and left the show at the end of the season. In 1987, she and Michael met again, on the New York City film set of "Bright Lights, Big City." This time, they fell in love for real, and were engaged within months.

Tabloid-writers and celebrity-hunters tried zealously to crash the wedding, and helicopters hired by TV news shows flew over the determined location. But Michael and Tracy succeeded in having the small-scale, simple and private affair that they wanted. The ceremony was held outdoors *under a tent* beside the West Mountain Inn in Arlington, Vermont. The heat inside the tent tempted the just-married bride and groom to step outside for a moment and wave to the circling paparazzi, but the newlyweds knew that one or two images would never have been enough.

Keeping their married life as private as possible is a decision Michael and Tracy have maintained ever since, and it has helped them handle the difficulties that have followed Michael's diagnosis of Parkinson's disease only 3 years later. The Michael J. Fox Foundation continues to raise millions of dollars for research.

After they'd been married 20 years, someone asked Michael what keeps a marriage happy and long. "Keep the fights clean and the sex dirty," he said.

# JULY 17

## SID CAESAR & FLORENCE LEVY

*'the most beautiful girl...'*

"OY VEY!" SAID FLORENCE'S FATHER.

"WHAT'S the hurry?" said Sid's mother before the wedding in 1943. Sid and Florence were each only 20 years old, and he was on active duty in the Coast Guard. Would Mr. Levy's son-in-law ever amount to anything? Within 10 years, the kid from Yonkers New York was one of the funniest men on television, starring in *Your Show of Shows* and *Caesar's Hour*.

In 1942, Sid and Florence met at the Avon Lodge, her uncle's Catskill Mountains hotel. She was a Hunter College student working for the summer, and Sid had just been hired as a comedian and saxophone player. "I saw her near the office and thought, 'Wow! That's the most beautiful girl I've ever seen,'" Sid wrote years later in *Where Have I Been?* Florence was tall, blue-eyed, blond, intelligent, and classy. Expecting no more than a summer romance, Sid promptly told her he was in love. Florence usually preferred more serious boys, but she was willing to go steady with Sid for a while.

In the evenings, they danced together whenever Sid wasn't performing, until her uncle told him to go dance with some of the "ugly girls." Soon Florence began to realize how bright Sid was. He knew a lot about classical music and loved to read history, explaining that understanding the habits, opinions and daily activities of people throughout the centuries often inspired great comedy routines.

That October, Sid was sent to a navy base in Brooklyn and got the chance to produce and perform in skits, shows, and musical revues for servicemen – including a ludicrous conversation between Donald Duck and Adolf Hitler – with Sid playing both parts. Off duty, he always saw Florence. The following summer they were married in a restaurant on Manhattan's Lower East Side. She always was Sid's most devoted audience and friend.

# JULY 18

## EDNA ST. VINCENT MILLAY & EUGEN BOISSEVAIN
### *She burned her candle "at both ends"*

"DO YOU REMEMBER MEETING EUGEN BOISSEVAIN one day in Waverly Place?" Edna wrote her mother in May 1923. When the red-haired, green-eyed poet composed her letter, she was confident that her mother had liked Eugen. It mattered a lot, for Edna had decided to marry him.

After living on her own for 10 years in Greenwich Village, 31-year-old Edna had fallen in love fast. She had already won fame for "Renascence" and other poems published when she was a student at Vassar College. Now, friends had introduced her to Eugen, a genial, spirited, and sensitive 43-year old Dutch-Irish coffee importer. Although he was not artistically talented, he loved being around creative people.

One evening, they participated in an impromptu skit by turning around the conventional plot of country bumpkins corrupted by life in the big city. Instead, Edna and Eugen played an innocent young couple from the city who fall prey to sinister and corrupt country folks. By the end of Act Three, Edna and Eugen wouldn't part from each other.

She won the Pulitzer Prize for Poetry shortly before they married, but poor health dampened the celebrations. After the wedding in Croton-on-Hudson, Edna underwent intestinal surgery and Eugen nursed her tirelessly. The following year they took a leisurely trip to the Orient, inspiring her to write poems including "For Pao-Chin," about the Chinese boatman who played his flute as they sailed along in his junk.

Eventually, Eugen would quit his business to manage "Vincie's" affairs. He took care of her and Steepletop, their home in Austerlitz, New York, handling all the chores and petty details of everyday life so Edna could work undisturbed. "Anybody can buy and sell coffee," he said, "but not anyone can write poetry."

# JULY 19

## DAPHNE DU MAURIER & SIR FREDERICK A.M. BROWNING

### *Her book and "Ygdrasil" brought them together*

I N LATE SUMMER OF 1931, DAPHNE fixed her field glasses on a motorboat cruising Fowey harbor in Cornwall, England, and caught sight of Grenadier Guard Major Browning. She couldn't hear his voice, but the handsome 35-year old helmsman was telling his fellow officers that he'd recently read her novel, *The Loving Spirit*, and wished he could meet the author.

"Tommy" came back the following spring and sent Daphne a note, saying he was pretty sure their fathers used to know each other and would she come for a ride on his boat the next day? She wrote back that she would be "delighted."

Friday, April 8, was a "fine bright day with a cold wind," she recounted in *Daphne du Maurier: Enchanted Cornwall*, her pictorial memoir. He told her that everyone called him Tommy, and that his boat was named *Ygdrasil* after the Tree of Fate in Norse mythology. He returned to see Daphne again and again, "hatless, brown-leather jerkin, grey flannel trousers thrust into sea-boots… green eyes, and a smile that curled at one corner. Yes, no doubt about it, he was good."

The 25-year old storyteller who would continue to write award-winning tales about Cornwall had found a soul mate almost as passionately in love with the region as he was with her.

Daphne married Tommy in 1932 and began writing *Frenchman's Creek*. Five years later she completed *Rebecca*, her gothic novel about a woman's obsession. It won the National Book Award and was made into a film directed by Alfred Hitchcock. *Rebecca* also provided Daphne and Tommy with enough compensation to purchase and move into Menabilly, the supposedly haunted 70-room mansion that had inspired her to write her book about it.

# JULY 20

## PETE SEEGER & TOSHI-ALINE OHTA

### *Ballad of a long and happy marriage*

A FTER PETE CAME TO NEW YORK City in 1939, the future song-writer and folk singer lived on the Lower East Side while studying painting and looking for work as a journalist. Sometimes, he made money playing his banjo for a folk dance troupe; Toshi was at one of the get-togethers.

Her name meant "beginning of a new era." The daughter of a Japanese father and a Virginia-born mother, Toshi's American roots went back to Jim Bowie, the 19th century Texan who fought at the Alamo. Pete's family had been in the United States for 300 years, but he and Toshi always felt connected to outsiders and protest movements in America.

Pete was 24 and Toshi was a few years younger when they married in a Greenwich Village church in 1943. He'd been performing with Woody Guthrie and the Almanacs until he was drafted in 1942. During World War II, Pete served in the army's Special Services, singing and performing for troops. After his discharge, Pete, Toshi, and other singers set up People's Songs, a union of songwriters and a clearing house for folk songs. A few years later, he sang with a new group called the Weavers, performing old favorites such as "On Top of Old Smoky" and new tunes including "Kisses Sweeter Than Wine." In tents, concert halls, churches, meetinghouses—anywhere people would listen to him—Pete sang ballads, spirituals, lullabies, and work songs.

In 1949, Pete and Toshi built a house overlooking the Hudson River near Beacon, New York. Songs such as "Where Have All the Flowers Gone?" and "If I Had a Hammer" would follow, as would Pete and Toshi's efforts to clean up the Hudson by raising funds to build the *Clearwater*, a replica of a 19th century sloops that sails up and down the river, promoting conservation.

# JULY 21
## EDWARD MACDOWELL & MARIAN NEVINS
### *"Thy Beaming Eyes"*

EDWARD AND MARIAN WERE YOUNG AMERICANS in Germany when they met in Frankfurt's Conservatory of Music in 1881. He was a 19-year old composer, with bright blue eyes, black hair, and a reddish mustache, and she was a country-bred 23-year old from New England who hoped to become a concert pianist. During Edward's first two years at the Conservatory, he had already been noticed by composers such as the great Franz Lizst, and would become America's first internationally known composer.

Recently, Edward had been hired as head piano teacher at a conservatory in the town of Darmstadt. Finding it to be a dreary place, with dull, uninspiring students, he went back to Frankfurt regularly. There, Marian's aptitude and talent impressed him, and he offered her private lessons.

At first, the gifted teacher and his promising pupil talked only about music, but as the time approached for her return to America, they confessed their love for each other. In 1884, they married in Waterbury, Connecticut and honeymooned in London, where they saw Shakespeare's *Much Ado About Nothing*. Edward and Marian loved the play, and particularly enjoyed the gentle sparing between Beatrice and Benedick, another couple powerfully drawn to each other.

For a few years, the MacDowells lived in Germany, where Edward composed concertos, symphonic poems, and pieces for pianoforte, including *Opus 19: Forest Idyls*, which he dedicated to Marian. Eventually, he became the first professor of music at Columbia University in New York. He and Marian built a log cabin in the pines – "a house of dreams untold" – in Peterborough, New Hampshire, providing him with all the peace and solitude he needed for work. Kneeling before the newly finished fireplace hearth, he wrote, *"Edward – Marian – 1899"* in the damp cement. Many years later, Marian established the MacDowell Colony for artists in Peterborough; it's been a home and inspiration for countless artists ever since.

# JULY 22

## HARRY HOUDINI & BEATRICE RAYMOND

### *"The Master Monarchs of Modern Mysteries"*

T HE 1894 MARRIAGE OF 18-YEAR OLD "La Petite Bessie" and "Mysterious Harry" (Erich Weiss), the legendary 20-year old magician who walked through walls and escaped from straitjackets, leg irons, locked trunks, and Scotland Yard, was sudden, but not surprising.

He was 5 feet, 5 inches tall, with a winning smile and mesmerizing eyes. Bess was much shorter, was curvaceous and slim, had wavy brown hair and looked terrific in tights. She was one of the Floral Sisters, a song-and-dance act at Coney Island on the same bill with the Houdini Brothers.

One evening, Harry and his brother Theodore made a date with the sisters after the show. As they walked along the beach, Harry and Bess fell in love fast. Two weeks later, they disappeared… and came back married! The exact date of this event is debatable, although they celebrated it on June 22, and the *Coney Island Clipper* reported it, too. After getting married in a civil ceremony near Coney Island, the couple subsequently exchanged vows in two religious ceremonies to appease their Catholic and Jewish families. "I'm the most married woman I know," Bess used to say. "I've been married three times and all to the same man."

Soon, Bess replaced Theodore and joined Harry's show as his assistant. Within a year, they received their first major booking at Tony Pastor's Theater in Manhattan. They traveled extensively, and by 1904 they lived at 278 West 113th Street whenever they were in New York.

Some women joked that they envied Bess: how many wives spent their lives blindfolding, handcuffing, and padlocking their husbands inside watertight containers? Of course, Bess had other duties, too. She fell into trances, let Harry read her mind, and climbed into boxes so he could "saw her in half!"

## JULY 23
## PADRAIC COLUM & MARY MAGUIRE
*"Marry me," he suggested*

I N 1912, MARY WAS IN NO hurry to marry. "I did not have any taste for exchanging the independent and interesting life I was leading for pottering around in a kitchen, planning meals, hanging curtains and so on," she explained in her autobiography. A 24-year old university graduate, her circle of young talented Irish writer-friends in Dublin included the poet William Butler Yeats as well as the playwright and poet Padraic Collum.

One evening, a young man who wouldn't take no for an answer showed up at Mary's flat with an engagement ring and told her "that I had better accept my destiny." Mary had thought a great deal about the inferior position of women in the world, and was offended by the concept of someone else determining her "destiny." She threw the young man out and collapsed on the sofa.

A few minutes later, Padraic stopped by. They had met frequently at literary gatherings, and Mary wrote literary criticism for his journal, *The Irish Review*. Padraic was 30, soft-spoken and sensitive. He never felt threatened by competitive, bright women. After Mary told him what had happened, he came up with a way to get all the other fellows to stop bothering her: "I think that to save yourself trouble, you should marry me," he advised. Padraic's suggestions made perfect sense to Mary.

They were married by "an old scholarly bearded priest" in Dublin in a church called Star of the Sea, and then traveled to London for a few days. Two years later they sailed for the United States where Mary wrote literary criticism for well-regarded publications such as the *Saturday Review* and Padraic wrote plays, poetry, and children's books. He later taught comparative literature, she gave special lectures at Columbia University, and they collaborated on a biography of their friend, James Joyce.

## JULY 24
## MARIAN ANDERSON & ORPHEUS FISHER
### *Amazing grace*

"KING" WAITED 20 YEARS TO MARRY Marian. He first heard her sing at a benefit concert in Delaware, when she was a high school student from south Philadelphia. They chatted afterwards at a reception held in the Fisher home. It didn't take long for the tall, African-American architectural student to propose marriage to Marian, but he accepted her decision to fulfill her dream of becoming a great concert singer before she settled down.

Eventually, her extraordinary voice, combined with her quiet dignity and firm resolution to sing even under the most stressful conditions, brought Marian accolades and the title, "The World's Greatest Contralto." Her correspondence with King and their relationship during those years provided her with immeasurable support through glorious as well as appalling experiences. After Marian became famous, she refused to sing in segregated southern concert halls unless "vertical" seating arrangements were made, giving African-American ticket purchasers their own sections in every part of the auditorium.

In 1939 the Daughters of the American Revolution denied Marian the use of Washington's Constitution Hall, so she sang outdoors for more than 75,000 cheering Americans in front of the Lincoln Memorial. She would become the first African-American singer to perform at the White House and in New York City's Metropolitan Opera House; she also performed at the inaugurations of Presidents Eisenhower and Kennedy.

She and King were married at last at the Bethel Methodist Church in Bethel, Connecticut, in 1943. They bought 105 acres of land in nearby Danbury, and he built a dream house for them called Marianna Farms. There was room for horses, cows, chickens, a pond, and an apple orchard, as well as a separate music studio where Marian and her accompanist practiced freely – and loudly. "Marriage to King was worth waiting for," she said after their wedding.

# JULY 25

## MARC CHAGALL & BELLA ROSENFELD

*"blue air, love and flowers entered with her"*

"WHO IS THIS CHAGALL?" BELLA'S PARENTS asked in 1915. "An artist? He'll never earn a good living! You'll starve with him," they warned her. They knew she had been seeing Marc in his studio in Vitebsk, their tiny Russian village. She brought him sweet cakes, milk and fish to eat, and boards to use as easels. What they didn't know was that sometimes she also posed in the nude for him.

The Rosenfelds were well-to-do merchants who owned three jewelry stores. Marc's father was poor and worked in a herring warehouse. "What will people say?" Mrs. Rosenfeld fretted. But that summer, she acquiesced and stood proudly beside her husband when Bella married Marc under a bright red wedding canopy.

Five years earlier, Marc had gone to Paris to study art and had met many painters including Picasso, Braque, Modigliani, de Chirico, and Leger. Everyone inspired everyone else. They painted in riotous colors, shattering old conventions by breaking down images and reassembling them into unbelievably new combinations. It was a wonderful time to be an artist! Still, Marc missed Bella deeply. She sent him letters from college, saying she loved his enthusiasm, his laughter, and his sense of color, which inspired him to continue his studies. On one of his many trips home, he painted "Portrait of My Fiancée in Black Gloves," in which Bella poses confidently in a formfitting white dress.

Shortly before their wedding, Marc painted "Happy Birthday," commemorating one of Bella's visits to his studio. In the picture, he leaps into the air to kiss her. She, too, is on the verge of flying; the young lovers will remain blissfully entwined all their lives.

Bella was every bride Marc ever painted. "Her... eyes. How large, round, black they are!" he wrote. "They are my eyes, my soul."

## JULY 26
## MARIE SKLODOVSKA & PIERRE CURIE
### *"no better life companion"*

NEITHER MARIE NOR PIERRE BELIEVED THAT a life of scientific research could be combined with marriage… until they met at the Sorbonne in Paris in 1894. She was 27 and considered herself a spinster. He was a 35-year old professor and laboratory chief who had written, "women of genius are rare." But Pierre fell in love quickly with the physics and mathematics graduate student from Warsaw. He sent her a copy of his latest publication, "On Symmetry in Physical Phenomena." Not only did Marie understand it – she enjoyed it! They spent hours in her garret apartment in the Latin Quarter, sipping tea and discussing complicated theories.

Marie, whose family was extremely poor, had intended to work in Poland after completing her studies. Marriage to Pierre would mean settling in France instead. She went home that summer, but he begged her to come back. If she wouldn't marry, perhaps they could share an apartment, he suggested, "divided into two independent parts." The following winter Marie relented, telling a friend, "Fate has made us deeply attached to each other and we cannot endure the idea of separating."

Freethinkers, she and Pierre were married in a civil ceremony in Sceaux, his parents' village, in 1895. A relative offered to buy Marie a wedding dress, but she chose a practical navy blue suit "so that I can put it on afterwards and go to the laboratory."

The newlyweds purchased two bicycles with their wedding money and set off the following day on a month-long "wedding tramp" across the French countryside. Years later, after they made their Nobel Prize-winning discoveries in chemistry and physics, their daughter, Eve, wrote about their marriage and described their honeymoon, when "two hearts beat together, two bodies were united, and two minds of genius learned to think together."

## JULY 27

## HENRY MOORE & IRINA RADETZKY
### *"with love and kisses"*

I RINA WAS STUDYING PAINTING AT LONDON'S Royal College of Art when she met Henry in the autumn of 1928. She was 22-years old, slim and graceful, with limpid dark eyes and rich long hair. As she passed by the sculptor's studio one day, Henry looked up and thought, That woman is incredibly beautiful. Later, he would say that he married her because of her magnificent shoulders.

An English miner's son, Henry was 30 and already a well-known British sculptor who based much of his work on organic shapes found in natural rock formations and the landscape. A Royal College graduate, he taught students on a part-time basis, frequently declaring that "really serious artists shouldn't get married" and should remain devoted to their art, as did Michelangelo and Beethoven. But after Henry fell in love with Irina, he began talking about Rembrandt, who adored his wife, and Johann Sebastian Bach, who fathered 20 children!

Irina had immigrated to England with her mother and stepfather after their family lost everything during the Russian Revolution. Henry found her imperfect English charming. They parted at the end of the semester, and he wrote her many long letters. His first salutations were "Dear Irina," then "My dear," then "Dearest," she recalled. He closed with "my best wishes," then "with love," and then, "with love and kisses." "By the time the holiday was over, we were thick."

He courted her for nine months while he worked on "West Wind," a commissioned sculpture, followed by "Reclining Figure" for the city of Leeds, a piece that has been called his finest stone carving.

They married in 1929, three days before Henry's 31st birthday, and spent their honeymoon near Tintagel by the Cornish coast, at a boardinghouse that could be reached only by boat.

# JULY 28

## PRINCESS ANNE OF ENGLAND &
## PRINCE GEORGE OF DENMARK

### *Good friends*

SOON AFTER KING CHARLES II OF ENGLAND began thinking about a husband for his 18-year old niece, George's marriage proposal arrived from Denmark and was promptly accepted. Although the 1683 match had been arranged, the dark-haired, gentle-mannered princess who would become known as Good Queen Anne, the last and most beloved of the Stuarts, really did fall in love with the 30-year old tall, blond, sweet-natured prince.

Anne's childhood had been subdued and lonely. What she wanted most in a husband was constancy and companionship. At first, George spoke only a little English, making their conversations brief, but the betrothed couple seemed happy just spending time together, strolling in the gardens, playing cards, horseback riding, and visiting the zoo at the Tower of London. Evenings, they watched theatrical productions in the Cockpit, a small playhouse inside Whitehall Palace, overlooking St. James's Park.

Anne wore George's gift, a magnificent pearl necklace, when they married at 10 o'clock in the evening in the Chapel Royal at St. James's Palace. The bishop of London officiated and read from the Book of Common Prayer, reminding everyone that matrimony should be taken "reverently, discreetly, advisedly, soberly, and in the fear of God." When the ceremony ended, church bells rang all over London and bonfires were lit in celebration.

Anne and George spent their first summer at Windsor Castle, which Samuel Pepys described as "the most romantique castle that is in the world." The newlyweds often sat on a sheltered seat at the far end of a stone terrace built a century before by Queen Elizabeth. There, Anne helped George with his English and encouraged him to say as little as possible to members of the court... until he knew just what he was saying!"

# JULY 29

## POTTER PALMER & BERTHA HONORE
### *Worth waiting for*

POTTER WAS A MIDDLE-AGED SELF-MADE MILLIONAIRE when he married Bertha in 1870. She was the 21-year old daughter of a Chicago real estate developer who often invited Potter to their home. He'd made his fortune in retailing with the "Palmer system," which pampered customers and permitted them to try out merchandise before purchasing it. In 1867 Potter sold his store to his partners and constructed the Palmer House Hotel and other buildings on State Street. Bertha was only 13 when they first met, but he quickly sensed her intelligence and self-confidence, and silently decided to marry her when she grew up.

Some people thought the Honores had wheedled Potter into marriage because he was so wealthy. Others said the older man had to "buy" his wife. The Chicago *Tribune* defended everyone's motives, declaring "It is stated that the bridegroom… offered to settle a million dollars on his intended bride but she nobly and persistently refused."

At 6:00 P.M., they married in the Honores' Michigan Avenue home. Forty friends and relatives attended the ceremony, but 700 came to the reception. Potter and Bertha slipped away on a train to New York, heading for an ocean voyage and honeymoon in Europe. In Italy, Bertha purchased two wedding chests which she would always keep in her boudoir.

Fourteen months later, the Great Chicago Fire destroyed most of downtown. Hundreds of people died and 17,000 buildings were reduced to rubble. Only 5% of Potter's buildings remained, and he probably wouldn't have had the strength to rebuild if Bertha hadn't encouraged him. She participated in all the facets of reconstruction, including the acquisition of new building materials which were difficult to locate.

Bertha became a legendary hostess and collected early Impressionist paintings which were displayed three rows high on the walls of their Lake Shore Drive mansion. She and Potter promoted many worthy causes, including educational and business opportunities for women.

# JULY 30*

## KING CANUTE OF ENGLAND & EMMA OF NORMANDY

### *He fell for the "Gem of the Normans"*

EMMA WAS THE BEAUTIFUL WIDOW OF Ethelred the Unready when she married Canute in 1017, eight months after he became King of England. Soon he would also be king of Norway and Denmark, where his father had ruled. Canute had been a bellicose warrior, but now he humbly refused to wear a gold crown, asserting that kings were merely human and only God was perfect.

Emma liked this bright new monarch, and welcomed the chance to share the throne a second time. She didn't miss Ethelred, who'd been an unfaithful brute most of the time. She even encouraged her chroniclers to call her "virgo," although she was the mother of two sons. Canute also had a few children by a previous marriage, but he agreed to Emma's one stipulation when he proposed – that the throne should pass eventually only to Canute's children by her.

She'd gone back to Normandy when Ethelred died, and here she was crossing the English Channel as a bride-to-be again. The last time, Emma had been much younger. Now she was a mature woman tying the knot with a 22-year old. Canute wore his hair and beard untrimmed, Danish style, and had definitely won her heart. He also hoped that their union would help him win the affection of his English subjects... and it did.

In a gesture of hope for the future, Canute dispensed earldoms to worthy constituents, including Leofric of Mercia, whose wife was Lady Godiva, another strong-willed woman. Canute also brought security to England's borders. With Emma behind him, he became a great statesman and munificent ruler who established a code of laws for England. Some people balked at his abolition of tree worship, but for the most part, they accepted it!

---

*Date approximate.

# JULY 31
## STEVE ALLEN & JAYNE MEADOWS
*A highly entertaining team*

WHEN JAYNE MET STEVE IN 1952, he already was a television host and was two years away from becoming the first emcee of the *Tonight Show*. Steve had been a writer, composer, and disc jockey, but his radio monologues were often more entertaining than the music he played. Eventually he began ad-libbing, playing the piano, and inviting celebrities to join him on the air. When a guest star didn't show up one night, Steve left the stage and began chatting with members of the audience.

One night, he sat beside a beautiful red-haired actress at a dinner party in New York City, but never said one word to her. Later, Jayne recalled saying, "'Mr. Allen, you're either the rudest man I ever met or the shyest.' His face turned beet red and his head slumped. I had my answer."

In his autobiography, *Mark It and Strike It*, Steve said that meeting Jayne "was like being exposed to the Statue of Liberty or the Grand Canyon for the first time; one is apt to just stand and look." They were married in Waterford, Connecticut in 1954, shortly before the *Tonight Show* permanently changed late-night television.

The show was "live" every night from 11:30 P.M. to 1:00 A.M. Steve introduced routines that have since become staples of the talk show format: conversing with the band; strolling into the audience; and sitting behind a desk while gabbing with his guests. He also took chances with zany routines such as trying out new and complicated recipes, and jumping into a giant bowl of Jell-O. Occasionally Jayne came up with ideas for Steve's shows and performed with him. Only later did she tell him what she'd been thinking when they first met: if he wasn't already married, he was going to marry her someday.

# AUGUST

# AUGUST 1

## CHARLES FRANKLIN KETTERING &
## OLIVE WILLIAMS
### *"Ket" and "Ollie"*

I N 1900, THE FUTURE INVENTOR OF "Delco" automobile products "test called" an Ohio telephone customer while installing a new exchange. Miss Williams had a delightful sense of humor, and what should have been a brief call turned into a long conversation. When Charles hung up, he was determined to meet "Ollie."

Charles had once predicted that he would marry a red-headed girl who could play the piano. Ollie's hair was brown, but she was a pianist. He began dropping by her house to try out new gadgets and listen to her play. He even installed a telephone beside her piano so she could entertain listeners on the party line.

Eye ailments had caused Charles to drop out of Ohio State University, but with Ollie's support he returned for mechanical and electrical engineering degrees. They married in 1905, shortly after he was hired by the National Cash Register Company in Dayton. Honeymooning in Detroit, they rode in an automobile for the first time after Charles fixed the grateful owner's ignition system and helped him crank up the engine.

Back in Dayton, Ollie handled all their bookkeeping and finances once she realized that Charles was oblivious to such matters. "She was the general manager," Charles said years later. "A perfect supplement to an absent-minded inventor." He focused on other things, such as inventing the first electrical cash register, illuminating indicators, and adding machines for N.C.R. After 3 years, Ollie suggested that he quit his job and work independently because they could manage on the money she had saved.

Eventually, Charles sold his company, Delco Labs, which made automobile starters, batteries, and spark plugs, to the United Motor Company. When it became General Motors under his friend, Alfred Sloan, "Ket" had amassed so much money that they endowed the Sloan-Kettering Institute for Cancer Research in New York City.

# AUGUST 2

## ROBINSON JEFFERS & UNA CALL KUSTER
### *"Dearest-in-the-universe"*

ROBIN AND UNA MET IN 1905 when they were students at the University of Southern California. He was 18, filled with the shy intensity of the poet he would become, and she was 20, self-assured... and married. Men were easily attracted to this petite young woman with thick chestnut hair. Like Robin, Una devoured books. They talked endlessly about literature, philosophy, and music.

Robin's parents tried to divert him by taking him to Europe, where he studied at the University of Zurich. Returning to USC, he studied medicine for 3 years – not to become a doctor but a better poet, he said. Next, he took courses in forestry in Seattle. Everything interested Robin, but he couldn't forget Una.

In 1912 his grandfather died and left him a small legacy. In Los Angeles, Robin saw Una driving in an open car as he was crossing the street. They stared at each other and smiled. Soon afterward, they began corresponding and meeting in secret.

"I need you so much," he wrote. "There's no living – no delight or adventure – nothing but a bad blank – until we're together – for good." The following year, Una's husband agreed to a divorce, and she and Robin married.

"She gave me eyes, she gave me ears," Robin wrote, quoting Wordsworth. "And she arranged my life," he added. Una would be Robin's inspiration, amanuensis, and audience.

Impending war in Europe discouraged them from going abroad, so they headed instead for the Sur coast of California, a region that would inspire many of his poems. "When... we looked down through the pines and sea-fog on Carmel Bay, it was evident that we had come without knowing it to our inevitable place," he recollected. He built Tor House on Point Sur, overlooking the ocean, and they stayed there for the rest of their lives.

# AUGUST 3

## DIETRICH BUXTEHUDE & ANNA MARGARETHA TUNDER

### *A perfect fit*

A NNA'S FATHER, FRANZ TUNDER, WAS THE organist at St. Mary's, the most prestigious church in Lubeck, Germany. When he died in 1667, auditions were held for a replacement. Dietrich was 30 and had already established a reputation as a fine organist and composer in Denmark.

Young men in 17th century Europe frequently married the daughters or widows of their predecessors. Dietrich's brother, Peter, had married the widow of the town barber and taken over his business. But Herr Tunder hadn't made such an arrangement with Dietrich; if he had, there would have been no need for auditions. Consequently, St. Mary's got the best organist and *werkmeister*, and Dietrich and Anna married because they were in love.

They probably met in spring, 1668, when he arrived in Lubeck. As the 21-year old daughter of a musician, Anna knew well the responsibilities involved at St. Mary's. Her older sister had married the church cantor, so Anna's betrothal to Dietrich that summer ensured that the church "business" remained happily within the family. She and Dietrich were married at St. Mary's, of course, and celebrated at a friend's home across the street. Like all citizens of Lubeck, their wedding was controlled by strict sumptuary laws that dictated the number of guests, the kinds of refreshments, the bride's trousseau, and the value of the newly married couple's wedding gifts.

Dietrich and Anna were given second-floor apartments in St. Mary's Werkhaus, on the south side of the church yard and only a short walk from the bustling marketplace. For the remainder of what would be a long and fruitful life, Dietrich and Anna lived in Lubeck, where his fame as a composer and performer continued to grow. Years later, the young Johann Sebastian Bach would tramp 200 miles just to meet Dietrich and listen to his sacred music.

# AUGUST 4
## WOLFGANG AMADEUS MOZART & CONSTANZA WEBER
*"I love her and she me with all our hearts!"*

O NE OF MUSIC'S GREATEST COMPOSERS of symphonies, operas, and concertos grew up with an overbearing father. Leopold Mozart was a musician, too, and he soon realized that Wolfgang was a musical prodigy and a genius. By the age of 4, the little boy could play the violin, keyboard, and organ, and he had written a minuet! At 5, he was performing in public.

Leopold gave up his own musical career and concentrated on "Wolfie." But by the time Wolfgang was in his twenties, he needed to break away (or at least, back off) from his father's domination. Most of the time, he performed and composed in Vienna, and boarded at a home maintained by Mrs. Weber, a widow with 4 daughters.

First, he fell in love with Constanza's sister, Aloysia, but he gave up when she rejected him. Within a year, he turned his attentions to Constanza. Like Wolfgang, she had dark eyes and curly hair. She also had a lively spirit. Rumors flew in Salzburg: had Constanza really lifted her skirts just a little so a young man could measure the size of her shapely calves with a ribbon?

People are talking, Papa wrote to Wolfgang. You must leave the Webers' home. But "we are not in love," Wolfgang replied. "I play and joke with her… and that is all. If I had to marry all the ladies with whom I have jested, I should have 200 wives at least!"

Even so, he listened to his father, and vacated the Webers' home. But … he was lonely. And he was attracted to Constanza. "The voice of nature speaks as loud in me as in others," he wrote. "I am more inclined… to quiet domesticity than to revelry…."

For 8 months, Papa refused to give Wolfgang permission to marry. Finally, Wolfgang would wait no longer. He was 26 and Constanza was 19 when they married in 1782 at St. Stephen's Cathedral in Vienna, barely 2 weeks after the premiere of his opera, *The Abduction from the Seraglio*, which had been commissioned by Emperor Joseph II.

# AUGUST 5

## ALFRED SISLEY & MARIE LESCOUEZEC
### *"Madame Sisley" at last*

TWO DAYS BEFORE ALFRED AND MARIE married in Cardiff, Wales in 1897, they signed documents confirming that he was the father of their two children. This was no surprise to family and friends, however. The signing occurred thirty years after he and Marie began living together. Their "irregular liaison" had started in Paris in 1866. Nine years earlier, Alfred's wealthy English parents had sent him to France to study business. Instead, he became friends with Renoir, Monet, Bazille, and other early Impressionists. He studied art, set up a studio, and painted country landscapes and village streets. At 26, he was good-looking and serious, with a short dark beard and a pipe in his mouth.

Marie was 5 years older than Alfred, and came from a poor family in the village of Meurthe-et-Moselle. While learning to be a florist, she often posed for some of the painters. Renoir said that Marie had "a lovely little face… a very sensitive nature and was exceedingly well-bred." Since Alfred rarely painted figures, she is only an indistinct form in the landscape of his "Lady with a Parasol."

Alfred's parents disliked Marie and stopped sending money to him during the Franco-Prussian war, when his father's health and financial situation deteriorated. Now that art was Alfred's only means of income, he and Marie lived in villages outside Paris, and he began painting more steadily. "The Lesson" is one of the few pictures he made of his children.

In the summer of 1897, one of Alfred's patrons sent him to Wales for inspiration. Marie came too, for they had planned, at last, to marry. After a civil ceremony, they stayed at the Osborne Hotel on the Welsh coast near Langland Bay and walked along the beaches, gazing at the rocky cliffs. Alfred immortalized everything in what became his last great series of paintings.

# AUGUST 6

## WILLIAM S. GILBERT & LUCY BLOIS TURNER

*"Oh, happy day, with joyous glee, We will away and married be!"*

—THE PIRATES OF PENZANCE

"W.S." PROPOSED TO LUCY SHORTLY AFTER his play, *Dulcamara, or the Little Duck and the Great Quack* opened in London in December 1866. The play was a farcical parody of Donizett's *L'Elisir d'Amore*, and was so silly that even W.S. eventually called it "nonsense." But it gave the 30-year old playwright a taste of success and the courage to contemplate marriage.

"Kitten" was the 17-year old blue-eyed, blond daughter of an Indian Army officer when she married W.S. at St. Mary Abbot's church in Kensington in 1867. W.S. was always thinking up new plots and jotting down lyrics – even on their honeymoon in France. Kitten didn't mind; she was sweet-tempered, tactful, and devoted. Although W.S. could be easily exasperated, his rages were directed at sloppy stagehands and ill-prepared actors, not his "darling" wife.

They bought a large house at 24, The Boltons, in South Kensington and loved hosting parties for neighborhood children. They also lavished lots of attention on their pets. When a stout woman reporter commented that W.S.'s dogs seemed to like her, he couldn't resist saying, "Why not? It's rare that they see a bone with so much meat on it!"

W.S. admitted that his musical knowledge was limited to two tunes – "One is 'God Save the Queen,' the other isn't!" By 1870 he had teamed up with the young composer, Arthur Sullivan, whose music was as delightful, playful, and humorous as W.S.'s words. Their hits included *The Pirates of Penzance*, *The Mikado*, and *The Yeomen of the Guard*.

Gilbert and Sullivan enjoyed a lifelong, satisfying partnership, almost as perfect as W.S.'s marriage to Kit.

# AUGUST 7

## JOSEPH BOLOGNA & RENEE TAYLOR

### *"... I'm going with you!"*

The first time Renee and Joe married was in 1958, in a Stamford CT Catholic church. After that, the Jewish "bride" from the Bronx, and the Catholic "groom" from Brooklyn married again and again, in Protestant, Buddhist and Jewish ceremonies, too – including one on their 32nd anniversary in Manhattan, where they were performing in their play, *"Bermuda Avenue Triangle."* Actress Carol Channing was the maid of honor, and former congresswoman and social activist Bella Abzug was matron of honor. Bridesmaids included actress Nanette Fabray and Geraldine Ferraro, a former congresswoman and also the 1st woman nominated as a U.S. Vice Presidential candidate.

Throughout their marriage and long careers, Renee and Joe wrote and often starred in their own productions. Their first big hit, *Lovers and Other Strangers* (1970), was a semi-autobiographical Broadway play and later on a film about bringing Jewish and Italian families together for the short-notice wedding of their kids. Some relatives were given bit-parts as extras.

Renee has played Fran Drescher's TV mother, "Sylvia," on *The Nanny,* where Joe appeared in guest performances. More recently, she's been Mrs. Matsen, Ted Mosby's neighbor on *How I Met Your Mother.* Joe has also been in films such as *Blame it on Rio, My Favorite Year* and *Big Daddy,* and both stars have worked as voice-actors in animated films and TV shows.

In 1975 they bought a Beverly Hills Tudor mansion previously owned by former child-star Shirley Temple Black. Years later, in a 1997 newspaper interview, Renee confirmed that she and Joe were paired for life when she said "…I have always told him, if you ever leave me, I'm going with you!"

# AUGUST 8

## GEORGE WESTINGHOUSE & MARGUERITE WALKER
### *The seat beside her wasn't taken*

ALTHOUGH GEORGE HAD NOT YET INVENTED the air brake for railways, it was only fitting that he met the girl of his dreams on a passenger train. While traveling from New York City to Albany in 1867, he and Marguerite bumped into each other as their car lurched forward. She was deeply absorbed in *The Scarlet Letter*, and hadn't noticed the 20-year old man sitting beside her, although he was enchanted with her.

They began chatting about her book and the beautiful Hudson River outside, while stealing glances at each other. George also talked about some of his ideas, and pretty soon Marguerite realized that listening to him was more fascinating than Mr. Hawthorne's story. After serving briefly in the Civil War, George had come home to Schenectady full of ideas for practical inventions. He'd always been a bit of a daydreamer and had dropped out of college to work in his father's machine shop. Already, George had obtained a patent for a rotary engine, invented when he was 15 years old.

Before Marguerite disembarked from the train, she and George exchanged addresses. They started corresponding immediately, and he began shuttling between their homes in Schenectady and Roxbury, New York. Three weeks later, they were engaged.

They married in Roxbury and lived with George's parents until they could afford their own home. George's first major success was creating a single system of railroad brakes, powered by compressed air that drastically reduced the number of train wrecks. One of his customers was the railroad magnate Commodore Vanderbilt.

Within 4 years, George and Marguerite had moved to Pittsburgh where he established the Westinghouse Air Brake company. He also invented electrically-operated brakes for subway cars, turbine engines and shock absorbers for automobiles, and helped harness Niagara Falls for hydroelectric plants.

# AUGUST 9

## ANNE MARBURY & WILLIAM HUTCHINSON
*He always loved her*

ANNE AND WILL MARRIED IN 1612, long before she was banished from the Massachusetts Bay Colony because of her religious beliefs. They had grown up in Alford, England, overlooking the North Sea, where Will's father owned a dry goods business and Anne's father, Francis, was an outspoken, rebellious clergyman who was banned periodically from preaching.

Will was tall and thin, with freckles and a friendly smile. Five years older than Anne, he began noticing the self-assured young girl by the time she was 13. Sometimes, Will's father gave him spare bolts of cloth for the Marburys. Even after they moved to London a year later, Anne never forgot sweet Will.

When Francis Marbury was given his own parsonage at the Church of St. Martin's in the Vintry, it seemed as if bleak times were finally over. Anne heard many religious discussions in her home and she spoke her mind, which few women did. "There was nothing but the great mingle-mangle of religion" in England at that time, she wrote later. Everything – astronomy, philosophy, the arts, even literature – had religious overtones.

Sadly, Anne's father died, and the family made plans to vacate the rectory. One afternoon, Will appeared in the doorway, offering his condolences and help with the packing. What he wanted most was to convince the grief-stricken Anne to marry him. With his gentle, loving ways, he succeeded.

They married 3 weeks after Anne's 21st birthday, and returned to Alford. Will took over his father's business, and soon he and Anne were raising the first of their 14 children. Twenty-two years later, Reverend John Cotton, the fervent leader of their church in St. Botolph's, convinced his flock of separatists to immigrate to America. In 1634, the Hutchinsons boarded the *Griffen* and sailed for Massachusetts.

# AUGUST 10

## MOSS HART & KITTY CARLISLE

*"Moss was the most wonderful thing that
ever happened to me"*

A FTER ATTENDING PRIVATE SCHOOLS IN EUROPE in the 1920's, Kitty, who was from New Orleans, made her society debut in Rome. Her mother had hoped that her bright, charming daughter would capture a prince or other aristocrat, but after 2 disappointing "seasons," she encouraged her to find a career instead. She was glad when Kitty chose the theater, and confident that she could succeed in musical comedy. Her mother also predicted a fairy-tale ending: one day, Kitty would marry a man who also was part of the theater.

Back in the United States, Kitty performed in Broadway musicals and then went to Hollywood where she sang and acted in musical comedies and played the ingénue in the Marx Brothers' *A Night at the Opera*. In late 1945, she was 35 years old when she and Moss met at a party following a rally for World War II war bonds.

He was a tall, dark-haired, Bronx-born, 41-year old Pulitzer Prize-winning playwright and director who wrote the books for many plays with Irving Berlin, Cole Porter, and George S. Kaufman. By 1945, Moss was writing independently.

Kitty and Moss married 8 months later in New Hope, Pennsylvania, and spent their honeymoon performing in a road company production of *The Man Who Came to Dinner*, which Moss had written with Kaufman. Afterwards, the couple settled in New York City. Moss wrote the screenplays *Gentleman's Agreement* and *A Star is Born*, and would subsequently direct *My Fair Lady* and *Camelot*. Kitty became a panelist of TV quiz shows such as *To Tell the Truth*. She continued performing and singing, and in 1976 she became chief arts administrator of New York State.

# AUGUST 11

## JAMES MCNEIL WHISTLER & BEATRICE GODWIN

### *"Trixie is my luck"*

"JIMMIE" LOOKED OVER HIS SHOULDER NERVOUSLY when he married "Trixie," half expecting Maud, his former model and mistress, to show up at the parish church of St. Mary Abbot's, Kensington. But only a few friends knew about his wedding plans in 1888; everyone else read about it the next day. "The Butterfly is captive at last," reported the London *Times*, referring to the painter's distinctive signature and trademark.

Mrs. Godwin was the 32-year-old widow of the architect who had designed Jimmie's house in Chelsea. In 1884, she posed for his full-length portrait, "Harmony in Red Lamplight." Standing before a warm red background, Trixie radiates exuberance and pride. Her large figure is wrapped in a red cape, and she tilts her head and smiles confidently. After her husband's death two years later, she and Jimmie became romantically involved.

They might have continued as lovers indefinitely if close friends hadn't persuaded them to tie the knot and helped out with the arrangements. When Jimmie and Trixie arrived at the fashionable church, she was wearing a blue gown and hat and he – ever the dandy – was dressed in a tight-fitting frock coat, yellow gloves, and new hat. "After the ceremony," the best man recalled, "we adjourned to Whistler's studio, where he had prepared a banquet. The banquet was on the table, but there were no chairs. So we sat on packing cases." Café Royal catered the food and Buszard's supplied the tiered wedding cake, ordered by Trixie's sister Ethel. Jimmie thought it was too ugly to eat and refused to sit near it.

The honeymooners went to France for 3 months, and Jimmie painted 5 small paintings and etched more than 30 copper-plates. With Trixie, his life was relaxed as well as fulfilling. There had been many mistresses before her, but Trixie was the only woman Jimmie ever loved.

# AUGUST 12

## LORENZO DA PONTE & ANN GRAHL

*His "bella inglesina"*

AFTER YEARS OF MANY AMOROUS ADVENTURES, Lorenzo married "Nancy" in 1792. It was the 43-year old Venetian librettist's first and only marriage, and life with his "beautiful, fresh and adorable bride" would bring him 46 years of happiness.

He had left Italy 10 years before, after cavorting in escapades with his friend Casanova. Jealous husbands and religious oppression bore down on Lorenzo as he headed for Vienna, where he became Emperor Joseph II's court poet and the brilliant librettist for Mozart's operas *The Marriage of Figaro*, *Don Giovanni*, and *Cosi Fan Tutte*. But after Mozart's death, and more romantic dalliances, Lorenzo packed his bags again, in 1791.

In Trieste, a friend asked Lorenzo to make arrangements for him to marry a wealthy young woman, but the girl's father canceled everything when he sensed that the absent suitor was only interested in winning her large dowry. Nancy and Lorenzo were greatly relieved, for she had been giving him French lessons – in between vocabulary exercises and verb conjugations – and they had fallen in love.

"My joy," Lorenzo wrote later in his memoirs, "was so great... that neither of us could say a word for the … rest of the evening." They were married soon after, "and with the courage, or to be more exact, with the temerity of a young blade of 20," he took Nancy from Trieste after the wedding festivities. "That evening, we reached Leibach, where we stopped for the night, and … Amor and Hymen taught me to dry the tears of a tender girl who was leaving parents and friends, perhaps forever, to be mine."

Lorenzo wrote additional librettos as well as poetry and translations. Eventually he and Nancy came to New York, where they helped introduce Italian opera to the United States and he became Columbia College's first professor of Italian language and literature.

# AUGUST 13

## PETER STUYVESANT & JUDITH BAYARD
### *"Old Silver Leg's" sweet love*

PETER SAILED HOME TO HOLLAND IN 1645 for rest and recuperation after his right leg was shattered by a Portuguese cannonball on the Caribbean island of St. Maarten. The brave Dutch soldier and governor of Curacao had encouraged his men to keep fighting for 28 days until, at last, they retreated. Although Peter ended up losing his leg, the tragedy brought him a wife.

First, he moved in with his married sister Anna Bayard and her family in Alphen, not far from Leiden where Peter was fitted for a wooden leg. A plain, ordinary one wouldn't do; the war hero's peg leg sported wide bands of silver. Soon, "Old Silver Leg" was hobbling around the Bayards' house, enjoying the special attentions of Anna's sister-in-law Judith. She was fascinated by Peter's stories about his exploits, and he was deeply touched by her kind assistance. He also loved hearing her play for him on the Bayards' spinet piano.

They married that summer at the Walloon church in Breda, where Judith's late father had been the minister. On top of Judith's head was a small jeweled crown worn by every bride in her family for generations. On Christmas Day, 1646, she and Peter voyaged to the New World, where the Dutch West India Company had asked him to be director-general of the Nieuw Netherland colony. They stopped for a few months in Curacao and arrived in Nieuw Amsterdam harbor the following May, shortly before their first son was born.

The company gave them farmland which they called "Stuyvesant's Bouwerie," roughly from 5th to 17th streets and from the East River to Park Avenue in today's New York City. They also built a fine house farther downtown, near what is now Whitehall Street. Flower and vegetable gardens were laid out in neat rows and patterns behind the "Great House," long considered the grandest residence in Manhattan.

# AUGUST 14

## DANIEL BOONE & REBECCA BRYAN

*"my little girl"*

A CCORDING TO THE FAMOUS AMERICAN FRONTIERS-
MAN, a man needed 3 things to be happy – "a good gun, a good
horse, and a good wife." Years after Daniel married Rebecca in 1756,
he told their 10 kids that their courtship began on the day he decided to "try
her temper."

Daniel and Rebecca were sitting together under a tree while she sorted
fresh-picked cherries and he fiddled absentmindedly with his knife. He began
tossing it into the dirt, point first. One time, he aimed for the edge of Rebecca's white cambric apron, just to see if she'd get angry. When Rebecca didn't
complain, he knew she was the girl for him.

Daniel was 21 and Rebecca was 17 when they married in a triple wedding ceremony with 2 other couples from the Boone and Bryan extended
families. They probably celebrated afterwards at a wedding party held in their
first home, a cabin on the Boone family property. Quilts, linens, furniture
and other gifts were displayed, as well-wishers drank toasts of rum, cider, and
whisky. Following a popular tradition, wedding attendants escorted the bride
and groom upstairs to bed, tucked them in under the covers, and merrily
went back downstairs. There, everyone sang and danced loudly, made bawdy
jokes about "thumping good luck" for the newlyweds, and occasionally sent
up trays of food.

Soon Daniel was blazing trails in the Appalachian Mountains, carving his
initials into trees and marking the spots where "D Boon cilled A BAR." He
and Rebecca preferred living in the backwoods, away from the growing num-
bers of settlers. Although he was a hunter, he also was a Quaker, opposed to
war and usually sympathetic to Native Americans. When Daniel discovered
a "hunter's paradise" in Kentucky in the late 1700's, he and Rebecca headed
west through the Cumberland Gap.

# AUGUST 15

## JACK LEMMON & FELICIA FARR

### *His "Farfel"*

FELICIA AND JACK MARRIED IN PARIS in 1962 while he was film-ing *Irma la Douce*. He'd been a successful actor ever since his Broadway debut 9 years earlier. But in 1956, a year after he won an Oscar for his role as Ensign Pulver in *Mister Roberts*, Jack's first marriage ended. A few months later, he and Felicia met on a movie set, and he was immediately captivated by the beautiful actress. "I took one look at her and – that was it!" he recalled afterwards. Jack was smitten but reluctant to get involved. So was Felicia, whose first marriage also had ended in divorce.

Occasionally, they'd have tempestuous battles, although neither one doubted the other's love. Once, after Felicia refused to open her front door for Jack, he pounded on it so hard that his fist smashed through the plywood panel. Eventually, she framed the splintered piece and gave it to him as an anniversary gift.

After six years, Jack finally proposed on the telephone from Paris, and Felicia flew there from Los Angeles. At their wedding, he wore a dark suit and she wore a sleeveless lace dress with long white gloves. Her hair was swept up in a French knot and covered with a finely dotted veil.

They were married by the mayor and then drove off in a friend's white Rolls-Royce, dragging ridiculously oversized two-gallon cans behind them. That morning, Jack had performed in a scene requiring him to jump into the Seine River. Unfortunately, the unsuspecting bridegroom swallowed some polluted water and had an upset stomach throughout his honeymoon!

Felicia appeared in films including *Kiss Me Stupid* in 1964, and *Kotch*, which Jack directed, starring their good friend Walter Matthau. Sometimes, she and Jack acted together. In 1986 they appeared in Blake Edwards's com-edy, *That's Life*, along with Blake's wife, Julie Andrews, and children from both families.

# AUGUST 16

## JESSAMYN WEST & HARRY MCPHERSON
### *"I love thee"*

UNDULATING SAGEBRUSH COLORED THE SOFT BROWN hills of Yorba Linda, California, when Jessamyn and "Max" married in a Quaker ceremony at the Friends Church in 1923. Thirty years later, the region gained fame as the hometown of Jessamyn's distant cousin, Richard Milhous Nixon, for whom she used to babysit.

Jessamyn and Max met at Whittier College and were engaged by the end of her freshman year. Their first home was Hemet, where Max's parents had a fruit orchard. He finished his Ph.D. in education, and Jessamyn taught in a one-room schoolhouse. Max encouraged her to earn a Ph.D. in English literature, although it meant spending the summer studying at Oxford University in England. Few young women in the 1920's left their husbands to cross the United States and go to England, but Max knew that Jessamyn could handle it.

After she returned, Jessamyn contracted a dangerous form of tuberculosis shortly before she took her oral examinations at University of California, Berkeley, when she was 29. For the next 2 years, she lived in a sanitarium until doctors told her family that she would probably die. That's when Max and Jessamyn's mother, Grace, decided to bring her home. Steadfastly, they took care of Jessamyn. During her long recuperation, Grace told stories about her forebears. As Jessamyn recalled, "Grace knew… the limbo in which I lived…. Since I had no life of my own… she gave me her own life… as a Quaker girl on a farm in southern Indiana at the turn of the century."

Convalescing, Jessamyn began to write, adapting her mother's tales into poems and stories. With Max's encouragement, her work was submitted to publishers. *The Friendly Persuasion* takes place in the mid-19th century, and brought Jessamyn literary acclaim in 1945. Eventually, it was made into a motion picture and popular song.

# AUGUST 17

## HELEN HAYES & CHARLES MACARTHUR
### *Peanuts and emeralds*

IN 1924, AT A COCKTAIL PARTY IN a New York City art studio, Irving Berlin was playing his love song, *"Always,"* on the piano while George Gershwin hovered nearby, waiting for his chance to tickle the ivories. Helen had come with the playwright Marc Connelly, who explained that their hostess, a commercial artist, wanted lots of people milling about and posing, as if in a stage set, for a magazine cover she was producing.

Helen was a 24-year old actress with silky light brown hair and a magnificent smile. She rarely socialized and was dazzled by all the celebrities she saw. When a very handsome fellow approached her and asked, "Want a peanut?" she nodded, entranced, and he poured several nuts into her hand. Then he smiled and said, "I wish they were emeralds."

The fellow was Charlie. Helen's mother and friends had warned her about him; he was known as a drinker, a cad, and "bad news." If she got involved with him, sooner or later he'd leave her, just as he'd walked out on his wife 2 years before. Until that night, Helen's life had been devoted to stage performances. Her mother, who was her agent, also feared that a romantic involvement with a separated man could end Helen's promising career.

But Charlie became the love of Helen's life. "It is a miracle that he rescued me from the corner of that studio and from the shadows of an endless childhood," she wrote in *Helen Hayes: On Reflection*. They married in 1928, soon after his divorce was finalized. That same year, the hit play, *The Front Page*—written by Charlie and Ben Hecht—opened on Broadway.

Both Helen and Charlie were enormously successful in their chosen careers. Years later, Charlie returned from a trip to India, dumped a small bag of emeralds in Helen's lap and told her, "I wish they were peanuts!"

# AUGUST 18

## WILLIAM BLAKE & CATHERINE BOUCHER
*"when she speaks, the voice of Heaven I hear"*

CATHERINE INSPIRED, ASSISTED, AND MODELED FOR William, whose mystical poems and engravings still mesmerize art lovers today.

*Abstinence sows sand all over*
*The ruddy limbs and flaming hair*
*But Desire Gratified*
*Plants fruits of life and beauty there.*

She sketched William's "ruddy limbs and flaming hair," capturing his strong features and intense expression. He immortalized his "Sweet Shadow of Delight" in a picture of a lovely young woman sitting by their edge of their bed.

They met in 1781 after he'd been rejected by another girl. William roamed London aimlessly, stopping by the Boucher home to visit Catherine's father, a market gardener. He wasn't there, but his daughter was. She listened sympathetically to William's sad tale. "I pity you deeply," she said. "You do?" he replied. "Then I love you."

He was 24 and she was 20 when they married a year later, at St. Mary's, the parish church in Battersea. Catherine was dark-haired and spirited, but like most young women of her class, she was illiterate and could make only a cross under William's name on the marriage register.

Their first home was at 23 Green Street, Leicester Fields. William taught Catherine how to read and write, and he explained the secrets of engraving, bookbinding, and the coloring of prints. She also began to draw and paint. "My wife has undertaken to Print," William wrote to a friend, "which She does to admiration... In short I have Got everything... under my thumb."

They produced magnificently illustrated volumes such as *Songs of Innocence, Songs of Experience, Jerusalem,* and William's principal prose work, *The Marriage of Heaven and Hell.*

# AUGUST 19*
## DAVY CROCKETT & POLLY FINDLAY
### *"a sweetheart for me"*

IN DAVY'S AUTOBIOGRAPHY, THE LEGENDARY BACKWOODS-MAN remembered meeting "one of the prettiest little girls... I had ever seen" at a Tennessee reaping party in 1806. A few weeks later, he went to Polly's house, but when he found her sitting with another man, he "began to think I was barking up the wrong tree."

"Her mother was deeply enlisted for my rival and I had to fight against her influence as well as his. But the girl herself was the prize I was fighting for, and... she welcomed me."

One night, they accidentally met in the woods. Polly "had been traveling all day, and was mighty tired; and I would have taken her up and toated her, if it hadn't been that I wanted her just where I could see her all the time, for I thought she looked sweeter than sugar, and by this time I loved her almost well enough to eat her."

They decided to marry, but Polly's mother "appeared to be mighty wrathy and when I broached the subject she looked at me as savage as a meat axe." Fortunately, Mr. Findlay was friendlier than his wife, and said she just needed time to get used to the idea. Davy declared that he would return in a week with a horse for Polly, "and she must be ready to go."

When Davy came back, Polly's father begged them to get married at their house, saying her mother had come to accept their plans. Davy agreed, located the parson, "and got married in a short time, for I was afraid to wait long, for fear of another defeat....

"Having gotten my wife, I thought I was completely made up and needed nothing more in the whole world. But I soon found out this was a mistake – for now having a wife, I wanted everything else!"

---

*Date approximate.

# AUGUST 20

## ENRICO CARUSO & DOROTHY BENJAMIN

*"Credi all' amore... tu sei amato"*
*("Believe in love... you are loved")*

**—ANDREA CHENIER**

WHEN THE WORLD-ACCLAIMED OPERATIC TENOR ENCOUNTERED Dorothy at a party in Manhattan in 1918, "We both knew from that moment that our lives would be united," she wrote many years later.

They had met once before, at a gathering held in Enrico's honor. Dorothy had been accompanied by her family's housekeeper, a young Italian woman who hoped to become a professional singer. Enrico drove them home afterwards, and when Dorothy realized she had left her gloves behind, he graciously gave her his pair as a replacement.

Dorothy's stodgy and critical father already considered his 25-year old daughter to be a "spinster." In addition, Mr. Benjamin was a wealthy and prominent lawyer and editor who viewed entertainers with disdain. Although 45-year old Enrico had been a dinner guest several times, Mr. Benjamin thought he was a lowborn foreigner and hot-blooded "public singer." Even so, it didn't take long before Enrico and Dorothy declared their love and decided to marry.

At first, Dorothy's father said he would never approve such a union, then he demanded that Enrico pay *him* half a million dollars for the privilege of marrying his daughter! Dorothy was outraged. She stormed out of their house and went to Enrico's hotel. The next morning, they married at New York City's Marble Collegiate Church.

"I did not want my daughter to marry riches or a voice or an orator, just a man," Mr. Benjamin asserted. "However, she is a mature woman and Caruso is 45. Therefore, the match cannot be ascribed to the ardor of youth," he added snidely. Secretly, he adopted the housekeeper and left her everything in his will. He never forgave Dorothy, but the years she spent with Enrico were the best part of her life.

# AUGUST 21

## JAMES GARFIELD RANDALL & RUTH PAINTER
*Shared passions for life, and history*

RUTH'S FATHER, A HISTORY PROFESSOR AT Roanoke College in Virginia, began inviting young "Dr. Randall" to dinner in 1915. Ever since the sudden death of his wife, Jim had concentrated exclusively on teaching and research until he met Ruth, Dr. Painter's bright and beautiful daughter. She was full of youthful optimism and enthusiasm, and would become a well-known historian, specializing in writing biographies of famous American women. Eventually, Jim also would become a highly regarded Civil war historian and biographer of Lincoln.

Friends and relatives decorated the College Church in Salem, Virginia, with white flowers and tall white candles when Ruth and Jim married in 1917. Baked inside their wedding cake were a miniature silver thimble, symbolizing the "spinster," a silver button for the "bachelor," and a tiny silver heart for a happy marriage.

"Jim and I had all the ancient good-luck signs with us on our wedding day, bright sunshine, a cricket chirping on the hearth of the parlor that evening, and I myself got the little silver heart in my piece of cake. I still have it," Ruth wrote in her autobiography.

Within 3 years she and Jim had moved to the land of Lincoln, where he became a history professor at the University of Illinois in Urbana. Ruth helped with Jim's research and manuscript editing, and before long she was writing, too.

In 1947, when President Lincoln's private papers were finally made available to academicians, Jim and Ruth took the next train to Washington, DC and pored over documents at the Library of Congress. Jim's reputation as a Lincoln scholar soared, and Ruth wrote acclaimed biographies of Mary Lincoln, Elizabeth Custer, and other wives of famous men.

# AUGUST 22

## ULYSSES S GRANT & JULIA DENT
*"Remember I shall cling to you"*

"CAPTAIN GRANT WAS AS COOL UNDER the fire of the clergyman's questions as he had been under the batteries of the Mexican artillery," said Emma Dent after her sister's 1848 wedding. Julia had just married the 26-year old officer on a hot and rainy summer night in her parents' St. Louis, Missouri town house.

Candles shaped like stars lighted the 22-year old bride's way as she descended the narrow staircase in a white watered silk gown with a tulle veil and a "corsage bouquet" of white Cape Jessamine flowers. Her 3 bridesmaids also wore white. "Lyss's" 3 groomsmen wore their army dress uniforms. Seventeen years later, two of them would surrender to General Grant at Appomattox when the Civil War ended.

Lyss and Julia spent their wedding night in the Dents' home. The next day, friends followed a southern tradition by throwing bouquets of flowers at the newlyweds as they set off by boat to visit Lyss's family in Ohio. "He asked me to sing to him, something sweet and low, and I did," said Julia. "I do not remember any of the passengers on that trip. It was like a dream to me."

She was the pint-sized sister of one of his West Point classmates when they met. Lyss began visiting frequently, and one spring day after a rainstorm, he and Julia went riding in an open carriage and stopped before a bridge over a swollen ravine. "Now, if anything happens, remember I shall cling to you," she told him. Lyss smiled and nodded, and when they reached the other side, he proposed. They married soon after he returned from the Mexican wars.

Fifty years later, the president's wife recalled their early days together in St. Louis – "They were not dark but bright and charming, as it was always sunshine when he was near." She still had his wedding gift, a daguerreotype picture of himself, which she kept in a locket on a velvet wrist strap.

# AUGUST 23

## LEWIS HINE & SARA ANN RICH

*Working together, "armed" with a camera*

L EWIS BEGAN TAKING PHOTOGRAPHS IN NEW York City in 1903, a year before he came home to Oshkosh, Wisconsin and married his sweetheart, Sara. Like him, she was a schoolteacher. Lewis taught natural studies and geography at the Ethical Culture School in Manhattan where the principal, Frank Manny, convinced him that photography could be a powerful way to teach children about the world.

Lewis and Sara settled in Yonkers, north of the city, and he started taking pictures of classroom activities. After school, he and Frank rode the subway downtown and photographed immigrants arriving at Ellis Island. During the first decade of the 20th century, more than 10 million people emigrated, mainly from Europe, and "foreigners" were rarely considered worthwhile subjects for photography. But Lewis's camera eloquently captured the fear, exhaustion, and exhilaration of newly arrived immigrants in the noisy and often chaotic inspection halls.

By 1907 social welfare agencies were hiring him to photograph oppressive working conditions in coal mines and factories in cities such as Pittsburgh. Sara supported Lewis's decision to quit teaching, although it meant giving up a steady income.

For the next 10 years, Lewis was a staff photographer for the National Child Labor Committee's ongoing campaign to raise public awareness about the evils of child labor. He and Sara traveled from Maine to Texas, documenting children working in mills, factories, canneries and sweatshops. He took the pictures while Sara took notes and recorded important data.

Sometimes, Lewis's camera had to be smuggled inside, and interviews were conducted surreptitiously. The information gathered wasn't written down until after Lewis and Sara left a building, and before the bosses realized what had been going on. The unsettling and graphic results played a valuable role in developing legislative reforms to eliminate child labor.

# AUGUST 24
## ANTONIO STRADIVARI &
## ANTONIA MARIA ZAMBELLI
*Making music as well as love*

NTONIA WAS 36-YEARS OLD, WITH THE wide hips, small waist, slender neck, and curved shoulders of a magnificent violin. Why wouldn't Antonio notice her? In 1699, the widowed violin maker was 55, with grown sons and a successful business in the town of Cremona, Italy. And yet… Antonia's full skirt swirled and skimmed the cobblestoned street as she chatted briefly with a neighbor, then hurried off around a corner.

Some men said that all women were the same – like all violins. But Antonio knew that each one was unique. A violin's superiority was determined by specifics – the thickness of the wood, the height of the bridge, the arch of the back, the slope of the belly. What music could be brought forth from a fine violin, or a woman?

In his workshop, Antonio sat at his bench, surrounded by wedges of maple and pine, sandpapers, chisels, clamps, planes, varnishes, saws, glue pots, and other vital pieces with which he painstakingly built his creations. He would marry again, he decided, as soon as he could convince the lovely Antonia.

They were wed that summer, at the parish church of San Donato. Antonio's output had always been remarkable, even during his first wife's illness, but the violins he made during the years he spent with Antonia were even more astonishing. In time, the name Stradivari would become synonymous with all fine violins. Antonio's richly beautiful, wine-brown, orange-red, or golden wood creations – instruments that one's fingers ached to touch – would be given proper names, such as the "Lafont," the "Castelbarco," the "Ward," and the "Russian," after the fortunate few who played them. Paganini, Heifetz, Zimbalist and other great musicians would draw magnificent music from Antonio's violins for many years to come.

## AUGUST 25

## LAURA INGALLS & ALMANZO WILDER
### *The sound of sleigh bells*

THE TV CHARACTER LAURA GOT MARRIED on the popular show, *Little House on the Prairie*, but the real Laura wrote about it first, in *These Happy Golden Years* and *The First Four Years*, sequels to her series of fictionalized memoirs that began with *Little House in the Big Woods*.

The Ingalls family came west in a covered wagon and settled in DeSmet, South Dakota. "Manly" was 10 years older than Laura, and he and his brother had already established a homestead nearby. Sleigh bells signaled Manly's arrival when he drove Laura to and from a settlement 12 miles away during the time she held a temporary job as a teacher. Fierce winter weather and the distance required her to board with another family on weekdays, so the homesick 15-year old was deeply touched to see Manly outside her school-house on Friday afternoons, waiting to take her home for the weekend.

Afterward, Laura returned to school in DeSmet, but Manly continued to call for her on Sundays. Two years later, in 1885, they exchanged their first kiss when he offered her a garnet and pearl ring and proposed marriage. Joyfully, Laura accepted, as long as the word, "obey," was omitted from her vows, because she didn't think she could obey anyone "against my better judgment."

"And so on Thursday, the 25th of August, at 10 o'clock in the morning, the quick-stepping brown horses and the buggy with the shining top flashed around the corner at Pierson's livery barn… and drew up at the door."

In her finest dress, which was black cashmere, Laura rode with Manly to the preacher's, got married, and returned to her parents' home for a celebration dinner. She and Manly moved to a 2-room gray frame house he had built. Within 10 years, they had settled on Rocky Ridge Farm in Mansfield, Missouri, where Laura wrote about farm and country life.

# AUGUST 26*

## TIZIANO VECELLIO & CECILIA OF CADORE

### *"Marriage – Italian Style"*

SOMETIME IN THE EARLY 1520'S, "TITIAN," who was about 35-years old and already known as a great Venetian painter and portraitist, returned to his hometown, Cadore, an Alpine village in northern Italy. There he met Cecelia, the exquisitely beautiful daughter of the town barber. Titian sketched her, wooed her, and won her. In Venice, she became his housekeeper and mistress, and bore him 2 sons, Pompanio and Orazio.

In 1525, Cecelia became gravely ill. While no one knows for sure if she was really dying, everyone believed she was on her deathbed. Maybe she and Titian should marry, if only to legitimate the children? But the artist was reluctant; like most men, he was content with the way things were.

Cecelia knew her lover well: Didn't the 2 love goddesses he painted in his "Sacred and Profane Love" symbolize his visions of womankind? Their flesh was erotic, soft, and touchable, but it was the idealized Venus who represented eternal and divine love to him, not the well-dressed wife beside her. True, he also immortalized Cecelia in his magnificent "Madonna and the Rabbit;" how tenderly she looks at the young child. That man knew the joys of fatherhood and what it meant to be a loving parent.

Cecelia could barely lift her head from her pillow. If she couldn't live as Mrs. Vecellio, perhaps at least she could die that way. Marry me, she beseeched Titian, gasping. Reluctantly, he acquiesced. A priest was summoned, and the wedding was held in the bedchamber immediately.

Soon afterward, the new bride recovered, and the bridegroom – to his surprise – was sincerely overjoyed. Years later, when Cecelia really died, Titian mourned her deeply and never married again.

---

*Date approximate.

# AUGUST 27

## HENRY LOUIS MENCKEN & SARA HAARDT
### *"I have the most perfect husband"*

ALTHOUGH "H.L." WAS KNOWN FOR HIS satirical wit, biting criticism and combative journalism, the cigar-chomping, hard-boiled writer was always sweetly tender with Sara. When they met in 1923, he had already written widely about American society and the "boo-boisie," lambasting bigotry and hypocrisy, and condemning blue laws, Puritanism, and temperance crusades. Few literary figures of the Jazz Age and the Roaring Twenties were as influential as the Baltimore *Sun's* H.L. Mencken.

He was 42 when he guest-lectured about writing at Goucher College in Baltimore, and Sara was a young instructor who accompanied him to lunch. H.L. was attracted by her dry wit, literary knowledge, elegance, and beauty. He began taking her out for dinner and escorting her to literary soirees, but almost 7 years passed before the famous bachelor decided to tie the knot.

One problem was Sara's health. Within a year, she was fighting tuberculosis and was in and out of sanitariums. When she improved, she quit teaching and became a freelance writer. H.L. gladly provided practical advice, and soon Sara's stories and sketches were appearing in *Vanity Fair*, *Century*, and other popular magazines. By the time she and H.L. married in 1930, Sara had established her own literary reputation and was working on screenplays and novels.

Years earlier, H.L. had poked fun at marriage, but now he concluded, "I am a firm believer in monogamy…. It is comfortable, laudable and sanitary." He and Sara were married in Baltimore's St. Stephen the Martyr Church. After honeymooning in Canada, they moved into a 3rd-floor apartment at 704 Cathedral Street. Sara had decorated it tastefully with Victorian furniture and artwork, but she didn't blink when her new husband impishly "enhanced" the new dining room wallpaper with cartoon figures of Mutt & Jeff, and Krazy Kat, cut from the Sunday funnies.

# AUGUST 28

## JOHN HANCOCK & DOROTHY QUINCY

### *"I am yours forever"*

"IIS SAID THAT JOHN HANCOCK COURTS courts Dolly Quincy," wrote a local wag in Braintree, Massachusetts. But when King George III's troops marched into Lexington and Concord in April 1775, wedding plans were postponed as the groom-to-be – an outspoken patriot – fled to Philadelphia. Fortunately, his good friend, Paul Revere, had been out all night warning everybody that the British were coming, enabling John to skip town and join the Continental Congress, where he was made president.

Dolly remained in her parents' home, fretting about John. The parlor walls had been freshly covered with blue paper decorated with cupids and hearts for a wedding ceremony put off indefinitely. John pined for his "dear Dolly," and begged her to at least "write me often" and send "long letters." He sent her caps, stockings, thread, a summer cloak, and a white kid fan from Paris, which she would carry at their nuptials.

The British blockade of Boston prevented John from coming back, so in late summer Dolly married him at the Burr mansion in Fairfield Connecticut. John was 38, wealthy and good-looking. Dolly was 10 years younger, blond and beautiful. The festivities were simple, due to wartime shortages and the unsettling times. A few days later, bride and bridegroom rode by coach over dusty rutted roads to Philadelphia, where the congress reopened in September. The following spring, when John signed the Declaration of Independence, his name was the largest – so King George could read it without his spectacles!

John Adams, Thomas Jefferson, and Benjamin Franklin visited the Hancocks. Adams was particularly impressed by Dolly. "Among 100 men at this house, she lives and behaves with modesty, decency, dignity and discretion," he wrote. By 1780 the Hancocks had resettled on Beacon Hill in Boston. John was elected governor of Massachusetts (and would be reelected 9 times).

# AUGUST 29

## GUISEPPE VERDI & GIUSEPPINA STREPPONI
### *"Carisima"*

"NOT EVERYBODY CAN WRITE 'AIDA,' BUT somebody has to pack and unpack the trunks," said "Peppina." The great soprano did much more than that during her life with Guiseppe, but she often underplayed her position in light of his greater genius.

After Guiseppe's first wife died in 1840, the 27-year old composer doubted that he would ever write operas again. But when he read the libretto for *Nabucco*, he was deeply moved. "La Strepponi," already an internationally known prima donna, said if he composed the music, she would sing the leading role of Abigaille. Her enthusiasm was inspirational. *Nabucco* became Guiseppe's first major success, premiering at Milan's La Scala in March 1842, and performed 57 times that year, more than any other production.

Peppina's voice began failing a few years later, and she retired from the stage. But she and Guiseppe remained true collaborators. She had a wonderful ear and was a kind but firm critic. She helped him shape many arias, including "Sempre libera" from *La Traviata*. Another magnificent joint effort was the adaptation of the score of *Jerusalem* in 1847. They worked together, taking turns writing lines alternately—

Peppina: "Angel from Heaven!... May I die in the arms of a husband!"
Guiseppe: "Let me die with you! My death will be…"
Peppina: "… Sweet!"

They became lovers soon after, and eventually settled in Sant' Agata in northern Italy. In 1859 they were married in a brief ceremony in the village of Collonges-sous-Saleve near the French and Swiss border. Only their coachman and the village bell ringer witnessed the legalization of a union that lasted, altogether, more than 50 years. Back in Sant' Agata, the local band played selections from Verdi operas as grown men and women cried "Viva Verdi!" and wept with happiness.

*"Mio caro Verdi…"* Peppina said. "Without you I am a body without a soul."

# AUGUST 30
## ELIZABETH STEVENSON & WILLIAM GASKELL
### *"my bonny wee bride"*

ELIZABETH WAS 21 WHEN SHE MET William, an assistant minister in Manchester, England. He was struck by the dark-haired, intelligent and vivacious young woman. They both enjoyed nature walks, poetry, music, and art, and they became engaged within a few months. William was 25 and would become a devoted husband who applauded his wife's eventual success as a poet, novelist, and biographer. During their engagement, he told his sister. "You can't imagine how lonely I feel without her. I am now writing with her rings on my fingers... with her likeness lying before me."

They married in 1832 at the parish church in Knutsford, where Elizabeth had grown up. Friends followed a medieval wedding tradition called "well-dressing" by strewing red sand on the street and enhancing it with flower patterns made with white sand poured from funnels. They also recited:

> *"... Long may they live*
> *Happy may they be,*
> *And blest with a numerous*
> *Pro-ge-ny!"*

The newlyweds honeymooned in Ffestiniog in north Wales while William's sister fixed up their house at 14 Dover Street in Manchester. They moved in on Elizabeth's 22nd birthday, September 29.

William was not only a clergyman but also a professor of English history and literature. He and Elizabeth held literary gatherings for his students, encouraging them to write freely on whatever subjects pleased them.

Elizabeth gave birth to 6 children and performed social work with William in Manchester's sooty slums. Together, they wrote the poem, "Sketches Among the Poor." As "Mrs. Gaskell," she made her literary debut with *Mary Barton* in 1848. Two years later, chapters of her novel, *Cranford*, appeared in Charles Dickens's magazine, *Household Words*. After her friend Charlotte Bronte died in 1855, Elizabeth wrote her definitive biography.

# AUGUST 31

## JIM JORDAN & MARIAN DRISCOLL
### *Fibber McGee & Molly*

FOR ALMOST 30 YEARS, BEGINNING IN 1935, millions of Americans tuned in their radios on Tuesday nights at 9:30 and howled with laughter as Fibber, an outrageous but lovable prevaricator, was once again caught in a lie by his long-suffering wife, Molly. She always ended up proclaiming, "'Taint funny, McGee!" Jim played Fibber, and Marian played Molly. She didn't put her ladylike foot down often, but Fibber always jumped when she did. That's probably why their make-believe marriage lasted at "79 Wistful Vista."

"Fibber was a bum," Jim said years later. "He never worked and was constantly taking advantage of his friends. That was the mystery of the show: how he managed to keep any friends at all. But he was likable... in the same way that [TV character] Archie Bunker is."

Jim and Marian were teenagers in the St. John's Church choir in Peoria, Illinois when they first met. Even then, Jim hammed up his performances while Marian, who intended to become a music teacher, took her singing more seriously. Five days after they married in 1918, Jim left on an army troop train for Georgia and France, and returned home the following July.

For the next 6 years, he and Marian worked at odd jobs, sang in churches and lodges and on vaudeville stages. A major break came on a 1931 show called *The Smackouts*. Jim played a talkative but ineffectual grocer "smack out of everything" except long-winded, unbelievable stories. Four years later, the Jordans became "Fibber McGee and Molly."

Marian also portrayed other characters on the show, including Teeny, the exasperating neighbor child whose whiny "Why, mister, why, mister?" drove Fibber to tears, and the sorrowful Mrs. Wearybottom, who spoke in monotonous run-on sentences. Every week, Fibber horrified Molly by trotting down the hall to his famous overstuffed closet. When he opened it, everything – old shoes, tin cans, dumbbells, books, and more – tumbled out, prompting him to say, "Gotta straighten out that closet one of these days."

# SEPTEMBER

# SEPTEMBER 1

## BENJAMIN FRANKLIN & DEBORAH READ

*"Keep your eyes open before marriage,
half shut afterwards"*

"BEING CALLED ONE MORNING TO BREAKFAST," I found it in a China Bowl with a Spoon of Silver. They had been bought for me without my knowledge by my Wife, and had cost her the enormous sum of three and twenty shillings, for which she had no Excuse or Apology to make, but that she thought *her* husband deserv'd a Silver Spoon and China Bowl as well as any of his Neighbors," wrote Ben in his *Autobiography*.

The future inventor, statesman, and ambassador was munching on a roll when he first spotted Deborah in Philadelphia shortly after he arrived from his hometown, Boston. He rented a room in her parents' home, "made some Courtship," and proposed the following year, when he and Deborah were both 18. Unfortunately, her mother discouraged them. After all, Ben was going to England soon; why not wait until he returned?

While he was gone, Deborah married a cad who already had a wife and who eventually fled to the West Indies to escape creditors. By the time Ben came back, Deborah had been abandoned by her "husband" *and* her mother! Straightaway, Ben "took her to wife 1 September 1730."

They lived above his Market Street print shop, where Deborah assisted Ben and also ran their book and stationery shop next door. Her fear of ships and ocean travel prevented her from sailing to Europe with him, but she managed their business affairs whenever he went away. Ben's first publishing success was *Poor Richard's Almanack*, filled with recipes, weather forecasts, lunar charts, and the homespun wisdom readers still appreciate today. Deborah gasped when Ben flew kites in thunderstorms until he explained that he was learning about electricity… and promptly invented lightning rods. He also invented bifocals, established the first lending library, and founded Philadelphia's first volunteer fire department.

# SEPTEMBER 2

## BENJAMIN WEST & ELIZABETH SHEWELL

*Devoted to his art, and to Betsy*

SHORTLY BEFORE BEN MARRIED "BETSY" IN London in 1764, the 25-year old artist painted "The Choice of Hercules," depicting the Greek hero standing between a demure figure of Virtue and a seductive, voluptuous Vice. Classical themes were popular in 18th century England, where Ben had come to study art. He had saved every penny for this trip from Pennsylvania, and was assisted by a rich merchant who admired him.

There were no art schools or museums in colonial America at that time; even good art supplies were difficult to find. Ben and Betsy knew that he needed to study the old masters and develop his talents. Back home in Philadelphia, Betsy's well-to-do parents had been glad when the poor artist left town and went to Europe. But a few years later, the English were calling Ben "the American Raphael." Fame and financial success were his; now all he needed was Betsy – would she marry him in London? Yes, she wrote, even if her family objected.

Family legends recount that Betsy's older brother locked his 22-year old sister in her room when he learned about her plans, but one of Betsy's maids smuggled in a rope ladder. When Betsy found out that Ben's father and her cousin Matthew were sailing to England, she dropped the ladder out her bedroom window, climbed down, and ran off to join them.

She married Ben at the church of St. Martin-in-the-Fields, and they settled down on Castle Street in Leicester Square, London. Eventually, Ben became president of the Royal Academy of Art and was known as the "father of American art." Betsy kept a detailed diary of life in late 18th century London. Even 50 years later, she could look back and say her husband "never had a fault."

## SEPTEMBER 3

## SIR EDMUND HILLARY & LOUISE ROSE

*"Really, life is too good to be true"*

L OUISE HAD A PRETTY GOOD IDEA of what she was getting into when she married Edmund in 1953. The tall, good-looking 34-year old mountaineer had climbed to "the roof of the world" – Mount Everest's peak in the Himalayas – and had just been knighted by Queen Elizabeth for his achievements.

Louise's father was president of the New Zealand Alpine Club, and she and Edmund had known each other for years. The 11-year age gap between them had prevented them from becoming romantically involved previously. But now that Louise was almost 23 and studying the violin at the Sydney, Australia Conservatory of Music, Edmund decided to see her on his way home to New Zealand.

He wasted no time admitting his true feelings. He proposed forthwith and asked Louise to go with him to England, where he'd agreed to give some lectures. "Somewhat in a daze, she consented and I was overjoyed," he wrote in his autobiography. Then, the fearless adventurer, who'd taken more risks in a few years than most people take in a lifetime, added, "It certainly proved the most sensible action I have ever taken."

The wedding was held in New Zealand on Louise's birthday. Afterward, she and Edmund flew to London, with stopovers in Australia, Java, Singapore, and other exotic places. Louise's "bubbling enthusiasm" thrilled Edmund and charmed well-wishers and reporters along the way. She wrote their parents, "I'm really not sure if I'm dreaming or not…."

Edmund went on other expeditions including a 1958 "Race to the Pole" in Antarctica, and he supported many humanitarian causes for the people of Nepal. He and Louise trekked through the Himalayan mountains together, hiking along hillside paths bordered by orchids, magnolias, and wildflowers, and he felt the wonder of seeing familiar sights "through her delighted eyes."

# SEPTEMBER 4

## KEVIN BACON & KYRA SEDGWICK

### *Yin and Yang*

MANY YEARS AFTER THE STAGE, TV and film stars married in 1988, they learned that they were distant cousins. The news came as quite a shock on the TV show, "Finding Your Roots," when host Henry Louis Gates, Jr. made the surprising announcement: Kyra and Kevin were "10th cousins." Being on the same (albeit very large) family tree did not distress the two actors. Instead, they were rather pleased, and tweeted the information online to their fans.

They were married in a civil ceremony about a year after they met in 1987 on the set of Lanford Wilson's play, "Lemon Sky," to be shown on PBS television. Kyra was 23, had attended Sarah Lawrence College and was graduated from University of Southern California, where she majored in theater. Kevin was 30 and had first appeared on the TV soap opera, "Another World," when he was 16. Soon after that, he won a scholarship to the Pennsylvania Governor's School for the Arts at Bucknell University. Subsequently, he was known for his performances in "National Lampoon's Animal House" (1978), "Diner" (1982), and "Footloose" (1984) and she achieved stardom for her role as Deputy Police Chief Brenda Leigh Johnson in TV's "The Closer."

If not for Kevin's support, she wouldn't have taken the role, because it meant extended periods of filming in California while he and their two kids lived in New York. "There is a yin and yang to everything," Kyra said in a magazine interview. "... sometimes the universe is telling you, 'This is what you need.'"

And he still makes her feel like the "most beautiful woman in the room."

# SEPTEMBER 5

## FRITZ KAHLENBERG & INGEBORG WALLHEIMER
*Love in perilous times*

S HE WAS TALL, SLENDER, AND RADIANTLY beautiful. In her early 20's, Ingeborg was several years younger than Fritz, whose bright blue eyes and light-hearted manner belied the strain of being a Jew hiding in wartime Amsterdam. He and Ingeborg first met in the Dutch Underground, a resistance group of valiant men and women who dedicated their lives to ending the Nazi reign of terror by setting bombs, transporting munitions, forging documents, and delivering clandestine messages. Anyone caught was either killed or sent to a slave labor camp.

Fritz never stayed for long in his attic hideout at 36 Michelangelo Street or in other relatively safe havens throughout the region. Determined to let the world know what was happening, he recruited a group of photographers called the "Hidden Camera" who secretly took pictures – at great personal risk – of Nazi military movements, the persecution and deportation of thousands of Jews, resistance bombings and German reprisals, the brutally cold "Hunger Winter" of 1944-1945, and finally, liberation by the Allies.

Fritz taught Ingeborg how to operate a camera, which she carried inside her shoulder bag. As if rummaging for something, she would press the lens against a tiny hole cut in the leather and snap pictures of events on the streets. She also transported weapons to resistance fighters by pushing baby carriages loaded with Sten guns under the blankets. When the war ended, she and Fritz were honored by the United States government and General Eisenhower for "gallant service" in assisting the Allied defense.

In 1946, they were married in a civil ceremony in Amsterdam, followed by a reception at the Wallheimers' home. The celebrants danced to popular American tunes such as "Begin the Beguine," played on the family's record player. Eventually, Fritz and Ingeborg sailed to New York, where they produced many documentary and travel films.

# SEPTEMBER 6

## THOMAS WOOLNER & ALICE GERTRUDE WAUGH

*"Love comes divinely, gladdening mortal life."*

"TO MY WIFE, ALICE GERTRUDE, I offer this vision of the past," wrote Thomas in *Pygmalion*. Seventeen years after they married in 1864, he composed his book-length poem about the mythical Greek sculptor who fell in love with the beautiful statue of a woman, which ultimately came to life. Thomas was a sculptor as well as a poet, so it's only fitting that he was attracted to the legend. Thirty-one years later, George Bernard Shaw wrote a play about it. The musical, *My Fair Lady* was based upon it, too.

Thomas and Alice were married at St. James's Church, Paddington, and honeymooned on the British island of Guernsey. After traveling through Dartmouth, Exeter, and Salisbury, they settled at 29, Wellbeck Street in London's Cavendish Square and stayed there for the rest of their lives.

Like other pre-Raphaelite artists of his generation, Thomas chose uplifting themes for his work. He was thinking of his new bride when he wrote "Beautiful Lady" 6 months after their wedding:

*"I love my Lady; she is very fair…*
*How beautiful she is! A glorious gem,*
*She shines above the summer diadem*
*Of flowers!"*

England's poet laureate Alfred, Lord Tennyson, and his wife, Emily, Edward Lear, the Carlyles, and other talented English friends sent gifts and good wishes to the happy couple. Thomas immortalized them and other writers, statesmen, and monarchs in busts and statues. His statue of John Stuart Mill is on the Thames embankment, and his bronze statue of Captain Cook overlooks Sydney harbor in Australia. Occasionally, Alice posed for Thomas. He missed her terribly whenever she left Wellbeck Street and proclaimed "the house has received its soul again" when she came home.

# SEPTEMBER 7*

## ANNE KINGSMILL & HENEAGE FINCH

### *Her "much lov'd husband"*

ANNE AND HENEAGE MET AT KING Charles II's court and were married in 1684, when she was 22-years old. The orphaned young woman had been appointed maid of honor to Mary of Modena, the duchess of York. Heneage was the duke of York's gentleman of the bedchamber. When the king died the following year, the duke became King James II. In 3 years, he fled to France after unsuccessfully trying to convert England to Roman Catholicism.

Heneage and Anne refused to swear allegiance to the new monarchs, William and Mary, and swiftly lost their positions. Anne was deeply saddened to give up the "glorious show" of court life, but leaving was the best thing for her as a future author. She and Heneage retired to his family seat in Kent, where the sweet countryside was conducive to contemplation and writing. They became count and countess of Winchilsea when Heneage succeeded to the title.

"They err, who say that husbands can't be lovers," Anne wrote, inspired by Heneage's boundless affection and support for her writing. Whenever he returned home from journeys, Anne shared new poems, fables, and religious meditations with him. Through poetry, she conveyed her passion for Heneage at a time when few women revealed their amorous feelings in print. In "Mr. F., Now Earl of Winchilsea," she calls him "Dafnis" and herself "Ardelia," and concludes that when true love exists, a poet doesn't need the muses for inspiration.

Although Anne's work was respected by such writers as Alexander Pope, the world of 17th century literature still belonged to men. More than 100 years later, her talents were rediscovered by the great poet William Wordsworth, who said she had been "a wood lark among the town sparrows."

---

*Date approximate.

# SEPTEMBER 8

## KING GEORGE III & PRINCESS CHARLOTTE OF MECKLENBURG

### *"Ich will!"*

"YOU'RE GOING TO BE QUEEN OF England," Charlotte's mother said in 1761, when George's formal proposal of marriage arrived. Two months later, the German princess boarded a ship bound for Great Britain.

George, who was 23 and would rule for 60 years, had a fair amount of latitude in choosing a wife. Charlotte was 17, plain-looking but healthy, with a dignified presence and charm. Until she learned to speak English, she and George conversed in French and German.

Marriage plans were delayed when the king came down with chicken pox, but Charlotte sent him a lock of her hair to soothe him. She curtsied before George when at last they met, but he promptly picked her up and hugged her affectionately. After the royal family met her, George made sure that he and Charlotte dined alone. Then everyone got all dressed up and walked to the Chapel Royal, across the road from the palace.

It had been a very hot day, and the heat lasted into the evening. At 10:00 PM Charlotte, wearing a purple velvet cape trimmed with ermine atop a silver wedding gown enhanced by diamonds, stood under a domed canopy until the king came down the aisle to claim her. "Courage, Princess, courage!" whispered George's brother William, who noticed she was trembling. The Archbishop of Canterbury conducted the ceremony, and Charlotte confirmed her vows with "Ich will." Two weeks later, she was crowned in Westminster Abbey.

Although history remembers George primarily for losing the American colonies, he was a loving husband to Charlotte, and father to 12 surviving children. He and Charlotte liked being home with their kids, giving them a somewhat boring, traditional life. She devoted her spare energies to charitable causes, especially for the welfare of British women and children. He didn't discuss affairs of state with her… but he might have done better if he had!

# SEPTEMBER 9

## RICHARD STEELE & MARY SCURLOCK
### *"Yr Obedient Husband"*

ICK MET "MOLLY" IN LONDON AT his first wife's funeral in 1706. He had been married for only 2 years and it had been fairly common knowledge that he'd married the elderly widow primarily for the property she held in Barbados. One day, the 35-year old English dramatist and essayist would be immortalized with Joseph Addison for their periodicals, *The Tatler* and *The Spectator*, but now all Dick could think about was beautiful Molly.

At the Kit-Kat club and other coffeehouses he frequented, Dick described the 28-year old Welshwoman to friends such as writer Jonathan Swift. Dick nicknamed her "Prue" and "Molly" and pursued her intensely, although she did little to encourage him. Before long, he was proposing marriage and declaring in ardent letters that he was "tenderly, passionately, faithfully thine." He asked Molly's widowed mother to intercede, after overstating his assets and minimizing his debts. Maybe Dick was erratic, extravagant and impulsive; he also was brilliant and adoring. If only Molly's "fair lips" would say yes, giving him "in one monosyllable more than all the eloquence in the world could express."

At last, on September 8, 1707, they secured a marriage license. Dick was ecstatic: "Methinks I could write a volume to you; but all the language on earth would fail in saying how much and with what disinterested passion I am ever yours."

In truth, no records exist of a wedding ceremony. For some reason, the marriage was kept secret, but a month later, Dick and Molly moved into a house on London's Bury Street, "third door, right hand, turning out to Jermyn St." Molly saved hundreds of Richard's letters and eventually donated them to the British Museum.

To Dick, September 9 would always be the day "in which you gave me your hand and heart."

# SEPTEMBER 10

## RICHARD STRAUSS & PAULINE DE AHNA
### *"my Pauksl"*

"IN WEIMAR I WON MY BELOVED Pauline," wrote the German composer in his *Recollections and Reflections*. The magnificent singer "had followed me as a pupil and was... an excellent Pamina, Elvira, Elsa, Elizabeth and Evchen, and even had the pluck to sing Fidelio and Isolde."

They had known each other for 7 years when they announced their engagement to a stunned group of musicians in May 1894. While rehearsing Richard's opera *Guntram*, Pauline made a mistake and began arguing with him. At first only angry words flew between the stage and Richard's podium. Then she hurled the musical score, which struck him on the head. Pauline stormed off to her dressing room, and Richard followed, furious. The door slammed shut and their loud arguing continued. Then... silence. A few musicians tiptoed to Pauline's door and knocked on it timidly. Richard opened it, smiling broadly. "I have just become engaged to Fraulein de Ahna," he proclaimed.

Richard's parents thought the high-strung diva was unsuitable for their genius son, which saddened him greatly. But he was resolute. He told his parents that he and Pauline would see them as little as possible "so long as the woman whom after much deliberation I have chosen as my wife, and whom in spite of her faults I love and admire, irritates you and embitters your life."

Richard's wedding gift to Pauline was a group of German lieder, or songs – "Cacilie," "Secret Invitation," and "Tomorrow" – which he gave her soon after their wedding. She was 31 and he was 30 years old. Already he had completed his famous *Till Eulenspiegel*, based upon Flemish legends of an endearing prankster and folk hero. The years ahead would be filled with symphonic poems, songs, and operas he would compose, including *Salome* and *Der Rosenkavalier*. Even after Pauline retired from opera singing, she continued to be Richard's greatest admirer and the "model interpreter" of his songs.

# SEPTEMBER 11

## AGATHA MILLER CHRISTIE & MAX MALLOWAN
### *Second spring*

THE FAMOUS ENGLISH WRITER OF MYSTERY and detective novels met Max at a Middle Eastern archeological site in 1930. He was an Oxford classical scholar and the 24-year old assistant to the project leader at Ur, an ancient settlement not far from Baghdad. Agatha was 40 and depressed after a recent divorce.

They took long car trips to visit sites. Nothing fazed Agatha – not flea bites, nor brutally hot weather, nor car trouble that left them stranded in the Arabian desert without water or shelter. Their Bedouin driver set off on foot to seek help, leaving them alone overnight. By the time they returned to the main base, Max had fallen in love.

Agatha liked Max a lot, but marriage was out of the question. Once burned was bad enough; besides, the "very unsuitable" difference in their ages surely would doom any permanent relationship. Fortunately, Max pursued her anyway. After a romantic trip back to London on the *Orient Express* train, Agatha concluded (as she wrote in her autobiography) that "nothing in the world would be as delightful as being married to him."

Slipping away from family and friends, she and Max were married in the chapel of St. Columba's Church in Edinburgh, Scotland. Two days later, they crossed the English Channel by boat and took the *Orient Express* to Venice for a honeymoon before continuing to Greece and back to Ur.

In their frequent travels, Agatha helped Max by cataloguing and photographing finds he uncovered. He assisted her with archeological information for some of her stories, such as *Murder on the Orient Express* and *Murder in Mesopotamia*. Years later, Max summed everything up by saying, "After being stuck in the sand... we never looked back." Neither could have "guessed that the short journey from Baghdad would lead to a longer union... destined to last the best part of 50 years."

# SEPTEMBER 12

## JOHN F. KENNEDY & JACQUELINE BOUVIER

*"What I want more than anything in the world is to be married to him"*

THEY BOTH WERE INCREDIBLY GOOD-LOOKING AND driven to succeed. John's family was wealthier, but Jackie was classy and refined. She was an accomplished equestrian; he was allergic to horses. He loved touch football; she quit playing soon after she broke her ankle. Outgoing on the surface, deep down John was as insular and private as Jackie was.

They met at a Georgetown dinner party in May 1951. She was a 21-year old George Washington University senior, and the Massachusetts congressman was 33. "I leaned across the asparagus and asked her for a date," John recalled later. They didn't get serious until the following winter, when Jackie was a cub reporter for the *Washington Times-Herald*, and John's Senate race had begun.

Jackie's mother and stepfather, Janet and Hugh Auchincloss, wanted a small, dignified wedding but the Kennedys insisted that the senator they hoped would be president one day be married in a grand, elaborate affair. Parties began a week before. On the day of the 1953 wedding, thousands of people stood outside St. Mary's Church in Newport, Rhode Island. John's brother, Robert, was the best man, and Jackie's sister, Lee, was her matron of honor.

The wedding day was not entirely blissful. Jackie's stepfather escorted her down the aisle because her mother made sure that her alcoholic father didn't show up at the ceremony and embarrass everybody. The Auchinclosses threw a party for 1200 guests at Hammersmith Farm, their country estate. At nightfall, the newlyweds flew to New York to spend their wedding night at the Waldorf-Astoria Hotel. Honeymooning in a private villa in Acapulco, John caught a 9-foot-long sailfish, which was mounted and displayed on his Senate office wall; later it hung in the White House.

## SEPTEMBER 13

## SIGMUND FREUD & MARTHA BERNAYS

*"One is very crazy when one is in love"*

SOMETHING WAS DIFFERENT WHEN SIGMUND CAME home from work in April 1882. Usually, the 26-year old medical doctor raced to his room without stopping to chat with family guests in the dining room, but he was struck by the sight of an attractive young woman with long, dark hair and large, expressive eyes. Martha was tall, slim, and 21, with an air of self-assurance. Like Eve in the garden of Eden, she also was peeling an apple!

Love-struck, Sigmund began sending red roses to Martha and calling her "Princess." In late May they took their first walk together. They exchanged books, and she baked cookies for him to "dissect." Holding hands under his parents' table, they considered themselves unofficially engaged.

That summer, Martha's family moved from Vienna to Wandsbek, a Hamburg suburb, possibly to keep the young couple apart since marriage would have to wait until Sigmund's practice was established. In December, he bought Martha a garnet engagement ring. Until they married in 1886, he wrote more than 900 letters to his "precious darling," discussing his growing interest in patients suffering from symptoms with no known physical causes. Eventually, he became the founder of psychoanalysis.

They were married in civil and Jewish ceremonies in Wandsbek, and honeymooned for two weeks on the Baltic coast. Back in Vienna, Martha spent her small dowry to furnish their apartment and borrowed chairs from the porter who lived in the basement. Sigmund hung a sign by their doorway stating that he specialized in nervous diseases.

Two years later, he wrote a friend, "We live pretty happily in steadily increasing unassumingness. When we hear the baby laugh we imagine it is the loveliest thing that can happen to us." By 1891 they had moved to a more spacious apartment at Berggasse 19, and stayed there for the next 47 years.

# SEPTEMBER 14

## GERALD ISAAC STILLER & ANNE MEARA
### *"Hershey & Mary Elizabeth"*

THE FIRST TIME JERRY ASKED ANNE to go out for coffee, he never expected that she'd ask him to steal the silverware!

They had just met at a casting call in New York City for actors seeking work in a summer-stock company. As Jerry recalled, Anne was "a tall girl… with auburn hair and an angelic face." After neither passed muster at the audition, Jerry suggested that they go to a nearby cafeteria. In 1953 he had barely enough money to pay for the coffee, but she insisted on paying for herself and mentioned that her roommates kept misplacing the silverware.

Anne swiped a few spoons, and Jerry tucked a fork into his pocket. "I've just become her accomplice in crime," he thought. A year later, (and 6 days before her 26th birthday) he also became her husband. With family members standing by the bride and groom, they were married at City Hall in New York by Judge Ben Shalleck, a former husband of singer Lillian Roth.

Six years later, Anne studied Judaism and became a convert to it. Pretty soon, Stiller and Meara were a popular duo, performing as "Hershey Horowitz and Mary Elizabeth Doyle" in a comedy act on TV variety shows including 34 times on *The Ed Sullivan Show*. They also wrote and performed in radio commercials for Blue Nun wine.

Jerry gained fame as George Costanza's irascible father, Frank, on the TV show, *Seinfeld*. Anne had recurring roles in TV shows such as *All in the Family*, *Sex and the City* and *The King of Queens*, where Jerry attained major stardom as grumpy, quick-tempered Arthur Spooner.

Parents of actors Ben Stiller and Amy Stiller, Anne and Jerry lived in the same Riverside Drive apartment ever since Ben was born.

# SEPTEMBER 15

## JAMES MADISON & DOLLEY PAYNE TODD

*"this day I give my Hand to the Man who of all others I most admire."*

M UCH AS THE FUTURE PRESIDENT HATED sea travel, Dolley was the real reason he didn't sail to France with James Monroe in late spring, 1794. His former Princeton classmate, Aaron Burr, had introduced him to the 26-year old blue-eyed, black-haired, pink-cheeked young widow and mother in Philadelphia. James couldn't stop thinking about her. At 43, he had been reluctant to marry since being jilted 10 years before. He certainly kept busy – working on the Bill of Rights' creation and ratification, determining the roles of the president, forming an independent national judiciary, and other significant matters… but recently, he'd been feeling lonely.

Most probably, James proposed to Dolley in a letter, although none survives to confirm this. We do know that she became ill, probably with malaria. He went to Montpelier, his family's estate in Virginia, and attended to a sick houseguest. Weeks passed, and James didn't hear from Dolley. He'd shared his feelings with her cousin, however, who wrote Dolley that "he thinks so much of you that he has Lost his Tongue, at Night he Dreams of you and Starts in his Sleep a Calling on you to relieve his Flame for he Burns to such an excess that he will be shortly consumed & he hopes that your Heart will be callous to every other swain but himself."

At last, Dolley sent James a letter, accepting his proposal. They married at Harewood in the Shenandoah Valley, the plantation home of Dolley's sister Lucy and her husband, George Steptoe Washington. James wore a low-cut waistcoat with a lace jabot at the neck, and gave Dolley a necklace of medallions depicting scenes of Roman history. During the boisterous wedding supper, bridesmaids snipped off his lace ruffles to save as souvenirs.

# SEPTEMBER 16
## PAUL KLEE & LILY STUMPF
*"Dearest beloved heart"*

PAUL AND LILY HAD BEEN IN love for 8 years when they married in 1906. Her parents had opposed the match, doubting that the young Swiss artist could ever support a family. But nothing weakened Lily's devotion. When she first met Paul, he was a 19-year old student from Bern who came to Munich to study music, literature, and art. "It is not my task to reproduce appearances," he wrote, after he had decided to concentrate on painting. "For that there is the photographic plate… I want to reach the heart."

Lily was 22, an accomplished pianist and music teacher when Paul called on her father, a medical doctor. Dr. Stumpf discouraged his daughter from seeing Paul, at first gently, then adamantly. Lily protested; she and Paul were kindred spirits, passionately in love with books, music, and each other. At last she announced that they intended to marry. Paul begged Dr. Stumpf to accept their decision. Finally, he did, "though he asks sardonically what we plan to live on."

The answer was simple: Lily would work so Paul could paint. Their son, Felix, remembered, "In the little flat in Munich, my mother… gave music lessons from morning to night and her husband… had to see to the chores and look after the baby. The kitchen was his room; there his pictures and drawings saw the light…."

Afternoons, Paul took Felix to a park where the son played and the father painted. Much of Paul's work was fanciful and witty; he was inspired by primitive art and children's drawings, as well as Cubism and Surrealism. Thanks in part to Lily's willingness to work full-time in an era when few wives did, within 4 years of their marriage Paul's first exhibition was held, and his career was launched. Fanciful paintings such as "Twittering Machine," a pen-and-ink drawing tinted with watercolor, and "At the Mountain of the Bull," in watercolor and oil, influenced other artists of the 20th century.

# SEPTEMBER 17

## WILLIAM ABBOTT & BETTY SMITH
### *His first partner*

ABBOTT AND COSTELLO BECAME A TEAM years after "Bud" Abbott found his most lovable partner. As the son of a circus advance man and a bareback rider, he grew up in show business and was treasurer of Washington D.C.'s National Theater when Betty caught his eye in 1918. The pert 17-year old dancer from Buffalo, New York, had changed her name from Jenny Mae Pratt when she let home and joined an acrobatic act. She was working at the National when a well-heeled fan took the entire cast for a Sunday cruise on the Potomac. Suddenly, one of the female performers foolishly dived into the water. The current was treacherous, and while everyone stood on deck wondering what to do, Bud jumped in and rescued the hysterical girl. Seeing this, Betty was "hooked" too; 19-year old Bud was a hero!

A week later, they drove to Alexandria, Virginia after the midnight show, got married, and were back in time for the matinee. When the show closed, they developed their own comedy skits, with Bud playing the straight man unaware that Betty was getting laughs behind his back.

Eventually, Bud began performing with other comics, too. In 1936, he and Betty had dinner with Lou Costello and his wife at Reuben's, a New York City deli. When Lou's straight man became ill, Bud stepped in as a perfect (and permanent) replacement. "Abbott and Costello" found success first on the burlesque and vaudeville stages, then on radio shows, on Broadway, and in feature films.

Betty was happy to watch the new comedy team take off. She and Bud moved to Hollywood where they held parties for hundreds of people under huge circus tents. After 32 years of marriage, they renewed their wedding vows in a traditional Jewish ceremony – a tribute to Bud's mother, who never lost faith in her son or her daughter-in-law.

# SEPTEMBER 18

## SIR ARTHUR CONAN DOYLE & JEAN LECKIE
### *"Elementary," said Arthur*

"MY HONEYMOON BEGAN ON THE DAY I was wed, and will continue right through eternity," said the father of the modern detective story and creator of Sherlock Holmes years after he married Jean in 1907. They had met 10 years before, when she was 24 and the burly writer with a walrus mustache was 38 and married. Sadly, his wife, Louise, was gravely ill, and the strain of caring for an invalid was almost too much for Arthur.

Jean was warm and adoring. She had hazel green eyes, dark blond hair, and an untroubled acceptance that Arthur would never leave Louise or hurt her deliberately. Jean and Arthur fell in love quickly, but for a long time only Arthur's mother, "the Ma'am," knew about it, and she approved as well. When at last Louise died, Arthur waited a year to marry Jean.

A few close friends and relatives attended the quiet ceremony at London's St. Margaret's, Westminster. Arthur wore a frock coat, white waistcoat, and a white gardenia in his lapel, and looked "supremely happy," said a reporter. Jean wore a white silk gown appliquéd with Spanish lace and pearls over silver tissue. Arthur recited his vows "in a clear, fervent voice, but the bride's replies were barely audible."

The reception was livelier. Writers including Bram Stoker ("Dracula") and James M. Barrie ("Peter Pan") and 250 other guests watched 48-year old Arthur carry his new bride up the Hotel Metropole's red-carpeted stairs so she wouldn't get entangled in her train. They honeymooned on the Continent, traveling as far as Constantinople.

Settling down at Windlesham, a country estate in Sussex, Arthur wrote more Sherlock Holmes stories, as well as plays, adventure novels, and treatises on spiritualism. Jean said, "Whenever I heard my husband's dear voice in the distance, or he came into a room, something radiant seemed to enter and permeate the atmosphere."

# SEPTEMBER 19*

## ELIZABETH BARRETT & ROBERT BROWNING

*"How do I love thee? Let me count the ways"*

ONE OF THE WORLD'S MOST ROMANTIC love stories began in January, 1845 when Robert sent Elizabeth a note: "I love your verses with all my heart, dear Miss Barrett."

Five months passed before they actually met, but a lively correspondence between the two poets began immediately. Because of Robert, "the face of all the world has changed," wrote Elizabeth in *Sonnets from the Portuguese*.

She was almost 39, a fragile recluse in her widowed father's house at 50 Wimpole Street, London. Robert was 33, a handsome bachelor who'd already written "My Last Duchess," "The Pied Piper of Hamelin," and other poems and plays.

What weighed upon the two lovers most heavily was Edward Barrett's tyrannical demand that none of his children ever leave home or marry. He was "as immovable as stone," said Elizabeth, but nothing would deter her from seeing Robert. Not only did he bring passion into her life, he gave her the strength and will to venture outside for short walks and carriage rides.

On September 12, 1846, Elizabeth slipped out of the house and married Robert in St. Marylebone Church. The wedding ring was put on and quickly removed before the bride and groom exited through separate doors. Trembling, Elizabeth returned home and composed a farewell letter to her "dearest Papa," to be delivered after she and Robert had gone. From then on, Robert could not bear to call on "Miss Barrett" at her house when she was, in fact, Mrs. Browning. Letters flew back and forth for days, until Elizabeth wrote, "By tomorrow at this time, I shall have *you* only, to love me – my beloved!"

On September 19, "a delicious day," said Robert, they boarded a train for Southampton, then the ferry to France, where they honeymooned in Paris before continuing on to Florence, Italy. To Elizabeth, they were "living as in a dream… loving and being loved better every day."

---

*Date their marriage truly began.

# SEPTEMBER 20

## LEWIS LATIMER & MARY WILSON

### *"My Venus shall be ebony"*

BY THE TIME LEWIS AND MARY met in the early 1870's, the future inventor had been a draftsman for over 5 years. The son of fugitive slaves granted freedom in Massachusetts, Lewis had served in the Union navy when he was 16 and subsequently found employment at a patent law firm in Boston. Mary was from Fall River, and she encouraged Lewis to learn as much as possible at work. Although Lewis could be shy about expressing his growing love for Mary, he wrote about it easily:

> Let others boast of maidens fair,
> Of eyes blue and golden hair,
> My heart, like needle ever true,
> Turns to the maid of ebon hue.

They married in 1873, two weeks after his 25th birthday, and settled in Boston. Within a year, Lewis and a partner had secured their first patent, for a railroad car "water closet." Alexander Graham Bell also asked Lewis to use his self-taught draftsman's skills to make the necessary patent application drawings for his new "telephone." Bell would remain eternally grateful for this; thanks to Lewis's speed and competence, their submission was filed only hours before another inventor's.

In the 1880's, after Lewis formulated a way to make inexpensive long-lasting carbon filaments for lightbulbs while working for one of Thomas Edison's competitors, the great man convinced him to join his organization. In later years, Lewis volunteered at Manhattan's Henry Street Settlement House, helping new immigrants learn English and mechanical drawing. Unfortunately, most of Lewis's achievements were not fully recognized during his lifetime. Mary remained his most loyal admirer and the inspiration for his greatest poetry:

> O'er marble Venus let them rage.
> Who set the fashions of the Age.
> Each to his taste, but as for me
> My Venus shall be ebony.

# SEPTEMBER 21

## MAUD POWELL & H. GODFREY TURNER
*A deep love of music and each other*

FOR MAUD, BECOMING AN INTERNATIONALLY ACCLAIMED woman violinist in the late 19th century had required many sacrifices, including giving up an ordinary childhood to "train train train." It also meant forgoing activities that might damage her hands, and not wasting time with suitors. Opportunities to play professionally were limited, especially because sitting beside men in orchestras was deemed "improper," and women were considered too delicate for the rigors of rehearsals and performances. But Maud had abundant grit and talent. After all, her Uncle John had explored the Grand Canyon, and her Aunt Emma was the first woman to climb Pike's Peak. By the time Maud was 35, she had performed for European kings and queens as well as countless people in small towns across the United States.

Maud was 36 and performing in London when she met "Sunny," the genial 44-year old English manager of John Philip Sousa's band. Sunny knew a lot about music and had a wonderful knack for making Maud laugh. After Maud's tour concluded, she returned to America, and soon afterward, Sunny proposed. He understood Maud's life as a performer and promised to be a true companion and lover.

They married in 1904 at a farm near Pawling, New York. "Madame Powell," as she would be known professionally, always wore her gold wedding ring on her right hand, to keep her left hand as agile as possible. She and Sunny built a home by the water in Great Neck, New York, and called their boat *"Fiddle-Dee-Dee."* Sunny managed Maud's career, accompanied her on tours, and wrote advertisements proclaiming that she had "the Arm of a Man, the Heart of a Woman, and the Head of an Artist." Maud was the first instrumentalist to record for RCA Victor, and her recordings became worldwide best-sellers. In 1989 three compact disc recordings of her music were reissued by the Maud Powell Foundation, based in Arlington, Virginia.

# SEPTEMBER 22
## BARRY MORRIS GOLDWATER &
## MARGARET JOHNSON
*"There wasn't any escape" from his persistent proposal*

THE TALL, BLUE-EYED FUTURE SENATOR FROM Arizona proposed to "Peggy" in a telephone booth on New Year's Eve, 1933. Barry had been visiting her hometown of Muncie, Indiana, and "was running out of money and out of patience," he wrote, later, in his autobiography. "For the umpteenth time I asked her to marry me. She said yes."

They first met 3 years before, when Peggy and her mother were shopping in Goldwaters department store in Phoenix, Arizona. Barry was a $15-a-week junior clerk who thought Peggy was very pretty, with a good sense of humor, and a delightful laugh. Unfortunately, the petite blue-eyed brunette wasn't impressed with him or his "hick town." She dropped by again the following year, and Barry went back east to see her, too. He proposed in person, by letter, and over the telephone, but nothing – not even his gift of a caged lovebird – worked until that night in the phone booth.

Once Peggy accepted, Barry wanted to get married immediately, but first she and her mother took a 4-month-long cruise around the world, which they had been planning for a long time. Fearing that Peggy might fall for another guy in a shipboard romance, Barry sent lots of letters that greeted her at every port. When at last she arrived in New York harbor, he gave her his grandmother Sarah's wedding ring from 1854.

They married in Muncie in 1934 and settled in Arizona, which Peggy grew to love and where she and Barry began studying and collecting Native American Indian art. Even after he was elected to the U.S. Senate, ran for President, and became known as a leader of conservatism in America, for Barry nothing ever compared with the night that Peggy said yes.

# SEPTEMBER 23

## PAUL REVERE & RACHEL WALKER

*"the Fair One that is nearest my Heart"*

RACHEL MARRIED PAUL IN BOSTON IN 1773, two years before he took his "midnight ride" warning everyone that "the British are coming!" The previous spring, Paul chanced to see Rachel outside his gold and silversmith shop. She knew that Paul's wife had died recently, and offered to walk home with him and visit his young children. They took such a liking to the cheerful young woman that Paul began to court her. On the back of a bill for "mending a spoon," he composed a riddle spelling out Rachel's name:

*Take ¾ of a pain that makes traitors confess (**RAC**k)*
*With 3 parts of a place which the wicked don't bless (**HEL**l)*
*Join 4/7 of an exercise which shopkeepers use (**WALK**ing)*
*Add what bad men do when they good actions refuse (**ER**r)*
*These 4 added together with great care and art*
*Will point out the Fair One that is nearest my Heart.*

Two months after Paul and Rachel were married, colonists disguised as Indians boarded English ships and threw more than 300 chests of tea into Boston harbor to protest taxation without representation. It's likely that Paul was one of the "Indians" because he'd been active in the growing revolutionary movement. As a messenger for the Committee of Public Safety, he carried news about the "tea party" all the way to New York and Philadelphia.

Whenever he rode off, his "dear Girl" managed his business and their home. Like Paul, Rachel was energetic and feisty. Their marriage would be filled with love and devotion. In 1775, when British soldiers pursued him on his famous ride, Rachel sent him money and a letter warning him not to "attempt coming into this towne again." She closed by saying "adieu my Love," and eventually met him in Charlestown with his "little lambs," their children.

## SEPTEMBER 24

## HEINRICH SCHLIEMANN & SOPHIA ENGASTROMENOS

*"She loves me as a Greek, with passion, and I love her no less."*

HEINRICH FIRST SAW SOPHIA'S FACE IN a photograph. Her eyes were intelligent and her beauty was flawless. She also spoke classical Greek. A few years earlier, the 47-year-old self-made German millionaire and linguist had retired from business to fulfill his childhood dream – locating the ancient city of Troy. After completing his doctorate in archeology and ending a very unhappy marriage, Heinrich went to Greece and found his own "Helen of Troy."

Seventeen-year-old Sophia was everything he wanted. At first, she accepted Heinrich's proposal simply because her parents told her to marry the wealthy man. But this made Heinrich furious. What did *she* want? If a life filled with archeological discovery and adventure wasn't enough, he wanted nothing more to do with her. Sophia apologized profusely; of course, she wanted *him!* In 1869 they married in the tiny candlelit church of St. Meletios in Athens, near her parents' home. The festivities lasted until 1:00 AM, when Heinrich and Sophia sailed away on a ship aptly named *Aphrodite*.

Heinrich was brilliant, generous, and passionate. Although he could be high-strung and demanding, Sophia's gaiety softened him. She understood his determination to prove the basis for the legends of the *Odyssey* and the *Iliad*, and in 1873 they uncovered extraordinary treasures in Turkey, near what would be identified subsequently as King Priam's palace. Sophia evaded the local police by wrapping a dazzling array of gold, silver, and copper helmets, goblets, vases, diadems, and jewelry in an enormous red shawl and smuggling them out of the country. Years later, Heinrich told her, "I can never celebrate our marriage enough, for you have always been my beloved wife and at the same time my comrade... by Zeus! I will marry you again in the next world!"

# SEPTEMBER 25

## HELEN GURLEY & DAVID BROWN

*"The difference between David and me and some other people with ideas is that we sit down and do it."*

THREE YEARS AFTER HELEN MARRIED DAVID in 1959, her book *Sex and the Single Girl* became a best-seller and "how-to guide" for unmarried women in the new sexually permissive era. They had met in Los Angeles, where Helen was a 36-year old copywriter and the highest paid woman in advertising on the West Coast. David was a journalist and motion picture producer who'd been married and divorced twice. Much as he liked the "brown-eyed, smart" and "very sexy" woman who was financially independent because of her own hard work, he was not in a hurry to tie the knot again.

Helen waited more than a year before she brought up the subject. As she said in his book, *Let Me Entertain You*, "I tendered my ultimatum… it was time for marriage and I wanted *him*." When that didn't work, she told him she wasn't going to see him anymore. A few days later, he proposed.

One of the first things David did after he married Helen was to encourage her to write a book based on her experiences as a single working woman. David even suggested the dynamite title. In 1965 Helen became editor-in-chief of 79-year old *Cosmopolitan* magazine and turned it into an upbeat, splashy publication aimed at showing single women (and married women who "thought single") how to get as much as they possibly could out of life. She also created the first male centerfold.

David produced successful films such as *Jaws*, *The Sting*, *The Verdict*, and *Cocoon*, and also worked in publishing. But the best thing he ever did was marry Helen. "Stick a pin in me and she jumps," he would say. "If someone appears to hurt me, she cries out."

# SEPTEMBER 26*

## ARTHUR EVANS & MARGARET FREEMAN
### *"the find of a lifetime"*

ARTHUR HAD BEEN WORKING AT AN archeological site at
Ragusa (now Dubrovnik) when war broke out in the Balkans in
1877 and the dig was disbanded. The 26-year old English writer sent
war dispatches to London newspapers but he had not yet determined his life's
work – uncovering the ancient civilizations of Crete, including King Minos's
palace at Knossos – when he met the English historian Edward Freeman and
his 29-year old daughter.

Although Miss Freeman was dressed demurely in a tight-waisted dress,
white gloves, and a large hat, Arthur saw that she was lively, well-educated,
and an excellent listener. She found the thickset, dark-complexioned man
bright and energetic, poking the air with "Prodger," his walking stick, to stress
his points of view.

Arthur followed the Freemans back to England, brimming with stories
about life in the magnificent coastal region of Ragusa and fantasizing about
bringing Margaret there one day. It wasn't hard to convince her. In 1878 they
married in Nash Mills, his birthplace, and sailed for Casa San Lazzaro, their
home by the Adriatic Sea. Margaret learned the local Serbian language and
soon was playing music on a rented piano. Arthur brought relief supplies
to dispossessed families and continued to write dispatches about the war in
Bosnia and Herzegovina for the next 3 years. But the Austrians, who had
become embroiled in the battle, accused Arthur of spying and threw him into
Ragusa's ancient prison. He languished there for weeks until Margaret convinced the police that Arthur's maps were only of prehistoric sites. The men
visiting their house, she explained, carried ancient pottery shards and other
archeological finds, not ammunition or arms.

After Arthur was freed, he and Margaret returned to England. Subsequently, they set off for Greece, where treks to ancient ruins fired their dreams
of uncovering an ancient world.

---

*Date approximate.

# SEPTEMBER 27

## HUME CRONYN & JESSICA TANDY
### *"The odds were impossible...."*

BEFORE HUME WAS INTRODUCED TO JESSICA backstage after her 1940 performance in A.J. Cronin's *Jupiter Laughs*, he stepped outside the theater during intermission and watched her – still wearing her costume – leap into a taxi. That year, she had brought her daughter Susan with her to New York, leaving behind her husband, actor Jack Hawkins, and their shaky marriage. Every night, Jessica raced back to her hotel to check on Susan… and always returned in time for the next act.

Hume was divorced and briefly engaged to someone else before he realized that he loved the petite, blue-eyed actress. Jessica had a much harder time making up her mind. Hume courted her with lavish dinners and drives in his snappy Buick roadster. He also had the lead role in a dismal flop called *Mr. Big*.

He wasn't having luck with Jessica, either. "I had asked her to marry me so many times that I had almost lost count," he wrote in *A Terrible Liar*. "Her unequivocal nos lasted for about eighteen months." Then, in summer 1942, she went to Reno, Nevada for a divorce, and married Hume in Los Angeles after he completed filming *Shadow of a Doubt* for director Alfred Hitchcock.

Jessica wore a pink and gray suit at the wedding, held in a gardenia-filled chapel of the Beverly Vista Community Church and followed by a garden party behind Romanoff's restaurant. Hume was 31 and his next project was Hitchcock's masterpiece, *Lifeboat*. Jessica was 33 and had just signed a 5-year film contract. Within two years, they played a husband and wife in *The Seventh Cross*, a wartime thriller.

"You are the music to which my world is set," were the words Hume had inscribed inside Jess's wedding ring. They were husband and wife, actors, costars, and parents. And they would be very happy.

# SEPTEMBER 28

## ERNEST H. SHEPARD & FLORENCE CHAPLIN
### *"Kip" and "Pie"*

I N 1899 IT WASN'T EASY FOR men and women to get to know each other at London's Royal Academy School of Art, because their classes and lunchtimes were held separately. But Ernest and Florence kept running into each other at Robertson's Art Supplies store in Camden Town, and at Lyons tea shop across the street from school. Twenty-four year old Florence, whose grandfather had founded *Punch* magazine, was 3 years older than Ernest. He found her cleverness and talent greatly appealing.

"Oh my girl," he wrote after they admitted their love. "If I could hold your hand I shouldn't be so troubled and worried about money and things, the same old worry you know, that I shan't get rid of till I *do* something!" By 1902 he had sold his first oil painting and was selling cartoons and drawings to newspapers and magazines. The following year, Ernest was commissioned to do a painting for Morden College Chapel, and Florence worked on a mural for Guy's Hospital. As soon as they realized they could manage financially, they bought a double bed, Worcester china dinnerware, and were married in 1904.

Ernest remembered his own childhood well, and he had a knack of seeing things from a child's point of view. His favorite works would always be the illustrations he drew in the 1920's for A.A. Milne's stories about Christopher Robin and Winnie-the-Pooh, and Kenneth Grahame's *The Wind in the Willows*.

The Shepards settled in tiny Arden Cottage at Shamley Green in Surrey, and called each other by the childhood nicknames, "Kip" and "Pie." After their son and daughter were born, they moved to Red Cottage, a larger house where they continued sketching and painting. Kip used the real Christopher Robin's stuffed toys as models for the animals in Milne's books, but Winnie-the-Pooh was fashioned after "Growler," the chubby bear that belonged to Kip's own son, Graham.

# SEPTEMBER 29

## HENRY LOUIS GEHRIG & ELEANOR TWITCHELL
### *"My Luke"*

THE NEW YORK YANKEES' STAR FIRST baseman may have been an "Iron Horse" on the playing field, but Lou was shy and reticent when he was with women. He and Eleanor had been dating for 6 years, but he still struggled to find the right words about marriage. Finally, Eleanor asked, Do you want to propose to me? Yes, he answered, blushing and relieved. Well, I accept! She answered. That afternoon, he hit a home run at the stadium!

Lou's mother didn't like his fiancée, but Mrs. Gehrig didn't think any girl was good enough for her boy. She also thought that baseball was "a bunch of nonsense," although she'd grown to accept it. But Lou was only 30 years old. Why did he need to get married? Didn't his Mama always take good care of him? If you get married, I won't be at your wedding, she threatened.

So… she wasn't invited! Instead, Lou and Eleanor married suddenly, on the last day of the 1933 baseball season, in what the bride jokingly called the "classiest wedding ever held in Westchester County." Workmen were fixing up their apartment at 5 Circuit Road, New Rochelle, when the mayor arrived with the marriage license and a motorcycle caravan of cops.

After the short ceremony and a champagne toast to the "coatless groom" and his "besmudged bride," the police escorted the newlyweds to Yankee Stadium. Lou didn't hit any home runs that day, but at least he made no errors in the field.

Six years later, on Lou Gehrig Day, he said, "When you have a wife who has been a tower of strength and shown more courage than you ever dreamed existed, that's the finest I know." Referring to his serious illness, he added, "I might have had a bad break, but I have an awful lot to live for."

## SEPTEMBER 30

## P.G. WODEHOUSE & ETHEL NEWTON ROWLEY
### *"Plummie" and his "Bunny"*

PELHAM GRENVILLE, KNOWN AS "PLUM," MARRIED Ethel at New York City's Little Church Around the Corner less than 2 months after they met in 1914. Although the 32-year old British writer's stories were humorous and lighthearted, he was woefully inexperienced socially, and he longed to be married. Plum fell for Ethel right away; she was 29 and long-legged, with a delightful zest for life. She also was a widow with a young daughter named Leonora, whom Plum adored and nicknamed "Snorkles."

Like one of the bumbling characters in his comic novels, Plum's proposal of marriage was slightly calamitous. He had a nasty cold, which kept Ethel at arm's length. When it was time to utter those magic words, "Will you marry me?" Plum began sneezing uncontrollably. Even the wedding ceremony was "marred" when the minister arrived late, apologetic but also jubilant. Sorry I was detained, he said, but I've just made a pile of money in the stock market!

The next day, Plum and Ethel headed for the Long Island seashore where they had spent so much of their courtship that summer, riding the waves and lying on the beach. In November, they moved into an apartment at 375 Central Park West. Over the years, they kept many house pets, and established an animal shelter on Long Island.

"It was an awfully curious thing how everything altered just after we married," Plum said later. Ethel, who was gregarious and social, took charge of his affairs while he concentrated on writing. Besides magazine stories and play adaptations, he also wrote song lyrics for Irving Berlin, Jerome Kern, Cole Porter, and George Gershwin. Eventually, Plum wrote more than 100 novels about lovable characters with zany names like Bingo, Oofy, Pongo, Stiffy, Nobby, and Mugsy. Most famous was Bertie Wooster, a befuddled aristocrat who was invariably rescued from disaster by his levelheaded "gentleman's gentleman," the valet Jeeves.

# OCTOBER

# OCTOBER 1

## WILLIAM JENNINGS BRYAN & MARIE BAIRD
### *"Won, 1880. One, 1884."*

A YEAR BEFORE "MAMIE" MARRIED "WILL" in 1884, the lawyer and future Populist drafted a document certifying that "I... do love Marie E. Baird better than... any one else in the world... I always will love her, be good to her and contribute as largely as possible to her happiness and usefulness."

They had met when Will and other Illinois College men attended a tea party hosted by the women's division. The men called the place "Jail for Angels," because they were so strictly watched, but Will managed to chat with Mamie. A year later, when the principal realized that Miss Baird was being courted, he escorted her to the next train home. Right after her train departed from the station, Will, who'd stowed away in the baggage car, sat down beside her and proposed.

They waited 4 years to marry, until Will was earning more than $500 a year. Just before the wedding, he confessed that he'd been rehearsing "'with all my worldly goods I thee endow' so as to make it duly impressive. If you dare laugh when I say that, I won't kiss you when he tells me to salute my bride."

After honeymooning in St. Louis, the Bryans lived in Illinois. Mamie took care of their home, began raising their children, and studied law under Will's instruction. They moved to Nebraska, where she was admitted to the bar in 1888, and Will was elected to Congress 2 years later. Subsequently, he became a journalist and editor-in-chief of the Omaha *World-Herald*. At 36, he was the Democratic party's presidential nominee; he lost to McKinley, but his fame and influence were ensured.

In some ways, Will was ahead of his time, advocating women's suffrage and the regulation of banks and railroads in an era when robber barons were making fortunes. Will and Mamie never forgot the plights of ordinary people.

# OCTOBER 2

## JOHN CONSTABLE & MARIA BICKNELL

*"Nothing that can happen in this world can ever change or abate my love for you"*

MARIA'S GRANDFATHER, THE WEALTHY CHURCH RECTOR of East Bergholt in Sussex, England, threatened to disinherit her if she married that no-account landscape painter, John Constable, in 1809. Since Grandpa controlled all the money in the family, everyone was afraid of him. John's mother gave Grandpa one of John's drawings of his church, hoping this would appease him. Instead, he handed John a few coins and said, "Buy some little article by which you may be reminded of me, when I am no more." But like so many mean-spirited human beings, Grandpa lived on and on.

The Constables' flour mill barely supported the family, let alone a wife for John. He might have made a good living by painting portraits, which were popular at that time, instead of the landscapes he preferred. He painted the Constable gardens and mill often, and would also paint Salisbury Cathedral, Hampstead Heath, and other favorite places.

John was not prepared to give up Maria. When "Flatford Mill" was accepted by the Royal Academy, his paintings began to sell. "Be assured we have only to consider our union as an event that must happen, and we shall yet be happy," he wrote Maria.

John's parents died by 1816, leaving their son a small inheritance. Soon after, he and Maria married at St. Martin-in-the-Fields Church in London – without her grandfather's consent. Friends lent their country house in Dorset for a honeymoon, and John created a series of paintings of Weymouth Bay nearby. One day, his pictures would hang in London's National Gallery and the Victoria and Albert Museum.

P.S.: Grandpa died a few years later, and that's when they discovered that he wasn't very rich, after all – but he had managed to intimidate everybody just the same!

# OCTOBER 3

## BARACK HUSSEIN OBAMA & MICHELLE ROBINSON
*"an unbelievable life force"*

M ICHELLE WAS A FIRST-YEAR LAWYER at a Chicago law firm in 1989 when she was asked to mentor a summer associate named Barack. She was 25 and a graduate of Harvard Law School; he was 27 and had just completed his first year there after working as a community organizer for a few years. What was he like? His name was odd, his mother was white and his father was African, and he was from Hawaii. He also had a great smile. It didn't take long for other associates in the firm to notice how much these two enjoyed talking and listening to each other. Michelle was impressed by Barack's commitment to working with and for the poor, and they both shared a love of Stevie Wonder's music.

On their first date, they went to the Art Institute, and saw the film, *Do the Right Thing*. He returned to Cambridge, Massachusetts in the fall, but they stayed in touch (and fell in love) over the next two years. She wanted to get married, but he didn't. Finally, during dinner at a fancy restaurant in Chicago, he reiterated his negative feelings about marriage and caught her off-guard. When dessert was served, a surprising little box was also on the plate. Inside the box was an engagement ring.

She wore an off-the-shoulder white wedding gown when they married at Trinity United Church of Christ in Chicago in 1992. Afterwards, they celebrated with friends and family at the South Shore Cultural Center, once a country club closed to Jews and blacks. Their wedding song was "You and I," by Stevie Wonder.

Afterwards, a friend recalled it as being a very happy wedding, especially because "Everybody knew... together they were going to be so much more than they would have been individually."

# OCTOBER 4

## WILLIAM WORDSWORTH & MARY HUTCHINSON
### *"the blessed time of early love"*

"ON MONDAY, 4TH OCTOBER, 1802, MY brother William was married to Mary Hutchinson," wrote Dorothy Wordsworth in her journal. That morning she had sat by her window, watching William and Mary walk toward the village church in the parish of Brompton. Dorothy and William had been extremely close, and although she couldn't bear to witness his wedding, in time she welcomed her sister-in-law into the family fold.

The wedding day was low-keyed, in deference to Dorothy's dejection. The bride and groom received few gifts, and thought their friends didn't believe the marriage would last. Mary's uncle Henry called William a "vagabond" because he lacked a regular profession, but years later he admitted that he had read some of William's poems and thought they were very good.

Mary was sunny, tender, and devoted to Will, who called her "a Phantom of delight." Like the Wordsworths, Mary had been orphaned at a young age, and she grew up in her grandparents' care. Now, she and Will were each 32, and he had already written remarkable poems including "Lines Composed a Few Miles Above Tintern Abbey," and "Lucy Gray." Shortly before the nuptials, he wrote "A Farewell" to Dove Cottage, saying "A Gentle Maid... Will come to you... And love the blessed life that we lead here."

Their marriage lasted 48 years. On the rare times that Mary and Will were separated, she wrote impassioned notes to him—"my best friend, my soul," professing that "every nerve is full of thee." He confessed, "I love thee so deeply and tenderly and constantly... that I scarcely can bring my pen to write of anything else." Much of Will's best work, including completion of *The Prelude*, was written after his marriage. Eventually, he became poet laureate of England.

# OCTOBER 5

## GOWER CHAMPION & MARGE BELCHER
### *"May I have this dance?"*

GOWER SAT BEHIND MARGE IN JUNIOR high school in Los Angeles but the future dance team didn't fall in love until after he returned from coast guard service during World War II. They first met in the ballet school run by Marjorie's father, Ernest Belcher, soon after Gower and his divorced mother, a dressmaker, came to California from Illinois. Mr. Belcher's star pupils included Shirley Temple, Gwen Verdon, and Cyd Charisse. One day, Marge and Gower would also bring fame to his school.

At 16, Marge had been Walt Disney's model for the heroine in the movie, *Snow White and the Seven Dwarfs.* She also danced in a frilly tutu for cartoonists, in a role later performed by an animated hippo in *Fantasia.* She was fresh-faced, bubbly, and skilled in everything from ballet to tap. As Marjorie Bell, she appeared in the 1939 film, *The Story of Vernon and Irene Castle,* not knowing that within 10 years she and Gower would become as famous as the Castles had been earlier in the century.

Gower had quit high school after he won an amateur dance contest, and began dancing in clubs and in bit parts in Hollywood films. Following his coast guard tour of duty, the team of Gower and Bell was born. They both were 26 when they married in 1947, soon after Gower's performance in the film, *Till the Clouds Roll By.* His mother made all their costumes, including those worn at their smash-hit debut at the Waldorf-Astoria's Persian Room in New York City. MGM Studios signed the Champions to a film contract, beginning with *Mr. Music* and *Show Boat.* Later, they appeared on television variety shows and in a situation comedy, *The Marge and Gower Champion Show.* Gower excelled as a choreographer and director, and Marge also appeared in dramatic roles.

# OCTOBER 6

## GLENN MILLER & HELEN BURGER

### *"In the Mood"*

"TO GLENN, THE MEANEST MAN IN the world," Helen wrote on the photograph she gave him in 1926, after he quit the University of Colorado. Glenn had been in dance bands on campus, coming up with incredibly fresh sounds by playing popular tunes in new ways. It was pretty remarkable, especially since he'd failed a first-year course in harmony!

Besides music, Glenn also loved Helen, the serious, soft-spoken young woman he'd met in class. Someday, he promised, they'd get married, but right now he was taking his trombone and heading for California. After 2 years of long-distance phone calls, letters and brief reunions, Helen started giving up hope. Perhaps her parents were right, and Glenn was "unstable," like most musicians. Had he ever really proposed? She began dating other boys.

Glenn was working on the East Coast in 1928 when he heard that Helen was "practically engaged" to someone else. He sent her a telegram immediately, begging her to take a train to New York and marry him right away. Fortunately, she consented!

They married in a small ceremony and settled into a modest apartment at 30-60 29th Street in Astoria, Queens, with their pet bull terrier, Pops. Home was just a short subway ride from the Manhattan clubs and recording studios where Glenn was a freelance trombonist and arranger. He and Helen managed well financially, but she encouraged him to form his own band, even if it meant giving up a regular paycheck. Blending saxophones and clarinets, the Glenn Miller Orchestra developed unique musical renditions. "Moonlight Serenade" became their theme song. Other smash hits included "In the Mood," "Tuxedo Junction," and "Little Brown Jug." During World War II, Glenn formed the U.S. Air Force Band to entertain troops in Europe.

# OCTOBER 7*

## JOHN ALDEN & PRISCILLA MULLENS
*A triumph of romantic love*

"IN THE OLD COLONY DAYS, IN Plymouth, the land of the Pilgrims" begins Henry W. Longfellow's famous poem, "The Courtship of Miles Standish." Poetic license accounts for some of the details, but the story of a young man who is sent to propose marriage for his older friend and ends up winning the girl himself is charming and believable.

A brutally cold first winter killed many Pilgrims in Plymouth, including Priscilla's entire family. By the spring of 1621, the colony was quite small, and the 19-year old maiden was living with another family. She was known for her skill at the spinning wheel, and that's where John usually found her when he came calling. He was blond, blue-eyed, and about 22. They had met onboard the *Mayflower*, where John maintained the ship's water and beer barrels. The ship's Captain Standish was 35 and considered middle-aged. Soon after his wife died, he asked John to woe Priscilla for him, prompting her to pose what has become a legendary question: "Why don't you speak for yourself, John?"

Poor John was torn between his loyalty to Miles and his passion for Priscilla! Miles had spoken before John had his chance. But Priscilla's remark startled him, and "Into the open air John Alden, perplexed and bewildered/ Rushed like a man insane, and wandered alone by the seaside." Only after he had made his peace with Miles did John ask Priscilla for her hand.

They were married in a civil ceremony performed by William Bradford, governor of the colony. That summer, John and other colonists had built a common house, storerooms, and plank houses with thatched roofs, including a commodious one for himself and Priscilla. Subsequently, Miles married, too. Later, the two families lived near each other in Duxbury, which they founded, and much later the Aldens' daughter Sarah married the captain's son, Alexander.

---

*Date approximate.

# OCTOBER 8

## OSWALD NELSON & HARRIET HILLIARD
### *"The Adventures of Ozzie and Harriet"*

OZZIE PROPOSED TO HARRIET IN THE backseat of a sedan in 1935 as they drove across Texas with other members of his dance band. They had met 3 years earlier when Ozzie was searching for a female vocalist. Harriet – formerly Peggy Lou Snyder, a Des Moines beauty queen – was a specialty dancer and mistress of ceremonies in a restaurant, and "it took me about thirty seconds to decide that she was the girl I was looking for," he wrote in *Ozzie*.

Harriet had "a beautiful face, a fantastic figure, and a wealth of talent and experience," he said. She and Ozzie quickly developed a breezy style, singing boy-girl duets and making lighthearted banter. As they incorporated personal remarks into their performances, Ozzie added extra lyrics to popular songs.

They married at Ozzie's parents' home in Hackensack, New Jersey, in 1935, but they didn't take a honeymoon for 4 years. Right after the wedding, Harriet left for Hollywood and a singing role in *Follow the Fleet*. Soon after she returned to New York, she became pregnant with their older son, David.

The Nelsons moved to Hollywood in 1941, after Eric ("Ricky") was born, and they kept on working in films. When comedian Red Skelton canceled his radio show to join the army in 1944, *The Adventures of Ozzie and Harriet* – about an average American family – went on the air on October 8 – their 9th anniversary. Ozzie wrote most of the scripts, which generally dealt with problems and complications (usually caused and made worse by Ozzie) and resolutions (usually worked out by Harriet). He was 40 and she was 35 when they started, but they were billed as "America's Favorite Young Couple." Their address, "1847 Rogers Road" was fictitious, but the Nelsons' own white clapboard, green-shuttered colonial house in the Hollywood Hills was shown at the start of every show.

# OCTOBER 9
## PATRICK HENRY & DOROTHEA DANDRIDGE
### *An eager bridegroom*

BY THE TIME "DOLLY" MARRIED PATRICK IN 1777, the bold Revolutionary War statesman and orator had already brandished his ivory letter opener in Richmond, Virginia and staunchly proclaimed, "I know not what course others may take, but as for me, give me liberty, or give me death!"

Dolly was an old friend's daughter and Martha Washington's cousin. Patrick proposed in summer, after the Virginia Assembly had adjourned. He spent the next months in special meetings and racing back and forth to Hanover County to see Dolly. Perhaps the 41-year old widowed governor of Virginia feared that the 21-year old bride-to-be would change her mind. (After all, hadn't Patrick talked to her of liberty?) The dashing naval war hero, John Paul Jones, had also been a suitor.

Most couples published church banns announcing their impending nuptials for 3 consecutive Sundays, and then they married. Some paid 2 British pounds for a marriage license and married within days. That's what Patrick wanted: He left Williamsburg on October 7 and rode nearly 100 miles over bad roads to the Dandridge estate in upper Hanover to marry Dolly 2 days later.

Marriage to a governor meant a spirited but dignified wedding reception with hearty toasts and glorious feasting. For Patrick, it also meant allying his cause with aristocratic families in favor of the Revolution. After the festivities he and Dolly, and children from his first marriage, drove to their home in the Governor's Palace in Williamsburg.

"P.H. was perhaps the best husband in the world," wrote his sister Jane's husband, because "it is said that he never took any important step without consulting Dolly." Years later, when Patrick's daughter Anne was about to be married, he told her that "matrimonial happiness does not depend upon wealth... but in minds properly tempered and united."

## OCTOBER 10

## EDWARD, THE BLACK PRINCE, & JOAN OF KENT
*"My dearest and truest sweetheart"*

EVER SINCE EDWARD WAS BORN IN 1330, his parents, King Edward III and Queen Philippa had been talking about choosing an appropriate wife for him. Why not a French princess, or the Count of Flanders' daughter? Edward paid little attention to these discussions, preferring to put on his shiny black armor and throw himself into jousting tournaments and military battles. For years, he barely noticed "little Jeanette," his fair-haired, sweet-faced second cousin who fluttered about the 14th century court in ermine robes and silk dresses, bringing a smile to everyone's face.

Joan was sociable and merry and soon married off to Sir John Holland. When he died, she was left with vast property holdings and a handsome pension. Many suitors came calling on the 32-year old widow, who still had a joyful disposition and a comely figure.

At 30, the Black Prince was more handsome, dignified, and courageous than ever, but he was beginning to feel discontented and dejected. He'd played a decisive role at the battle of Poitiers in France, and yet… it wasn't enough.

At court, he spoke to Joan about her suitors' proposals. Tears filled her eyes. "I desire none of them," she said. Her heart was already bound to the most chivalrous knight on earth, someone – alas! – whom she could never tell. Edward put his arms around his cousin's shoulders and urged her to confess. Who was this knight? Perhaps, if Edward had not been so affected by her tears and womanly grace, he never would have heard his name.

They married at Windsor, in 1361, overriding his parents' concerns that the match was somewhat unsuitable. Edward became a devoted husband, and Joan never wavered in her love for him. Two years later, he was named Prince of Aquitaine and they moved to the south of France.

# OCTOBER 11
## WILLIAM JEFFERSON CLINTON &
## HILLARY RODHAM
### *"I loved being with her"*

BILL AND HILLARY WERE MARRIED IN 1975 by a minister named Nixon, just a year after she worked on the House Judiciary Committee's impeachment inquiry of President Richard Nixon. The Clintons had met 4 years before at Yale Law School. Bill first saw Hillary in class, and she noticed him in the lounge. He spotted her again in the library. Usually, Bill was easygoing and loquacious, but all he did was stare. Finally, Hillary walked up to him and said, If we're going to keep looking at each other, I ought to introduce myself. Bill was so stunned, he couldn't remember his own name! But "that's exactly how we met," he's said. "And we've been together ever since."

When Nixon resigned before impeachment proceedings began, Hillary left Washington. She taught at the University of Arkansas Law School and ran a legal aid clinic. Bill practiced law and taught at the law school, too, but his goal was to run for state office. The following year, he began campaigning for state attorney general.

In summer, 1975, Hillary went home to Illinois to sort out her feelings for Bill. He met her plane when she returned to Fayetteville in August, and drove her into town. En route, they passed a small brick cottage that she'd admired on California Street. Bill announced that he had bought it and furnished it... right down to flowered sheets on an antique bed. "So you're going to have to marry me!" he asserted, laughing.

After years of wanting no one else, that was all it took to convince Hillary. She and Bill were married in their own living room, and celebrated with hundreds of friends and relatives at an Arkansas state senator's home. The bride wore a Victorian-style cream-colored wedding dress she had bought the day before.

Three years later, Bill became the nation's youngest governor since the Great Depression. And that was just the beginning!

# OCTOBER 12

## LOUIS ARMSTRONG & LUCILLE WILSON

*"My house is filled with happiness"*

AFTER 3 FAILED MARRIAGES, THE 40-YEAR old jazz trumpeter and singer finally found someone who was *good* for him. "It was love at first sight with Lucille, because of the color of her skin," said the New Orleans-born musician. "When she danced at the Cotton Club, she was darkest in the company." "Satchmo's" band had begun a 6-month stint, and he couldn't take his eyes off 24-year old Lucille.

Even then, he'd mop his overheated brow with a white handkerchief as he blasted away at his trumpet, rousing the black and white crowd of nightclubbers into a joyful frenzy. Louis dated Lucille a few times, although she discouraged him; getting involved with a married man always meant trouble! So he got a divorce and convinced her to marry him in 1942.

The following year, when Louis was on the road, Lucille purchased a modest house on 107th Street in Corona, Queens, New York, and told Louis about it on the telephone. He didn't need a home, he said. Hotels were perfectly fine places to live. When he arrived, he told his cabdriver to wait outside while he checked out the new place.

In just a few minutes, Louis was beaming, and he invited the driver to join them for dinner. Once again, Lucille had Louis's best interests at heart. Most of the time, she stayed out of his professional life, although she traveled with him whenever possible. In 1950 they had a private audience with Pope Pius XII, who asked Louis if they had any children. "No, your Holiness," Louis answered. "But we keep on tryin'!"

In 1947 Louis began performing with other jazz all-stars and he developed a new group of fans among the younger, postwar generation. The popularity of his gravel-voiced rendition of "Hello, Dolly!" has outlasted many Beatles hits.

## OCTOBER 13

## HARRY ELLIS DICKSON & JANE GOLDBERG

*"my anchor, my protector, my nurturer, my life"*

HARRY AND JANE'S 1935 WEDDING CEREMONY lasted less than 3 minutes, causing the groom's mother to wonder, were they "really married?" They'd asked Rabbi Stephen Wise, who had offici-ated in his study at New York's Free Synagogue, to "make it as short as pos-sible," and he did.

It didn't take the future violinist of the Boston Symphony Orchestra much longer than that to fall in love with Jane 4 years before, after he arrived in Berlin to study music. His teachers at Boston's New England Conservatory of Music had warned the 23-year-old musician not to get romantically involved. Concentrate on your violin, they told him.

But Harry met Jane at a party and was immediately "smitten," he wrote years later in *Beating Time: A Musician's Memoir*. Jane was American but she'd lived abroad for so long that her German and French surpassed her English. She was 19 and a social worker at a home for retarded children outside Ber-lin. She and Harry attended concerts, the theater, and the opera, and he serenaded her privately with sweet melodies on his violin.

In 1933, they returned to America when the Nazis took over Germany. Harry supervised orchestras for the WPA in Boston, and Jane worked for an orphanage in New York. When she visited Harry, he proposed in Boston's Franklin Park. After their very quick wedding, they settled in Boston, where Harry began his lifelong association with the Boston Symphony Orchestra, and also became assistant conductor of the Boston Pops.

Twenty years later, Harry and Jane returned to Berlin and visited his for-mer German landlady. Frau Tils wasn't surprised that they had married; she'd known from the beginning that they were meant for each other.

# OCTOBER 14

## BEATRIX POTTER & WILLIAM HEELIS

### *"My Willie"*

SHORTLY BEFORE BEATRIX MARRIED WILLIAM IN 1913, the well-known children's book author wrote *The Tale of Pigling Bland*. It was her only love story, charming and somewhat autobiographical, about a pig who's locked up with another pig named Pigwig. When the 2 pigs escape, they race "over the hills and far away," hand in hand and in love.

The 47-year-old writer knew about restrictions: All her life, her parents had limited her freedom. Beatrix taught herself how to draw, paint, and write stories. When she was 40, she used the proceeds from sales of *The Tale of Peter Rabbit* to buy herself a 17th century cottage and working farm in England's Lake District.

As Beatrix's wealth increased, she asked William, a slightly younger country lawyer, to find more properties for her. He was fascinated by the writer in London who loved the north country as much as the "natives," and they began to correspond regularly. But when they became engaged in 1912, Beatrix's parents objected strongly. Her brother Bertram was rarely home these days. If Beatrix married, who would take care of them in their declining years?

Then Bertram confessed that he had been married secretly for the past 7 years, which explained his frequent (and long) absences. If his sister wanted to marry, no one should stop her! That winter, Beatrix became very ill and was bedridden for weeks. Gradually, her parents' feelings changed, and as Beatrix wrote abut Pigling Bland, she also began planning her wedding in the fall.

She and William married at St. Mary Abbot's church, Kensington, and settled down at Castle Farm, one of her country properties, where they raised prizewinning sheep. Although Beatrix insisted that Pigling Bland and "the portrait of two pigs arm and arm – looking at the sunrise – is not a portrait of me and Mr. Heelis," it's clear that their love inspired her delightful tale.

## OCTOBER 15

## GERALD R. FORD & ELIZABETH BLOOMER
*"standing by my side, as she always has"*

"WE CAN'T GET MARRIED UNTIL NEXT fall and I can't tell you why," "Jerry" told "Betty" when he proposed in February 1948. The 35-year-old Michigan lawyer had decided to run for Congress but had promised the local Republican party that he wouldn't announce his candidacy until June.

Right from the beginning, Betty always trusted Jerry. Unlike her first husband, Jerry was unaffected, honest, and sincere. Years later, when he became the 38th president, his forthright nature helped to heal the nation after the Watergate scandals.

They were married at Grace Episcopal Church in Grand Rapids, 2½ weeks before election day. Betty wore a dark satin dress and carried a large bouquet of roses. Some guests remembered that the groom, who'd been totally distracted by the upcoming election, showed up wearing one black shoe and one brown one, but Jerry always insisted that his shoes had been the same color... until he stepped in mud outside the church door.

The honeymoon lasted only a few days and included political rallies. Jerry resumed his campaigning with Betty, who took time off from her job as a department store fashion coordinator. Although many Midwesterners frowned on divorce, they still voted for Jerry and sent him to Washington.

In January 1977, shortly before Jerry's presidential term of office ended, he and Betty returned to the White House after attending a farewell party. Members of the Marine Band were there, so Jerry took his first lady's hand and asked for a last dance. As they spun around the floor to the bittersweet tune, "Thanks For the Memories," friends and supporters appeared on cue and began dancing around them. Betty "gave a gasp of surprise and then tears came to her eyes.... Seeing her so happy was one of the greatest joys of my life," Jerry recalled afterward.

# OCTOBER 16

## JOAN SUTHERLAND & RICHARD BONYNGE
### *"La Stupenda" and her "Svengali"*

B Y THE TIME THE AUSTRALIAN-BORN MUSICIANS married in 1954, Richard was devoting himself to guiding Joan's career as a coloratura soprano. "It was clear that hers was the greater talent," the gifted pianist realized, and "helping her would be a full-time occupation."

They had met as teenagers in Sydney, where he played the piano as she sang for the ladies of the Queen Victoria Club. Richard always loved opera, especially 19th century bel canto operas, and Joan had a perfect set of vocal chords. She debuted at the Sydney Opera House in 1947 and came to London 4 years later. Richard, a student at the Royal Academy of Music, convinced Joan to try becoming a dramatic soprano instead of a contralto. Easy for you to say, she laughed. You make music with your fingers; I have to do it with my throat!

Joan's mother feared that her daughter's voice could be ruined, but she permitted Joan to work with Richard. He wouldn't accept payment, so mother and daughter began inviting him for dinner. Soon he was at their flat daily, helping Joan prepare for her Covent Garden audition. He proposed after they decided he would move into their home. "This is silly," he told Joan. "You know your mother isn't going to like me living here like this. Why don't we get married?"

They did, at a Methodist church on the following Saturday, although few people – including Joan's mother – knew until afterwards. Twenty-seven-year old Joan wore a red velvet dress with a large gray hat. Richard was 24 and wore a gray suit and a large bow tie. They celebrated afterwards with champagne and homemade apple teacake. The groom's parents were thrilled, and even Joan's mother accepted the situation. She cabled, "You naughty children. Watch yourselves. Love, Mum."

# OCTOBER 17
## RUBE GOLDBERG & IRMA SEEMAN
### *"I'm the guy"*

WHEN IRMA MET RUBE AT A charity dinner at Delmonico's restaurant in Manhattan in 1915, his cartoons were syndicated in newspapers nationwide, and he earned more than many corporation presidents. But that didn't impress Irma, whose wealthy father owned the White Rose Tea and Grocery Company. What mattered to the 21-year-old Ethical Culture School graduate were Rube's good looks, self-confidence, and sweet nature. She also liked his animated film spoof, *The Boob Weekly* – "all the news that nobody wants to hear."

The 32-year-old artist courted Irma in his cartoons. She symbolized beauty and charm, while he was just an ordinary guy wooing his beloved dreamboat by strumming guitars underneath her window or performing other attention getting tricks. Rube's best jokes were always about himself or other poor "boobs" struggling through life.

The night before their 1916 wedding, Rube went drinking with some friends and ended up in jail for disorderly conduct. He managed to convince the cops that he was getting married in the morning, and they released him just in time for the ceremony. It took a 2-week trip to Jamaica to soothe his somewhat hysterical bride.

Irma's clothing, telephone conversations, and opinions inspired her artistic husband, as did married life and the births of their 2 sons. Nagging, unattractive women in Rube's cartoons were now replaced by bright young flappers with interesting ideas. Children became precocious and highly entertaining, and Rube began supporting women's right to vote.

His humor was best expressed in a unique blend of cartoon and commentary. He worked alone, often in their West 75th Street townhouse, with Irma as his only critic. One day, Rube's name would be in the dictionary to describe a contrivance that "by extremely complex roundabout means" (pulleys, ropes, dogs, revolvers, brooms, and you-name-its) achieves what could have been done simply.

# OCTOBER 18*

## JOSEPH HAYNE RAINEY AND "MME. SUZETTE"
*Together… through the best and worst times*

"THE PREVAILING SPIRIT OF THE SOUTH is either to rule or ruin," said Joseph in 1872, 2 years after he became the first African-American congressman from South Carolina during the Reconstruction Era. Ten years earlier, Joseph could have entered the Capitol only as a servant; now he was speaking on the floor of the House of Representatives, and would serve 4 consecutive terms. *All* Americans needed the federal government's protection from the Ku Klux Klan, he insisted, convincing his peers to enforce the 1866 Civil Rights Act and the Fourteenth Amendment.

Joseph's wife, Susan beamed with pride. They'd been through so much since marrying in Philadelphia in 1859. She was an accomplished dressmaker from the West Indies who spoke French and called herself "Mme. Suzette." Joseph's slave parents had purchased their family's freedom in Georgetown, South Carolina, and provided him with an education. He was 27 when he went "up north" and met and married Susan. That October, John Brown's raid on Harpers Ferry was on everyone's mind. No one knew when slavery would end, but at last it did seem possible.

Joseph and Susan settled in Charleston, where he became a barber. Three years later, when the Confederate Army began drafting free black men, the Raineys fled on a blockade-running ship to Bermuda, which had abolished slavery. Joseph opened a barber shop on Tucker's Lane in St. George, offering services "executed in artistic style." As "Mme. Suzette, Dress and Cloak Maker," Susan introduced the latest fashions and quickly developed a fine clientele and reputation.

Joseph's shop became a meeting place for sailors bringing news about America's Civil War. After it ended in 1865, Joseph and Susan headed for home. With faith in government and political action, he ran for office and became an active proponent of civil rights legislation.

---

*Date Approximate.

## OCTOBER 19
## FRANK GILBRETH & LILLIAN MOLLER
### *Cheaper by the Dozen*

WHEN LILLIAN MARRIED FRANK IN 1904, he said he wanted 6 sons and 6 daughters. She'd been working on her doctorate in psychology and hoped for a career as well as motherhood. "How on earth" would that be possible? She asked. Don't worry, said her confident 35-year-old husband. "We teach management and we shall have to practice it."

He'd already invented a gravity mixer for cement, and a moving scaffold that enabled bricklayers to work more productively. He and Lillian became known as "efficiency experts," establishing industrial engineering and management sciences. Their ideas also led to improved services for the disabled, and streamlined kitchens with labor-saving devices such as step-on trash cans and refrigerator door shelves.

They had met in 1903 at the Boston City Library. Lillian, who was 25, had come from California with other young women and a chaperone on their way to Europe. Frank was the chaperone's cousin and he showed them the sights, including M.I.T.'s Lowell Laboratory, which he had constructed ahead of deadline. The more the blue-eyed young man spoke about his time-and-motion studies, the more captivated Lillian became. He was at the dock in New York when her ship returned in the fall, and he escorted her to the theater – un-chaperoned for the first time in her life. Christmastime, Frank traveled to California and proposed to Lillian on the Golden Gate Bridge.

They were married on a Wednesday (Lillian's mother's "lucky day") at her parents' Oakland home and traveled across the country to Manhattan after stopping at the St. Louis World's Fair. Later they moved to Montclair, New Jersey, with their growing brood. In 1948, two of their 12 children wrote a book about their family, in which everyone participated in decisions and housekeeping, and kept track of work with charts and a follow-up system. There even was a "birthday gift buyer" whose job included remembering when everyone's birthday occurred.

N.B. See November 27 for another October 19 story.

## OCTOBER 20

## BENJAMIN HARRISON & CAROLINE LAVINIA SCOTT

*"A pious moonlight dude"*

BEN WAS 17 IN 1850 WHEN he fell in love with Carrie at Miami University of Ohio. As the grandson of the 9th president (and future 23rd president, with Carrie by his side), Ben took his schoolwork seriously and planned to become a lawyer.

Carrie's father ran the female academy affiliated with the all-men's college. He locked his school gates every evening until Carrie convinced him that get-togethers with the "men of Miami" might be a wholesome idea. Soon the good-natured young man with a sandy mustache began dropping by and taking Dr. Scott's brown-haired outgoing daughter for buggy rides. They talked about music and art – her greatest passions – and attended a dancing party that her parents would have considered "scandalous" if they'd found out about it. Within a year, the fellow whom his friends called the "pious moonlight dude" was secretly engaged to Carrie.

Ben studied law in Cincinnati after graduation, and Carrie taught music and sewing in Oxford. He missed her terribly and pestered the post office clerks daily to make sure he got all her letters. Love was a "mysterious disease," Ben said. The separation made Carrie sad and exhausted as well.

Dr. Scott married them in the family's front parlor on a cool autumn morning in 1853. Carrie wore a gray traveling dress, and Ben wore a black frock coat over a black satin vest. After the wedding breakfast, they left for The Point, the Harrison family's home outside Cincinnati.

By 1854 they had settled in Indianapolis. Ben practiced law and allied himself with the Republican party's anti-slavery group. Less than a week after their wedding, he wrote that Carrie "is now sitting at the fire plying her needle.... Her presence and the consciousness that she is my wife... afford an infinitude of quiet happiness."

# OCTOBER 21*

## SIR WALTER RALEIGH & ELIZABTETH THROCKMORTON

*"sweet empress of my heart"*

W HEN QUEEN ELIZABETH FOUND OUT THAT her favorite knight – oh, Ralegh! her gallant and loyal (until this!) captain of the Guard – had secretly married one of her ladies-in-waiting in 1591, she imprisoned them in the Tower of London.

The Virgin Queen was proud and vain, and almost 20 years older than Walter. He had caught her eye 10 years before when he placed his cloak over a muddy path to protect her royal feet. He was then about 29 years old, 6' tall, intelligent, bold, and muscular, and she rewarded him with a new wardrobe, honors, and extensive privileges. He became her Oracle and Wit, as well as a naval hero, New World explorer, statesman, historian, and poet.

Walter's platonic verses to his queen were read frequently at court, but now he was penning private lines filled with sexual allusions and passionate descriptions of "wanton kisses," "violet breath and lips of jelly" – for "Bess." Their romance had been fraught with danger from the beginning. At 27, she was blue-eyed, blond, and no empty-headed maiden but an accomplished, witty, and graceful woman who'd been serving the queen for years and was currently her maid of honor. Bess and Walter saw each other often, but usually under Elizabeth's watchful eyes. Hadn't they sworn their allegiance to their queen? She thought they loved her! Instead, they had been bribing guards so they could sneak away to make love.

They bore the consequences of their love bravely. After Bess became pregnant, she and Walter were married in a secret ceremony in autumn. Wagging tongues at court may have given them away, but Elizabeth didn't react publicly until late spring, after Bess's son was born. Enraged and deeply hurt, the queen locked up her traitorous servants. Several months later, she released them. Walter and Bess fled to his estate at Sherborne in Dorset, for what would be their happiest days together.

---

*Date approximate.

# OCTOBER 22

## CESAR CHAVEZ & HELEN FABELA

*Valiente y constante, for each other and La Causa*

THE FUTURE LEADER OF MIGRANT FARMWORKERS was 15 when he met Helen in 1942 at an ice cream shop in Delano, California. Cesar had endured another backbreaking day picking crops in the San Joaquin Valley with other Mexican-American migrant laborers when he noticed a girl with flowers in her hair. Helen was 14 and worked after school in a grocery store. She thought Cesar was handsome, although his dark eyes seemed sad. Ever since his family lost their Yuma, Arizona farm and became migrant workers, he had attended dozens of different schools. Now Cesar had quit school altogether. He and Helen married in Delano in 1948 after he returned home from service in the navy.

Their first "home" was a 1-room shack without running water or heat in a migrant labor camp. They left, going wherever work picking crops could be found. They tried sharecropping but couldn't make a living. For a while, they lived in *Sal Si Puedes* ("Escape if You Can"), a San Jose barrio, but work was scarce and sporadic. By the time 3 of their 8 children were born, Cesar had become a grassroots union organizer. Later he said, "If you're outraged at conditions, then you can't possibly be free or happy until you devote all your time to changing them."

In 1962 the National Farm Workers Association was established to help members find decent work and housing. Helen kept the books and managed the credit union. The association grew over the next 8 years, organizing non-violent strikes, marches, and consumer boycotts of grapes. Cesar fasted for *"La Causa,"* and Helen was arrested on picket lines. In 1970 contracts were signed with the biggest producers of California table grapes, setting fair wages, mandating increases and picking bonuses, health insurance for workers, and prohibiting the use of many pesticides.

# OCTOBER 23

## SARAH JOSEPHA BUELL & DAVID HALE
### *"unbroken happiness"*

I N 1813 MOST SINGLE MEN IN Newport, New Hampshire, kept their distance from the local schoolteacher, Sarah Buell, who always wanted to talk abut philosophy and literature. Someday, she would become the first woman editor of *Godey's Ladies' Magazine*, but at 24, Sarah was well on her way to becoming a spinster—until she met David. He was a brilliant young attorney from a neighboring village who'd recently hung up his shingle in town.

David started dropping by the Rising Sun Tavern, owned by Sarah's father, who introduced him to his daughter. Soon, David and Sarah were exchanging books and spending all their free time together. With David's encouragement, Sarah also wrote poetry and stories.

The day before her 25th birthday, Sarah married David in her father's tavern and they moved to a white frame house facing the village green. "We commenced, soon after our marriage, a system of study and reading… from 8 o'clock until 10 – two hours in twenty-four. How I enjoyed those hours!" she wrote. They studied French, natural sciences, the classics, and writing, for David had "that combination of intellectual and moral powers which make the perfectly balanced mind…. To me, the period of our union was one of unbroken happiness."

Five years later, Sarah was dying from consumption when David bundled her into their gig, took her for an extended ride through the mountains, and cured her with plenty of fresh air and wild grapes. Sarah ate grapes for the rest of her long life; like her beloved David, the fruit gave her strength to achieve more than most women of her day. She became an abolitionist, reformer, and champion of women's rights. In 1863 she convinced President Lincoln to establish a "national day of Thanksgiving."

Not everything Sarah wrote was high-minded and serious. She composed "Mary Had a Little Lamb" simply for her children's amusement.

# OCTOBER 24*

## ALICE THOMPSON & WILFRID MEYNELL

### *"My sweet sweet Wilfrid"*

ALICE WAS A WELL-KNOWN AND RESPECTED poet in Victorian England by the time she was 28. Soon after returning from a holiday in Tuscany, she met Wilfrid, a literary critic and journalist, at an afternoon party in London. He'd just read *Preludes*, Alice's first published volume of poetry, and lauded her in particular for "The Garden:"

> Come, my own,
> Into the garden; thine be happy hours
> Among my fairest thoughts, my tallest flowers...."

Wilfrid was fascinated by Alice. They began exchanging sonnets as well as lengthy letters in which she stated, "I should like never to receive any kisses but those I shall never part with." They became engaged on New Year's Day, 1877, and were married the following fall by the bishop of Nottingham, an old friend.

Alice continued to write essays and poetry (while rearing 8 children) and she worked with Wilfrid on the 2 periodicals he edited, *Merry England* and the *Weekly Register*. They labored together tirelessly in satisfying comradeship as editors, proofreaders, and authors (often using pen names), and still managed to give time to humanitarian causes, especially women's suffrage.

Years later, their children would recall how hectic Thursday – deadline day – always was in their home at Palace Court, London. Hectic? Perhaps, but also filled with the keen sense of purpose and fulfillment.

"To W.M.," Alice wrote, dedicating her poem, "At Night." One stanza reads:

> Oh, which are they that come through sweetest light
> Of all these homing birds?
> Which with the straightest and swiftest flight?
> Your words to me, your words!

---

*Date Approximate.

## OCTOBER 25

## JOHN ADAMS & ABIGAIL SMITH
### *"Lysander and Diana"*

THE FUTURE PRESIDENT WAS A 27-YEAR-OLD stocky, fair-haired, struggling lawyer when Mary Smith's fiancé brought him along to Weymouth parsonage, south of Boston. Reverend Smith's 17-year old middle daughter, Abigail, was clever and petite, with an oval face and luminous, wide-spaced eyes. She lacked John's education, but she had read all the books in her father's extensive library and enjoyed discussing everything with the brilliant Harvard graduate.

She and John were terrific letter-writers, adopting pen names from ancient history and mythology, as many young people did in colonial America. Abigail was "Diana" – "spreading Light and Beauty and Glory all around her," said John. He called himself "Lysander," after the great Spartan admiral and statesman. Within a year they were talking about marriage, with John declaring that he was "ready to *have you* at any Time."

Abigail's mother had considered him rough-edged, unpolished, and not entirely worthy of her daughter, but John predicted that their life together would be long and happy. Shortly before their 1764 wedding, he wrote, "You shall polish and refine my sentiments of Life and Manners, banish all the unsocial and ill natured Particles in my Composition, and form me to that happy Temper, that can reconcile a quick Discernment with a perfect Candor."

That summer, Abigail had purchased a white challis wedding gown embroidered with tiny red flowers. She was almost 20 and John was 29 when they were married in the Weymouth meeting house by her father, a Congregationalist minister. A lively reception followed, at which the men smoked, drank, and shared indelicate wedding-night stories while the women sat in another room, gossiping and giving the new bride advice.

John and Abigail moved into an old saltbox cottage on 10 acres of land across the way from his widowed mother's home in Braintree, now Quincy. John set up his law office in the front room so he could be close to Abigail all day long.

# OCTOBER 26

## NOAH WEBSTER & REBECCA GREENLEAF

*wed'ding (wed'ing) n. — nuptial ceremony,*
*nuptial festivities, marriage*

NOAH DIDN'T HESITATE TO GO TO Philadelphia when Ben Franklin invited him in 1787. *Webster's Spelling Book* was the first publication devoted to language in the new United States, and both men were highly pleased. "Becca," a wealthy Boston merchant's daughter, met Noah at a holiday party and was impressed by his intelligence and drive. His nickname at Yale had been "the walking question mark." Noah was fascinated by words; besides Becca, they were his strongest passion.

Shortly before she went home that summer, Noah confessed his growing love in a letter: "*Without you*, the world is all alike to me; and *with you* any part will be agreeable.... You must go, and I must be separated from all that is dear to me."

Marriage would have to wait for the struggling writer whose income was sparse and erratic. He worked hard, writing pamphlets and giving lectures in support of the recently completed Constitution of the United States. "I sometimes go to dances and other parties, where I see ladies," he wrote, "but there is not a Becca Greenleaf among them: no such tenderness, such delicacy, such sentiment, such unaffected goodness."

If his future brother-in-law hadn't lent Noah money in 1789, he could not have afforded to marry Becca then. She was 23 and he was 31 when they married at her parents' home. Fifteen years later, Becca encouraged Noah to devote himself full-time to linguistics and lexicography, even though it meant financial risk. In his upstairs study overlooking the future site of Amherst College, which he would help establish, Noah worked at a wide semicircular table piled high with reference books, grammars and small dictionaries, and a bowl of fruit and nuts, regularly refilled by Becca. Three years later, he completed his *Compendious Dictionary of the English Language.*

# OCTOBER 27

## EDWARD R. MURROW & JANET BREWSTER

*"Love and luck"*

"YOUR SON EDWARD JOYFULLY ANNOUNCES THE acceptance of Miss Janet Huntington Brewster of a personal permanent fellowship, providing board, room and tuition... till death do us part," Ed wrote in 1933. The 25-year old future radio news commentator and analyst knew just the right words to please his parents. They were very happy, especially since Janet's photo implied that she didn't "look like a flapper."

They'd met in New Orleans at a convention of student activists. Ed was 24 and Janet was 2 years younger. Afterward, they corresponded regularly. He was glad that his blond "Hunka" (so nicknamed because Janet was part-Swedish) also cared about social and political issues. By the time they were engaged, Ed was working for an educational exchange program for students that set up international debates among scholars and also helped German-Jewish displaced scientists and academic refugees come to the States.

An Episcopal minister married them at the Brewsters' Middletown Connecticut home. Janet and Ed spent their honeymoon driving to the West Coast and parts of Mexico. A year later, they moved to London where Ed managed Columbia Broadcasting's European news bureau. By hiring correspondents such as William L. Shirer and Eric Severeid, he collected information that became invaluable once war was declared. Ed also broadcast eyewitness accounts from London, and Janet assisted him by reporting on such matters as the evacuation of British children from the city. She also headed the Bundles for Britain relief program.

With the impassioned honesty and moral tone that infused Ed's radio broadcasts through the London blitz and other World War II crises, he wrote Janet, "Above all else, there must be nothing cheap and nothing small in our lives. They must burn with a clear bright light."

# OCTOBER 28

## EDOUARD MANET & SUZANNE LEENHOFF
### *"Ma cherie Suzanne"*

"**M**ANET HAS JUST ANNOUNCED THE MOST unexpected news," said his poet-friend, Charles Baudelaire, in Paris in 1863. "He's leaving this evening for Holland, from which he will bring back *his wife*!... It seems that this wife is not only beautiful but very good and also a talented musician." And she had been Edouard's mistress for the past 12 years.

The 31-year-old painter knew how to keep a secret. Edouard first met the fair, blue-eyed Dutch pianist 13 years before, when his parents hired her to teach music to their 3 sons. It was the teacher, not her sonatas, that captivated him. "Maman" figured out very quickly what was going on, but no one ever told "Papa," who would have been horrified by his son's indiscretion.

Papa died in 1862, leaving Edouard enough money to paint and support a family, which was particularly important because one of the wedding guests was 11-year-old Leon-Edouard Koella, known as Suzanne's younger brother but really their son. Leon appeared in many of his father's paintings including "Reading," in which he reads to his mother in their Paris apartment.

Although Edouard couldn't bear scandals in his private life, he was perfectly comfortable with them in his art. The year he and Suzanne married, his painting, "Olympia," was accepted by the Salon, a welcome surprise after the rejections of his magnificent and equally sensational "Luncheon on the Grass," 2 years earlier. In "Olympia," a blatantly nude young woman reclines on a bed, wearing nothing but a flower in her hair, a bracelet, a black velvet ribbon around her neck, and one silk slipper. The painting was extremely realistic, causing many Parisians to call it immoral.

Suzanne worshipped Edouard and deeply respected his work. His devotion to her was equally strong. "I kiss you as much as I love you," he wrote, long after their affair began.

# OCTOBER 29

## THOMAS ASSHETON SMITH & MATILDA WEBBER
### *"Tally-ho, Matilda!"*

MATILDA MET TOM AT A FOX hunt, which wasn't surprising since practically all he ever did was ride with his hounds. Away from his horses and stables, Tom cared little for what he wore, but in his bright red riding coat, black hat, and boots, the immensely wealthy English sportsman and squire of a huge Hampshire estate looked particularly spiffy.

Matilda was from Binfield Lodge in Berkshire. She loved the hunt almost as much as Tom. They decided to marry in late October 1827, when the hunting season began. From then on, they hosted lavish get-togethers for foxhunting friends, including the Duke of Wellington. After eating beef pasties, hashed mutton, and other breakfast delights, riders mounted their horses and prepared to take off in pursuit of "Reynard."

The first half of the 19$^{th}$ century were the "golden years" of foxhunting, before the rise of wire fences and railways that cut across open fields. By the time Tom married Matilda, he was known as a great leaper, guiding his horse over the hedges at full gallop. He also had earned the title, Master of the Hounds.

Matilda and Tom remodeled and expanded the stables at his estate, Tedworth, to accommodate more than 50 horses. They built airy and spacious kennels for 100 hounds, including Tarquin, Trimbush, Trimmer, and Tomboy, who could always be counted on to bring home the fox's head. Also constructed on the grounds was a glass-enclosed conservatory 315' long, and 40' wide; it was high enough for birds to fly indoors, and big enough for Matilda and Tom to ride indoors during the winter! He kept riding at least 4 times a week into his 80's, sometimes putting his head into a bucket of water if he began to procrastinate.

They were lucky, he told Matilda. Life was good, and it was "Thank God for everything!"

## OCTOBER 30

## FEDERICO FELLINI & GIULIETTA MASINA
### *"Fefe" and his "Cuccina"*

THE FUTURE FILM DIRECTOR AND HIS favorite leading lady met in Rome during the harrowing days of World War II. "Fefe" was a 23-year-old radio and film scriptwriter whose military records had been destroyed in a bombing. This enabled him to avoid conscription and usually elude German occupation troops. "Ciccina" was 22, a university student, actress and pantomimist.

A few years earlier, Fefe's sketches about a married couple named Cico and Pallina had formed the basis for a humorous radio series. When plans developed to turn it into a film, he decided to meet the actress currently playing Pallina. Introducing himself to her on the telephone, he said, "I am fed up with life, but before I die I would like to see what my heroine looks like." Ciccina hoped he was kidding, but she agreed to have lunch, rather than "risk having a corpse on my conscience."

Amid wartime bombings and destruction, the young couple soon found a tiny haven of peace and romance in each other's arms. They were married in 1943 by a monsignor living next door to Ciccina's aunt on the Via Lutezia. Within a week, Fefe escaped capture when he and other Italians were rounded up by the Germans near the Spanish Steps. In a scene as heart-stopping as those he would write and direct, Fefe hopped off the transport truck and boldly embraced a German officer as if they were long-lost friends – before disappearing into an ancient alley.

After the war, Fefe and Roberto Rossellini used stolen Nazi cameras to film *Open City*, a powerful anti-fascist story. Additional extraordinary films followed, including the Oscar-winning *La Strada*, starring Cuccina as Gelsomina, *La Dolce Vita*, *8 1/2*, and *Amarcord*. "When you marry in your early twenties, you grow up together," Fefe said, adding, "Guilietta has told me a few times… that I didn't grow up at all."

## OCTOBER 31

## WILL DURANT & IDA KAUFMAN

*"My dear sweet terrible beloved"*

THE FUTURE AUTHORS OF THE AWARD-WINNING *The Story of Civilization* and other "biographies of mankind" met and fell in love in 1912, when 26-year-old Will taught English at a progressive school in Manhattan, and Ida was his teenaged student. He had recently quit the Catholic seminary and "seemed more a poet than a teacher," said Ida, a precious Ukrainian Jewish immigrant enthralled by Will's passions for Whitman and Shakespeare. She was bursting with opinions and questions. As she recalled later, in their *Dual Autobiography*, although Will was older, he was very naïve "and here I was, close at hand, crazy with life and energy, and physically in full bloom."

Will quit teaching but continued to see Ida, after convincing Mrs. Kaufman that he was trustworthy. The young couple spent long afternoons holding hands and sitting in the park. Finally Will said he had to get away to think. He rode 150 miles to Albany on a bicycle, traded it in for a canoe, and paddled back to New York City on the Hudson River. It was storming when Will arrived. Exhausted and wet, he stumbled into the Kaufmans' apartment and fell asleep at Ida's feet. "When he awoke," she recalled, "we quietly assumed that we were pledged to each other forever."

Swinging her roller skates over one shoulder, Ida met Will at City Hall and married him in 1913. Afterward, she tried teaching Will how to skate, but he said it was more difficult than reading Plato. Ida's mother, who ran a newsstand near the newly-opened Grand Central Station, encouraged them to live with her until they could manage financially. Ida continued her schooling, and Will, who lectured to help support his "Ariel" and their family, won a scholarship to pursue graduate studies at Columbia University.

# NOVEMBER

# NOVEMBER 1*

## AGNES SURRIAGE & SIR CHARLES HENRY FRANKLAND

*Local girl makes good*

PULLING YOUR LOVER OUT OF EARTHQUAKE rubble may not be the only way to get him to marry you, but it worked for Agnes in 1755.

Initially, she had captured the baron's heart with a soulful glance in the summer of 1742. "Harry" was the 26-year-old British collector of customs at the port of Boston. One hot day, he dropped by the Fountain Inn in Marblehead, where Agnes was scrubbing the tavern floor. She was 16 and winsome, with long black ringlets, but her dress was skimpy and her feet were bare. Harry was enthralled and offered to buy shoes for Agnes. He also convinced her impoverished parents to let him take their fair daughter to Boston and pay for her education.

After a few years, she probably became his mistress, and they moved to a grand house in Hopkinton. Agnes's sweet devotion suited Harry's sensitive and scholarly nature perfectly. They loved each other dearly but knew that his aristocratic family would never approve of a marriage.

A decade later, they sailed to England and then on to Lisbon, Portugal. On the morning of November 1, 1755, an earthquake rocked the city. Thousands of people, including Harry, were buried in ruins. Agnes searched for him frantically and finally extricated him from piles of masonry and debris. Possibly, Harry had been stuck in the head by a large rock, because the traumatic event shocked him to his senses. They *would* marry, he declared, regardless of his family's objections!

Thankfully, his parents also came to *their* senses; Agnes had saved their precious son, and now she would become their beloved daughter-in-law. Back in Boston, Lord Frankland and his new lady moved into a mansion on Garden Court Street in the north end of town and became leaders of Boston society. Subsequently, they returned to Lisbon, where he served as the British consul-general.

---

*Date approximate.

# NOVEMBER 2

## MILTON ABORN & MARJORIE PRESSER
*Love for light opera, and each other*

E VEN BEFORE MARJORIE FELL IN LOVE with Milton, she was charmed by the lanky, dark-haired young man's recitations of lines from great plays and renditions of popular songs, especially those by Gilbert and Sullivan. Whatever Milton was doing, he'd also be warbling, humming, or singing a tune. His days as a traveling salesman were over, he told her in 1892. He'd been star-struck by musical theater.

Soon after Milton arrived in Boston with his sample case, he headed for the theater district, naively hoping that his talents and enthusiasm would get him a role in some production. When no one offered him a part, he boldly organized his own company and put on Andrian's *The Mascot*. An up-and-coming theatrical manager named B.F. Keith was so impressed that he hired Milton as a comedian and stage manager for his vaudeville shows. Milton also stepped in to sing melodies by Victor Herbert and other popular composers, and he convinced Keith to do condensed versions of popular operettas.

Milton and Marjorie were married in Boston that year, shortly before they left for New York, There, Milton and his brother founded the Aborn Light Opera Company, offering light operas at affordable prices. They produced operas "for those who love it and not for those who come to compare clothes," Milton said, making a not-so-subtle jab at Metropolitan Opera-goers more interested in those people sitting in the "diamond horseshoe" than in what was happening on the stage.

For years, the Aborns were the only ones keeping standard light opera alive. If one of the soloists failed to show up, Milton stepped in to perform on short notice, and he loved every minute. He and Marjorie lived on West 57th Street, not far from Broadway, and she attended all his shows, applauding her husband as well as his productions.

# NOVEMBER 3

## ELIZABETH HARMAN & FRANK PAKENHAM, EARL OF LONGFORD

### *"the literary Longfords"*

EARS AFTER FRANK AND ELIZABETH MARRIED in 1931, she was gathering material for her biography of Queen Victoria when she came across a sweet note the young monarch had sent her beloved Albert on the night before their 1840 wedding. How similar that message was to the one Frank had written right before he married Elizabeth: "My darling, Just a line to say that I love you…. Your loving loving Frank."

Their wedding day began "in a whirlwind of flying autumn leaves and white tulle," Elizabeth wrote in her memoir, *The Pebbled Shore.* She wore a cream satin dress decorated with love knots and a wreath of orange blossoms. Her 12 bridesmaids wore white satin dresses under jewel-toned velvet jackets. They arrived somewhat late at St. Margaret's church in London, which was just as well, since Frank got there only moments before the ceremony. He and his best man had gone "next door" to Westminster Abbey by mistake, and only realized their error because so few people were there!

The bride and groom had met at Oxford in 1927, when she was a philosophy and classics student and he was a young don. Theirs would be a life intimately connected to English power, politics, and literature. Elizabeth wrote biographies of British rulers, a 2-volume biography of Lord Wellington, who had married a family ancestor, and books such as *Jameson's Raid* about a settlers' revolt in 19th century South Africa.

Frank served in the English government as lord-in-waiting to King George VI, first lord of the Admiralty, and leader of the House of Lords. He also was a respected publisher and writer, concentrating on religious and biographical books. Their large family would be called "the literary Longfords" because 5 children (including Antonia Fraser and Rachel Billington) and other relatives became writers, especially in the field of British history.

# NOVEMBER 4
## BETSY GRISCOM & JOHN ROSS
*Always rebels*

MRS. GRISCOM DEFINITELY HAD MIXED FEELINGS when her 20-year-old daughter ran off and married John Ross in 1773. But you never could stop Betsy from doing what she wanted! John was a nice enough young man but... he wasn't a Quaker. If that didn't bother Betsy, it certainly upset her parents.

On the other hand, John adored Betsy, and he *was* an upholsterer. They'd always have a good steady income. Betsy was an excellent needleworker – just look at her beautiful quilts and samplers. Like John, she had apprenticed with Mr. Webster after school, and the two of them could make anything – draperies, coverlets, swags, flounces, gimp, and the occasional flag. Not too much call for flags these days, what with a war brewing against England. But you never knew. One day, they might become popular again....

Why were my parents unhappy when I married John? Betsy wondered as she stitched fabric in their Arch Street shop in Philadelphia. If they didn't want me to know non-Quakers they shouldn't have sent me to the public school on 4th Street.

By the time Betsy's parents forbade her from seeing John, the couple were too much in love to stop. If they couldn't meet openly in town, they could always take walks in the woods or sit on the banks of the Schuylkill River. It was cold, that November night, when John rowed their small open boat across the Delaware River to New Jersey. They dashed to Hugg's Tavern where a justice of the peace married them in front of the fireplace. John kissed his new bride passionately before they headed back to Philadelphia.

He worked beside her for the next 2 years until he enlisted to fight in the Revolution. And then one day, George Washington and a few compatriots came to the shop and asked Mrs. Ross to sew something really special – a new flag for their cause.

# NOVEMBER 5

## JAMES ALFRED WIGHT & JOAN CATHERINE DANBURY
*A marriage filled with all things bright and beautiful*

"AS I CRAWLED INTO BED... IT occurred to me... that there are few pleasures in this world to compare with snuggling up to a nice woman when you are half frozen," James wrote in *All Things Bright and Beautiful*, but his wife wasn't the least bit upset. If not for Joan's prodding, "James Herriot" might never have written anything.

They had married in 1941 on the same day the 25-year-old veterinarian joined a Yorkshire, England practice. He and Joan moved to an apartment above the ivy-covered Georgian medical building. As the daughter of a local farmer, she wasn't surprised to spend their honeymoon testing cows for tuberculosis.

James kept a daily journal about the animals he tended, and he also recounted tales of his experiences to family and friends at the dinner table. Pausing at the conclusion of a particularly exhilarating story, James often said one day he would write a book. Usually, Joan nodded sweetly, as if to say, Of course, you will dear. But after 25 years, she'd had enough. "Who are you kidding?" she asked. "Vets of 50 don't write first books!"

That was all he needed to hear. James bought a typewriter and taught himself how to use it. He wrote stories, sent them to publishers, and got them back, rejected. He read books on how to write, and read good literature with a critical eye. Still working 7 days a week, sometimes all night long, he finally completed *If Only They Could Talk* and sold it after Joan convinced him to ignore the rejections and keep submitting his manuscript.

"The thing that had changed everything was the tranquil basis of my home life," James wrote. He called Joan "Helen" in his books, and said her "presence was a warm infinity, a measureless peace."

# NOVEMBER 6

## BERNARD MALAMUD & ANN DE CHIARA

*"Too many are afraid to take their chances with love"*

"NOT LONG AFTER PEARL HARBOR, WHILE I was teaching at night and writing... I met a warm, pretty young woman at a party," said Bern years after he met Ann in 1942. The 28-year-old Brooklyn-born writer had been working at various jobs. What mattered most was having time to write. He taught evening classes to immigrants in Flatbush, Brooklyn, and started seeing Ann, who lived in Manhattan. They began going out on weekends and writing to each other during the week. Ann's letters were bright and clever, revealing a deep sensitivity for literature.

He'd thought about marriage before, but feared it would hurt his career, especially since he wasn't sure he'd succeed. Besides, could a wife ever understand what was going on inside his head? And could she manage their family when he needed to work?

Ann could, he realized. Soon after they married in 1945, they settled down in Greenwich Village. Bern wrote articles and short stories, and taught at a high school in Harlem. He also began reading African-American history and fiction, which later inspired him to write his novel, *The Tenants*. Ann worked, too, until their first child was born.

Four years later, they headed west. Bern began teaching English composition at Oregon State College and wrote primarily about Jewish-American life in New York. He also completed *The Natural*, an allegorical novel about baseball. Bern revised his work repeatedly – sometimes more than a dozen times – and Ann typed new drafts from his handwritten copies. The rewards would be great: a lifetime of powerful novels and short stories and awards, including the Pulitzer Prize and National Book Award.

# NOVEMBER 7

## CHARLES DANA GIBSON & IRENE LANGHORNE

*His very own "Gibson girl"*

IRENE'S LONG SATIN GOWN SWISHED SEDUCTIVELY as she crossed the floor at Delmonico's restaurant and approached Charles's table in 1894. The talented young illustrator was dining with 2 friends who also felt the perfumed presence of the blue-eyed blonde as she passed by. One of Charles's companions, who'd met Irene before, jumped up to say hello and returned to the table. What luck, he said, I'm giving a tea tomorrow and she's agreed to stop by.

Irene knew quite well who "C.D. Gibson" was because his delightful and sophisticated magazine illustrations and cartoons had captivated her during her finishing school year in New York. Everybody knew his "Gibson Girl," the epitome of decorum, charm and good breeding whose fame would continue until World War I. Many women claimed to be the model, but actually she was an idealized composite of many well-bred young ladies whom Charles knew… until he met Irene, who became the "real thing" for him.

Now his sketchbooks were filled with lovers picnicking or standing in the pouring rain, gazing with adoration into each other's eyes. Irene was 1 of 4 gorgeous and spirited Langhorne sisters from Richmond, Virginia. When she went home, Charles wrote to her constantly and visited her as well. Then he sent her a picture of his Gibson Girl pensively wondering, "Yes or no?"

"Yes!" They were married in 1895 at St. Paul's church in Richmond where a crowd of New Yorkers and local friends and relations were so exuberant they knocked over an elaborate canopy hanging above the church door.

Wherever the Gibsons went on their European honeymoon, their fame and love were so apparent that people stared. This inspired Charles to sketch "The Wedding Journey," in which newlyweds sitting at their breakfast table notice a pair of eyes in their morning eggs.

# NOVEMBER 8

## PHINEAS TAYLOR BARNUM & CHARITY HALLETT

### *"the most wondrous woman I have ever seen"*

"I DO NOT APPROVE OF EARLY marriage," "P.T." said 50 years after he married "Chairy" in 1829. "But, although I was little more than 19 years old when I was married… if I had waited 20 years longer I could not have found another woman so well suited to my disposition and so admirable… as a wife, a mother and a friend."

The future circus impresario was a store clerk in northwestern Connecticut when he was asked to accompany a young lady back home to Bethel. She'd just purchased a new bonnet and the weather looked particularly ominous. "I assented," he said, "and was introduced to Chairy Hallett, a fair, rose-cheeked buxom girl with beautiful white teeth."

She hoped someday to travel. He said that New York City was bustling with energy and excitement; one day, he would take her there. P.T.'s enthusiasm was irresistible. Chairy laughed easily and made quick comebacks to his jokes. They became engaged in the summer of 1829 but kept it a secret because their parents disapproved. In November, P.T. and Chairy could wait no longer. They skipped off to New York City and were married in her uncle's parlor on Orchard Street.

Soon, they moved into a boardinghouse in Bethel, and P.T. pursued a variety of enterprises, including operating a fancy goods store, selling lottery tickets, running for office, and publishing a newspaper – which brought him 60 days in jail on a libel conviction. Everything he did was done boldly, with the same cocky spirit that marked his future career of turning the circus into the greatest show on earth. Even his book, *Struggles and Triumphs of P.T. Barnum*, became one of the best-known autobiographies of its time.

# NOVEMBER 9

## ANNA MARY ROBERTSON & THOMAS SALMON MOSES

### *"we were a team"*

"GRANDMA MOSES" WAS AN OLD LADY in her 70's when she became a painter, but she'd been artistic and creative all her life. Ever since she married Tom in 1887, Anna had found time in between her household and farm chores to make a quilt, sew doll clothes, or stitch something fancy out of wool.

She was a 27-year-old "spinster" when she met her tall, blue-eyed husband-to-be. They both worked as hired hands for a farmer in upstate New York. Thomas was a decent, industrious man, which meant a lot to Anna. "In those days, many of the boys were chicken thieves!" she wrote in *Grandma Moses: My Life's History*. They were married in the minister's home in Hoosick Falls, a town she later memorialized in many of her paintings. Thomas put on his only suit, and Anna wore a dark green dress with a high collar, and black high-buttoned shoes. With her intuitive sense of color, she stuck a bright pink feather in her dark green hat.

For the first time in her life, she traveled more than 12 miles from home when they boarded a train heading south to work on a North Carolina horse farm. They changed their minds in Virginia, however, after falling in love with land in the Shenandoah Valley. Eighteen years later, they resettled on a farm in Eagle Bridge, New York, not far from the Vermont border. When Anna ran out of wallpaper while decorating the parlor, she painted a large picture on the firescreen to help beautify the room.

Partners in everything, she and Thomas took care of each other. She worked as much as he did, she said, "Not like some girls, they sit down, and then somebody has to throw sugar at them."

# NOVEMBER 10
## LOUIS JACQUES DAGUERRE & LOUISE GEORGINA SMITH
### *Worth a thousand words*

AT A PARIS SOIREE IN 1809, Louis sipped his wine and wondered who was speaking French with such a delightful foreign accent. Turning around, the 22-year-old scene painter saw a sweet-faced young woman chatting with several men. Louise was 19 and lived in Paris with her English parents. Her smooth dark hair was parted neatly above her creamy white forehead, and soft ringlets dangled saucily over her ears. Wonderful cheekbones, Louis observed, thinking he'd like to sketch her merry expression. One day, he would develop a new process for fixing images on paper, but now he could do only what artists had always done – paint the attractive mademoiselle's portrait.

He and Louise married the following year, at the Reformed Church of Paris. Louis was charming and talented, with boundless energy and perseverance. Sometimes he showed up at parties walking on his hands! He loved to dance and occasionally got small parts performing in crowd scenes at the opera house.

Using the camera obscura, an artists' device dating from the Renaissance, Louis painted tiny 3-dimensional scenes in dioramas, as well as 360-degree panoramic spectacles of battlefields and exotic places. By 1824, he was studying lenses and other optical equipment, figuring out how to transfer pictures seen in the camera obscura onto translucent glass. Other inventors were also thinking of ways to fix images from the camera obscura.

By the 1830's Louis's process was a success, and the ancient dream of preserving how people and places actually looked at a specific moment in time had been attained. "Daguerreotypes" weren't better than fine paintings, but everyone agreed they were definitely more "real."

Of course, no photographs were taken at Louis and Louise's wedding, but ever since his great invention was popularized, virtually all brides and grooms have commemorated their special day by smiling for the camera, and… saying "cheese!"

# NOVEMBER 11

## KING HENRY I OF ENGLAND & PRINCESS EDYTHA
### *"Lion of Justice" and "Maud"*

NO SOONER DID HENRY BECOME KING of England in 1100 than he made plans to marry a Saxon princess. As William the Conqueror's youngest son, the good-looking 32-year-old monarch had been expected to "marry well," but he chose Edytha because he really loved her. Besides, intermarriage between Normans and Saxons would help appease the locals.

Edytha was the golden-haired daughter of the late King Malcolm of Scotland, and one of the few remaining descendants of the exalted King Alfred. Others had sought her slim white hand, but none lured her away from the convent where she'd grown up – until Henry. Besides being handsome, he also read Latin and believed that "an unlettered king is no better than a donkey with a crown."

Many nobles opposed the union, and they pressured the abbess to declare that the princess had already taken her religious vows. Forthwith, the archbishop formally questioned Edytha to decide if she should return to the convent or become queen of England instead. (Some choice!) Edytha claimed that she wore her veil primarily to discourage unworthy suitors and – she paused, glancing toward her antagonists – to preserve her virginity against violent Normans! Thankfully, the archbishop believed her and decreed that she and Henry could be married right away.

The ceremony was held in the grand stone chapel of Westminster Abbey. Edytha changed her name to Matilda (her late mother-in-law's name) and became known as "Good Queen Maud." After years of wearing dark colors and a nun's black hood, now Maud favored blues, reds, and greens in her clothing and in the royal apartments. She also started a trend by unbraiding her long hair and wearing it loose over her shoulders. Above all, her fairness and intelligence were admired, and everyone recognized the positive influence she exerted on Henry, who repudiated the absolute rule of his older brother Rufus, and paved the way for the Magna Carta of 1215.

# NOVEMBER 12

## JULIE ANDREWS & BLAKE EDWARDS
### *"Life is tremendous fun with him."*

"I'D HATE TO BE MARY POPPINS," Blake would say, describing Julie's public image – a blend of the perky, wholesome characters she's played – as a tremendous burden. But the Oklahoma-born film writer, director, and producer was comfortable with "Blackie," the nickname Julie gave him. It pretty much summed up his dark sense of humor and his devilish zeal and creativity.

He was 40 and almost divorced in 1963 when he met Julie at a Hollywood party thrown by Peter Sellers, star of Blake's comedy, *A Shot in the Dark*. Afterwards, they ran into each other occasionally. Blake thought that Julie was pristine and proper, like her screen image. But at 27, she was feistier than she seemed and would divorce her first husband a few years later. With her glorious singing voice, she'd been the toast of Broadway in *My Fair Lady*. But *Camelot*, which opened in December 1960, would be her last play for a long time. She took her young daughter and moved to Hollywood to make films and, eventually, fall in love with Blake.

They were married in 1969 in a small private ceremony at 1 o'clock in the afternoon beside a waterfall in their Beverly Hills garden. Life centered on their new family, which included his and her children as well as 2 adopted Vietnamese daughters.

In 1995 Blake produced a musical stage version of their 1982 smash-hit film, *Victor/Victoria*. Julie returned to Broadway after an absence of more than 30 years, and gave a show-stopping performance time after time.

# NOVEMBER 13

## E.B. WHITE & KATHARINE SERGEANT ANGELL

### *"Dear Katharine (very dear....)"*

"ARE YOU ELWYN BROOKS WHITE? KATHARINE asked "Andy" in *The New Yorker* magazine's reception area in 1926. She was happy to meet the 26-year old author of fine prose pieces she'd been editing regularly. One day he'd also write children's classics such as *Stuart Little*. Katharine was gracious, intelligent, and 7 years older, and he deeply appreciated her kind manner which made him feel at ease. Years later Andy couldn't remember exactly when he fell in love with Katharine, although he was "half in love with her for a long time."

But Katharine had 2 children, and she was married to someone else. It took a few more years for her unhappy marriage to end, and for Katharine and Andy to reach what he called "the most beautiful decision" of his entire life.

Things fell into place quite suddenly in 1929. After getting a marriage license at City Hall in Manhattan, they ate lunch in a midtown speak-easy and drove 50 miles north to Bedford Village, accompanied only by Katharine's Scottish terrier, Daisy. Unable to find a justice of the peace, they convinced a Presbyterian minister to marry them in his church – while his dog got into a fight with Daisy!

Just married, they were back in the city by dinnertime and returned to work the following day. Less than 2 weeks later, a short trip out of town inspired Andy to write the poem, "Natural History." Not only is it about the silken, spidery threads connecting him to Katharine, but it also presages his children's book, *Charlotte's Web*.

Katharine stayed on at *The New Yorker*. Eventually, she and Andy bought a farmhouse in Maine where they lived, wrote, and edited many books, including *The Subtreasury of American Humor* in 1940.

# NOVEMBER 14

## MERCY OTIS & JAMES WARREN

*"the best friend of my heart"*

SIXTEEN-YEAR-OLD MERCY COULDN'T WAIT TO ATTEND her brother's Harvard graduation in 1744. Although she lacked his formal schooling, the young girl from Barnstable Massachusetts had read every book he owned and had no trouble keeping up with other college-educated men. At a commencement day picnic, Mercy began talking with James Warren, a sandy-haired junior from Plymouth. Thus began a rich intellectual relationship that lasted the rest of their lives. Like his friend John Adams, James actually preferred women with bright minds and scholarly abilities.

Ten years later, Colonel Otis gave away his eldest daughter in a small wedding ceremony in Barnstable. The following day, Mercy put on a richly embroidered "second-day" dress for extended festivities that lasted a few more days. Then she and James headed 25 miles north to his farmhouse by the Eel River in Plymouth. Settling into married life, they rearranged his bookshelves, mixing her books with his, and added more volumes to an ever-growing library.

Later on, after Mercy became the mother of 5 sons, it would have been easy for her—the only woman in the household—to suppress her own creativity and channel all her energies into family life. But she also found time to write poetry, plays, and commentaries. John Adams praised her cleverness and humor when he read her satirical poem about the Boston Tea Party, published in the Boston *Gazette*. Like John and Abigail Adams, Mercy and James were deeply committed to the Patriots' cause. They spoke out in favor of independence long before many members of the Continental Congress were bold enough to do so.

Their marriage remained true and strong, in deeds as well as in writing. Years later, Mercy would write to her beloved James, "I take up my pen, which as the needle to the pole, immediately directs itself toward you, the powerful magnet, the center of my early wishes and the star which attracts my attention."

# NOVEMBER 15

## HERNANDO DE SOTO & ISABELLA DE BOBADILLA
### *"I will wait for you all my life, darling"*

WHEN HERNANDO WAS A LITTLE MUCHACHO, Isabella's wealthy and powerful father, Don Pedro Arias Davila, took the boy into his home, educated him and let him play with his own children. In the early 1500's, no one knew that Hernando would grow up to be a famous and rich conquistador but years later, when he was 36-years-old, he returned from Peru with Pizarro and was worth more than 4 million dollars.

He was handsome, athletic, with brooding dark eyes, a well-trimmed black beard, and a reputation for bravery and tenacity, and he went to see Isabella immediately. She was 6 years younger, a passionate senorita so trustworthy, astute, and wise that one day he would appoint her acting governor of Cuba.

For years, they had hidden their love, fearing the don's fury if his favorite daughter became romantically involved with someone "beneath" her class. Secretly, Hernando carried one of Isabella's handkerchiefs and wore her small gold cross under his armor. He knew that Don Pedro Arias had arranged for the murder of his explorer son-in-law, Vasco Balboa, husband of Isabella's sister Maria.

Soon, the don died, and Isabella's mother, Dona Isabel Bobadilla, gladly made the arrangements for a sumptuous wedding in 1536. Isabella and Hernando were married at the Bobadilla family chapel in Valladolid Spain the day after Isabel deeded a large ranch in Panama to Hernando as part of her daughter's dowry. Although the groom rarely wore elaborate clothing, it's likely that he dressed like all the wedding guests who were decked out in decorative armor, velvet and taffeta suits, scented gloves, satin leggings, colored leather boots, and plenty of heavy gold rings, buckles, and neck chains.

The newlyweds stole away to Segovia and wandered blissfully around Roman aqueducts and Moorish castles. Hernando loved making love to Isabella night after night, and taking long walks with her in the gardens of their mansion in Seville… but after a few years he yearned to go exploring again. Within 5 years he was the first European to see the Mississippi River.

# NOVEMBER 16

## GOODMAN ACE & JANE EPSTEIN

### *A pair of "Ragged Individualists"*

B Y THE TIME *MR. ACE AND JANE* began broadcasting in 1948, radio listeners already knew they could expect nonstop hilarity from the zany couple who'd been making them laugh for more than 20 years. The petite, hazel-eyed blond first met her tall, sandy-haired husband-to-be in Kansas City, where "Goody's" dry wit enlivened the high school newspaper and helped him get a job on the Kansas City *Post*. He changed his last name to Ace from Aiskowitz around the time he married Jane in 1922, and also began doing short stints on the radio.

*Easy Aces*, their most famous show, evolved about 7 years later when Goody's station director frantically signaled him to stay on the air. Performers for the next program hadn't shown up; could Goody fill the time? Yes! Not missing a beat, Goody introduced the audience to "my roommate," Jane, and they started ad-libbing about a gruesome local murder that had happened recently, during an argument over a bridge game.

"Would you care to shoot a game of bridge, dear?" Jane asked casually. Their banter was quick and punchy. Delighted listeners begged the producers to keep the entertaining duo on the show. Eventually, it became a clever and urbane sitcom about a New York City advertising man and his wife, and was a nationwide success for the next 15 years. The 2 stars moved to New York, where they continued to write most of the scripts and were on the air 2 or 3 nights a week.

Goody also wrote comedy routines for other hit shows, and Jane kept coming up with hilarious malapropisms. "I've been working my head to the bone," she said often, and wearily. Many of her expressions, such as "Time wounds all heels" and "You could have knocked me down with a feather" are classic one-liners even today.

# NOVEMBER 17

## LYNDON BAINES JOHNSON & CLAUDIA ALTA TAYLOR

*I'm ambitious, proud... and very madly in love with you"*

"WELL, HONEY, YOU'VE BROUGHT HOME A lot of boys, but this time I think you've brought home a man," said "Lady Bird's" father when he met Lyndon in 1934. As secretary for a Texas congressman, the 26-year-old "man" from Johnson City, outside Austin, was making frequent trips back and forth to Washington, D.C. He was "tall and gangling," Lady Bird recalled years later, and he "talked quite incessantly."

Lyndon pursued the shy, 22-year old small-town girl from East Texas relentlessly, although his enormous energy and drive almost overwhelmed her. "It was like finding yourself in the middle of a whirlwind," she said. Two months after they met, the even-tempered young woman who would later be called "the knot of the family" agreed to take the plunge with her strong-minded suitor.

Bird and Lyndon were married on a Saturday night in St. Mark's Episcopal Church in San Antonio. Friends attended, but no family members were present. The groom forgot to buy a ring until the last minute when he asked a friend to purchase one at Sears, Roebuck right before the ceremony.

In their haste to leave for a honeymoon in Mexico, the newlyweds neglected to take their marriage certificate. Twenty years later, a friend who worked in the San Antonio courthouse discovered the document and gave it to the Johnsons. When LBJ became president, he made his friend the postmaster of San Antonio.

A month after their wedding, Bird and Lyndon moved into an apartment on Kalorama Road in Washington. Two years later, he was elected to Congress. Long before she became First Lady, Bird ran her husband's office whenever he was away, lobbied for his causes, and escorted visiting constituents around town with her unqualified grace and charm.

# NOVEMBER 18

## PETER MARK ROGET & MARY TAYLOR HOBSON

*"My ever precious friend, my darling husband"*

ALTHOUGH PETER'S GREATEST FAME WOULD BE achieved with his *Thesaurus of English Words and Phrases*, he didn't complete the enduring reference book until he was 71 years old, long after he married Mary in 1824. Years before, Peter had become a doctor of medicine at the age of 19, and had devoted his life to his work, his ailing mother, and spinster sister. He was 45 when he met Mary in Liverpool, where she was the only daughter of a wealthy cotton merchant.

Mary was well educated, idealistic, warm, and self-confident – which suited the highly respected physician, scientist and educator. Like many tall, thin men, Peter was somewhat stooped, but his mind was brilliant. Even if Mary didn't understand everything he talked about, she was a wonderful listener with a keen grasp of his work.

Their wedding in the parish church of St. Philip, Liverpool, was followed by a reception hosted by Mary's parents. Afterwards, she and Peter left for their London home at 39 Bernard Street, where stacks of congratulatory notes and gifts were waiting for them on the marble-topped hall table. Mary began keeping a daybook in which she fondly described afternoons visiting sick patients together, "R" teaching algebra to her in the evenings, and she reading aloud to him from a book while he made sketches of optical illusions. Peter worked on his thesaurus for years, and also contributed many scientific articles to journals and the *Encyclopedia Britannica*.

A few years after their marriage, Mary grumbled to her twin brother that Peter spent too much time doing research to earn a great deal of money. She described pangs of jealousy she felt for the clothes and lifestyle of a wealthy woman they both knew… until the woman's rich but boring husband appeared. Then, Mary wrote, "I looked at my best of husbands by my side, and all my envy vanished."

# NOVEMBER 19

## JACK LONDON & CHARMIAN KITTREDGE

### *His idea "male-woman"*

JACK MARRIED CHARMIAN IN CHICAGO IN 1905, the day after his divorce from his first wife was final. His novel, *The Call of the Wild*, had been published the previous year, and at 29, he was one of America's best-known young writers. When word leaked out about the quick wedding ceremony arranged by Jack's publisher, William Randolph Hearst, reporters surrounded the couple at the Hotel Victoria, asking them if their marriage was legal.

"If my marriage is not legal in Illinois, I shall remarry my wife in every state of the union!" Jack contended. Charmian hated all the publicity, but she had "Jack adorable – my perfect bridegroom and lover, at last." She was 35, prim... and rebellious, ladylike... and lustful. And she had been his mistress for 2 years. Jack exulted in their "wonderful physiological affinity, that makes the feel of our flesh good and a joy." Earlier that year, Charmian had typed and edited his adventure-love story, *The Sea-Wolf*, while he covered the Russo-Japanese war as a newspaper columnist. He had modeled the plucky character Maude Brewster after Charmian, a pattern he followed in many of his works.

Charmian was Jack's comrade in adventure – unafraid to ride a horse astride, wield a pistol, and sail around the world on the *Snark* with her "mate man." Later, she would keep journals of their ventures to the South Seas, and eventually she would become Jack's biographer. He loved her deeply for the rest of his life, and penned these precious words to her:

> Sometimes I just want to get on top of Sonoma Mountain to shout to the world
> about you and me.
> Arms ever round and around.
>
> Mate Man.

## NOVEMBER 20

## PRINCESS ELIZABETH OF THE UNITED KINGDOM & PHILIP, DUKE OF EDINBURGH

*Quite the royal wedding*

TWO HOURS BEFORE ELIZABETH AND PHILIP were married at Westminster Abbey in 1947, her diamond tiara frame snapped and was sent out for emergency repairs. Then her white orchid bouquet disappeared, until a maid remembered it had been stuck in a porter's icebox for safekeeping. And at the last minute, 2 pearl necklaces – wedding gifts from her parents – were retrieved from St. James's Palace. They had been on display with more than 3000 other gifts, including 500 cans of pineapple from Australia and a loincloth made by Mahatma Gandhi himself!

The future queen and her prince consort had met shortly before World War II. "Lilibet" was 13 and immediately attracted to her good-looking 18-year-old third cousin, who had been exiled to Paris with other members of the Greek royal family. Philip served in the Royal Navy and corresponded with Lilibet until the war ended. The day before their wedding, he was created Duke of Edinburgh. Although it's been said that he, with ancestors going back to Charlemagne, had more "blue blood" than Elizabeth, she definitely had more money.

Elizabeth was granted extra ration coupons for her white satin wedding gown covered with crystal stars and roses made of pearls. Philip's widowed mother, who had become a nun, took off her black habit and wore a lace dress for the occasion. After the ceremony, crowds showered the bride and groom with rose petals as they rode off in their coach. The weather was a bit chilly, so they snuggled beneath small rugs and tucked their feet under hot-water bottles and one of Elizabeth's corgi dogs on the floor.

Within six years she became the queen of England, causing Philip to chuckle when someone asked him if he was a male chauvinist. "I'd find it a bit difficult, in my position, wouldn't I?" he replied.

# NOVEMBER 21
## PEARL ZANE GREY & LINA ELISE ROTH
*"the most adorable and wonderful of women"*

ON A LAZY SUMMER AFTERNOON IN 1900, Zane kissed the girl he called "Dolly" on the banks of New Jersey's Delaware River. The 28-year old dentist had been canoeing with his younger brother, Romer, when they paddled by 3 girls sitting on the shore, and flirted with them.

Dolly was 17 and a college student in Manhattan. Zane lived there, too, not far from his office at 100 West 74th Street. He wrote when he could, and dreamed of giving up dentistry entirely. He told Dolly that his happiest times at the University of Pennsylvania had been spent playing baseball and reading adventure novels. Soon, she was dropping by his office and helping to proofread Zane's manuscripts.

"A Day on the Delaware," about fishing, was his first published piece in 1902. Slowly, Zane's success and confidence grew. With Dolly's approval and support, he quit dentistry when they married in 1905 and moved to a cottage in Lackawaxen, Pennsylvania. Six weeks later, they took a honeymoon trip to California by train, stopping at the Grand Canyon and other western sites.

Back east, Zane sold more articles about fishing as well as "wild west" stories that combined situations of brutal violence with romantic interludes. He continued to make trips with Dolly or by himself, gathering material for stories and finding peace in the vast open spaces. "I need this wild life, this freedom, and I'll come back to love you to death," he wrote Dolly while he was traveling to a ranch in Arizona.

*Riders of the Purple Sage* was a 1912 best-seller that popularized the western frontier. The Greys moved to California, and eventually Zane wrote more than 80 books and hundreds of stories. Many were adapted as motion pictures. Dolly negotiated all his sales, and she always got top dollar for them.

# NOVEMBER 22
## THOMAS CRAPO & JOANNA STYFF
*His "plucky sailor"*

THOMAS HAD SAILED ALL OVER THE WORLD by the time he married Joanna in 1872, but she became his best "mate" and probably the first woman to cross the Atlantic in a small boat.

When they first met, in Marseilles, France, Thomas was 30; Joanna was 18, Scottish, and full of youthful enthusiasm for adventure. After they were married on board ship, he brought her home to Massachusetts. Within a few months, they returned to the sea on cargo ships, enduring ice storms, heavy winds, gales, and fog. Thomas dreamed about winning fame and perhaps fortune by sailing solo from the United States to England.

He commissioned the construction of the *New Bedford*, a 2-masted dory that was 19'7" long, 6'2" wide, and 30" deep. Too small to carry a chronometer, it would be steered by dead reckoning. But Joanna "was all anxiety about my intended trip," he said, and she insisted "that if I went, she should go too."

When they set sail in May 1877, the docks were filled with cheering crowds. The *New York Times* predicted failure because "when nature placed men's offices in towns and their homes in the suburbs she made provision for temporary separations which are absolutely necessary" for married couples. Instead, Tom wrote later, "the little boat skimmed over the surface of the water like a duck," and "the welcome voice of my partner" soothed his ears. With barely enough room to sit or lie down, he and Joanna took turns sleeping and steering their dory.

They pushed on for 23 days, through storms, sunshine, and near-collisions with sperm whales puffing vapor through their blowholes "like steam from the spout of a teakettle." When they reached England, Thomas's steering hand was temporarily paralyzed and Joanna was feverishly ill. Crowds surrounded them when they debarked, and women reached out to touch Joanna's hand. She was the "lion of the hour," said Thomas. Even Queen Victoria was impressed!

# NOVEMBER 23

## CLARE BOOTHE & HENRY ROBINSON LUCE

*Passionate about writing, work, and each other*

"HARRY" AND CLARE'S 1935 MARRIAGE IN Old Greenwich, Connecticut brought together 2 strongly competitive and ambitious people. She was a 32-year-old divorced writer and editor whose 1936 play about husband-snatching, *The Women*, would be called the most brilliant social satire of its time. Harry was 37, just-divorced, and worth millions, having established Time and Fortune magazines. With Clare's help, he would create the photo-magazine *Life*, as well as *Sports Illustrated*.

They'd met a few times before they became involved with each other. Clare finally got Harry's attention at a party honoring Cole Porter at the Waldorf-Astoria's Starlight Roof. Since Harry had snubbed her before, that night she decided to be brazen and outspoken. Steering him aside, Clare spoke boldly and directly; to her surprise… he liked it!

At evening's end, they rode down in an elevator together, and Harry blurted, "Do you know that you are the great love of my life?" Three days later, he showed up at her home and suggested that they spend the next year getting to know each other. They'd get married if she fell in love with him, too.

Somewhat astonished, Clare didn't reply right away. Instead, she left town and took a lengthy cruise with a girlfriend. When Clare returned to New York, she saw a lot of Harry. He was hardworking, gruff, and serious, but also fascinating, brilliant, and intense. She was intelligent, outgoing, and gorgeous. The following spring, he told his wife that he wanted a divorce.

After honeymooning in Cuba, the Luces got back to work in New York. Harry was probably the most innovative publisher of his time, and Clare was his equally talented spouse. In the early 1940's she became a Europe-based correspondent and wrote news stories about conditions there as war drew near. Clare was elected to Congress from Connecticut in 1943, and later became a U.S. ambassador to Italy and Brazil.

# NOVEMBER 24

## WILLIAM HARVEY, M.D. & ELIZABETH BROWNE

*"A blessing goes with a marriage for love"*

EVEN BEFORE WILLIAM FIGURED OUT HOW blood circulated through human bodies, looking at Elizabeth made his heart beat faster! A month before their 1604 marriage, he was admitted to the London College of Physicians, enabling him to practice medicine and lecture on anatomy and surgery.

William was 26 when he married Dr. Lancelot Browne's 24-year-old daughter at the Church of St. Sepulchre in London. Brides didn't start tossing their bouquets until the following century, but Elizabeth and William's friends probably indulged in another popular and somewhat similar custom – flinging a stocking at the newlyweds! First, they were escorted to the bridal chamber, and tucked into bed. Then, friends sat down at the foot of the bed and took turns tossing a stocking over their shoulders at the bride and groom. A hit meant that the lucky "tosser" would be married soon.

"My wife had an excellent and well-instructed parrot, which was long her delight... and so tame that it wandered about freely all over the house," William wrote years later. The bird, a "splendid talker," sat on a perch near their dinner table and "conversed" with William and Elizabeth while they sipped hot coffee, a new beverage from Turkey. Female parrots rarely spoke or sang, so they believed the parrot was a male until it died and a postmortem revealed an unfertilized egg inside its oviduct. The parrot's death saddened the Harveys, but it taught William not to trust his opinions until they could be proved.

Dissections also helped William understand the inner workings of the heart and its system of valves. Until he presented his discoveries, most people though that blood ebbed and flowed through the body like the tides of the ocean. Instead, William explained, the heart is a muscle that moves blood along by squeezing and relaxing.

## NOVEMBER 25

## WILL ROGERS & BETTY BLAKE

*"The day I roped Betty, I did the star performance of my life!"*

"MY DEAR BETTY... I AM NOT 'smoothe' like boys you have for sweethearts, but I know you have not one that will think any more of you than I do," Will wrote Betty before she married him in 1908. "I am yours with love," he concluded, and he remained a devoted husband even after he became America's "Poet Lariat," philosopher-cowboy star, and folk hero.

He first met Betty in Oologah, Oklahoma, where she was visiting her sister. Although Will was sweet on Betty right away, he also wanted to be a trick rope performer. She went home to Arkansas and he went into vaudeville, but he kept in touch, sending letters, books, sheet music and other gifts to Betty until finally, she agreed to marry him.

A Congregationalist minister in Rogers, Arkansas conducted the short ceremony in the Blakes' home. Afterward, Will and Betty boarded a train for New York City, stopping in St. Louis to celebrate Thanksgiving.

Throughout the 1920's and '30's, Will was the widely quoted, beloved conscience of America, telling hard truths about political and social issues with an easy grin and low-keyed charm and humility. One-quarter Cherokee Indian, he liked to point out, "My ancestors didn't come over on the *Mayflower* – they met the boat!" He wrote a syndicated newspaper column, and starred in movies and on the radio. When he performed in the *Ziegfield Follies*, he'd start by swinging a lariat and saying, "Well, I only know what I read in the papers." With a bemused look on his face, he'd talk about the news and chew gum while roping inanimate objects, small animals, and an occasional member of the audience. "Swingin' a rope's all right," he'd kid. "If your neck ain't in it!"

Will laughed when people said he ought to run for President, but eventually, his statue was placed in the U.S. Capitol building.

# NOVEMBER 26

## GEORG VON TRAPP & MARIA AUGUSTA KUTSCHERA
### *"God's Will Hath No Why"*

F ANS OF "THE SOUND OF MUSIC" will never forget the touching love story of Georg, the wealthy Austrian baron, and Maria, the
22-year-old religious novice hired to tutor his 7 children. After Georg's
wife's death, the decorated World War I submarine commander had moved
with his family to a villa near Salzburg. A kind but formal housekeeper pre-
sided over everyone, and she expected Maria to keep her high spirits under
control. Besides, it was whispered, the baron was "practically engaged" to
Princess Yvonne, another believer in rigid standards of behavior – for example, children were never welcome at weddings.

The baron was polite, but Maria sensed great sadness beneath his pleasant
manner. "Dear Lord," she prayed, "send him a good wife who will be a good
mother to his dear children, and let him be happy from now on." Little did
she know that *she* would be that wife.

Maria's exuberance was impossible to suppress, and at last the baron realized that she, not Princess Yvonne, had brought joy back to his heart. With
the children's help, he proposed marriage to Maria. After the reverend mother
convinced the novice that turning away from the convent didn't mean turning away from God, Maria accepted Georg.

They married in 1927 in the church of the convent where Maria had
been sequestered. Her stepsons-to-be escorted her down the aisle, and Georg
walked with his older daughters. Within 10 years he lost his fortune, and the
entire Trapp family began singing folk songs, carols, and religious and secular
music at festivals and concerts.

They fled Austria shortly after the Nazis invaded, and came to the United
States. After World War II, the Trapps organized an Austrian relief program,
and a music camp and lodge in Stowe, Vermont. They performed for many
years, until the children's marriages and separate careers made it impossible
to continue.

# NOVEMBER 27*
## JOHN CHARLES FREMONT & JESSIE ANN BENTON
*Married life began the day Dad found out about it*

WHEN THOMAS HART BENTON, THE FIERY Senator from Missouri, learned that his 17-year-old daughter had secretly married a penniless explorer, he was furious. Lieutenant Fremont was a 28-year-old "nobody" whom the senator had tried to get rid off by sending him out west to explore government properties. It made no difference that his daughter adored the army lieutenant, who was as romantic and impetuous as she.

On October 19, 1841, Jessie slipped away from her parents' Washington D.C. home. After a short wedding ceremony performed by one of the few clergymen in town not afraid of Senator Benton, the bride and groom parted. More than a month passed before they walked into her father's study and announced the big news. Benton exploded, sent Jessie to her room, and told John to leave the house and never come back. But Jessie wouldn't budge. She clutched John's hand and quoted Ruth in the Bible: "Whither thou goest, I will go...."

Hearing his beloved daughter's heartfelt words, the thunderstruck senator calmed down and asked his wife to prepare a suite of rooms upstairs for the newlyweds. If Jessie was going to stand by her husband, her father was going to stand by her.

On November 27, he placed an announcement in the papers stating that Jessie Ann Benton had married John Charles Fremont. Usually, the groom's name is listed first, said the editor. "Damn it, sir!" Benton retorted. "John Fremont did not marry my daughter; she married him!"

Eventually, John surveyed most of the territories between the Mississippi River and the Pacific Ocean, became the first senator from California, and was territorial governor of Arizona. Jessie wrote books and articles and also turned John's notes about routes to Oregon into useful reports and invaluable guides for pioneers heading west.

---

*Date of their public announcement.

# NOVEMBER 28

## HENRY FIELDING & CHARLOTTE CRADOCK
### *"the most excellent of women"*

"HER HAIR, WHICH WAS BLACK, WAS… luxuriant…. Her black eyes had a lustre in them, which all her softness could not extinguish…. Her cheeks were of the oval kind, and in her right she had a dimple, which the least smile discovered…. Her complexion had rather more of the lily than the rose; but when exercise or modesty increased her natural colour, no vermilion could equal it…. Her neck was long and finely turned; and here… I might justly say, the highest beauties of the famous *Venus de Medicis* were outdone."

Henry wrote these words to describe his lovely wife, Charlotte. Like his literary heroines – Sophie Western in *Tom Jones*, and Amelia Booth in *Amelia* – she was spirited, beautiful, loyal, and affectionate. Henry fell in love with Charlotte in Salisbury, England, where his family was residing. He'd been born in Glastonbury, Somerset, and usually spent the winters in London writing poetry, plays, and dramatic criticism.

Henry would become one of the first English novelists, but for many years he had a hard time making ends meet. He ate and drank too much, and was often in debt because he spent most of his money as soon as he earned it. But basically, he was an honest man who enjoyed heaping contempt on hypocrisy, sham, and meanness through his writings. Henry also was passionate, bright, and bursting with an enthusiasm for life. At 27, he was mad about Charlotte, and she couldn't resist him.

They married in 1734 in St. Mary's, a small Norman church at Charlcombe near Bath, and left for London and the theatrical season. Their first home was in Buckingham Street, just off the Strand. Charlotte's mother had died recently, and her small legacy helped them weather the unpredictable income of Henry's undependable profession. For him, Charlotte would always be the "one from whom I draw all the solid comfort of my life."

# NOVEMBER 29
## THEODOR SEUSS GEISEL & HELEN PALMER
### *She had the right idea!*

MILLIONS OF CHILDREN SHOULD BE GLAD that the future "Dr. Seuss" listened to Helen when they were at Oxford University together. The former editor-in-chief of Dartmouth College's humor magazine intended to acquire a Ph.D. in English... until Helen noticed his doodlings. She was a Wellesley College graduate with a keen eye and a hearty enthusiasm for life, and now she advised "Ted" to become an artist, not a professor.

That was an amazing suggestion, especially since Ted's high school art teacher had told him he'd never learn to draw. Within a year, he had thrown in his "doctoral towel" and headed for Europe. Helen completed her master's degree and met her mother on the Continent. They traveled with Ted for a while before sailing back to the states, where Helen taught school in New Jersey and waited for his return.

He was 23 and Helen was 28 when they exchanged wedding vows in her mother's Brooklyn apartment in 1927. Wedding cake and punch were followed by a rowdy champagne supper hosted by Ted's father in a nearby speakeasy. Four months earlier, *The Saturday Evening Post* magazine had purchased Ted's first cartoon.

The newlyweds moved into a walk-up apartment at 319 West 18th Street in New York City. Ted's cartoons caught the eye of an ad executive who hired him to draw ugly insects for a pesticide campaign, "Quick, Henry! The Flit!" For the next 17 years, Ted's artwork appeared on billboards and in periodicals. But when he sold his children's book, *And to Think That I Saw it on Mulberry Street* in 1937 (after 27 rejections), his life's work really began.

He called himself "Dr.," poking fun at the degree he never earned, and used his mother's maiden name so he could use his last name for more serious work! Helen wrote books and often assisted Ted with story ideas. They created documentary films during World War II and won 2 Academy Awards.

# NOVEMBER 30

## LUCILLE BALL & DESIDERIO ARNAZ Y DE ACHA III

*He loved Lucy!*

ON A BRIGHT FALL MORNING IN 1940 Lucy and Desi drove from Manhattan to Greenwich, Connecticut and got married. The ceremony was brief because Desi's band was performing 5 times a day in New York.

They'd met earlier that year on the Hollywood movie set of *Too Many Girls*, and fallen for each other like a ton of bricks. The future famous red-headed actress was a blonde with gorgeous blue eyes. At 29, Lucille had already been in quite a few movies. Twenty-three year old Desi was a film newcomer repeating his Broadway role of a Cuban football player. She nick-named him "Dizzy" and he called her "Lucy." Their romance was passionate and tempestuous. After 7 months, he convinced her to marry him.

All the jewelry stores were closed, so they bought a ring at Woolworths and were married by a justice of the peace in the Byram River Beagle Country Club. As they stood before a blazing fireplace, the twosome kissed their marriage license as well as each other. Then they raced to New York City and "were back at the Roxy a few hours later," Lucy always remembered. "The audience yelled and screamed. It was terrific."

They stayed at the Hotel Pierre until the band's engagement ended, and then took a cross-country train back to Hollywood. Their first home, a ranch in the San Fernando Valley, was called Desilu, the same name they gave the production company they established in 1950. Their show, *I Love Lucy*, began in 1951, shortly after their daughter, Lucie, was born.

For a while, they had wondered if they would ever have children. Desi's mother declared the reason they were childless was because they had not been married in a Catholic church. To appease her, Lucy and Desi married again in a religious ceremony with Mama as Lucy's matron of honor. And guess what? At the age of 40, Lucy became pregnant!

# DECEMBER

# DECEMBER 1

## WILLIAM SHAKESPEARE & ANNE HATHAWAY

*"such as I am, all true lovers are"*

W ILL FELL IN LOVE WITH ANNE in 1582, when he was 18 and she was 26-years old. Ardent yearnings sent the precocious lad back and forth between his home in Stratford-upon-Avon and hers in nearby Shottery… and eventually produced the timeless result – Anne became pregnant. They made plans to marry, but Will was still considered a minor who needed his parents' consent. But the young couple's news would not have shocked their families or the local folk, who knew about many similar unions. A special marriage license was granted by the local bishop on November 27 or 28, and the banns were called immediately, before Advent. It's likely that the ceremony was performed on December 1st.

"William Shagspere" and "Anne hathwey" were married at a church in Temple Grafton, a small village near Shottery. For a while, they lived with Will's parents on Henley Street in Stratford. Susannah Shakespeare was born the next May, and twins followed 3 years later. Will probably worked with his father, a glover, until London's theaters and Elizabethan court life drew him to the big city more and more. Will loved his family deeply, and although he spent a great deal of time acting and writing plays in London, he came back to Stratford whenever he could.

Perhaps, when he married Anne, he told her what King Henry V would declare to Katherine of Valois in Will's future play, *Henry V*. Marry me, he asks, and as time goes by, I shall try to become a better and better husband:

*The elder I wax, the better I shall appear… thou hast me,*
*if thou hast me, at the worst; and thou shalt wear me,*
*if thou wear me, better and better.*

# DECEMBER 2
## THEODORE ROOSEVELT & EDITH CAROW
### *"tender, gentle… and always loving"*

EDITH WAS STARTLED WHEN TEDDY SHOWED up for their wedding in Hanover Square, London wearing bright orange gloves, a gift from his best man. But since fog blanketed St. George's church, as well as the entire city, this made it much easier to spot the 28-year-old bridegroom.

Four days after the future president lost New York City's mayoralty election in 1886, he sailed for England to marry Edith. Six years had passed since his first wife died after a brief marriage. Edith had hoped to win back the love Teddy had shown her during their childhood years. She'd loved him all her life, ever since she and her sisters called him "Tweedie" and they played together in his family's Manhattan townhouse.

For almost 2 years, Teddy had grieved for Alice and kept busy reading Tolstoy's novels, writing a biography of Senator Thomas Hart Benton, hunting wild game, and cattle farming in the Dakota Badlands. He had avoided seeing Edith until he encountered her one day in his sister's home. Edith noticed that Teedie had grown a droopy reddish-brown mustache, but he still had the same toothy grin and exuberant blue eyes behind his round spectacles. She was still slender yet shapely, with a poise and graciousness that would serve her well through the White House years. He proposed a month later, but they agreed to wait another year before marrying.

Few people attended the ceremony, but word leaked out back home. After a 4-month honeymoon on the Continent, the newlyweds returned to a rousing welcome. In the spring they moved to Sagamore Hill on Long Island's Oyster Bay, and had a blissful time with Teddy steering their "jolly rowboat" through channels and coves as Edith read to him from the works of Browning, Matthew Arnold, and Thackeray.

# DECEMBER 3
## JOHANN SEBASTIAN BACH & ANNA MAGDALENA WULKEN
### *"meine Frau liebste"*

J OHANN WAS FORTUNATE AND FLATTERED WHEN his patron, the German Prince Leopold of Cothen, permitted him to marry Anna in Bach's own home in 1721. The prince controlled everything, and he also helped procure Rhine wine at a discount for the nuptial celebration. The 36-year-old composer had recently completed his Brandenburg Concertos and had been widowed for the past 18 months. Now, he was marrying a woman 16 years his junior, with whom he would form one of the most significant partnerships in the history of musical composition.

Anna Magdalena, a court trumpeter's daughter, was an accomplished soprano whom Johann had probably met during one of her guest appearances at Cothen, where he was the musical director. Like her serious, stocky husband, she was a brilliant musician. Their passion for each other was intense; over the next 19 years she bore him 13 children, and several became eminent musicians.

They remained in Cothen for a year and then moved to Leipzig where Johann became musical director and teacher at St. Thomas's church and school. He knew that he had not been the town fathers' first choice for the position, so he composed a new cantata every week – an incredible feat; most composers would have been worn out producing one cantata a month.

Anna Magdalena copied all of Johann's scores, in between housework, childbirth, and child care. She probably wrote some music as well. Manuscripts of the couple's music notebooks still exist, and in some cases it's impossible to tell who composed what. Whether or not Johann wrote the following poem in Anna Magdalena's notebook, it echoes his adoration and love for his "Frau liebste" (most beloved wife):

> Oh, how my heart with joy is filled
> to see your beauty blooming,
> Till all my soul with music's thrilled
> My heart with joy overflowing.

# DECEMBER 4

## JEAN-AUGUSTE-DOMINIQUE INGRES & MADELEINE CHAPELLE

*"My excellent wife"*

"HE'S A PAINTER, NOT A HOUSE painter, but a great history painter, a great talent," Madeleine wrote to her sister shortly before she married Jean-Auguste in 1813. Furthermore, he didn't drink, gamble, or stay out late, and he was known as a kind and decent man.

Trusting to luck and optimism, Madeleine had left her home and millinery business in Gueret, France, and set off for Rome to meet her intended husband. They had been corresponding for several months, ever since her cousin suggested they might suit each other. As a way of introduction, Jean-Auguste sent her a small self-portrait he had sketched.

The 33-year old French artist, who would become known for painting luminous skin tones in exquisite portraits and sensuous nudes, had been living in Italy for 7 years. Work was going well, but he ached for a wife and family. He had been engaged twice before but had broken off with women he believed would not respect his devotion to art.

Madeleine met him by Nero's tomb. Jean-Auguste saw her first as she descended from a coach. She was slim and small-boned, with a round face and eyes he would immortalize again and again.

"I have joined my fate to an excellent wife who makes me perpetually happy," Jean-Auguste wrote after they were married at the church of San Martino in Rome. Madeleine became an adoring helpmate, model, business manager, and protector. Knowing that ugly sights upset her husband terribly, at times she would cover his eyes with her shawl and lead him past beggars through the streets of Rome.

"My private life makes for an unrivaled happiness," he told friends. With Madeleine, it always was that way.

## DECEMBER 5

## DAVID BEN-GURION & PAULINE MUNWEIS
*"I want only two things – Eretz Israel and you"*

FEW BRIDES WOULD BE HAPPY TO HEAR what David told "Paula" shortly before their 1917 marriage: Leave America and come with me to a small, impoverished country without electricity, gas, or automobiles. Thirty years later, he became a founder and the first prime minister of the state of Israel.

Paula was a nurse working for a Manhattan doctor when she met David at the doctor's home in 1916. A Russian immigrant from Minsk, Paula was cheerful and outgoing, more anarchist than Zionist. But the 31-year old curly-hairy activist from Plonsk, Poland impressed her, and she offered to help him do research for a book.

Their life together would be hard, and dedicated to David's stalwart commitment to the establishment of Israel. Immediately after David and Paula were married at City Hall in lower Manhattan, she returned to work and he went to a committee meeting. He also placed an announcement in a Yiddish newspaper, stating that they were married on 20 Kislev 5678, according to the Hebrew calendar.

They moved into an apartment at 531 Bedford Avenue in Brooklyn, and Paula began her lifelong occupation of taking care of David. After 3 months, he wrote, "I feel as if I were in love with you for the first time." Usually the founding of Israel was foremost in his thoughts, but there were moments when all he wanted was "to give myself up to your arms, and forget everything but you."

Five months later, he joined the Jewish Legionnaires, fighting alongside the British in Palestine and wrestling control from the Turks by the end of World War I. "Be strong in body and spirit," David wrote Paula. A great future was in store for the man often called the "George Washington of Israel," and his wife.

# DECEMBER 6

## PETER PAUL RUBENS & HELENA FOURMENT

*"At home, very contented"*

" I HAVE MADE UP MY MIND to marry again… and have taken a young wife of honest but middle-class family… one who would not blush to see me take my brushes in hand," wrote Peter Paul in 1630. After his first wife died in 1626, one of the greatest painters of his century left Antwerp, Belgium, and wandered through Europe to escape loneliness and despair. Returning home, the 52-year-old Flemish artist designed "Life of Achilles" for tapestry merchant Daniel Fourment, and became enchanted with his youngest daughter.

Helena was dreamy-eyed, blond … and 16-years old. When she married Peter Paul in the Church of St. Jacques, he bestowed strings of pearls, diamond earrings, gold chains with diamonds, and a large diamond ring on her. Like many young spouses in "May-December" marriages, she instilled joy, vitality, and passion into her husband's life and work. The art he produced during their years together is considered his most mature and remarkable.

Helena enjoyed posing for Peter Paul. She wore plumed hats, regal gowns, quaint caps, Old Testament robes, loose negligees, and stiff satin dresses. He painted her often, beginning with a wedding portrait of her in a sumptuous gown with a sprig of myrtle – the flower of Venus – in her hair. Next was a scene depicting Peter Paul escorting Helena toward an ornate pavilion in their garden. She wears a yellow and black gown and a large straw hat decorated with flowers. Clearly, she is the focus of the picture. Her stepson, Nicolaas, follows along and watches an elderly servant feed 2 peacocks symbolizing Juno, the goddess of marriage.

In "Little Fur," Helena is naked except for a skimpy fur wrap. It's a very personal picture, probably begun when Peter Paul surprised her as she was getting dressed one day. It was also the only painting he left, specifically, to Helena in his will.

## DECEMBER 7

## ROBERT PENN WARREN & ELEANOR CLARK

### *"the happening that is you"*

WHEN ELEANOR MET "RED" IN THE spring of 1944, she had been unhappily married, and he was still unhappily married. The Kentucky-born, 39-year-old author of the Pulitzer Prize-winning novel, *All the King's Men*, was introduced to Eleanor at a party thrown by author Katherine Anne Porter. Eleanor was 30 and working for the Office of Strategic Services in Washington. After the war, she became particularly well-known for her essays, book reviews, and literary works including *Rome and a Villa*.

Red wrote superb fiction, but he could no longer compose good poetry. That changed, however, after he divorced his first wife and married Eleanor in 1952. When they traveled in Italy, he "felt freer" than ever, and developed "a whole new sense of poetry." Within 2 years, he completed *Promises: Poems*, which he dedicated to their 2 young children, and which won him his second Pulitzer Prize, as well as other awards.

Usually, Red and Eleanor worked apart in their 17th century converted barn in Fairfield, Connecticut. Most days, they began at 9 AM and wrote for about 5 hours. Eleanor tended to type her material, and Red wrote in longhand. The family cat liked to snooze beside Eleanor, and their dog stayed with his master.

Most of Red's stories were based in the South, and they projected strong feelings of time and place. Eleanor was descended from New England forebears, and he kidded her by saying, "My wife's a Yankee girl, she's as Yankee as they get, they don't get any Yankier." Although she only worked part-time while raising their son and daughter, *The Oysters of Locmariaquer* won her the National Book Award. In later years, Red read great works of literature aloud to Eleanor in the evenings, and they knew that for them, being writers was the best kind of life.

# DECEMBER 8*

## JOHN DONNE & ANNE MORE

*"Thou art the best of me"*

I
N 1601, WHEN ANNE'S FATHER LEARNED that she had secretly married Lord Egerton's poet and secretary, he practically dragged his daughter back home. Then the irate father insisted that John be fired, and imprisoned (briefly) at Fleet Prison in London. All this for love – but it was worth it. One day, John would become an Anglican priest and dean of St. Paul's, but now his love for Anne inspired him to write wonderfully sensual and romantic poetry.

After expeditions to the Azores and Cadiz, John had entered the service of the Lord Keeper of the Great Seal of London, and subsequently met his 17-year-old niece. No one sensed the fiery passion beneath the very proper conversations that Anne and John exchanged publicly. At night, he slipped upstairs to her bedroom where she welcomed him with warm embraces and sweet whispers of delight. Their clandestine trysts were perilous; how long, they wondered, before her powerful father discovered what was going on?

> *Though he hath oft sworn, that he would remove*
> *Thy beauty's beauty, and food of our love,*
> *Hope of his goods, if I with thee were seen,*
> *Yet close and secret, as our souls, we have been.*

A few weeks before Christmas, the lovers – 18 and 27-years-old – found a sympathetic clergyman who married them. Anne's father flew into a rage, declaring that not only had John violated civil and canon law by marrying a minor without her parents' consent, but she had married *beneath her class!*

John's imprisonment was brief, but he never found steady employment again. Faced with public humiliation, he retreated into poetry more and more. Relatives, friends, and patrons helped to support the Donnes for a while. By 1605 they managed to procure a small house in Mitcham.

> *Only our love hath no decay:*
> *This no tomorrow hath, nor yesterday...*

---

*Date approximate.

# DECEMBER 9
## OSSIE DAVIS & RUBY DEE
### *"best friends"*

I N 1948, TWO YEARS AFTER OSSIE met Ruby, he proposed to her in a telegram because he didn't feel brave enough to ask her, face to face. "What a way to propose!" Ruby laughed. But she didn't hesitate to say yes!

In 1946, the talented African-American actors met on the Broadway stage. Ruby had grown up in Harlem, and changed her last name from Wallace. She was a 22-year-old Hunter College graduate who acted primarily in radio plays. Ossie was 27 and from Georgia. After attending Howard University, he served in World War II and then got a part in the New York production of *Jeb*, about a wounded African-American soldier who encounters prejudice when he returns home. The play had a very short run, but it introduced Ossie and Ruby to each other. They also appeared together in *Anna Lucasta*.

They married during a break from rehearsals for *Smile of the World*, which opened on Broadway a month later. Subsequently, they staged a benefit show to aid African-American victims of racial prejudice. Over the years, Ossie and Ruby fought hard for civil rights and never accepted stereotypical roles that insulted African-Americans. "I have a rule," Ossie said, "never to sell more of myself than I can buy back before the sun goes down."

The 1959 award-winning production of *Raisin in the Sun* was one of the many shows in which they performed together. In 1961 they starred in Ossie's own Broadway play, *Purlie Victorious*, about an African-American minister who wants to build a church where blacks and whites can pray together.

The play was a major hit, enabling Ossie and Ruby to become more outspoken champions of social justice. As Purlie (and, indirectly, Ossie and Ruby) said, being black was "a thing of beauty: a joy; a strength; a secret cup of gladness...."

## DECEMBER 10

## KAROLA RUTH SIEGEL & MANFRED WESTHEIMER

### *The perfect mate for "Dr. Ruth"*

T HE WELL-KNOWN SEX THERAPIST AND AUTHOR met "Fred" on a ski weekend in New York's Catskill Mountains in 1961. The first thing she noticed was that he wasn't very tall, which meant that pint-sized Ruth didn't have to look way up in the air just to talk to him! Although she'd been married and divorced twice, she still hoped to find the perfect husband. Fred was good-looking, easy-going, and intelligent. He also liked kids and he owned a car. They dated frequently, even though some of Fred's relatives discouraged him from getting involved with a divorcee with a young daughter. But Fred affectionately called Ruth "my little skiing accident," and he proposed to her within the year.

They both were German-Jewish refugees who had lost many relatives in the Holocaust. Fred came to the United States in 1941 and joined the army. Ruth spent the war years in a Swiss orphanage and then immigrated to Israel, where she fought in the war for independence. She came to the states in the late 1950's. By the time she met Fred, she had earned a master's degree in sociology from the New School of Social Research in Manhattan.

Not above using "feminine wiles" to win her new beau, Ruth invited Fred for dinner, even though she barely knew how to boil water. The meal was superb, thanks to a talented friend who had done all the cooking! The day before the wedding, Fred's parents came to Ruth's apartment and won her heart by not criticizing her casual housekeeping style.

Ruth and Fred were married at the Windermere Hotel on Manhattan's Upper West Side, and honeymooned in Pennsylvania's Pocono Mountains. Nine years later, she earned her doctorate in family counseling at Columbia University, and began helping other people enjoy "good sex."

# DECEMBER 11

## GEORGIA O'KEEFFE & ALFRED STIEGLITZ
*"Oh Georgia – we are a team!"*

"AT LAST, A WOMAN ON PAPER!" said Alfred the first time he saw Georgia's drawings in 1916. Her friend had secretly shown them to the well-known photographer at "291," his Fifth Avenue art gallery in Manhattan. At 52, Alfred was a major figure in photographic art, prophet of the machine age, guide, teacher, and discoverer of new genius. Although he was married, the most passionate relationship of his life had just begun.

He hung up Georgia's drawings and was shocked when she insisted that he take them down. Most young artists were awe-struck before the great Stieglitz, but here was 29-year-old Georgia, arguing with him! At last, she let him become her exhibitor and promoter... and then her trusted friend and lover. Even his letters were inspiring, "like fine cold water when you are terribly thirsty," she told him.

They were an eye-catching couple, Alfred in his black loden cape that set off his bright white hair, and Georgia in a white blouse and black skirt, with her jet-black hair pulled back tightly. He liked being in the bustling city, but she preferred being by herself. He loved her angular, exotic features, and photographed her many times.

Alfred left his wife, but it took years to get a divorce. At last, on a cold, foggy day in 1924, he and Georgia took a ferry to Cliffside Park, New Jersey, and were married at the home of John Marin, a close friend and painter. For a while, they lived in a Manhattan skyscraper named the Shelton, which inspired some of Alfred's photographs and Georgia's paintings such as "The Shelton with Sunspots."

Alfred continued to promote Georgia's work and guide her career. She became an internationally known abstract artist whose paintings of greatly enlarged flowers and desert scenes are mesmerizing, erotic, and mystical.

# DECEMBER 12*

## RICHARD HENRY STODDARD & ELIZABETH DREW BARSTOW

*"That sweet sweet love of thine"*

RICHARD AND ELIZABETH MADE THEIR WAYS to New York City independently, and met one summer evening in 1851 at the home of mutual friends. But as Richard recalled, 50 years later, "nothing remarkable happened. It never does when it is expected to.... I was a penniless young man about 25, good-looking, it was thought, with a knack for writing verses, but ill-dressed, careless in my personal appearance, and with no manners to speak of. She was... about the same age... handsome... and had been accustomed to be tenderly cared for all her life. The only thing we shared in common was a love of books."

Even so, Elizabeth invited Richard to her parents' home in Massachusetts for the Independence Day holiday. They "read and talked and walked and rode together" constantly. The following December, they went to Manhattan's Church of the Good Shepherd where the pastor "found it easier to marry the poet than to praise his verses." Five years later, Richard wrote:

> The bridal flower you gave me
> The rose so pure and white—
> I press it to my lips, dear,
> With tears of soft delight....
>
> Then this may fade and wither
> No longer kissed by me,
> For these, my burning kisses,
> Will then be showered on thee!

The Stoddards settled in lower Manhattan and devoted themselves to their young sons and literature. After a volume of Richard's poems was well-received, Nathaniel Hawthorne helped him find work as a customs inspector at the port of New York; the job offered a good living and gave the Stoddards time to write. But their works would not be as significant as the literary salons they hosted at their home at 329 East 15th Street. Richard and Elizabeth offered erudite criticism and influenced great writers such as William Cullen Bryant, Henry Longfellow, Amy Lowell, and Herman Melville.

---

*Date approximate.

# DECEMBER 13
## MARGARET HILDA ROBERTS & DENIS THATCHER
*"I was just lucky with Denis. Absolutely marvelous!"*

ENGLAND'S FUTURE PRIME MINISTER DIDN'T WEAR white at her 1951 wedding because the groom had been married before. Twenty-five years passed before that fact was publicly admitted, but that's why Margaret came down the aisle of Wesley's Chapel in East London in a bright blue, floor-length velvet gown and matching hat and ostrich feather. Wedding guests stared, but no one realized that the bride's outfit – which, incidentally, was the Tories' official color – had been immortalized in a painting by Sir Joshua Reynolds. Afterward, Margaret, ever practical, turned her wedding gown into a dinner dress.

She and "D" had met almost 3 years earlier, when he drove her back from London after a political party meeting in the country. D was good-looking, 33, and the director of his family's paint and chemical business. Until then, 23-year-old Margaret's passions were only for politics. Years later, he recalled that she was "beautiful, very kind and thoughtful. Who could meet Margaret without being completely slain by her personality and intellectual brilliance?"

Before their marriage, she had been a research chemist, but D's substantial income now enabled Margaret to study law and become a barrister. Queen Elizabeth's recent succession to the throne increased Margaret's determination to advance as much as any man. She was a tax lawyer and the mother of twins when she entered the House of Commons in 1959.

Twenty years later, she became Prime Minister of the United Kingdom and served for 11 ½ years – the longest term held in the 20th century. Along the way, D was always there to help Margaret. At times, she was called the Iron Lady, but he remained her constant friend, sometimes the only one she could definitely trust. "He's not my second fiddle," Margaret said. "He's first fiddle in his own orchestra. In fact, he's his own conductor."

# DECEMBER 14

## ALEXANDER HAMILTON & ELIZABETH SCHUYLER

*"Beloved by you, I can struggle with every*
*embarrassment of fortune"*

IN 1780 GEORGE WASHINGTON'S WARTIME AIDE-DE-CAMP, Colonel Hamilton, married the girl of his dreams in the sumptuous drawing room of her parents' Albany, New York mansion. "Betsey" was the only one of 4 Schuyler daughters who gave her parents the chance to throw a wedding: all the others eloped!

The good looking 23-year-old soldier from St. Croix lacked wealth and social position, and was probably born out of wedlock, but Philip Schuyler was sufficiently impressed by Alexander's financial acumen. Schuyler's respect for his son-in-law continued to grow, especially when Alexander refused any monetary help at times when his family's finances were strained.

"I love you more and more every hour," he wrote Betsey a few months before their wedding. "You not only employ my mind all day, but you intrude on my sleep. I meet you in every dream."

White candles encircled by holly branches highlighted Betsey's face on her wedding day. Standing before the minister, she wore her grandmother's lace veil over her own fashionable white wig, and glanced at the expectant groom wearing a black velvet coat, white silk stockings, and breeches. Alexander's glittering rhinestone shoe buckles were a gift from his friend, the Marquis de Lafayette.

A year later, Alexander led his troops in the Revolution's last battle at Yorktown. Then he galloped home to Albany and the waiting arms of his pregnant wife. They moved to a house at 57 Wall Street in New York City, next door to his law office. Betsey was Alexander's secretary and assisted him with his speeches. He promoted various causes, including the abolition of slavery, and restructuring the economy. "It is impossible to be happier than I am in a wife," he wrote years later. Nothing ever dimmed the future secretary of the Treasury's devotion to his Betsey.

# DECEMBER 15

## FREDERIC AUGUSTE BARTHOLDI & JEANNE-EMILIE BAHEUX DE PUYSIEUX

*Jeanne-Emilie, ma cherie*

JEANNE-EMILIE POSED FOR THE BODY OF the Statue of Liberty, which Frederic designed and constructed during the 1870's and '80's, but Miss Liberty's dour face is probably modeled after the sculptor's long-suffering mother.

The 40-year-old bachelor spotted his wife-to-be after a wedding outside Paris in 1873. The first thing Frederic noticed were Jeanne-Emilie's elegance, poise, and graceful arms. He'd been looking for a model who would willingly stand for hours with one arm upraised....

Frederic lived with his widowed mother, who discouraged him from thinking about marriage. He was crushed when he found out that Jeanne-Emilie was only a dressmaker's assistant: Maman would never sanction such a relationship! After all, he'd been commissioned to create a huge monument representing freedom and independence, to be given by France to the United States.

Jeanne-Emilie moved to Paris, found a job, and posed for Frederic. She watched his supple fingers transform clay into a 4-inch model of a well-proportioned, dignified Roman woman in classical attire. Before long, she and Frederic fell in love, but they agreed to put off marriage until Maman got used to the idea.

In 1876 Frederic was in New York City studying Bedloe's Island, where his copper and steel statue would be placed, when he wrote to Jeanne-Emilie and convinced her to come to America and marry him at last. The ceremony was held at the Newport, Rhode Island home of her distant cousin, painter John LaFarge. Celebrations lasted until New Year's Day. The new bride loved everything about America, including popcorn made by the fireplace.

Jeanne-Emilie stood proudly beside Frederic 10 years later, when "Liberty Enlightening the World" was unveiled in New York harbor. His monumental work still welcomes countless travelers and immigrants.

# DECEMBER 16

## SHIRLEY TEMPLE & CHARLES BLACK

*His sweetheart, as well as America's*

BY THE TIME SHIRLEY WAS 21, the world's most famous child actress had earned $10,000 a week during the Great Depression. She also had rescued a major film studio from bankruptcy, and was treated like royalty everywhere she went. Shirley also had ended a sorrowful, 4-year marriage and was the mother of a young daughter.

While on vacation in Hawaii a few months before her 22nd birthday in 1950, Shirley met a "tall, deeply tanned" man "with a brilliant smile and thick black hair." As she recalled in her autobiography, *Child Star*, Charlie was 30 years old and knew very little about her. He also disliked name-dropping, causing Shirley to conclude, "Either he knew no one of importance or had no desire to impress me" – until a few weeks later, when he gave her his World War II military silver star.

The press spied on the lovers relentlessly, and announced their engagement before they had decided it themselves. Once Shirley and Charlie realized it was futile to deny it, they made plans to get married before the year was over. Their families were the only guests at the wedding, held at Charlie's parents' home in Monterey, California. He and Shirley exchanged their vows at 4:30 in the afternoon before a fireplace decorated with Christmas boughs. The officiating judge said he'd never seen a happier couple.

He may have been right. Shirley could have become one of those "has-been" actresses who suffer through a series of unhappy marriages. Instead, she had found a dependable and devoted husband who encouraged her to pursue other careers besides acting. Eventually, she became involved in worthy civic and political causes. Later on, she became a delegate to the United Nations, and ambassador to Ghana and Czechoslovakia.

# DECEMBER 17

## EBENEZER BUTTERICK & ELLEN AUGUSTA POLLARD

*Necessity—and Yankee ingenuity—were the "mothers" of their invention*

THE DAY THAT ELLEN THREW DOWN her chalk and scissors and told Eben she was tired of creating patterns every time she had to make new pieces of clothing, they started thinking of a way to standardize patterns so they could be used over and over again.

They first met in Sterling, Massachusetts when Ellen began working at Eben's tailor shop. Right away she knew that he was enterprising and smart, and he realized that she would be a valuable business assistant. She was 19 and he was 24 when they married in 1850. Ellen continued to help out even after their children were born, and Eben listened when she said there probably were lots of mothers who'd like patterns from which to make their own family's clothing.

Until then, worn-out shirts, dresses and suits were usually taken apart and used as models for new ones. It was a time-consuming activity, especially when patterns had to be adjusted for size changes for growing children. Furthermore, unless a dressmaker was particularly talented, styles rarely changed and the same old fashions were duplicated over and over again.

The first patterns Eben and Ellen made were for boys' shirts, and were cut from sturdy cardboard. Using their own children and nephews as models, the Buttericks devised a system of standardized paper patterns in a variety of sizes. Everyone in the family – aunts, uncles, and cousins – pitched in when they moved to Fitchburg in 1863 and began marketing tissue paper patterns in batches of 100, assembled and folded by hand. But making a lot of money wasn't the only important thing in Eben and Ellen's lives. Eventually, the thriving Butterick Company also published magazines such as *The Delineator*, which focused on serious issues such as women's suffrage and aid to orphans and other dependent children.

# DECEMBER 18
## PETER COOPER & SARAH BEDELL
*"my nearest, and best earthly friend"*

ONE OF 19TH CENTURY NEW YORK'S most revered inventors, manufacturers, and philanthropists, Peter started out as a poor man who succeeded in virtually everything he pursued, with the support of "Sally, the guiding star of my life." Their most enduring monument would be Cooper Union for the Advancement of Science and Art, established in the 1850's.

He and Sally met in 1813 and were married at her father's home in Hempstead, Long Island, where Peter worked briefly in the textile trade. Sally operated looms and spinning wheels and was the perfect wife for an up-and-coming businessman. They were a prudent couple who never bought anything they couldn't pay for in cash. Soon, Peter invented a simple but effective lawn mower and a self-rocking cradle operated by a pendulum and equipped with a small cloth that fluttered and "kept the flies off the little one."

A few years later, they opened a grocery store in Manhattan opposite the eventual location of Cooper Union. Sarah rose every morning at 3:00 AM to bake what Peter called "the best bread in New York," and she also created recipes for the calf's-foot jelly he manufactured. Subsequently, Peter established an iron works in New Jersey, where he built the Tom Thumb steam engine for the Baltimore & Ohio Railroad and perfected iron that was strong enough to fireproof buildings.

As the Coopers' wealth increased, Peter and Sarah helped many relatives find jobs and manage through hard times. As a city alderman, Peter advocated paid police and fire departments, an improved water supply system for the city, and better public schools. Cooper Union provided free lectures and courses in arts and engineering to working-class people. Women were particularly encouraged to attend and develop marketable skills, so they would not have to marry "bad husbands."

# DECEMBER 19

## ROBERT FROST & ELINOR WHITE
*Kindred spirits*

IN 1892, WHEN ELINOR SUBMITTED SOME of her poems to Rob, chief editor of their high school's literary magazine in Lawrence, Massachusetts, she already knew he was brilliant. He was impressed by her beauty and intellect, and would eventually recall their encounters in his poem, "Meeting and Passing." They were co-valedictorians at graduation, when they exchanged rings and became secretly engaged. Rob was mad about Elinor and wanted to marry, but she insisted on going to St. Lawrence University first. He headed for Dartmouth, but he longed for Elinor and found schoolwork uninspiring.

After a few months, Rob came home to write poetry and work in a mill. He also taught Latin at his mother's private school, and wrote to Elinor, begging her to return. She told him she would marry him if he could earn enough money to support them, but "we *must* not be a burden to either of our families." Grief-stricken and frustrated, he recovered slightly when one of his poems was published in a national magazine.

Rob's first publication in book form was *Twilight*, a leather-bound volume of 5 poems printed privately, at Rob's own expense. Only 2 copies were produced: he kept one and gave the other to Elinor. At last she understood Rob's incredible need to write poetry. Completing her education in 3 years, she began teaching at his mother's school. Evenings, Elinor read every poem he wrote.

In 1895 they were married by a Swedenborgian minister and friend in one of the empty schoolrooms during the winter vacation. In January, they returned to their teaching jobs, and struggled financially for years. Rob became a schoolteacher, journalist, and farmer. By 1915, he was known as one of America's best-loved poets. He was U.S. Poet Laureate from 1958 – 1959.

# DECEMBER 20

## SANDRA DAY & JOHN JAY O'CONNOR III

*"We liked each other immediately"*

MORE THAN 30 YEARS BEFORE SANDRA became the first female justice of the U.S. Supreme Court, she was working on the law review at Stanford University Law School when she ran into another student editor in the library. John was from San Francisco, 2 months older than Sandra, and a member of the class one year behind her.

Very few women attended law schools in 1951, and he was immediately taken with the blond young woman with hazel eyes. They chatted together often, and she laughed easily at his funny stories. Pretty soon, they were dating steadily. As their romance blossomed, Sandra brought John home to the Lazy B, her parents' 155,000 acre ranch in southeastern Arizona. "We like John," said her father. "But we've seen better cowboys!"

Sandra was 22 when she graduated third in her class in June 1952, and she married John the following December in her parents' living room. After a spirited reception for 200 wedding guests in a new barn, the newlyweds flew to Acapulco for their honeymoon. Then they came back to Stanford, and John completed his final year. Sandra looked for a job at a private law firm, but all she was offered was the position of legal secretary! Not willing to settle, she found work in the public sector as deputy attorney of San Mateo County in California.

A year later, John was drafted. He and Sandra went to Germany where he served as an army lawyer. She worked, too, as a civilian lawyer for U.S. forces in Frankfurt. For the next 3 years, the O'Connors traveled around Europe as much as possible, and skied in the Austrian Alps. When they returned to the United States they began practicing law in Arizona and stayed there until President Reagan invited Sandra to Washington D.C. in 1981.

# DECEMBER 21

## CAPTAIN JAMES COOK & ELIZABETH BATTS

*A winter solstice wedding*

MARRYING A SEA CAPTAIN AND EXPLORER, Elizabeth knew that James would be away a great deal. But she gave him the best gifts any wife could offer: peace of mind that things would be all right at home, and assurances that she was proud of him. Most important, she always loved him – on dark nights when thick fog crept over London and stars lit the southern skies above the Pacific, and on long summer days when sweet birds chirped and flowers bloomed gloriously in elegant English gardens, but men at sea saw nothing but more sea. Like most seafarers' wives, she never slept well on stormy nights. Elizabeth would lie awake, twisting the ring she always wore, which contained a lock of James's hair.

They met in 1762, soon after he came back from North America where he'd been mapping safe channels in the St. Lawrence River. James was 34 and considered the best navigator and surveyor in the Royal Navy. Elizabeth was 21 and had been visiting relatives in Shadwell, a popular sailors' neighborhood near the Thames where James had found lodgings.

They fell in love quickly, and after 2 months they bundled up in warm cloaks and high boots and walked across open fields to St. Margaret's Church in Barking, where a minister married them. They remained in Shadwell until James sailed off to survey Newfoundland. He returned the following November, and they settled into a 3-story brick house at 88 Mile End Road in a suburb east of London.

Over the years, their house was filled with furniture, maps and curiosities that James brought back from his voyages. In fragile wooden ships he crossed the Antarctic Circle, rounded the Cape of Good Hope and the Horn, and explored New Zealand, Australia, Hawaii, Tahiti, and other parts of Polynesia.

# DECEMBER 22

## BERTHE MORISOT & EUGENE MANET

*"the most cherished woman in the world"*

THE SPRING BEFORE BERTHE MARRIED EUGENE in 1874, the first Impressionist exhibition was condemned by the established art world for being too revolutionary. Few people liked Impressionism, and fewer were interested in Impressionist paintings by a woman. But Berthe, who had studied with Corot, couldn't stop searching for something new in art, any more than Degas, Monet, Renoir, or Eugene's brother Edouard could. These close friends influenced and posed for each other and even purchased each other's work to stay afloat financially.

Eugene painted, too, but he lacked the others' talents and dedication. He had a fine critical eye, however, and was impressed by Berthe's work. Light and shadow were brilliantly balanced, and her feathery brushstrokes and unblended hues created sweet harmonies of spirit and color. She wanted marriage and children – but not if it meant giving up her art. This he understood and always respected. When a newspaper reviewer called the Impressionists "lunatics," Eugene almost challenged him to a duel. Finally, one afternoon, as he and Berthe sat and painted by the water's edge in Normandy, he confessed his love and proposed.

She was 33-years-old and he was 40 when they married in Passy, a Paris suburb. Eugene described himself as a "man of property" in the church registry, for in truth he lived off family money and had no clear profession. But Berthe was content and told her brother, "I have found an honest and excellent man, who I think loves me sincerely."

Edouard painted a charming, whimsical portrait of Berthe relaxing in a chair and covering her face with a fan. Although it's hard to see her long dark hair and intense green eyes, a gold ring is prominently displayed on her finger. Eventually, Eugene worked in civil service and wrote a novel, and Berthe continued to paint her glorious pictures.

# DECEMBER 23

## MICKEY MANTLE & MERLYN JOHNSON

*"We were best friends"*

MARRYING MERLYN WAS MUTT MANTLE'S IDEA almost as much as it was Mickey's. Mutt thought his bashful, country-bred son needed the stabilizing influence and love of his devoted hometown girlfriend once he became a major league baseball player.

They'd been dating since Mickey returned to Oklahoma after playing for the New York Yankees' farm team. Before long, he and the high school majorette were going steady. Being with the cute brunette was distracting for an 18-year-old boy; one cold night they raced to a movie theater so fast, Mickey locked the car doors of his '47 Chevy but forgot to turn off the engine. Hours later, they had to find a policeman to pry open one of the car windows.

They got engaged at Christmastime the following year, when they passed a jewelry store on their way to the movies (again!) and saw a quarter-carat diamond engagement ring that cost Mickey a month's salary. It was money well spent on the woman who stuck by him through good years and bad ones, 18 in the limelight of Yankee stardom and professional baseball, and other times facing the tough, sobering realities of illness and tragedy.

Mickey didn't want a church wedding, so in 1951, after his first season as a full-fledged Yankee, he and Merlyn were married by a minister in the Johnsons' Picher, Oklahoma, living room. With no aisle to walk down, Merlyn came out of a bedroom and Mickey came out of a bathroom. He wore a dark suit, and she wore a pearl-trimmed champagne silk dress and a green hat.

After a wedding cake and punch celebration beside the Christmas tree, they spent their wedding night at a nearby motel and then drove to Arkansas with recently married friends. Within 2 years, Mickey had replaced Joe DiMaggio as the Yankees' starting center fielder.

# DECEMBER 24

## WALTER SCOTT & CHARLOTTE CARPENTER

*"Dear dear Charlotte, how I adore you!"*

"I HOPE THE RING IS WIDE enough…. I dare say I shall blunder putting it on," Walter fretted to Charlotte in 1797. She had the jitters, too, and begged Walter to make sure that she didn't see his judgmental parents the night before the wedding. Nervously, she reminded him, "I shall be yours *for ever*; does not that sound awful?"

"Did you ever know a man go mad with joy?" replied the future author of *Ivanhoe*, *Rob Roy*, *Lady of the Lake*, and other tales of Scottish romance, history, and chivalry. He'd been in love before and was deeply hurt when the young lady jilted him for someone else. Then, at the age of 26, Walter spotted Charlotte on horseback near Carlisle, by the English border of Scotland. She was French-born and 27, with large dark eyes and jet-black hair. That night they both attended a dance, and he escorted her to dinner afterwards. "I admire of all things your laughing Philosophy," he told her. Charlotte was good-natured, lively, and confident of Walter's abilities. He immortalized her years later in the character of Julia in his popular novel, *Guy Mannering*.

Walter slipped Charlotte's ring on her finger without a mishap when they married on Christmas Eve in Carlisle Cathedral. Subsequently, they settled into a thatched cottage outside Edinburgh. He practiced law but felt the pull of poetry more and more. Two years later, he was appointed sheriff deputy of Selkirkshire and began writing for publication. Popular lines from his works include "a miss is as good as a mile," "as old as the hills," and "Tell it to the marines – the sailors won't believe it."

Their financial life was not always easy, but neither one every forgot Walter's fervent prediction when they met: "When care comes we will laugh it away, or if the load is too heavy we will sit down and share it between us till it becomes almost as light as pleasure itself."

# DECEMBER 25

## JEROME SEINFELD & JESSICA SKLAR

*He made her laugh at a time when nothing seemed funny*

J ESSICA'S BRIEF, FIRST MARRIAGE WAS "BROKEN" before she met Jerry in fall, 1998. They had known each other, briefly, before her June wedding to a Broadway producer earlier that year. The newlyweds soon left for Italy, but by the time Jessica returned to New York, the honeymoon wasn't the only thing that was "over;" so was her marriage.

It's not surprising that she was feeling sad (and looking that way) when the famous bachelor/comedian approached her at a fitness center on Manhattan's Upper West Side. Being Jerry, he tried to make her laugh... and he succeeded! Soon afterwards, they began dating, and publicity surrounding their budding romance drove her separated and incensed husband to quickly file for divorce.

Brooklyn-born Jerry had been raised in Massapequa, New York, and was graduated from Queens College. Jessica (whose birth name was Nina) spent her childhood in nearby Oyster Bay until her family moved to Burlington, Vermont where she went to high school and the University of Vermont.

November 1998, Jerry proposed to Jessica at Balthazar, a bistro-restaurant on Spring Street in Greenwich Village. On Christmas Day 1999, they were married by a rabbi in a Jewish ceremony that took place after sundown because it was a Saturday. She was 28, and he was 45 years old. Jerry wore a traditional tuxedo instead of his usual button-down shirt and blue jeans. Jessica's white empire-waisted wedding dress was designed by her employer, Tommy Hilfiger.

Five years later, she told *Vogue* magazine that when she and Jerry first met, "his friendship gave me strength... at a time of desperate need...."

Jerry's TV show, *Seinfeld*, ended in May 1998 but he continues to perform stand-up comedy and work on films. After their second child was born, Jessica established Baby Buggy, a charity that provides gently-used clothing, baby gear and products for needy families in New York City.

# DECEMBER 26

## JAMES RUSSELL LOWELL & MARIA WHITE
### *"happy as two mortals can be"*

*The snow had begun in the gloaming,*
*And busily all the night*
*Had been heaping field and highway*
*With a silence deep and white.*

J AMES WROTE "THE FIRST SNOWFALL" 5 years after he married
Maria in 1844. Their wedding day in Massachusetts was much like the
poem, when horses pulled sleighs through the snow as friends and family gathered in the parlor of the Whites' Watertown home. The poet Henry
Wadsworth Longfellow came with his wife, Fanny, who wondered why Maria's
dress was exceedingly plain.

If Fanny had known Maria better, she would have realized that the 23-year-
old poetess cared little for worldly possessions. She and James had postponed
their marriage until they could manage on their own, but even now the struggling 25-year-old lawyer had few clients. Deep down, he yearned to quit the
law and devote his life to writing lines such as "And what is so rare as a day
in June?" With Maria's blessing and support, that would be possible after all.

They met when he was a Harvard student and she was the serenely beautiful sister of a classmate. Maria was a descendant of the martyred religious
leader Anne Hutchinson, and an ardent abolitionist whose poem, "Africa,"
would be called her greatest achievement. She encouraged James to cultivate
lofty ideals. He wrote anti-slavery tracts and essays, and his *The Biglow Papers*
is a satirical denunciation of the Mexican wars. For a short time, James and
a friend published a literary magazine with stories and poems by Poe, Hawthorne, and Elizabeth Barrett Browning.

The Lowells gave money to needy friends and strangers even when they
had little to spare. But nothing ever spoiled the happiness James knew when
being with his "glorious girl." With Maria he had found "the perfect joy of
loving and being loved."

# DECEMBER 27*
## FREDERICK PHILIPSE & MARGARET HARDENBROOK
### *The "Prince of Traders" and "Margaret the Commercial"*

IN COLONIAL AMERICA, MANY DUTCH-BORN WIVES were shrewd businesswomen, but Margaret was particularly talented. When she and Frederick married in 1662, she was a wealthy and beautiful young widow who maintained her late husband's company shipping furs to Holland in exchange for Dutch products sold in Nieuw Amsterdam. Undaunted by ocean travel, she often accompanied the pelts on her own fleet of ships to the Netherlands, which eliminated the need for profit-cutting middlemen.

Like Margaret, Frederick loved commerce as well as investing in real estate. He was an architect-carpenter for the Dutch West India Company when he first arrived in the New World, but soon he was making a small fortune by speculating in wampum used for trade with the Indians. He also dealt in Indian coats, horses, grain, liquors, feather pillows, furs and other staples.

Nothing topped sitting with Margaret in front of his large open fireplace, sipping mulled cider while talking about futures, commodities, and other business affairs. Frederick couldn't believe his good luck: Here was a well-educated woman who could share her husband's responsibilities as he enlarged his overseas trade. Margaret liked this ambitious man who didn't object to his wife using her maiden name in her commercial enterprises.

They married in December, probably right before New Year's Day when family members and friends usually visited each other. No doubt, the church deacon joined in the wedding festivities and collected well-wishers' donations to help those who were less fortunate. In time, Frederick became one of the founders of the city of Yonkers and built a fine manor house on highlands overlooking the Hudson River. By 1674 he was the wealthiest citizen of the city of New York.

---

*Date approximate.

# DECEMBER 28

## JOHN STEINBECK & ELAINE ANDERSON SCOTT
### *The third time was a charm*

"BEING MARRIED TO ME IS A very hard thing," the internationally acclaimed author wrote Elaine in 1949. His novels, *The Grapes of Wrath* and *Of Mice and Men,* had inspired countless readers to protest social injustices, but now it was John who was sad and depressed. His second wife had taken their 2 young sons away and divorced him, after admitting that she had never really loved him. Not only that, his best friend had just died.

He was 47-years-old, exhausted creatively, and tapped out financially. While struggling to write the film-script for *Viva Zapata!* he met Elaine, who became his salvation. She was 35 and Texas-born and had worked on Broadway in casting and stage management. Her marriage to actor Zachary Scott was virtually over and she, too, was searching for a peaceful, loving attachment.

Soon after Elaine's divorce was finalized in 1950, she and John were married at his publisher's home in New York, and spent their wedding night at the St. Regis Hotel. After a week-long honeymoon in Bermuda, John was back at work at their Manhattan brownstone at 206 East 72nd Street. Within 2 years he had completed another masterpiece, recalling the story of Cain and Abel and man's ancient struggles with good and evil. When Elaine read the manuscript and realized its biblical tone, she suggested the title: *East of Eden,* from Genesis.

In 1962 John was awarded the Nobel Prize for Literature. He and Elaine first heard the news at their summer cottage in Sag Harbor, New York. She was so flustered, she put the bacon she was frying into the refrigerator! A few years later, for her birthday, John placed a stepping-stone on the grass and inscribed these words in the wet cement: *"Ladye, I take recorde of God, in thee I have myn erthly joye."*

# DECEMBER 29
## JOHN NICHOLAS RINGLING & MABLE BURTON
### *Lovers of art, and each other*

"T HE CIRCUS KING" WAS 39 BEFORE he decided to settle down and marry, and 30-year-old Mable was smart enough not to try and change that. Like the circus that he and his brothers founded in 1884, John was bursting with physical power and energy. His arms were as thick as a wrestler's, and his voice was very deep. But like many large men, John spoke softly and maintained an air of dignity and decorum. If the self-made businessman smoked too many cigars and was occasionally egotistical and imperious, so be it. Mable adored her big bear of a husband, and by accepting his imperfections, she won his steadfast adoration.

They probably met in Atlantic City, New Jersey, where the attractive, diminutive young woman was living and working after coming east from a small town in Ohio named Moons. Whatever attracted the intensely private couple to each other, they kept it to themselves.

They were married in the Hoboken city clerk's office in 1905. A few days later, they sailed to Europe, where they looked at new circus acts and visited many cathedrals and museums. The trip sparked John and Mable's interest in art and culture, which eventually developed into a lifelong love. They studied art between the circus seasons, and began purchasing works at auctions.

By 1911 John and Mable were spending their winters in Sarasota, Florida. Ten years later, construction began of Ca'd'Zan ("house of John"), a grand waterfront mansion built in the style of a Venetian palazzo. In an outrageous gesture of fun, they commissioned life-size bas-relief panels of themselves dressed (actually, *undressed*) like Adam and Eve. Much of the artwork that enhanced the palazzo was later displayed in the John and Mable Ringling Museum of Art, which they built on the grounds beside their home.

# DECEMBER 30

## JOHN PHILIP SOUSA & JANE VAN MIDDLESWORTH BELLIS

*"When you change your name to mine…"*

ON FEBRUARY 22, 1879, AMERICA'S FUTURE "March King" was rehearsing the Philadelphia Church Choir in *H.M.S. Pinafore*, by Gilbert and Sullivan. He noticed "a remarkably pretty girl with the loveliest complexion I had ever seen." She sang in the chorus, but they had never met. Today, however, was her birthday, just like President Washington, she pointed out. When rehearsals ended, her colleagues congratulated her and introduced her to the conductor.

"Jennie" was 16 years old. He was 25, and known as Philip. When he looked into Jennie's eyes under "a cloud of chestnut hair," bells rang, cymbals clashed, and every musical metaphor he could imagine popped into his head! Although Jennie's singing abilities were limited, he managed to keep a spot for her in the choir.

They became engaged the following fall, after Philip convinced her father that he had $150 in the bank and could afford to hire a cook. More important, Mr. Bellis had faith in Philip. He was always humming something, and drumming his fingers on the table. He had composed the "International Congress" fantasy for Offenbach's orchestra 3 years before. Now he was working on operettas, orchestral pieces, and songs. He composed the song, "When You Change Your Name to Mine…" and dedicated it to Jennie shortly before they were married by a Baptist minister at the Bellises' home. Within a year, Philip became the youngest leader of the United States Marine Corps Band, and took it (and Jennie) on tour through the United States and Europe.

Eventually, Philip composed more than 100 stirring marches, including "Semper Fidelis," which became the Marines' official march, and "The Stars and Stripes Forever," his most famous work and personal favorite. Philip liked to stand up while composing, often beside the big square piano in the living room. Usually, Jennie sat nearby, handing him fresh quill pens.

# DECEMBER 31
## ROY ROGERS & DALE EVANS
### *"King of the Cowboys" and "Queen of the West"*

B ACKSTAGE AT A CHICAGO RODEO SHOW in October, 1947, Roy asked Dale what she was doing on New Year's Eve. Since they were sitting on horseback, she thought this was an odd time to pose such a question. Then, using his well-known cowboy charm, Roy took a ruby ring out of his pocket and put it on Dale's finger. "Why don't we get married?" he asked his stunned costar. The lights dimmed in the arena, and they rode out into the spotlight. "Yes," she whispered, right before they sang the National Anthem to a crowd of cheering spectators who had no idea what had happened.

When they did find out, they went wild. The famous yodeling cowboy and western hero had gone and married that cute gal who did so much singing and riding with him. It would be a marriage made in heaven – and in the barn. Even their horses, Trigger and Buttermilk, got along.

One of the first times Roy and Dale met was on the movie set of *The Cowboy and the Senorita*. She hadn't been on a horse since childhood, and she gratefully accepted Roy's riding tips and advice. After 2 failed marriages, she wasn't looking for romance, but when Roy's wife died suddenly, Dale helped him work through his sadness.

The former Leonard Slye and Frances Smith were married at a friend's Oklahoma ranch during a snowstorm that delayed the minister for hours. Instead of a 10-gallon hat and chaps, Roy donned a real suit. Dale wore a powder blue dress and carried roses.

Since horse years are usually counted every New Year's Day, it's not surprising that the following morning the quintessential cowboy told his bride they'd already been married 1 whole year.

*"YIPPEE-EYE'O-KI-AY!"*

# BIBLIOGRAPHY

M ore than 2000 books, magazine and newspaper articles, corporate archives, historical societies and online sources were consulted for this book. I was assisted also by descendants of notable couples, staff personnel at many public and private libraries, museum curators and archivists. A more comprehensive bibliography may be provided upon request.

# TIMELESS WEDDING TOPICS

S ome things about weddings never change, and the updated edition of WEDDING DAYS includes categories which anyone in love will enjoy, and anyone planning a wedding will appreciate, along with pages of dates where they can read all about it. To conserve space, only one spouse's name appears here.

COUPLES WHO WORKED TOGETHER: Burns 1/7; Roebling 1/18; Ward 2/22; Curie 7/16; Benny 1/14; Roebling 1/18; Ward 2/22; Beard 3/8; Cassavetes 3/19; Lennon 3/20; Susann 4/2; Ducrow 5/24; Pennell 6/5; von-Suttner 6/12; Houdini 7/22; Hine 8/23; Gurley/Brown 9/25; Durant 10/31; Moses 11/9; Butterick 12/17; Cooper 12/18; Rogers/Evans 12/31.

COUPLES WHO WERE VERY SUPPORTIVE AND INSPIRED EACH OTHER OR ONE: Cooper 1/1; Herriot 11/5; Darwin 1/29; Dali 1/30; Benton 2/19; Howe 3/3; Kipling 3/18; Rossetti 3/31; Susann 4/2; Agassiz 4/25; Opie 5/8; Fanshawe 5/18; Kollwitz 6/13; Ginsburg 6/23; Hutchinson 7/3; Klee 9/16; Gurley/Brown 9/25; Wight 11/5; Morisot 12/22.

COUSINS WHO MARRIED: Wedgwood 1/25; Darwin 1/29; Poe 5/16; Sedgwick/Bacon 9/4.

15+ YEARS DIFFERENCES IN AGE: Rush 1/11; Hearn 1/16; Friedrich 1/21; Cameron 2/1; Allen 2/9; Lind 2/5; Roosevelt 2/17; Morris 3/2; Jenner 3/6; Justinianus 4/8; Renoir 4/14; Carnegie 4/22; Houston 5/9; Bogart/Bacall 5/21; Cleveland 6/2; Palmer 7/29; Durant 10/31; Rubens 12/6; OKeeffe/Stieglitz 12/11; Seinfeld 12/25.

GREAT & QUOTABLE ROMANTIC POETRY: Nevin 1/5; L'Engle 1/28; Revere 9/23; Nevin 1/5; Key 1/19; Lamb 2/27; Bradstreet 3/24; Moore 3/25; Carnegie 4/22; Smith 5/31; Spenser 6/11; Blake 8/18; Freud 9/13; Latimer 9/20; Cronyn/Tandy 9/27; Wordsworth 10/4; Henry 10/9; Raleigh 10/21; Adams 10/25; London 11/19; Shakespeare 12/1; Bach 12/3; Donne 12/8; Stoddard 12/12; Scott 12/24.

GREAT QUOTES ABOUT MARRIAGE: Berlin 1/4; Wedgwood 1/25; Mott 4/10; Finch 9/7; Gehrig 9/29.

INTERMARRIAGES ARE NOTHING NEW: Weill/Lenya 1/28; Pocahontas 4/5; Sullivan 4/28; Ross 11/4.

MARRIAGES THAT TOOK YEARS TO HAPPEN: Burton 1/22; Riis 3/5; Baker 3/11; Khurram 3/27; Anderson 7/24.

MARRIAGES THAT ENDURED VERY TOUGH TIMES: Roebling 1/18; Trumbo 3/13; Lafayette 4/11; Fanshawe 5/18; Kahlenberg 9/5.

OVER-THE-TOP WEDDING CELEBRATIONS: QueenVictoria 2/10; Eliz&Fredrk 2/13; Franz Joseph 4/24; Duke of York 4/28; Presley 5/1.

OVER-THE-TOP WEDDING GIFTS: EdwConfessor 1/23; Berlin 1/4; Queen Elizabeth 11/20.

PARENTS WHO THOUGHT NO ONE WAS GOOD ENOUGH FOR THEIR "PERFECT" CHILD: Pushkin 2/18; Houston 5/9; Bartholdi 12/15.

PARENTS WHO THOUGHT THEIR SON/DAUGHTER'S CHOICE OF A SPOUSE WAS BENEATH THEM: Berlin 1/4; Thomas 1/15; Calder 1/17; Chagall 7/25; Burton 1/22; Pushkin 2/18; Benton 2/19; Stevenson 5/19; Caesar 7/17; Crockett 8/19; Benjamin 2/20; Fremont 11/27.

PARENTS AND GRANDPARENTS WHO TRIED TO CONTROL THEIR CHILDREN WITH MONEY... BUT FAILED: Berlin 1-4; Constable 10/2.

PETS AT THE WEDDING &/OR IN THE MARRIAGE: Napoleon/Josephine 3/9; St. Exupery 4/12; White 11/13.

"QUICKIE" MARRIAGES THAT LASTED: Boyer 2/14; Johnson 11/17.

ROYALTY & ROYAL WEDDINGS: Edward the Confessor 1/23; Edward III 1/24; Queen Victoria 2/10; Prince Khurram 3/27; Justinian 4/8; Duke of York 4/26; Prince William 4/29; Malcolm Canmore May 7; Duke of Windsor 6/3; George VI 7/6; Wm of Normandy 7/14; Princess Anne 7/29; Canute 7/30; George III 9/8; Black Prince 10/10; Queen Elizabeth 11/20; Henry I 11/11.

SECRET LOVE / IN LOVE ON THE SLY: Digby 1/13; Fremont 11/27; Donne 12/8.

THE THIRD (AND BEYOND....) TIME'S A CHARM: Houston 5/9; Armstrong 10/12; Westheimer 12/10; Steinbeck 12/28.

TWO WEDDING CEREMONIES – RELIGIOUS AND CIVIL: Maria 4/8; Loren 4/9; Kelly 4/18-19; Taylor/Bologna 8/7; Freud 9/13.

UNUSUAL WEDDING TRADITIONS: Franz Joseph 4/24; Grant 8/22; Gaskell 8/30; Madison 9/15; Harvey 11/24.

UNEXPECTED VOWS: Earhart 2/7; CadyStanton 5/11.

WEDDING CEREMONY & DRESS DETAILS: Marshall 1/3; Washington 1/6; Darwin 1/29; Lind 2/5; Roosevelt 2/17; Taylor 3/15; Roosevelt 3/17; Lennon/Ono 3/20; Penn 4/4; Pocahontas 4/5; Duke of Windsor 6/3; Madison 9/15; Longford 11/3; Hamilton 12/14.

WEDDING JITTERS AND MISHAPS (REAL OR IMAGINARY): Verne 1/10; Pushkin 2/18; Edison 2/24; Chekhov 5/25.

WOMEN OVER FORTY WHO FOUND TRUE LOVE: Potter 10/14; Christie 9/11.

WHY THEY PICKED THAT DATE: Roosevelt 3/17; Gilbreth 10/19.

AND... DON'T MISS: Chang/Eng 4/13; Titian 8/26.

ADVENTURERS & EXPLORERS: Byrd 1/20; Earhart 2/7; Johnsons 5/15; Lindbergh 5/27; Boone 8/14; Crockett 8/29; Hillary 9/3; Schliemann 9/24; Evans 9/26; DeSoto 11/15; Crapo 11/22; Cook 12/21.

ACTORS & ACTRESSES: Weill/Lenya 1/28; Taylor/Burton 3/15; Mitchum 3/16; Gable/Lombard 3/29; Martin 5/5; Bogart/Bacall 5/21; Lunt/Fontanne 5/26; Castle 5/28; March/Eldridge 5/30; Chaplin 6/16; Guinness 6/20; Oakley 6/22; Bologna/Taylor 8/7; Hart/Carlisle 8/10; Lemmon 8/15; Hayes 8/17; Sedgwick/Bacon 9/4; Stiller/Meara 9/14; Cronyn/Tandy 9/27; Champion 10/5; Nelson 10/8; Fellini 10/30; Ball/Arnaz 11/30; Dee/Davis 12/9; Seinfeld 12/25; Rogers/Evans 12/31.

ARTISTS, ARCHITECTS, SCULPTORS: Matisse 1/8; Peale 1/12; Rouault 1/27; Dali 1/30; Soyer 2/8; Hals 2/12; "Maria" 2/26; Renoir 4/14; Rockwell 4/17; Vermeer 4/30; Opie 5/8; Stuart 5/10; Borglum 5/20; Leystar 6/1; Rembrandt 6/10; Kollwitz 6/13; Pissarro 6/14; Fragonard 6/17; Monet 6/26; Eiffel 7/8; Disney 7/13; Gainsborough 7/15; Moore 7/27; Sisley 8/5; Whistler 8/11; Titian 8/26; West 9/2; Klee 9/16; Constable 10/2; Manet 10/28;

Gibson 11/7; Moses 11/9; Ingres 12/4; Rubens 12/6; O'Keeffe/Stieglitz 12/11; Bartholdi 12/15.

ATHLETES: Ashe 2/20; Gehrig 9/29; Mantle 12/23.

COMEDIANS: Rickles 3/14; Youngman 5/4; Cantor 6/9; Caesar 7/17; Allen 7/31; Jordan 8/31; Stiller/Meara 9/14; Abbott 9/17; Seinfeld 12/25.

INVENTORS & SCIENTISTS: Edison 2/24; Howe 3/3; Pasteur 5;29; Gillette 7/2; Bell 7/11; Curie 7/26; Kettering 8/1; Westinghouse 8/8; Latimer 9/20; Gilbreth 10/19.

MUSICIANS, SINGERS & COMPOSERS: Berlin 1/4; Tucker 2/11; Steinway 2/25; Mahler 3/10; McCartney 3/12; Lennon/Ono 3/20; Goodman 3/21; Mendelssohn 3/28; Autry 4/1; Welk 4/19; Starkey 4/27; Presley 5/1; Berg 5/3; Hammerstein 5/14; Anderson 7/24; Buxtehude 8/3; Mozart 8/4; Gilbert 8/6; DaPonte 8/12; Caruso 8/20; Stradivari 8/24; Verdi 8/29; Strauss 9/10; Powell 9/21; Miller 10/6; Armstrong 10/12; Dickson 10/13; Sutherland 10/16; von Trapp 11/26; Bach 12/3.

POLITICIANS & REFORMERS: Monroe 2/16; VanBuren 2/21; Davis 2/24; LaGuardia 2/28; Reagan 3-4; Riis 3/5; Roosevelt 3/17; Mott 4/10; Houston 5/9; CadyStanton 5/11; Johnson 5/17; King 6/18; Taft 6/19; Cleveland 6/2; Truman 6/28; Wells 6/27; Lee 6/30; Eisenhower 7/1; Greeley 7/5; Carter 7/7; Darrow 7/16; Hutchinson 8/9; Stuyvesant 8/13; Grant 8/22; Hancock 8/28; Franklin 9/1; Kennedy 9/12; Madison 9/15; Goldwater 9/22; Bryan 10/1; Obama 10/3; Clinton 10/11; Ford 10/15; Rainey 10/18; Chavez 10/22; Hale 10/23; Adams 10/25; Johnson 11/17; Ben-Gurion 12/5; Thatcher 12/13.

WRITERS & POETS: Cooper 1/1; Clemens 2/2; Dostoyevsky 2/15; Pushkin 2/18; Trumbo 3/13; Tolkien 3/22; Bradstreet 3/24; Fitzgerald 4/3; Wallace 5/6; Opie 5/8; Rabinowitz 5/12; Poe 5/16; Smith 5/31; Trollope 5/23; Chekhov 5/25; Milne 6/4; Nash 6/6; Muir 6/7; Marquis 6/8; Spenser 6/11; Sandburg 6/15; Thurber 6/25; Bronte 6/29; Joyce 7/4; Hawthorne 7/9; Beeton 7/10; Millay 7/18; DuMaurier 7/19; Colum 7/23; Jeffers 8/2; Melville 8/4; West 8/16; Blake 8/18; Randall 8/21; Ingalls 8/25; Mencken 8/27; Gaskell 8/30; Finch 9/7; Steele 9/9; Christie 9/11; Doyle 9/18; Barrett/Browning 9/19; Meynell 10/24; Durant 10/31; White 11/13; London 11/19; Geisel 11/29; Shakespeare 12/1; Donne 12/8.

# PERMISSION FOR TEXT

GRATEFUL ACKNOWLEDGMENT IS MADE FOR PERMISSION TO
QUOTE FROM THE FOLLOWING:

Excerpts from three Carl Sandburg poems: *"Cool Tombs," from CORN-
HUSKERS (1918), "Dream Girl," from CHICAGO POEMS (1914), and
"Paula," from SMOKE AND STEEL (1920) are printed by arrangement with
John Steichen, Paula Steichen Polega and The Barbara Hogenson Agency. All
rights reserved. For more information about Carl Sandburg visit www.nps.gov/carl*

# INDEX

Please note: Stories about these people are found on the dated pages, but in some cases, they are not the couple's exact wedding date.

# Index

# Index

*Index*

CPSIA information can be obtained
at www.ICGtesting.com
Printed in the USA
BVHW041129020220
571200BV00015B/327